WHAT IS PHILOSOPHY OF EDUCATION?

CHRISTOPHER J. LUCAS

University of Missouri–Columbia

THE MACMILLAN COMPANY

COLLIER-MACMILLAN LIMITED
London

To
my wife,
TERRIE,
in appreciation
for her patience
with professorial
foibles

First Printing

Library of Congress catalog card number: 69–11586

THE MACMILLAN COMPANY
COLLIER-MACMILLAN CANADA, LTD., TORONTO, ONTARIO

PRINTED IN THE UNITED STATES OF AMERICA

PREFACE

This work should have been made available to students of philosophy of education several years ago. For some time a need has existed for a convenient compilation of writings addressed to a narrow but important topic: the nature and function of educational philosophy. Courses in the subject have become rather firmly entrenched in the curricula of professional teacher preparation programs throughout the country. In many states such a course or its equivalent has become a requirement for state certification. Most institutions require students preparing to teach to enroll in a course in philosophy of education or "social foundations" of education to complete the undergraduate degree program. Elsewhere, a course devoted to general theorizing about broad educational issues is offered as a first, introductory course or in graduate-level instruction.

Recent decades have witnessed a proliferation of textbooks written to satisfy the demands such courses provide. Among those that devote themselves explicitly to philosophy of education, the pattern of topical organization has been to present in the first chapter a discussion of the nature and utility of general philosophy. Because most students in educational philosophy courses come with little or no philosophical background, such a strategy has been deemed essential. Following this, a section is usually devoted to an analysis of the meanings of "education." This is concluded with an exploration of the nature of the conjunction "philosophy of education." The present work is intended for use as supplementary reading in the initial portions of courses concerned, broadly speaking, with the philosophical dimensions of education. It may also serve as an introductory text for specialized seminars where a detailed examination of this topic is appropriate.

The question of what is philosophy of education opens a Pandora's box of other questions. It seems sometimes that one cannot answer this question without first entertaining a host of other problems. The selections included here constitute a retrospective look at the best that has been written on these problems. The writings span several decades. They are drawn largely from the pages of *Educational Theory*, the publication of the John Dewey Society and the Philosophy of Education Society, and from the *Harvard Educational Review*, which has sponsored symposia on the aims and content of philosophy of education, although a number of other sources are represented as well. Grateful appreciation is expressed to Professor William O. Stanley, editor-in-chief of *Educational Theory*, for his cooperation in granting permission for the reprinting of many of the articles here, and to Mrs.

iii

Margaret K. O'Hara of the permissions department of *Harvard Educational Review* for her assistance. Thanks are also due to the editors of the other journals from which selections have been made and to the authors here represented, many of whom volunteered expressions of support and encouragement for this effort. Special thanks must be expressed to Mrs. Joan Collison and her staff for the valuable secretarial help rendered in compiling this anthology of readings.

The Introduction to this work reverses the ordinary sequence of ideas by outlining ways in which philosophy of education can be taught rather than considering the logically prior questions of the nature of philosophy, of education, and the hybrid: philosophy of education. Since the answers to the latter query depend upon the two former questions, it is hoped that a description of how educational philosophy is presented in courses will show differing ways of looking at philosophy and its function in education. Thus, a look at teaching strategies becomes the prolegomenon to the essays that follow.

Part I consists of contrasting views on the nature of philosophy. The intent is to illustrate how and why controversy in this regard constitutes a predicament for philosophical thought in the modern world. By implication, views about educational philosophy will be heavily influenced by whatever stance a theorist adopts concerning what is general philosophy. Students with no previous work in philosophy may find this section especially pertinent when reading the subsequent essays.

Part II affords some perspectives on the historical development of philosophical thinking on education, particularly in the twentieth century. In the 1920's and 1930's, most educational philosophy was dominated heavily by the pragmatism of John Dewey and his followers. Many theorists found philosophical support for progressivist educational reforms in this pragmatist philosophy. Representative statements by leading lights in the early development of twentieth century educational theory are included, as well as commentary on the nature of philosophy of education written in reaction to the dominance of pragmatism.

Parts III and IV are closely related since the same topics are considered in each. A justification for the separation into two sections is found in the relative emphasis of the discussions in each part. Part III is comprised of essays whose primary focus is defining philosophy of education. The authors appearing in Part IV focus more on what philosophy of education does—that is, assessing the benefits to be garnered from the philosophical approach to education. A list of suggested readings is appended for the benefit of the reader who may wish to pursue questions further than the scope of the present work allows.

One cautionary note: much depends upon the spirit in which these readings are evaluated. Philosophizing about education is not the same as theorizing about philosophy of education. In a very real sense, this is not a book *in* philosophy of education; it is *about* it. In the last analysis, the merits of philosophy of education must be judged on how well it helps to illuminate the educational scene, not on how eloquently its practitioners explain the character of that illumination.

C. J. L.

CONTENTS

INTRODUCTION

Philosophy is in a state of crisis today. The nature of the function of philosophy has always been a philosophical problem generating controversy since the first disagreements between Socrates and Anaxagoras. "Philosophy," it has been said, "is its own first problem." [1] So it always has been. But in the twentieth century discussion has been raised to a new pitch as a result of sharply divergent views as to what philosophy is, what it offers modern man, and what it might aspire to do. The net effect of such controversy has been to produce widespread skepticism as to the legitimacy of philosophy itself. There have always been skeptics happy to offer obituaries for philosophy, but not until this century have these critics been so numerous or so vocal.

Susanne Langer has argued persuasively that we are at the end of a philo-sophical epoch with the exhaustion of its motive concepts. [2] Philosophical thought has become moribund. The characteristic symptoms that mark the end of an epoch are in evidence everywhere. There has been a shift from live philosophical issues to peripheral concerns: methodology, apologetics, treatises on the philosopher's place in society, and the like. Philosophical thought rigidifies into dogma, and various "isms" proliferate. The public comes to expect little or nothing from philosophers and treats their counsel with impressive indifference. Philosophers cease to raise problems that matter outside their academic community and retreat into purely procedural matters. "When philosophy, for one reason or another, has run dry," one philosopher notes, "when it has ceased to have anything to say, or fears to have anything to say, it turns inward upon itself, and proposes as a self-sufficient task, to analyze the meanings of terms. . . . When [this] becomes identified with philosophy, it seems to me to have been transmuted into a device for repressing philosophical questions." [3]

Since the seventeenth century, Anglo-American philosophy has been strongly influenced by empiricism, in particular the classical empiricism of Locke, Berkeley, and Hume. Their work led to the traditional division of

---

[1] G. Simmel, *Hauptprobleme der Philosophie*. Leipzig: Göschen Verlag, 1910, p. 9.
[2] Susanne Langer, *Philosophy in a New Key*. New York: Mentor, 1959, pp. 20–23ff.
[3] Lewis S. Feuer, "The Aims of A Philosophy of Education," *Harvard Educational Review*, 26 (Spring, 1956): 113.

1

knowledge as truths of fact and truths of reason. Logicians and philosophers of mathematics elaborated upon rational knowledge and epistemologically oriented philosophers pursued the empirical truths of fact founded ultimately in sensory experience. The growth of modern experimental sciences in the last two centuries cast doubt on the supposed truths of empiricism until science replaced philosophy as an accredited empirical discipline. It seemed that a better way of describing the nature of knowledge and facts about reality had been discovered by the sciences, hence philosophy, no longer able to offer itself as empirical, had to withdraw into semantic and methodological concerns.[4] *A priori* principles, speculative metaphysics, and rationalist ontologies went by the board. It looked as though philosophers had better close shop.

In the meantime, the ancient tradition of speculative philosophy as a guide to moral, religious, political, and social living persisted, especially with the public at large, although how philosophy can be a practical guide to daily life has never been especially clear among nonphilosophers.[5]

A philosophical revolt against the popular, traditionalist view arose in this century. It began with the movement known as logical positivism and it was continued later by linguistic analysis movements. This revolt sharply criticized the legitimacy of speculative metaphysics and dismissed it as, literally, nonsense. The term *nonsense* assumed a technical meaning: meaning depends upon usage and verification. This became the credo for a new generation of philosophers. Briefly, the logical positivists contended that for a statement to be meaningful it must be verifiable. They concluded that there are but two kinds of statements: (1) analytical statements whose validity depends upon the definitions of the symbols they contain (such as two plus two equals four), and (2) empirical statements verifiable by sense experience. Thus, metaphysical statements purporting to yield information about man, God, the meaning of human existence—being neither analytic nor empirical since they cannot be validated through observation—can be neither true nor false; they are "non-sense."

These developments underwent considerable modification as later philosophers such as Wittgenstein and Russell introduced refinements. Under their influence, a new view of philosophy emerged. The questions of philosophy, as Wittgenstein argued, do not arise from ignorance of facts but from confusion about what is in one way familiar. Philosophy is a response to that sense of bafflement about what we know but do not understand. The confusion is akin to that of a child's who knows what a finished picture puzzle

---

[4] See John W. Yolton, *Thinking And Perceiving*. LaSalle, Ill.: Open Court, 1962, pp. vii*ff.*
[5] This is not to prejudge the issue; the comment is intended to indicate merely that ambiguity and confusion attend this concept of the function of philosophy.

should look like but does not know how to fit the pieces together. Philosophy yields no new facts or theorems; it "proves" nothing in the scientific sense of proof. Instead, since (as the linguistic analysts said) the source of such confusion is the way in which language is used, the new view advanced was that philosophy's primary function is to examine our misuses of language.

Two sorts of reactions took place. On the one hand, some philosophers became concerned with expanding and liberalizing a theory of language in order to readmit traditional philosophical problems. The way in which this program was carried out need not be considered here except to say that its effect was to soften the impact that linguistic analysis had had on philosophers' own understanding of what it meant to "do" philosophy. On the other hand, certain philosophers more or less by-passed the concerns of their analytical colleagues to forge yet another conception of the nature and function of philosophy. This second orientation became known as existentialism. Between the two approaches—one analytical and the other existential—a number of hybrid varieties of philosophizing grew up. Among the various factions acrimonious and often bitter controversy arose, which continues today. At the center of debate, the question of the nature and function of philosophy has not received any decisive answer. The result has been almost unmitigated confusion.

But is all this merely a scholar's quarrel of no possible interest to the ordinary layman? Someone once remarked sarcastically that if all the philosophers in the world were stretched end to end they would still not reach an agreement. In the final analysis, does it really matter what people think about philosophy?

In the present context, two observations need to be made. First, if philosophy has something to offer modern man in the way of enlightenment and understanding, it might seem judicious to explore the nature of the contribution philosophy can make in resolving problems in a troubled world. Since, traditionally, philosophy has performed this service, we owe it to ourselves to find out something about the nature of philosophy and its function. We need to know where we can look for guidance and instruction as we confront the pressing difficulties of our time. There is always the possibility that philosophy has something to offer.

Secondly, since our concern here is education as well as philosophy, we want to know if philosophy can be of assistance in resolving educational issues. Or, alternatively, can philosophy applied to education contribute something toward a better understanding of education in all of its ramifications? Even the most objective, impartial observer of the American educational scene today must note the chaos of irresponsibility, the inefficiency, the fads, the vested interests, and the confusions that exist in various degrees and at various levels in American education. This is not to say that there are no strengths to be taken into account. It seems evident, however, that there are shortcomings and deficiencies in education. How we conceive of the nature and function of philosophy will affect profoundly how we answer the question, can philosophy of education help?

Philosophy of education has been around since time immemorial. Men have philosophized about education almost since the beginnings of philosophy itself. But questions about what is philosophy of education are embarrassingly unwieldly. Such questions form the content of the articles that make up this work. Since the intent here is to let the various authors speak for themselves, no separate discussion is required. Instead, a better beginning is to describe *strategies* for the *teaching* of philosophy of education. A necessarily cursory look at the way courses in philosophy of education are organized within the context of teacher preparation programs will go far toward providing a framework for subsequent reading. By looking at ways in which philosophy of education is taught, a sense of the different ways philosophy is conceived can be gained and hence an improved understanding of what is philosophy of education may result.

The "Great Minds" Approach.   As one examines the corpus of thought recorded by philosophers throughout history, from Socrates to Russell, it becomes clear that many philosophical giants have ventured into those areas of educational inquiry that lend themselves to general theorizing. The larger issues of the nature of human nature, the purposes of schooling, or the ways in which men can realize their potential as human beings have received thoughtful attention. Sometimes the recorded observations are integral with a systematic philosophical position, as in Plato's *Republic*. This far-reaching treatise on the nature of reality, knowledge, and value incorporates a systematic theory of education within the larger philosophical structure in such a way that philosophical and educational problems become continuous. Similarly, John Dewey's philosophy of pragmatism or experimentalism builds much of its substructure out of educational concepts following from that "mind-boggling heresy" that philosophy and education are but two aspects of the same endeavor—the forming of those fundamental dispositions toward nature and our fellow man that the world of experience demands of us.[6]

With Dewey, and his adherents in particular, the notion found credence that general theorizing about educational objectives and methodologies inevitably leads to the application of philosophical thinking to all dimensions of education, including curriculum construction, teaching strategies, and

[6] See Van Cleve Morris' Foreword in *Philosophy and Educational Development*, George Barnett (ed.). Boston: Houghton Mifflin Company, 1966, pp. vii–viii.

administrative decision-making. Conversely, Dewey stressed the reciprocal influence of pedagogical themes upon philosophical theorizing.

On the other hand, among those who have speculated philosophically about matters educational, the observations may appear to bear less of an organic relation to their "pure" philosophical writings. Immanuel Kant's pedagogical works, for example, or Rousseau's *Émile*, constitute writings by philosophers on education. Neither are vital components of a larger whole, however; the educational theories advanced may "follow from" the respective philosophies in some ill-defined sense, but the former certainly are not central to the latter. Jacques Maritain's *Education at the Crossroads*, to cite another example, is a work devoted to education viewed from the perspective of neo-Thomistic philosophy, but in no sense are the observations on education "built into" the total philosophical position espoused by Maritain elsewhere.

Other philosophical savants have largely ignored specific educational problems or concerns, although their writings may seem to suggest fruitful ways of looking at pedagogical issues. The scholastic philosopher Aquinas produced an enormous mass of writings, but only a small part of them has to do explicitly with what might be considered problems of education. Because he wrote as a theologian, questions about God are at the core of his study of universal reality. Only the short discussion called the *De Magistro* and a few places in his *Summa Theologiae* deal to any real extent with formal educational matters. Again, Karl Marx wrote little or nothing that could be characterized as educational works. In both cases, however, many have professed to find an incipient philosophy of education or, at the least, the logical cornerstones upon which a philosophical theory of education might be constructed.

Given this rich source of wisdom, insight, and knowledge, it would seem unwise to neglect it when considering contemporary educational issues in their fullest theoretical dimensions. Whether or not a particular individual has discussed education explicitly may not, in the final analysis, make any significant difference. Any full-blown philosophy, it can be argued, traditionally deals with the questions of the nature of knowledge and knowing, the nature of reality or existence, and the question of the nature and status of values. The connection with education of these epistemological, ontological, and axiological issues is fairly obvious. Philosophizing about what can be known, how we know, what is most worth knowing, and so on, is not too far away from asking what are the proper aims of education and the nature of learning and teaching. Therefore, the "great minds" approach emphasizes the need to consult the creators of the best, most profound, and most comprehensive philosophies of our cultural heritage. As a teaching strategy, students are required to devote themselves to a careful analysis of the great philosophers, past and present, culling their writings for concepts, proposals, and recommendations essential for understanding education today. In the case of a Plato or Dewey, this is a more or less straightforward procedure. Where a philosopher has neglected to supply specific educational theories, the student is asked to derive implications that seem consistent with the larger precepts of the general philosophy.

It seems reasonable to assume that salutory consequences will follow when this approach is followed and done well. It can be an enlightening and liberalizing experience when the student successfully confronts the challenge of coming to grips with a better mind—a thinker whose matured wisdom, penetration, and thoroughness of thought have earned him a place of honor in the intellectual history of our civilization. Aristotle's notion of education as disciplined cultivation of the intellect or Whitehead's thesis of a "rhythm" in education are marvelously subtle, intricate, and productive perspectives from which to view education. But there are several important qualifications that need to be made.

In the first place, no criteria for selecting *which* philosophical giants are to be considered suggest themselves as self evident. Although not a devastating criticism in itself, the content of a course in philosophy of education so conceived is very much a function of the predilections of the instructor. One might look to Plato, Aristotle, and Socrates, or to Dewey, Russell, and Kant, or any other similar grouping of thinkers. There seems no clear-cut way of deciding which great philosopher is most instructive, and because one cannot consider all partisans (except at the risk of becoming hopelessly superficial) a final selection is bound to be somewhat arbitrary.

Secondly, it remains unclear in most cases how a philosopher's educational ideas are related to his general philosophy. Particularly since philosophers may address educational themes with varying degrees of specificity, it is difficult to envision what detailed proposals an individual might offer on a given topic—for example, the scope and sequence of an ideal curriculum. Whereas Plato presents a fairly detailed picture, Hegel or Spinoza or Hume assuredly does not. Even had all philosophers writing on education left parallel or even similar recommendations for the educator, whether those recommendations are inevitably related in some meaningful way to their metaphysical, epistemological, and axiological persuasions is very much open to question. This much is certain: philosophical theories of education are not deductive theorems following from postulates in a philosophical system since (with one or two possible exceptions) philosophies generally are not constructed in this way. Hence, it becomes almost impossible to say assuredly what a philosopher's views might be on some topic in education unless he did, in fact, consider that topic.

Thirdly, the kind of proposals for education that typically have been advanced pose peculiar problems for the educator seeking guidance and direction in dealing with today's educational issues. If the reflections are confined to broad generalities concerning the nature of human growth and development, the "good life" for which men ought to be educated, and the like, considerable ambiguity attaches itself to finding ways of translating such generalizations into policies and practices for the classroom. The situation is no better when it is reversed—that is, when a philosopher has framed detailed proposals. They are likely to be the products of a special time and place which, when viewed in retrospect, appear obsolete and irrelevant. Most recommendations reflect the limited knowledge available in such fields as psychology, biology, sociology, and other disciplines at a particular point in time; they encompass more than the basic philosophical posture assumed by a philosopher. Therefore, discussions about education frequently are a function of a social, cultural context that is outdated.[7] Thus, Locke's or Montaigne's views on education are advanced with the presupposition that private, tutorial instruction is the norm. Educators functioning within a public school system discover little relevance to their needs and difficulties. The educational utopia of Plato's *Republic* bears scant resemblance to the modern school and the society which supports it. Similar difficulties inhere in many other schemes advanced by philosophers discussing education. Hence, the student in a course utilizing the "great minds" approach is not altogether blameworthy when he concludes that philosophy of education is inspiring as moral uplift but wholly impractical for assisting in the everyday problems of education he confronts.

The "Systems" or "Schools of Thought" Approach. Mindful of the difficulties endemic in the "great minds" approach, many teachers have sought to accomplish the same ends through an examination of the significance for education of the various *systems* or *schools* of philosophy rather than the writings of individual philosophers. Because philosophers differ in their comprehensiveness, in the kinds of questions selected for emphasis, and in the way basic questions are formulated in their philosophies, to say nothing of their educational theories, one way of removing these difficulties is to consider the alternative bearings of groups of philosophers who espouse similar positions with respect to the perennial questions raised in philosophy. As Raphael Demos has phrased it,

---

[7] This point is borrowed from Philip G. Smith, *Philosophy of Education, Introductory Studies.* New York: Harper & Row, 1965, p. 54. Much of the following discussion is structured along lines suggested in Smith's analysis, *op. cit.*, Chapter 3.

Though at no one time is there unanimity among philosophers on any theory, there are several doctrines which are bound to have a good number of devoted followers at all times. The history of philosophy is the continuous recurrence and resuscitation of certain well-defined points of view, such as empiricism, rationalism, mysticism, realism, idealism, etc.; in these the mind seems to have achieved a final insight into the nature of things, in the sense that they represent permanent possibilities of explaining the universe.[8]

Here again, however, the problem arises that when spokesmen for a philosophical position promulgate specific educational proposals, these will be functions of a special point in place and time as well as of the basic school of thought. A contemporary proponent of realism or idealism or pragmatism might well advance ideas differing drastically from those offered ten, fifty, or a hundred years earlier by some other adherent of the same fundamental philosophical position. Two unhappy conclusions might appear to follow: (1) there is no single philosophy of education that can be derived from a school of thought; there are only philosophies of education advanced by men who happen to share some common philosophical presuppositions, and (2) the underlying philosophical assumptions are not indispensable as a rationale for someone's particular theories, though they be represented as "idealist" or "realist" or "pragmatic" educational philosophies. In point of fact, these observations raise some knotty, technical problems, which are considered at length by writers elsewhere in this work. Suffice it to say, the question of how educational proposals or theories are related to more general philosophical ideas is a crucial issue in any approach to philosophy of education.

Another pressing difficulty in the "systems" approach concerns the labels used to identify the various schools of philosophy, or "well-defined points of view," to which reference has already been made. Experience suggests that students lack the sophistication to view classificatory schemes in philosophy as convenient fictions of limited utility. Philosophical labels do not refer to alternate groups of common answers and questions. Taxonomies invariably oversimplify in philosophy for the sake of providing "handles" for different viewpoints. Unfortunately, most students and many teachers forget this and come to consider the various schools as isomorphous. The presumption is, for example, that an existentialist philosophy of education is identical in scope and conception to a realist or perennialist educational philosophy, which is, in fact, far from the truth of the matter. The synoptic character of philosophical thought that confounds any attempt to classify is disregarded.

[8] Raphael Demos, introduction to *Plato Selections*. New York: Charles Scribner's Sons, 1955, pp. xlvii–xlviii. (Quoted with permission of the publisher.)

Seen in this light, any blanket classifications appear arbitrary and over-simplified. It could be argued that the labels that have come into common usage are the creations of textbook writers in the field of educational philosophy, more than faithful reflections of the philosophical scene. Until quite recently, if one picked up such a text one could expect to find a comparative discussion of the educational bearings of standardized "schools" of philosophical thought.

The misuse of labels, some will argue, has had the result of surrounding courses in philosophy of education with an aura of unreality. Students finding themselves unable to give their allegiance to any single school of thought pick and choose bits and pieces from one position, now from another. This eclecticism cannot help but be superficial; inevitably it does serious damage to whatever cohesive unity and internal logic a position may possess. Worse yet, when the individual gets into a classroom for the first time, the airtight philosophical categories begin to dissolve—and finally disappear.

There are more sophisticated variants on this theme. To avoid gross over-simplifications, sometimes teachers of philosophy of education have picked broad themes and, depending on the questions asked, grouped philosophical positions around an issue (for example, "What is the nature of knowledge?"). Philosophers can then be grouped according to their epistemological orientations.

It must be said that despite its difficulties, students have found the "systems" approach useful both in engaging in serious examination of philosophical issues and in defining a self-concept or philosophically grounded role through which their teaching tasks make more sense. For all of its draw-backs, this general way of studying philosophy of education has enjoyed tremendous popularity and is followed frequently today.

The "Problems" Approach.   Both the method of comparing philosophical positions for their educational implications and the method of looking to great individual philosophers for instruction place the emphasis upon the *products* of inquiry rather than the *process*. Philosophy is regarded primarily as something to be learned, not as something one does. The "problems" approach, so-called for want of a more descriptive label, represents an attempt to get students involved in the *activity* of philosophizing about important problems of education. The focus of attention may differ. It can be directed to education as a social institution in society, in which case one might consider broad sociological issues such as the proper locus of direction and control, religion in the schools, federal aid to education, student rights, and similar controversies. Or attention may fasten on education considered as a teaching and learning process, wherein students explore the meaning of

instruction versus indoctrination, teaching role models, rationales for the
maintenance of class discipline, or the criteria for building a curriculum.
Either way, the fundamental attempt is to think philosophically, to examine
education with the depth and scope that such thought can afford. The
ultimate hope is that teachers will become more thoughtful in their dealings
with problems as they are met in practice and less inclined to rely on narrow
habitual modes of response.

Sometimes the conventional categories of philosophy—epistemology,
axiology, ontology—are placed in service to provide a structure for problem-
centered inquiry. One might begin with the question, "What is the nature
of knowledge that teachers impart?" From a consideration of ideas about
different kinds of knowledge one is soon led to examine differing epistemologies, or the meaning of meaning, the logical characteristics of concepts, ways
of knowing, and related topics. An initial question might be, "How shall we
adjudicate conflicts involving value claims in education?" It is a short leap
to questions about the nature of values, how can they be justified, how do
values differ from factual assertions, *ad infinitum*. Students soon realize that
similar philosophical issues underly virtually every significant dimension of
education.

One crucial difficulty with this approach is that students usually lack
sufficient background in general philosophy as a foundation for further
inquiry. Hence, the terminology is likely to appear formidable, the concepts
far removed from more familiar experimental ideas, the relations between a
specific problem and its more basic philosophical foundations tenuous and
unclear. On the other hand, philosophy as a discipline may become in the
student's mind a vital, important mode of questioning instead of an esoteric
body of relatively unintelligible ideas. Finally, it is worth mentioning that
textbooks utilizing the problems approach have been few in number. Moreover, they have enjoyed a decidedly mixed success. One common complaint
is that they contain far too much second-hand philosophy and too little
education. In other words, so much attention is devoted to philosophical
considerations that the educational significance of those considerations
receives insufficient analysis. Courses utilizing the "problems" approach
may accordingly suffer the same defect.

The "Didactic" Approach. Philosophically unsophisticated persons often
speak about the need to have "a philosophy" of life, of education, of child
rearing, or—*mirabile dictu*—of cooking, sewing, or farming, *ad nauseum*.
"Philosophy" comes to mean anything and hence nothing, although it may
be equated vaguely with "theory" or "reasons" or "general objectives."
The philosopher's idea of a systematic discipline with a special conceptual
apparatus and methodology becomes, in the popular consciousness, a poorly

organized array of half-understood generalizations and unexamined assumptions.

In point of fact what does this . . . philosophy come to? It comes to something having less kinship with anything to be called a philosophy than with the job lot of odds and ends in Tom Sawyer's pocket. Insofar as the vast majority of us are equipped with anything resembling an outlook upon life and the world, it consists of a substratum of superstition about the supernatural, a smattering of social theory, a nest of group prejudices, a few wise saws, a rumor or two from science, a number of slip-shod observations of life. To call this hodge-podge a philosophy is to take unwarranted liberty with language.[9]

   Students enrolling in a philosophy of education course often expect to find philosophies of education up for sale; they are the customers waiting to select some merchandise to their liking.
   On a much more sophisticated level, the "didactic" approach tries to provide a reasonable facsimile of a philosophy for the teacher. A sustained attempt is made to refine, systematize, and give depth to one's outlook and transform it into something approximating a philosophy. The strategy employed is similar to the "great minds" approach in that the student is exposed to philosophies or programs for reform initiated by writers who have ventured some recommendations for the improvement of existing educational practices or have submitted an original vantage point from which education may be viewed. The teacher of the course may attempt to plumb for a particular partisan position, or he may simply be interested in having the student accept a position that the individual finds persuasive. In contrast with the "problems" approach, here the objective is to come to definite conclusions and to adopt a point of view on an issue rather than simply to analyze problems philosophically. The student is encouraged to range freely across the domains of philosophical discourse until he arrives at a set of foundational assumptions upon which a philosophy of education can be set. Sometimes—perhaps more often than not—the novice will adopt *in toto* someone else's views and become a discipline of that person. More rarely, the thoughtful individual will generate a philosophy of his own. Although it may lack something in depth, it can be a comprehensive viewpoint that is intellectually and emotionally satisfying for the student involved.
   The Metaphilosophical approach.   If one examines a textbook on educational theories, three logically different kinds of statements can be discerned (although sometimes only after intensive analysis), which are put forward as

---

[9] Max C. Otto, *Things and Ideals.* New York: Holt, Rinehart and Winston, 1924, p. 34. (Quoted with permission of the publisher.)

a basis for educational practice.[10] They differ in that they need to be supported in quite different ways, although usually they are inextricably bound together so that their differences are not readily apparent. First there are *metaphysical* judgments whose truth is not readily tested by the methods of experimentation and observation. In fact, the legitimacy of such propositions and the extent to which they convey intelligible meanings is, as has been noted, a topic of controversy in contemporary philosophy. Metaphysical propositions such as "Education involves the realization of the divine potential of each child," or "Teaching is the art of the enrichment of experience," are definitional or stipulative in that they purport to offer a clarification of the nature of something. According to one view at least, no matter how much these may look like ordinary factual assertions, they are basically unlike them in that they cannot be either refuted or confirmed by evidence that is collected and assessed by established, publicly recognized methods. Thus, there seems to be no universally accepted way of deciding whether education *is* in fact the bringing to fruition of a student's "divine potential," or that teaching *is* the art of experiential enrichment.

A second type of judgment found in educational writings is *normative* in character. Such statements as recommendations about desirable ends, principles, means, methods, subject matter, etc. of education are "ought" statements, that is, they enjoin action for the realization of a different, "good" state of affairs as opposed to what actually obtains. An injunction such as "The teacher *ought* to strive to meet pupils' needs" provides one clearly recognizable example of normative proposition. Sometimes, however, such statements may be disguised as factual assertions about education; for example, "The teacher is a resource person for her students." The latter statement is ambiguous in that it does not necessarily state what is the case but covertly recommends how a teacher ought to function. Such statements raise questions as to how values can be justified, how values differ from facts, and a host of other difficulties.

Talk about education will usually include factual or *empirical* propositions whose truth can, in principle at least, be uncovered by the application of ordinary methods of experimentation and observation. A statement such as "Students learn more through individualized instruction" is susceptible to investigation to discover whether students *do* learn more through the use of certain instructional techniques.

Although the above analysis is something of an oversimplification since there may be more than these kinds of statements and some may combine

---

[10] See D. J. O'Connor, *An Introduction to the Philosophy of Education*, London: Routledge & Kegan Paul, 1957, pp. 90–91, 104*ff*.; William K. Frankena, *Three Historical Philosophies of Education*, Chicago: Scott, Foresman & Co., 1965, pp. 1–12; and Edward Best, "Common Confusions in Educational Theory," in Archambault, *Philosophical Analysis and Education*, New York: Humanities Press, 1965, pp. 39–56.

the logical characteristics of more than one kind of assertion, enough has been said to illustrate how theorizing has different kinds of components. Moreover, the *level* at which discourse takes place can differ.

Most articles or books that could be classified as writings in philosophy of education are made up of several types of observations and comment running from specific proposals for school practice and policy to a philosophic analysis of various educational problems. Such writing usually involves some comment upon the historical setting of the points at issue and frequently involves considerable logical, psychological, and sociological analysis and argument. All of this is less commonly interspersed with some more or less philosophic observations about things in general— about the nature of man, of society, of democracy, or what not.[11]

The metaphilosophical approach to philosophy of education takes account of this confusing array of statements about education. It notes that there are differing kinds of propositions that need to be seen for what they are. Talk in education may refer to practices (what happens in classrooms); policies (directives to guide practice); and theories, scientific and nonscientific. Furthermore, there are metaphysical, empirical, and normative statements promulgated, which cut across the theory–policy–practice continuum. The metaphilosophical approach then consists of the analysis of education into its various aspects, with attention to the sorts of distinctions herein introduced.

A course in philosophy of education utilizing this approach is likely to concern itself with second-order questions—not a discussion of substantive issues of the aims, methods, and issues of education, but instead the problems of how education as a scholarly discipline is to be studied and what kinds of inquiry are thus entailed. In brief, the metaphilosophical approach seeks answers to questions about how educational inquiry itself should be conceived and conducted rather than to questions about the ends and means of educational practice. In large measure, the readings in this book represent metatheorizing about education, philosophy, and their mutual interrelationships.

Little can be said with any assurance regarding the strengths and weaknesses of the metaphilosophical approach to education as a teaching strategy since it is a relatively new orientation. A course so conceived may aspire to clarify and refine the procedural and conceptual problems inherent in any philosophizing about education. If students can be sensitized to the ambiguities and confusions involved in the study of education, considerable progress might be made toward clearer thinking on the part of educators working on professional problems. On the other side, students in courses structured

---

[11] Philip G. Smith, *op. cit.*, pp. 61–62. (Quoted with permission of the publisher.)

around metatheoretical issues may become impatient to engage in discussion
of substantive issues more familiar to them. Although it can be argued that
the former is a logical propaedeutic to the latter, from the average student's
point of view metaphilosophy of education may appear hopelessly remote
from any real problems with which they are engaged as teachers-to-be.

The "Social Foundations" Approach. Courses with titles such as "Contemporary Issues and Problems in American Education," or "The School and
Society," or simply "Social Foundations of Modern Education" have appeared in the curricula of teacher-preparation programs for many years.
Recently, the approach reflected in these course titles has enjoyed a resurgence
of popularity. It remains to sketch briefly the outlines of this foundational
orientation.

Education as a social, political, and economic institution does not exist in a
vacuum. It is created, nurtured, and supported by society. What happens in
society influences what happens in education. The revolutionary changes
that convulse our social structure have effects on the schools. The way they
are supported and by whom, what sources of financial and intellectual
support schools receive (or fail to receive), teacher-student relations, the
content of the curriculum and how it is taught—all these are intimately
bound up with the far-reaching developments in the larger societal context.
Teachers cannot adequately understand the changing nature of society, it is
alleged, unless they comprehend the social foundations of the educational
endeavors of our society. The impact of automation, rising demands on the
part of students for a greater control of institutions of higher learning, team
teaching techniques, the phenomenon of alienation, nongraded instruction,
and an almost infinite host of other issues need to be examined. The foundational approach tries to meet this need.

Education has an historical dimension. Historical investigation is one way
of looking at educational issues in relation to society. There is a psychological
dimension to education that goes beyond such considerations as child and
adolescent psychology or learning theory. Psychology thus provides a tool
for examining certain issues. Education encompasses a sociological aspect;
hence the dynamics of sociological change need to be investigated for their
education bearings. Education has political and economic ramifications so the
disciplines of political science and economics deserve consideration. If teacher
preparation programs tend to be method-centered and narrowly illiberal in
conception, as some would argue, studies in the social foundations of education can serve as valuable, even indispensable, correctives.

The role of philosophy in the foundations approach seems somewhat
unclear. In one sense, philosophy becomes a method to impose order and
structure on the issues considered and the ways questions get raised. But this

approach represents a drastic, radical movement away from the more familiar categories of thought, which traditionally have been the philosopher's stock-in-trade. The grist for the philosophical mill in this case becomes the data generated by the social sciences and humanities. The major virtue of this approach is that the substance of a course in social foundations is likely to involve topics with which students are familiar. Rather than the ostensibly esoteric subjects of philosophical discourse, students are plunged into controversies that get attention in the popular mass media—issues such as compensatory education for the culturally disadvantaged, discovery-oriented curricula, the innovative use of techniques such as programmed instruction, and other developments that engage the attention of people everywhere.

One chronic problem with this entire approach is finding a plan of organization or structure for courses. Textbooks in the field present a bewildering array of topics. An instructor is likely to find an embarrassment of riches for subject matter since almost anything can be shown to have some bearing on education. Then, too, it is questionable whether anything akin to social philosophy comes out of discussions. More frequently what is left is a residue of undigested generalities, precepts, and imperatives for action. Nonetheless, this way of utilizing philosophy to look at pressing, "real-life" problems has an ancient lineage going back to the midwifery of Socrates and Plato. Partially in reaction to the passion for precision and clarity, which animates the metaphilosophical approach to the study of philosophy of education, the social foundations approach tries to barter a little order for a sense of involvement from students in such courses. One educational theorist reflects this spirit as follows:

If Socrates had devoted his dialectical talents to systematizing the code of educational theory and practice current in Athens (thus producing something like the less inspired parts of Plato's *Laws*), he would merely have been voted a dull fellow ("Respectable, of course; but who can endure to read such stuff?"). No one would have dreamt of demanding that he be tried and put to death—for blasphemy, i.e., for offending against moral and spiritual values![12]

The social foundations approach dares to offend while it seeks to provide more comprehensive perspectives for understanding education in the confusing world of today.

The five ways of teaching courses in educational philosophy characterized above do not exhaust the full range of possibilities. But each represents a more or less distinctive effort to help teachers understand more adequately

[12] Rupert C. Lodge, "The Essence of Philosophy of Education," *Educational Theory*, 3 (October), 1953, p. 354. (Quoted with permission of the publisher.)

what education is all about. It should come as no surprise that each strategy has its deficiencies. The awesome responsibility to help prepare teachers and administrators for their professional tasks is always a formidable business. To engender a sense for the philosophical significance of education among teachers is a still more difficult matter. The following discussions may illuminate the full dimensions of what is involved.

PART I

THE
PREDICAMENTS OF
CONTEMPORARY
PHILOSOPHY

It is often said that a compelling need of the modern era is a sense of direction and purpose. Amidst the confusions engendered by man's loss of self identity, his alienation from himself and from the technological edifice he has constructed around him, the growth of scientific knowledge unharnessed by moral wisdom, and a consequent sense of futility and meaninglessness, man finds himself in confusion and despair. We have lost collectively our sense of perspective in devoting ourselves to questions of method while eschewing the more difficult questions of ends or goals. It is contended that we are animated by the impulsive passions of the moment rather than a healing vision of long-range possibilities. What has been lost, in the final analysis, is the ability to see life steadily and to see it whole. Thus, modern man and his society suffer from an illness of mind and spirit. The predominating images and themes of the day reflect decay, decadence, isolation, and estrangement. We need new visions and reconstructed values. We require the healing balm of a deeper wisdom which will lead us from our contemporary predicament. Philosophy, some will argue, ought to provide the purpose, direction, and integration so sorely needed at the present time. Today as never before, as the argument has it, the job of philosophy is to restore personal cohesion and social stability.

Harold Titus argues eloquently in favor of this view of the nature and function of philosophy in our contemporary life. Philosophy, he says, is

17

both an attitude and an activity. It is represented by the critical, searching quest for answers to the questions that matter most ultimately in the scheme of things. Philosophizing is a sustained effort to become aware of life in its wholeness and totality. Both speculatively and analytically, philosophical thought moves to more adequate understandings of those ideas and values that guide our lives. Finally, philosophy holds out the promise that we can gain a sense of the meaning of human existence itself. Titus suggests that nothing less will suffice in a world convulsed with revolutionary changes that undermine the very foundations of human life and society.

Yet, what if philosophy is dead? Perhaps the visions of the philosopher are empty delusions. Could it be that the methods of philosophical inquiry lead not to greater wisdom but merely to idle, useless speculation? Can philosophy provide the guidance so sorely needed in modern life?

Among many professional philosophers, the answer has been negative. As indicated previously, a revolution of sorts has taken place in the present century involving an altered conception of the nature of philosophy, a view that rejects the notion of philosophy as "vision" or as a guide to practical life. The essay from *Time* magazine outlines in summary fashion this revolution and the consequent split of philosophy into two warring camps. The analytic revolt represented a move away from the traditional understanding of what philosophy is and what it can do. The existentialist and phenomenological groups, on the other hand, adhere to an older perspective, although with emphases that are distinctive to the twentieth century. The possibilities of a reconciliation or *détente* between the "logicians" and the "lotus eaters" are considered. The dichotomy posited may appear overly simplistic to some. The variegated species of philosophical thought do not admit of such simplified classifications perhaps. The virtue of the *Time* essay, nonetheless, is that it throws into stark relief at least one important contrast characteristic of the philosophical scene today.

Lewis Feuer suggests that the rise of analytic philosophy reflects the altered nature of our bureaucratic society and the character of our educational institutions in particular. He distinguishes between "academic philosophy," by which he refers to analytical philosophy, and "philosophy" proper, by which he seems to mean the search for deeper "meanings of the human status." The rise of the former, he contends, has eclipsed the latter. Thus man's persistent search for a sense of the significance of life and his attempts to answer the larger philosophical questions reassert themselves not in the familiar categories of philosophy, but through the forms provided by theology, literature, and the arts.

Two very different selections follow. D. J. O'Connor reviews the development of Western philosophy to the present century while arguing that the traditional conceptions of method and subject matter have been thrown into question by new advances in the logic of scientific inquiry and by new ways of understanding the functions of language. In particular, the status of metaphysical speculation is left open to doubt. Philosophy can no longer presume to answer the global questions of man's destiny nor perhaps to even raise such issues. The very questions themselves may prove, upon critical analysis, to be pseudo-problems bearing no cognitive meaning whatever. O'Connor concludes that the grandiose claims of philosophy to provide a picture of the universe and of man's place within it must be rejected. On a more modest scale, the practice of philosophy may assist us in keeping our minds free of nonsense. A careful consideration of the meaning of concepts and ideas with attention to their logical behavior constitutes the proper activity of philosophy. Such an effort may not yield up satisfying answers to the more difficult and important questions of human existence, but clear-headed thinking, purged of ambiguities and confusions through the good offices of philosophy, is enough. It is, O'Connor alleges, all that we can legitimately expect from philosophy.

Reflective of the dichotomy between those who reject philosophy as a source of wisdom or special insight and those like Feuer and Titus who maintain a broader view of philosophy, Sidney Hook argues for the latter perspective. While acknowledging the importance of philosophy as an activity of logical analysis, he denies that this is its primary or even sole function. The study of philosophy is an indispensable aid in understanding both the past and the present. Ideas—including philosophical ideas—have left their impress in the development of our civilization. Similarly, contemporary intellectual movements are grounded in philosophical themes that need to be uncovered and made explicit. Only by becoming aware of these themes in an intellectually responsible fashion can one have genuine understanding of our civilization.

Philosophy has another use: it can assist in promoting an enhanced understanding of vital issues and controversies whose resolution can be furthered by understanding the meaning of the terms in which ideas are couched. Still further—and this is a point emphasized by philosophical traditionalists—philosophy involves a search for truth as well as meaning. We are not simply concerned with the meanings of the things we say; we want to know if they are true. Philosophy, Hook argues, is the pursuit of true knowledge also, in particular that knowledge of human values that constitutes wisdom. At this point, the fundamental divergence of Hook's views from those of O'Connor's becomes apparent. Finally, the possibility of philosophy as an avenue to new visions and unexplored horizons is examined.

It might seem, then, that the discussion has gone full circle, concluding with the arguments that initiate this section. What is important to note throughout is the contrast between two opposed orientations toward the question of what is philosophy. Depending upon which position is emphasized, the implications for the philosophical study of education will differ accordingly.

PHILOSOPHY AND THE CONTEMPORARY SCENE

HAROLD H. TITUS

CONFLICTING TRENDS IN A REVOLUTIONARY AGE

We are living through what many people call a "world revolution." Changes are occurring which reach to the very foundations of human life and society. There has recently been a "shortening of the time-span between notable changes" in society.[1] In the past men could expect to live under relatively fixed conditions; the time-span of significant changes was considerably longer than that of a human life. Now great changes are taking place within a fraction of the life-span of single individuals, and this situation creates unprecedented problems in both human living conditions and human thinking. We are living in a period which resembles the late stages of the Graeco-Roman civilization, the Renaissance, the Reformation, and the Industrial Revolution, when basic shifts took place in the thinking, values, and practices of men. But in our age the changes are world-wide, and they are happening at a greatly accelerated rate.

Yet in spite of our amazing advances, many thoughtful people are disturbed and anxious. They are concerned over a situation in which our physical power, scientific knowledge, and wealth stand in sharp contrast with the failure of governments and individuals to come to grips with the pressing intellectual and moral problems of life. Knowledge seems divorced from values; it is possible to have great power without insight. With few exceptions, the many books on the philosophy of history and civilization that have appeared during the last few decades agree that, though our civilization is making progress in science and technology, in other areas, including the ethical and nonmaterial, there is widespread confusion and possibly disintegration. While these writers differ as to what they feel can and should be done, most of them believe that revival is possible and

FROM Harold H. Titus, *Living Issues in Philosophy* (4th ed.). New York: American Book Company, 1964. (Reprinted by permission.)

[1] Alfred North Whitehead, *Adventures of Ideas* (New York: New American Library of World Literature, 1953), p. 99. (Mentor ed.) See also Ch. VI, pp. 110–126.

that dangerous trends can be discovered and controlled if men have vision, courage, and determination.

Many older ethical standards, as well as interpretations of life and the universe, have been weakened or destroyed, and many people find it difficult to establish new and stable foundations for living. In speaking about the "personal fragmentation." that leads to insecurity, one writer says, "There is in the climate of the modern world a sense of impending disaster, a rootlessness of the person, a pervasive tenseness which points to certainties dissolved and emotional centers displaced." [2] After speaking about the uneasiness which exists today and saying that "we are not living up to our moral capacity in the world," the editor of *The Saturday Review* goes on: "We have been living half a life. We have been developing our appetites —but we have been starving our purposes. We have been concerned with bigger salaries, bigger television screens, bigger cars—and now with bigger missiles— instead of with the big ideas on which our lives and freedoms depend." [3]

The concern in our time is not only about what is happening to many individuals, but about the very future of our type of civilization and perhaps of civilization itself. James P. Warburg says, "The decline of the West is undeniable, but in the writer's opinion it is by no means irreversible. The renaissance of Western civilization must begin within Western society. The key element in Western society is Individual Man." Again he says, "Our civilization has for centuries practiced neither the Jewish teaching of justice under moral law nor the Greek teaching of rational thought and behavior, and least of all the Christian teaching of love, compassion, and human brotherhood." [4] Lewis Mumford speaks about "the invisible breakdown in our civilization," the "erosion of values, the dissipation of humane purposes, the denial of any distinction between good or bad, right or wrong, the reversion to sub-human levels of conduct." [5] A psychologist, after consulting other psychologists, psychiatrists, and social scientists in many countries of the world in an attempt to discover the reasons for the tension and anxiety gripping the world, says: "The melancholy truth about the course of world history is that we are well along the road to disintegration." He concludes that there has been a "deterioration of personal, political, and social morals." [6]

The events of recent decades have made it clear that something has indeed gone tragically wrong with human affairs. Man has gained great new powers in science and technology, but too frequently these powers have been used for destructive purposes. Man has rapidly extended the range and quantity of his knowledge, but he has advanced little if at all toward happiness and well-being. He has devised numerous plans and organizations for gaining greater security and comfort, yet he suffers from intellectual and emotional insecurity because he is uncertain about

---

[2] Albert William Levi, *Philosophy and the Modern World* (Bloomington: Indiana U. Press, 1959), p. 5.

[3] Norman Cousins, "Is America Living Half a Life?" *The Saturday Review*, 40 (November 16, 1957): 26.

[4] *The West in Crisis* (Garden City: Doubleday, 1959), pp. 16–17, 26.

[5] *The Conduct of Life* (New York: Harcourt, Brace & World, 1951), p. 148.

[6] George W. Kisker (ed.), *World Tension—The Psychopathology of International Relations* (Englewood Cliffs: Prentice-Hall, 1951), pp. 296–297.

the meaning of life, the nature of the world in which he lives, and the kind of life he wants to live with his fellows.

World War II was a war of ideas, as well as of men, materials, and conflicting national interests. It was in large part a conflict between two irreconcilable philosophies competing for the allegiance of men. The difference between life in the democratic and in the fascist countries was not so much a difference in technology, or in science, or even in general education; it was a difference in ideas, ideals, and loyalties. The "cold war" that has existed since the end of World War II is a similar conflict between philosophies of life. Communism challenges our traditional beliefs and intensifies the struggle for the minds and hearts of men. If in this conflict our civilization has appeared weak at times, it is not because large numbers of leaders in the "free" societies have been communists or have wished to be "soft" toward communism. The real reason appears to be a lack of a strong sense of direction.

After calling attention to the lack of a sense of national purpose, to the overwhelming drive for personal comfort, amusement, and new gadgets, to industrial stoppages due to a lack of social discipline, to an educational system which all too frequently sacrifices quality to quantity, and to other conditions which tend to weaken our society, George F. Kennan, one of our outstanding diplomats who has served under both political parties, said, "If you ask me—as an historian—whether such a country has, over the long run, good chances of competing with a purposeful, serious and disciplined society such as that of the Soviet Union, I must say that the answer is 'no.'"[7]

All the men quoted above speak of the need for a revitalization of our society. They feel that our trouble is mainly intellectual and moral confusion leading to cultural instability. For some, however, "the prospect of the coming quarter-century is exhilarating," since we are likely to see and to participate in "centuries of development telescoped into a brief span."[8] One student of philosophy comes to the defense of modern man. While admitting that "it is frightening when intelligence is applied in a moral void," and acknowledging that something very fundamental has gone wrong and that "an extraordinary number of men and women . . . are asking whether our civilization has not been on the wrong path for a long time," he thinks that the "doom-filled prophecies are unwarranted."[9]

Civilization is basically a set of ideas and ideals by which man lives. These ideas and ideals are embodied in rules of living and in institutions. They give life its unity and meaning. When they are lost sight of or fail to motivate, the civilization either changes or tends to decline. Medieval civilization was inspired primarily by a belief in salvation and a supernatural order. During the late Middle Ages this belief apparently ceased to be, of itself, sufficient motivation for a living society, and we can conjecture that if other beliefs had not emerged, Western civilization would have died.

[7] Quoted by Steve Allen in *The Saturday Review*, 43 (August 20, 1960): 14.
[8] David Sarnoff, *The Fabulous Future: America in 1980* (New York: Dutton, 1956), p. 14.
[9] Charles Frankel, *The Case for Modern Man* (New York: Harper, 1956), pp. 2, 196.

Changes in ways of doing things and in history usually begin with people who are convinced of the worth of some ideal or who are captured by some vision of a different way of life. Following the Middle Ages, many people began to conceive of a way of life motivated to a much larger extent by a belief that life on this earth is worthwhile in itself. In the broadest sense, this belief made possible the Renaissance, the Reformation, and our modern world, with its factories, mass production, money and banks, rapid transportation and, more recently, atomic power and exploration of outer space. All these things are calculated to make this world better and to give man more control over it. But unless we develop some fairly consistent view of the nature of man, the nature of the total order within which man lives, and some reasonable scale of values based on an order beyond mere human desires, such things are not likely to provide an enduring basis for our world.

With man's rapidly increasing knowledge and power over the physical and intellectual world, his potentialities for good as well as for evil are greater than ever before. We may come to live in a better world than man has ever known. What our world becomes depends in large part on whether we have the intelligence, the sense of responsibility, the courage, and the determination to reconstruct a set of values in which we can believe. Philosophy, in conjunction with other disciplines, plays a central role in personal integration and social reconstruction and stability.

WHAT IS PHILOSOPHY?

In a general sense, a person's philosophy is the sum of his fundamental beliefs and convictions. In this sense everyone has a philosophy, even though he does not realize it. All people have some ideas concerning physical objects, man, the meaning of life, nature, death, God, right and wrong, and beauty and ugliness. Of course, these ideas are acquired in a variety of ways. Especially during the early years of our lives, we are continuously engaged, with varying degrees of consciousness, in acquiring views and attitudes from our family, from companions, and from various other individuals and groups. These attitudes may come to us through custom and tradition as expressed by behavior in home, school, and church. They may be influenced by the movies, radio, television, and books. They may be the result of some thinking on our part; or they may be largely the result of convention and emotional bias. This broad, popular, or man-in-the-street view of philosophy is not adequate for our purposes. It does not describe the work and task of the philosopher. We need to define philosophy more specifically, since the broad view does not distinguish philosophy from many vague, confused, and superficial beliefs.

The word *philosophy* is derived from the Greek words *philos* ("loving") and *sophia* ("wisdom") and means "the love of knowledge and wisdom." But philosophy can be approached or defined from a number of different points of view. Here we present five that are supplementary rather than contradictory, although some philosophers may wish to exclude one or more of them. Each approach must be kept in mind for a clear understanding of the many meanings of *philosophy* and what particular philosophers may say about the nature and function of philosophy.

1. *Philosophy is a personal attitude toward life and the universe.* When a person goes through some crisis or unusual experience, often we inquire, "How does he take it?" or "How does it affect him?" Sometimes the answer is, "He takes it philosophically." This means that he sees the problem in its broad perspective or as a part of a larger scheme of things; hence he faces the situation calmly and reflectively, with poise and composure.

The mature philosophical attitude is the searching and critical attitude; it is also the open-minded, tolerant attitude expressed in the willingness to look at all sides of an issue. It includes a readiness to accept life and the world as they are, and to try to see life in all its relationships. This does not mean enslavement to the present or to what exists now, however, because philosophy is willing to look beyond the actualities to the possibilities.

To philosophize is not merely to read and to know philosophy; it is also to think and to feel philosophically. Philosophy begins in wonder, doubt, and curiosity. It grows out of our developing awareness of the problems of human existence. Consequently, philosophy is in part the speculative attitude that does not shrink from facing the difficult and unsolved problems of life.

2. *Philosophy is a method of reflective thinking and reasoned inquiry.* This method is not the exclusive property of philosophy, as will readily be seen; it is the method of all careful and accurate thinking. Philosophy, however, is more inclusive or synoptic than are the various sciences. Philosophical method is reflective and critical. It involves the attempt to think through one's problems and to face all the facts involved. The accumulation of more knowledge does not by itself lead to understanding, since it does not necessarily teach the mind to make a critical evaluation of facts or enable a person to live his life according to consistent principles.

3. *Philosophy is an attempt to gain a view of the whole.* Philosophy seeks to combine the conclusions of the various sciences and long human experience into some kind of consistent world view. The philosopher wishes to see life, not with the specialized slant of the scientist or the businessman or the artist, but with the over-all view of someone cognizant of life as a totality. In speaking of "speculative philosophy," which he distinguishes from "critical philosophy," C. D. Broad says, "Its object is to take over the results of the various sciences, to add to them the results of the religious and ethical experiences of mankind, and then to reflect upon the whole. The hope is that, by this means, we may be able to reach some general conclusions as to the nature of the universe, and as to our position and prospects in it." [10]

Since the direction of learning during the past century has been toward analysis, specialization, and the fragmentation of knowledge, it is well to keep in mind that many of the great philosophers have refused to confine their attention to some one or even a few aspects of experience. Plato, Aristotle, Aquinas, Hegel, Bergson, Dewey, and Whitehead, to mention only a few, have sought to gain a comprehensive vision of things.

While there are difficulties and dangers in setting forth any world view, there are also dangers in confining one's attention to fragments of human experience.

[10] *Scientific Thought* (New York: Harcourt, Brace, 1923), p. 20.

"The dangers of the sort of narrow specialization which either refuses to look beyond its own little province or treats as nonsensical attempts to go beyond it far outweigh the risks of attempting a world view."[11]

4. *Philosophy is the logical analysis of language and the clarification of the meaning of words and concepts.* Certainly this is one function of philosophy. In fact, nearly all philosophers have used methods of analysis and have sought to clarify the meaning of terms and the use of language. There are some philosophers, indeed, who see this as the main task of philosophy, and a few who claim this is the only legitimate function of philosophy. Such persons consider philosophy a specialized field serving the sciences and aiding in the clarification of language rather than a broad field reflecting upon all of life's experiences. This outlook is recent and has gained considerable support during the last half century. It would limit what we call *knowledge* to statements about *observable facts* and their interrelations—that is, to the business of the various sciences. All linguistic analysts, however, do not define *knowledge* so narrowly. While they do reject and try to "clean up" many non-scientific assertions, many of them think that we can have knowledge of ethical principles and the like, though this knowledge is also experientially derived. Those who take the narrower view neglect, when they do not deny, all generalized world views and life views, as well as traditional moral philosophy and theology. From this more narrow point of view the aim of philosophy is to expose confusion and nonsense and to clarify the meaning and use of terms in science and everyday affairs.

The discussions centering around "philosophical analysis" as the function and method of philosophy are involved and technical. . . . We do not need to emphasize here that there are no philosophical schools which do not rely on analysis in some form. We are using the terms *philosophical analysis* and *linguistic analysis* to describe those philosophers who see this as the sole or at least the major task of philosophy.

5. *Philosophy is a group of problems as well as theories about the solution of these problems.* There are certain perennial problems which interest mankind and for which philosophers have always sought answers. Philosophy presses its inquiry into the deeper problems of human existence beyond what eye hath seen or ear heard. Some questions raised in the past have been answered in a manner satisfactory to most men. For example, the existence of innate or inborn ideas has been denied since the time of John Locke in the seventeenth century. Many questions, however, have been answered only tentatively, and many problems remain unsolved.

What are philosophical questions? The question "Did John Doe make a false statement on his income tax return?" is merely a question of fact. But the questions "What is truth?" and "What is the distinction between right and wrong?" have philosophical importance.

Most of us stop at times—sometimes because of startling events, often out of sheer curiosity—and think seriously about fundamental life issues: What is life and why am I here? What is the place of life in this great universe? Is the universe friendly or

---

[11] Lewis E. Hahn, "Philosophy as Comprehensive Vision," *Philosophy and Phenomenological Research.* 22 (September, 1961): 16–25.

unfriendly? Do things operate by chance or through sheer mechanism, or is there some plan or purpose or intelligence at the heart of things? Is my life controlled by outside forces or do I have a determining or even a partial degree of control? Why do men struggle and strive for their rights, for justice, for better things in the future? What do concepts like "right" and "justice" mean, and what are the marks of a good society?

Often men and women have been asked to sacrifice their lives, if need be, for certain values and ideals. What are the genuine values of life and how can they be attained? Is there really a fundamental distinction between right and wrong, or is it just a matter of one's own opinions? What is beauty? Should religion still count in a person's life? Is it intellectually respectable to believe in God? Is there any possibility of a "life after death"? Is there any way we can get an answer to these and many related questions? Where does knowledge come from, and can we have any assurances that anything is true?

These questions are all philosophical. The attempt to seek answers or solutions to them has given rise to theories and systems of thought, such as *idealism, realism, pragmatism, logical empiricism, humanism,* and *materialism.* Philosophy also means the various theories or systems of thought developed by the great philosophers—men like Socrates, Plato, Aristotle, Augustine, Aquinas, Descartes, Spinoza, Locke, Berkeley, Kant, Royce, James, and others. Without these men and their thoughts, philosophy would not have the rich content it has today. Even though we may be unconscious of the fact, we are constantly influenced by ideas that have come down to us in the traditions of society.

So far we have been talking about philosophy in general. However, philosophy also deals with the systematic body of principles and assumptions underlying a particular field of experience. For example, there are philosophies of science, education, art, music, history, law, mathematics, and religion. Any subject pursued far enough reveals within itself philosophical problems.

THE RELEVANCE OF PHILOSOPHY TO EVERYDAY LIVING

Occasionally we hear it said that it does not matter what a person believes so long as he does the right thing. Some people, in other words, have a tendency to value action or deeds over beliefs and convictions. But ideas are the foundation of action, and a person is not likely to make any determined effort to act unless he believes something. Communism as we know it would probably not have come into being if Marx had not laid its foundations in his philosophy; once men accepted his ideas, it was almost inevitable that these ideas should be expressed in action. There is a deep tendency in us all to become whatever we think ourselves to be; as a result, ideas have a decisive power in human history. One writer says:

This capacity to believe is the most significant and fundamental human faculty, and the most important thing about a man is what he believes in the depth of his being. This is the thing that makes him what he is; the thing that organizes him and feeds him; the thing that keeps him going in the face of untoward circumstances; the thing that gives him resistance and drive. Let neutrality, confusion, indifference or skepticism enter this inner place, and the very springs of life will cease to flow. Men will quit, lose heart, yield, give up, become bitter or cynical, become sunk in bleakness or emptiness, commit suicide, turn to criminality, or retreat into a realm of phantasy.[12]

Let us summarize briefly some of the things that philosophy can do for us, showing why it is that a person needs a philosophy.

1. *Each person must make decisions and act.* If we are to decide wisely and act consistently, we need to discover values and the meaning of things. Life forces us to make choices and to act on the basis of some scale of values. We have to decide questions of truth and falsity, of beauty and ugliness, and of right and wrong. The search for standards and goals is an important part of the task of philosophy. Philosophy is interested in the qualitative aspect of things. It refuses to disregard any authentic aspect of human experience and seeks to formulate standards and goals in the most reasonable way.

After asking the question, "What is the use of philosophy?" Jacques Maritain says that it reminds men "of the supreme utility of those things which do not deal with means, but with ends. For men do not live only by bread, vitamins, and technological discoveries. They live by values and realities which are above time and are worth knowing for their own sake."[13]

2. *Our conduct is our own, and we are really free only when we rely upon inner controls or self-chosen ends.* If a man acts as he does merely because of custom or tradition or the law, he is not genuinely free. When asked what good his philosophy did him, Aristotle remarked that it enabled him to do willingly what other men did merely because of fear of the law. That man is free who is the author of the principles and the laws by which he lives. In an ideal society, each person would agree with every law or, if he did not like the law, would criticize it and agitate for a change. He would do this on the basis of facts and principles which were consistent.

3. *Philosophy is one of the best means to foster the habit of reflection.* Philosophy can help us to enlarge the areas of our awareness—to become more alive, more discerning, more critical, and more intelligent. In many specialized fields of knowledge there is a definite and specific body of facts, and students are given problems so that they will gain practice in arriving at the right answers quickly and easily. In philosophy, however, there are different points of view to be considered, and there are unsolved problems which are important for life. Consequently, the student's sense of wonder, his curiosity, and his speculative interest are kept alive.

4. *We live in an age of uncertainty and change, when many of the older beliefs and ways of doing things are inadequate.* Under such conditions we need a scale of values and a sense of direction. Just as we feel physical discomfort when we are in the midst of material disorder and moral discomfort when we are confronted with cruelty and

[12] From Hugh Stevenson Tigner, *No Sign Shall Be Given* (New York: Macmillan, 1942), p. 109. By permission of The Macmillan Company, publishers.
[13] *On the Use of Philosophy* (Princeton: Princeton U. Press, 1961), pp. 6–7.

injustice, so there is intellectual discomfort in the presence of fragmentary and confused views of the world. Without some unity of outlook and response, there may result, as Irwin Edman has pointed out,[14] a divided self, which in turn may lead to psychological tensions or nervous collapse. One way we can gain unity in a world in turmoil is to achieve an inner integration, to know what to approve and what to disapprove, and to gain a sense of the meaning of human existence.

WHAT (IF ANYTHING) TO EXPECT FROM TODAY'S PHILOSOPHERS

There is an old saying that philosophy bakes no bread. It is perhaps equally true that no bread would ever have been baked without philosophy. For the act of baking implies a decision on the philosophical issue of whether life is worthwhile at all. Bakers may not have often asked themselves the question in so many words. But philosophy traditionally has been nothing less than the attempt to ask and answer, in a formal and disciplined way, the great questions of life that ordinary men might put to themselves in reflective moments.

The world has both favored and feared the philosophers' answers. Thomas Aquinas became a saint, Aristotle was tutor to Alexander the Great, and Voltaire was a confidant of kings. But Socrates was put to death, and Giordano Bruno was burned at the stake. Nowadays, Historian Will Durant has noted, no one would think of doing that—"not because men are more delicate about killing, but because there is no need to kill that which is already dead."

Philosophy dead? It often seems so. In a world of war and change, of principles armed with bombs and technology searching for principles, the alarming thing is not what philosophers say but what they fail to say. When reason is overturned, blind passions are rampant, and urgent questions mount, men turn for guidance to scientists, psychiatrists, sociologists, ideologues, politicians, historians, journalists— almost anyone except their traditional guide, the philosopher. Ironically, the once remote theologians are in closer touch with humanity's immediate and intense concerns than most philosophers, who today tend to be relatively obscure academic technicians. No living U.S. philosopher has the significance to the world at large that John Dewey or George Santayana had a generation or two ago. Many feel

---

FROM *Time*, 87 (January 7, 1966): 24–25. Copyright Time, Inc., 1966. (Reprinted by permission.)

[14] "Philosophy," in *On Going to College: A Symposium* (New York: Oxford U. Press, 1938), pp. 196–198.

that philosophy has played out its role in the history of human culture; the "queen of sciences" has been dethroned.

Once all sciences were part of philosophy's domain, but gradually, from physics .o psychology, they seceded and established themselves as independent disciplines. Above all, for some time now, philosophy itself has been engaged in a vast revolt against its own past and against its traditional function. This intellectual purge may well have been necessary, but as a result contemporary philosophy looks inward at its own problems rather than outward at men, and philosophizes about philosophy, not about life. A great many of his colleagues in the U.S. today would agree with Donald Kalish, chairman of the philosophy department at U.C.L.A., who says: "There is no system of philosophy to spin out. There are no ethical truths, there are just clarifications of particular ethical problems. Take advantage of these clarifications and work out your own existence. You are mistaken to think that anyone ever had the answers. There are no answers. Be brave and face up to it."

REVOLT OF THE LOGICIANS

Before such chilling views took hold, philosophers always were men who thought, says Yale's Professor Emeritus Brand Blanshard, that "they could sit down in their studies and arrive by reasoning at a knowledge of the ultimate nature of the world." Perhaps in no other age had philosophers greater confidence in their capacity to do this than in the 19th century. Hegel tried to encompass all aspects of life within his dialectical logic of thesis-antithesis-synthesis, in 18 ponderous tomes. His idealistic principle that the material world exists only in relation to the Absolute mind led to the metaphysics of F. H. Bradley, who denied—even during the course of an hour's conversation in an Oxford chamber—that time or space had objective reality.

By the turn of the century, science and common sense alike dictated a shift away from idealism. "Damn the Absolute," roared William James, and the American pragmatists turned from principles and categories to results and facts. But the most effective rebellion against Hegelianism was carried out by two groups— the analytic philosophers, who prevail in U.S. and British universities, and the partisans of phenomenology and existentialism, who predominate in Western Europe. On some U.S. campuses, they are known as "the logicians and the lotus-eaters."

The analytic revolt began with two convictions: first, that experience contradicted the idealistic theory that material objects are not in themselves "real"; second, that philosophy could not compete with science as a way of studying the real world and thus would have to turn to other tasks. The analytic thinkers decided that philosophy's true job was to answer that old Socratic question "What does it mean?"

The study of meaning takes many forms. One stems from G. E. Moore of Cambridge, who argued that the business of philosophy was simply the analysis and clarification of common sense beliefs. Moore's colleague Bertrand Russell tried to eliminate fallacies by using an artificial language of symbols into which the truths of science and ordinary descriptive statements could be translated in order to test their accuracy. The "Vienna Circle" of logical positivists—who carried their ideas to Britain and the U.S. in the 1930s—declared that the criterion of meaning was verifiability; if the meaning of a statement could not be verified by empirical procedures, it was literally nonsense. But, as Russell pointed out, this criterion was itself a philosophical principle.

Finally Ludwig Wittgenstein, an Austrian-born Cambridge don, and such Oxonians as J. L. Austin and Gilbert Ryle decided independently that philosophy was concerned not so much with meaning as with use, and should seek to establish the rules of the various "language games" that men played with ordinary words, describing when a word was used legitimately, and when it was not. About all the various analytic schools had in common was the belief that philosophy has nothing to say about the world and that clarity and straight thinking will dissolve most of the classical metaphysical problems.

THE RISE OF THE LOTUS-EATERS

On the Continent, the philosophical revolt took a different form. Germany's Edmund Husserl developed a "descriptive science" that he called phenomenology. His method was to examine and describe a particular experience—at the same time mentally blocking off any speculations about its origin or significance, any memories of similar experiences. By this act of epoche, a deliberate suspension of judgment, Husserl felt that the mind could eventually intuit the essence of the object being studied. Husserl's bafflingly difficult approach influenced such modern existentialist philosophers as Martin Heidegger and Jean-Paul Sartre.

What the existentialists emphasize about man is that he, alone among other beings, is a decision-making creature blessed, or cursed, with the freedom to choose among a variety of possibilities in an absurd and mysterious existence; to be truly human, man must accept this freedom and conquer the anxiety and despair that threaten it by "commitment" to a way of life. This message can be bracing, notably in the religious version of existentialism, in which the commitment is directed toward a spiritual goal. It can also be nihilistic, notably in the atheistic version, in which commitment is demanded for its own sake only and the despair of the human situation is emphasized more than its conquest.

Both movements, the logicians as well as the lotus-eaters, appear to do away with what has usually been considered the very heart of philosophy: metaphysics, the attempt to comprehend through reason the nature of reality. In *The Conditions of Philosophy*, a current examination of the discipline, Mortimer Adler charges that the analytic thinkers abandon "first-order questions" that metaphysics used to ask —such as the nature of being, causation, free will—and are concerned mostly with second-order problems of method. The existentialists, on the other hand, continue to ask large-size questions, but because of their man-centered approach they are indifferent to systematic thinking. Thus, for both movements, a question such as "What is truth?" becomes impossible to answer. The logical positivist would say that a particular statement of fact can be declared true or false by empirical evidence; anything else is meaningless. A language philosopher would content himself with analyzing all the ways the word true can be used. The existentialist would emphasize what is true for a person in a particular situation.

THE WAR OF THE SCHOOLS

Both movements have turned philosophy into a private game for professionals. Laymen glancing at the June 10, 1965, issue of the *Journal of Philosophy* will find a brace of learned analysts discussing whether the sentence "There are brown things and there are cows" is best expressed by the formula $(\exists x)Exw \cdot (\exists x)Exy$ or by $(\exists x)Bx \cdot (\exists x)Cx$. And while the existentialists speak dramatically enough about the condition of man in novels and plays, their philosophical writing is so dense that Brandeis' Henry Aiken complains: "Reading Heidegger is like trying to swim through wet sand." One typical passage of Heidegger's alleged masterwork, *Being and Time*, reads: "If the Being of everyday Being-with-one-another is already different in principle from pure presence-at-hand—in spite of the fact that it is seemingly close to it ontologically—still less can the Being of the authentic Self be conceived as presence-at-hand."

Philosophy cannot and need not make sense to the layman in every detail; excerpts from Aristotle or Hegel (or, for that matter, Einstein) may also seem like gibberish to the uninitiated. But it is significant that the analytic and phenomenological thinkers don't even understand one another.

As a result, philosophy today is bitterly segregated. Most of the major philosophy departments and scholarly journals are the exclusive property of one sect or another. Harvard, U.C.L.A. and Cornell are oriented toward analytic thinking, for example, while Penn State and Northwestern are among the minority leaning toward phenomenology. Despite much academic talk about the horrors of conformity, some philosophy departments are rigidly conformist. Instructors or students with the "wrong" approach are forced out. The attitude at U.C.L.A., for instance, is that "a lot of nice young people who might be wholesome philosophers of the nonanalytic kind can't get through our requirements."

Many students who do make the grade in analytic courses are disappointed because they had expected more from philosophy. To some, the analytic approach is now old hat, while the older, unfashionable philosophies take on a new excitement. There are many older-line philosophers left in the U.S. who belong to neither of the two warring sides, including Yale's Paul Weiss, Chicago's Richard McKeon, the University of Texas' Charles Hartshorne, and Michigan's Abraham Kaplan, who states wryly: "The word philosophy means the love of wisdom. And the love of wisdom, I suppose, is like any other sort of love—the professionals are the ones who know least about it."

There are signs that, hesitantly and sometimes unintentionally, professional philosophers are beginning to take such reproaches to heart. At long last, philosophy may have stopped attacking the Hegelian bogey and be about ready to put its analytic tools to work on the real issues facing man.

Suggesting the glimmer of a *détente*, French Phenomenologist Paul Ricoeur now teaches a course in linguistic analysis at the University of Paris. Yale's John Wild recently published an article suggesting that the *lebenswelt*, the "life world" of experience that phenomenology investigates, is the world of "ordinary language" that the linguistic philosophers are studying.

Some analytic philosophers are even daring to "do metaphysics" again. P. F. Strawson, one of the most respected of Oxford's analytic philosophers, boldly subtitled his latest book, *Individuals, An Essay in Descriptive Metaphysics*. The book is partly concerned with the difference between material objects and human beings, a highly technical question that, by extension, has to do with the very real problem of whether man can be explained like a flesh-and-blood object or whether he is an organism with a purpose. Another, younger Oxonian, Anthony Quinton, is completing a philosophical treatise, grandly titled *The Nature of Things*, that starts from the problem of identity and reference: Is a given object simply a bundle of qualities, or is it something more than that? Quinton points out that the question is as old as Aristotle, who grappled with the meaning of "substance." Strawson, as well as such U.S. figures as Harvard's Morton White, emphasizes that analytic technique is a means rather than an end.

The early analytic thinkers believed that with the clarifying of language the old questions of philosophy would simply disappear, but their intellectual offsprings are wiser. "Once you see that language permeates the world," says Morris Kaplan, a Ph.D. candidate at Yale, "all the problems you had with the world come back." Strawson agrees that "the insatiable appetite of philosophers for generality has reasserted itself." In other words, the philosophers are beginning to re-invent philosophy.

In Britain, philosophers are newly concerned over such ancient issues as the relationship of body to mind and the problem of causation in human behavior. David Wiggins of Oxford is currently exploring "the entire concept of event identity—what makes it right to say that event A is the same as event B?" An American illustrates Wiggins' problem with a homely example: "Is my act of flipping on the light switch the same act as my act of alerting the prowler, if in fact by flipping on the switch and illuminating the room, I do alert the prowler?" Although the question sounds as relevant as the medieval puzzler about how many angels can dance on a pinhead, Wiggins notes that it has highly practical implications in fixing intention and responsibility, and theoretical ones in helping to solve the age-old puzzler of free will *v.* determinism. Free will is back in philosophical style, and Wiggins concedes that the traditional way of stating that problem "wasn't after all in quite such a mess as had recently been supposed."

TIME TO WAKE UP

In the Middle Ages, the questions that philosophy asked were determined largely by theology; today major philosophical issues are posed by science. Says Chicago's McKeon: "The new priests come from the lab and hand us the tablet—how do we handle it?" Philosopher Hubert Dreyfus of M.I.T. is wondering about the possibility of creating a computer that would be completely determined by programming but would behave as if it were a free, intelligent agent. "If something that we knew was just a machine could behave intelligently," he muses, "it would tend to suggest that maybe we are just machines." Would such computers have to be considered conscious beings? Would they raise a civil liberties problem? To some, such questions suggest that science is creating more problems than philosophy can readily cope with; and concepts like antimatter and the expanding universe make some philosophers quite nervous.

Chances are, however, that philosophy will learn to coexist with science and (in Mortimer Adler's phrase) reach its delayed maturity, provided it resolutely insists on being a separate discipline dealing publicly and intelligibly in first-order questions. Caution is bound to remain. Instead of one-man systems, philosophy in the future will probably consist of a dialogue of many thinkers, each seeking to explore to the fullest one aspect of a common problem. Says Oxford's James Urmson, a visiting professor at the University of Michigan: "It is just like Galileo experimenting with little balls on inclined planes before he addressed the heavens."

The question remains: Will philosophy ever again address the heavens? Will it contribute anything to man's vision, rather than merely clarifying it? Caution and confusion are not necessarily signs of disaster, and even Hegel remarked that "the owl of Minerva spreads its wings only with the falling of the dusk." But the shadows are deep and the time for an awakening is at hand.

AMERICAN PHILOSOPHY IS DEAD

LEWIS S. FEUER

Seventy years ago America was enjoying its Golden Age of Philosophy. At Harvard, William James was expounding the new pragmatism and looking at the

FROM *The New York Times Magazine* (April 24, 1966): 30–31*ff*. © 1966 by The New York *Times* Company. (Reprinted by permission of the author.)

classical questions of man's place in the universe with an unparalleled freshness of perception. At Chicago, John Dewey was fashioning with the help of teachers at the Laboratory School a new answer to Pontius Pilate's query, "What is truth?" Truth, said Dewey, was an instrument for reforming and remaking the world.

The America of open, unrealized possibilities took on cosmic proportions in James's pluralistic universe, with its challenge of human freedom. And in Dewey, the renaissance which was beginning in a Chicago of immigrant confusion, violence and financial chicanery found a philosopher who retained his faith in the creative potentialities in crude human experience.

American philosophers spoke for and to the American people at large, and they tried continually to write in their fellow citizens' language. In the case of William James, a clarity and vigor of philosophical writing was achieved which remains unsurpassed. What philosopher today would have the democratic effrontery to write, as James did, of the God of science as one "who does a wholesale, not a retail, business"? What philosopher today could write theology with this candor and Churchillian sweep:

"In this real world of sweat and dirt, it seems to me that when a view of things is 'noble', that ought to count as a presumption against its truth, and as a philosophic disqualification. The prince of darkness may be a gentleman, as we are told he is, but whatever the God of earth and heaven is, he can surely be no gentleman."

Today the Golden Age is a closed chapter in the history of philosophy. Three generations of academic philosophers have intervened, and one asks with the advent of the fourth, why do we no longer have a James or a Dewey or a Josiah Royce? Not only have we had an end of ideology in America (at least for a brief while) and an end of God in theology, but we have also witnessed evidently an end of philosophy. For the intellectual history of contemporary America could be written today virtually without mention of its 2,100 or so professional philosophers. With the lone exception of Sidney Hook, their work attracts almost no notice among general readers, while among themselves, at their professional meetings, they are mostly telling each other privately what a waste of time it all is, that nothing significant is being said and that they don't know what it's all about. What has happened to philosophy?

More than a decade ago, a philosophical dialogue took place between Andrei Gromyko, the Soviet diplomat, and Christopher Mayhew, until recently the British Labor Government's Naval Minister. "What philosophy do your philosophers teach?" asked Gromyko. "Philosophy in Britain," replied Mayhew, "is concerned mainly with the meanings of words." Perhaps it was not very constructive, he added, but it helped in understanding the errors of Marxism. Gromyko was puzzled. "But what is your own philosophy?" he persisted. "Are you a materialist? Is this glass I am holding real or not?" Mayhew was not sure.

Perhaps we have in Mayhew's responses the worst and best of academic philosophy. It is essentially a training in disputation in the medieval tradition. But the disputationist rarely has a philosophy of his own to advance or defend; he will argue, challenge, criticize. Conventions of philosophers today are occasions for jousts and tourneys, quite unlike the less forensic meetings of scientific investigators which are more concerned with fact. Consequently, when young thinkers, for instance, in the Soviet Union look for an alternative to the official doctrine of dialectical materialism, they rarely turn to the writings of our academic philosophers, with their treatises on language and morals. They read instead Camus, Berdyaev or Niebuhr. They are looking for a philosophy, not for a compendium of word usages, and they do not find philosophy among the academic philosophers.

For what has happened, indeed, is that academic philosophy has become the antagonist of philosophy; the two are, in the long run, incompatible with each other. The great figures who founded modern philosophy were not academicians but men such as Descartes, Leibnitz, Spinoza, Locke and Hume—physicists, mathematicians, political scientists who had almost no connection with the universities.

Academic philosophy was very much the creation of the German universities. The professor, a kind of ideological bureaucrat, explicated a system. Nowadays in its linguistic form, it is cultivated by eccentric disputationists in the common rooms of Oxford and Cambridge and imported by academic admirers into the United States.

When philosophy, however, becomes academic, the results are much the same as when art becomes academic. What great novel could have been written to satisfy a Ph.D. requirement in Creative Writing? Or what great painting could have been done to secure a Ph.D. degree in Creative Art? It is quite otherwise in the sciences where the methods and techniques of verification and experiment on the whole provide a common ground upon which almost all will meet.

When philosophy becomes academic, it tries to emulate the sciences, to employ methods and criteria which the profession in general will accept. The pressures in the universities to be "scientific" are now overwhelming. Therefore, academic philosophers look for some device which will seem to make their "discipline" as objective, scientific and examination-gradable as physics or mathematics. A generation ago mathematical logic was the favored device. Today, as this is being discarded, the study of ordinary language, a kind of descriptive lexicography, is taken as the examinable core of philosophy. Would a James, Kierkegaard or Nietzsche ever have been able to get his mature philosophical works accepted for a Ph.D. degree? Probably not.

How would Freud have fared with his theory of the unconscious if he had been examined by today's academic philosophers? "Your notion of unconscious mental events," they would have said, "plainly contravenes ordinary language; a mental event must be conscious." How would young Einstein have survived the mighty gauntlet of the ordinary-language philosophers? "Your ideas of spacetime," they would affirm, "are simply excluded by the ordinary usage of "'space' and 'time.'"

By contrast, an original contribution to physics will pass muster through the universal criteria of science. Einstein would have had small reason to expect rejection at the hands of university science faculties. But academic philosophy, on the other hand, tends to become a crushing force inhibiting fresh philosophical thought.

As a result, professional philosophers have been losing a sense of their vocation. There have been numerous symptoms of the decline of philosophy in the universities. Departments of philosophy have dwindled in relation to departments of sociology, political science and psychology (which, 30 years ago, was usually a small section under the aegis of the philosophers). Moreover, subdomains are gradually being ceded to other disciplines, leaving the academic philosophers with little "scientific" which they can call their own.

Mathematical logic is being absorbed by departments of mathematics, where indeed it belongs; inductive logic has found its way to statistics. Even the history of philosophy is studied most constructively by intellectual historians who have a sense of the interrelations of ideas often lacking among academic philosophers. Similarly, the philosophy of science is probably best pursued by scientists who work on the frontiers of research, where the philosophical discussion becomes most significant.

The number of able Americans who study philosophy constantly declines. Therefore, whenever a major post is vacant in a graduate department of philosophy, the tendency is to import an Englishman from the home breeding grounds. In sociology, on the contrary, the United States exports professors to Britain.

The decline of philosophy has not been wholly an American phenomenon, of course. In Britain, the lifetime of its most eminent thinker, Bertrand Russell, has seen it decline from significance to triviality. Russell today mourns the change of philosophy into an academic cult of linguistic analysis; he regards it as snobbish talk by silly people asking what they mean when they say silly things. Yet Russell himself is the grandfather of this cult, for it all began with his own notion that philosophy "analyzes propositions" and that language is decisive in shaping a philosophy.

Most people think of Russell, first, as the author of those classical essays, "A Free Man's Worship" and "Mysticism and Logic," and secondly, as the man who, in his nineties, speaks for the collective conscience of mankind against nuclear destruction. But those writings and activities have nothing to do with Russell's philosophy. The essays were the *obiter dicta* of a young man indulging his human weaknesses in ways irrelevant to philosophy, while his preference, as an old man, for life rather than death, is, from the standpoint of his philosophy, a concession to prejudice.

Philosophy, according to Russell, was a dull, dry, austere study devoted to the analysis of logical relations, and with nothing to say on such subjects as human destiny or God. Russell began the separation of academic philosophy from philosophy; his descendants to his regret have completed it. They have reached the apex of dullness.

Bereft of a sense that they have something to say, a curious style of writing has developed among academic philosophers. They seem to delight in conspicuous boredom; they multiply pages to explain what it is they are not going to discuss; they convey the sense of having an endless time to say what they feel it's not really worth saying. As content declines, the preciosity of their style increases. Young academics vie with each other at philosophy clubs in giving fatuous titles to papers, taking as their models "Chinks and Clinks" and "On Three Different Ways of Spilling Ink."

At times, embarrassing incidents take place, as when the risk arises that scientific colleagues will see that the emperor is wearing no clothes. A few years ago, a great Eastern university undertook to invite a leading figure in English philosophy to a special visiting lectureship. In accordance with the usual procedure, his appointment had to be approved by an interdepartmental committee which included several scientists. They read the essay or two which constituted the philosopher's works, and said quite frankly that they thought them silly and trivial; they were puzzled that these meager essays could be regarded as a momentous contribution to anything.

The academic philosopher on the committee assured them that the essays were momentous for philosophers. The scientists, still unconvinced, felt the lectureship was a waste of university funds. But there is, on such matters, an academic as well as a Senatorial courtesy, and they decided to humor the strange ways of philosophers.

No student is as disoriented and bewildered as the average graduate student in philosophy. The young student comes to philosophy with a certain enthusiasm, moved usually by some personal religious problem or quest for a way of life. He spends a year or two in a mishmash of studies. For a while he may cultivate the standard mannerisms of the linguistic analyst—walking around clutching his head and indulging in tedious verbalisms. Then he wakes up one day and wonders what it has all added up to. Existentialist students especially tend to be bitter about the System, and to regard their professors (in the Sartrean idiom) as touched with bad faith.

The desperate search by the philosophers for a method which could render their discipline "scientific" has had the powerful consequence of dephilosophizing philosophy. For every time a "method" is proposed, it turns philosophy into something else—whether it be psychology, sociology, mathematics or linguistics.

The existentialists have argued that the method of philosophy is phenomenology; that is, a close description of man's consciousness as he makes his choices, hopes, suffers, loves, triumphs and fails. A revival of richly introspective psychology has taken place, a welcome sign that a generation of behaviorism has failed to obliterate the psyche. But can one accept introspective psychology as a master key to ultimate reality? Or was Freud right in thinking the human experience of its freedom an illusion? Not all the literary skill and introspective genius of existentialists can avail as a method for solving the ultimate philosophical problems.

Then there have been the logicians who, following Russell, have said that logic was the essence of philosophy. But then it transpired, as Russell acknowledged, that the classical philosophical problems of man and God were simply going to be ignored or legislated out of existence as meaningless. Why mathematical logic was to be called philosophy was never made clear; it could be called economics just as well.

Then there were those who felt philosophy was methodology, that its primary function was to analyze scientific methods. It turned out, however, that scientists, statisticians and sociologists could take care of their own methodological worries. In any case, a textbook on scientific methods was no substitute for trying to answer problems which were outside the purview of any given science.

The latest proposal to make the method of philosophy the study of linguistic usage may advance the knowledge of linguistics but it altogether begs the philosophical questions. Knowing how different peoples use their different ordinary languages will not answer these questions for us, unless we arbitrarily assume that some given language gives us a privileged insight into ultimate realities.

In one respect, linguistic philosophy might perhaps be regarded as an ideology of the bureaucratic society, especially the bureaucratic university. Not only does it cultivate a professional way of writing, with a specialized idiom in which "paradigm case" and "language games" sound as imposing as the "simulated model" and "war games" in military parlance, but it raises no moral challenges nor pretends to a moral critique; it takes the moral rules and speech of society as it finds it.

To a bureaucratic order, we are all ordinary people with ordinary usage; the fugitive insight is exiled. The interchangeable man is the norm. In a bureaucratized world, the ideologist analyzes bureaucratic language and expects standard results. The individual perspective on existence is obsolete. Arthur Lovejoy, America's greatest historian of ideas, remarked to me shortly before he died that the dominance of "ordinary language" showed philosophy was "on its last legs."

But, as I have suggested, it would be as much a mistake to identify philosophy with academic philosophy as it would be to regard the whole of American society as a bureaucratic order. The revival of the concept of "alienation," of Marx's youthful philosophy when he was not yet a Marxist, is evidence among America's younger generation of a search for a deeper philosophy than the academics provide. And, curiously, this word has become the philosophical slogan of a generation not only in the United States but in the Soviet Union, Poland, Japan and Latin America.

If the conflict of religion and science was the provocative agent for most philosophy 75 years ago, then the conflict of the individual with bureaucratic pressures may inspire in our time the search for new meanings of the human status. In Poland, the young philosopher Leszek Kolakowski, struggling to impart a religious sense and liberal values to a rigid, bureaucratic Marxism, has become the only young thinker widely read and representative of his generation's longings.

In the Soviet Union, as the official ideology declines, young thinkers revolt against a doctrine planned to economic specifications, and their own philosophies emerge. Ideology is socially determined; a philosophy is a personal achievement which surmounts the social circumstances. The young Soviet thinkers are trying to liberate philosophy from their academic Marxism-Leninism.

Though academic philosophy withers in the colleges and universities, philosophy itself cannot be suppressed. While our professional philosophers practice their respective nonphilosophies, the function of philosophy itself has been assumed by religious thinkers, historians, scientists, novelists. A historian or physicist who within his own work has already demonstrated his scientific capacity will not labor under the compulsion to make his philosophy "scientific." The historian or physicist is far more likely to allow full range to his speculative imagination on ultimate questions. He does not have to repress his philosophical instinct as a defense-mechanism against his scientific colleagues.

Religious thinkers and novelists likewise have committed themselves to explore the nature of man without benefit of scientific orthodoxy. The initiative in the philosophy of history has thus passed to such a man as Arnold Toynbee, who has dared to sink himself in facts and nonetheless emerge with a vision.

You could look through a whole library of academic philosophy in the United States between the two World Wars and not realize what had taken place. The philosophers were arguing whether it was meaningful to talk of another's tooth-ache; in the midst of the Depression they thought it was nonsense, though on the eve of the Second World War some doubts had arisen. Today, after the holocaust, the academics still fill scholastic pages with the old ontological argument that a perfect God must exist because the very definition of a perfect object involves its necessary existence. How much more wisdom and honesty there is in the groping "death of God" theology.

During the post-World War II era, such political theorists and historians as Arthur Schlesinger Jr. certainly found a greater inspiration in the theology of Reinhold Niebuhr than in any of the formalistic treatises on historical statements. Why was this? Because the basis on which a whole generation finally rejected Marxism and pragmatism was in terms of the false character which they imparted both to one's emotions and beliefs. The all-sufficing social dedication, when one looked deeply within oneself, turned out to be a repressed, partially sublimated religious feeling. When one realized that ideological causes were attempts at a secular equivalent of religious experience, old abandoned beliefs began to return in a chastened, simpler form—the belief, for instance, in human freedom in more than a political, social or psychological sense. Are there any methods of philosophy other than being most honest with oneself concerning one's spontaneous, uncoerced beliefs? And don't we reject doctrines finally because we feel behind the facade of pedantic profession a certain dishonesty?

Novelists have been the primary philosophers in modern times. Koestler's "Darkness at Noon" depicted the dramatic return of the "I," which the academic positivists had reduced to a "grammatical convenience" and the Marxists had ostracized as a bourgeois vestige. Rubashov, facing death, and adding up his sociological accounts, asks himself: What of the infinite?

Camus unravels the destructive drive which can permeate the metaphysical rebel; Graham Greene's characters find themselves wondering if a divine element can intrude into their everyday lives. The nihilism of the drug-directed beatnik poets, tinkling Tibetan bells on bewildered peace parades, with their frantic, directionless search which always ends compulsively in the nothingness of things, is an undeniable symptom of America's need for a philosophy.

Would it help revive philosophy in the universities if departments of academic philosophy were gently allowed to end their days? The young student with the spirit of a genuine philosopher would then press his interest within the more fruitful context of some science, literature or history. A committee on philosophical thought, composed of persons from different departments who, on the basis of their lifetime's work had something philosophical to say, could help him. Philosophy is far too important to be left in the hands of the academic philosophers.

THE NATURE
OF PHILOSOPHY

D. J. O'CONNOR

The work of the philosopher has traditionally been supposed to consist of three connected tasks. In the first place, he has been expected to provide a compendious overall view of the universe and of man's place in it. Secondly, he has been expected to do this by rational procedures and not, for example, by intuition or poetic imagination. Lastly, men have looked to the philosopher to give them or at least justify for them, a religious point of view that would also be defensible by reason. Philosophers have thus been expected to combine the aims and achievements of scientists, moralists and theologians. But these expectations have proved far beyond what they have been able to accomplish. On rare occasions, a philosopher of genius like Aquinas [1] or Spinoza [2] has given us a map of the universe that many people have found both intellectually and spiritually satisfying. But in such cases it has proved only too easy for the philosopher's critics to attack the logic

FROM D. J. O'Connor, *An Introduction to The Philosophy of Education.* New York: Philosophical Library, 1957, pp. 16–23, 30–32, 35–38, 39–40, 44–45. (Reprinted by permission of Routledge & Kegan Paul, Ltd. and Philosophical Library.)

[1] St. Thomas Aquinas (1225–74), a medieval theologian and philosopher.
[2] Baruch Spinoza (1632–77), a Jewish philosopher who lived in Holland.

of his system or the truth of his premises. They have shown in this way that, however fascinating and persuasive his picture of the world may be, there is no good reason to believe that it is a true one.

At the present day, philosophers would state their aims very much more modestly though, naturally enough, a philosopher's view of the scope of his discipline will depend on his own philosophical opinions. A few of them might still want to maintain the traditional view. But most would agree that the traditional philosophers promised more than they were able to deliver and that their claims to interpret the universe on a grand scale must be rejected for just the same reason that the claims of alchemists, astrologers or magicians are now rejected. The reason is the simple and fundamental one that the results of any sort of enquiry are acceptable in so far as they are publicly testable, reliable and coherent with the rest of public knowledge. Traditional metaphysics,[3] like astrology and alchemy, cannot meet these requirements. It may perhaps be objected that the requirements themselves are arbitrary if they are applied to philosophy since these are standards by which we test scientific knowledge. We may return to this objection after we have looked at the way in which philosophy has developed.

The history of western philosophy started in fifth-century Greece. If we examine the doctrines of the Greek philosophers, we see that they cover an enormously wide field. We find discussions of characteristically philosophical problems like the existence of God, the nature of human knowledge and the good life for man. We also find interest in questions of mathematics and astronomy, physics and chemistry of a primitive kind, biology and the social sciences. Moreover we do not find that any clear distinction was made between those questions that we nowadays recognize as philosophical and those that we class as scientific. Not only was knowledge not departmentalized as it is today but it was not even divided into the main *logically distinct types of enquiry* that we now recognize. We distinguish nowadays between physics, chemistry and zoology, for example, but this kind of distinction is largely a matter of administrative convenience, so to speak. The field of scientific knowledge has become far too detailed and complex for one man to deal effectively with more than a very small area. The division and subdivision of natural science into specialities is thus a practical device to meet the limitations of man's mind and the shortness of his life. There is however a more basic distinction between branches of knowledge. This depends not on the kind of material that we study but on the *sort of evidence* by which we advance our knowledge. Botanists study plants, geologists the history and structure of the earth's crust, astronomers the planets and

---

[3] A statement is metaphysical if it assumes the existence of entities or facts which lie outside the range of human observation and experience. An argument is metaphysical if it purports to prove the existence of such entities or facts. Note that statements are not metaphysical because they cannot *in fact* be checked by observation, but because they cannot *in principle* be checked in this way. Compare the following statements: (1) On January 1st, 1567, there were 6537 crocodiles in the River Zambesi. (2) Some good actions are the result of divine grace. (3) Julius Caesar had blood belonging to group AB. (4) Julius Caesar had an immortal soul. (2) and (4) are metaphysical; (1) and (3) are not, because, although we do not know whether they are true and can never find out, the sort of evidence which would confirm them is within the range of human observation.

stars. But all of them get their material by observing nature through the senses. Indeed this is one of the characteristic features of the sciences. Pure mathematics and formal logic on the other hand do not derive their material from observation of the world nor are the findings of these sciences proved or supported by this kind of evidence. Anyone who has taken a school course of elementary geometry is aware that we do not *prove* that the three angles of a plane triangle total two right angles by drawing a selection of triangles and measuring their angles. We prove such propositions by deductions from axioms or postulates conventionally accepted as a starting point. And when we turn to the problems of philosophy, it is easy to see that they cannot be decided either by the observational methods of the natural sciences or the deductive methods of mathematics and formal logic. For if they were decidable in this way, some of them at least would long since have been decided. (It is not merely a truism to say that *what is provable can be proved*. Indeed, we can read in this statement one reason for the failure of traditional metaphysics and natural religion.)

This very important logical point that different kinds of statement demand different kinds of evidence is not one that the Greek or medieval philosophers would have denied if it had been put to them. They were, in a sense, aware of the point but the presuppositions of their thinking and the state of knowledge in their time did not require them to bring it into focus and concede it any importance. But this situation was radically altered by the rise of natural science and the renaissance of mathematics during the seventeenth and eighteenth centuries.

All the sciences started as branches of philosophy in the sense that the Greek word 'philosophia' was originally used in a very general sense to cover all investigations into the nature of man and of the universe. But in the sixteenth and seventeenth centuries a discovery was made about scientific method which seems to us nowadays trivial and obvious, perhaps because it is the unquestioned foundation of a civilization based on the achievements of natural science. This was the discovery that if you want to know what the world is like, you have to look and see. As a practical maxim, this was not always a commonplace. There have been long periods in the history of the world and no doubt there will be again, when people were discouraged from looking either by the intellectual fashions of their time or because the prevailing religious or political outlook might conflict with what observation would tell them. And of course mere observation of the world of nature was not enough to lay the foundations of science. The results of observation had to be refined by experiment and by measurement and the direction of observation controlled by hypothesis. But once men had learned the lesson of what has been called 'respect for fact,' natural science started on that brilliant epoch of development which has marked off the last three hundred years from all other periods of history. This lesson was first thoroughly, though slowly, learned by the scientists of western Europe during the seventeenth and eighteenth centuries.

Thus science became emancipated from philosophy by the discovery of its proper method; and the only relic of the long association between the two is the title of 'Professor of Natural Philosophy' which adorns the holders of chairs of physics in some of the older British universities. The method of observation and experiment had of course been practised in Greek and medieval times but in a half-hearted and sporadic way; and it had not usually been practised in conjunction with the language of mathematics, the language in which, in Galileo's famous epigram, the book of nature is written. But with the systematic adoption of the experimental method and the translation of natural laws into mathematical modes of expression, men were at last developing a large body of reliable and testable knowledge. They were moreover acquiring it with the aid of a method whose power they recognized and which they consciously applied to the solution of the problems of nature. Philosophers could now compare the uncertain powers of their own speculative methods with the method of hypothesis and experiment. Though it is a method that needs slow, laborious and piecemeal application, it gives answers that can be progressively corrected, tested and communicated and leads in the end to generally accepted results. Like many other important revolutions, this one did not take place overnight. Indeed its full impact has not been felt by all educated men even at the present day. But most philosophers since the seventeenth century, many of whom were also men of science, saw clearly enough what the new way of explaining the world meant for them. It was a challenge to find a method of tackling the problems of philosophy which would be appropriate to those problems and so would enable men to agree when a solution of them had been reached.

There is one important way in which the success of the natural scientists helped the philosophers to focus their difficulties more clearly. It became obvious with the rise of the scientific method that the attention of philosophers in ancient and medieval times sometimes had been taken up with questions that had not properly been matters for them at all, since they were questions decidable only by the methods of the scientists. Aristotle, for example, discussed not only philosophical questions such as origins of human knowledge, the nature of morality and the relations between mind and body but also scientific questions about the mechanism of sensation, the constitution of the physical universe, the nature and organization of the heavenly bodies and the like. There is no reason why a man should not be both a scientist and a philosopher but unless he clearly distinguishes his scientific questions from his philosophical ones, both his science and his philosophy are likely to suffer. Aristotle failed to make this distinction and in this he was followed by nearly all the medieval philosophers.

And so, in the seventeenth century, the physics of Aristotle were not corrected but rather replaced by the physics of Galileo and Newton. Philosophers were henceforth relieved of the duty of trying to solve problems about the observable facts and regularities of nature. But this restriction of their responsibilities was an embarrassment rather than a relief. If all questions of observable fact were questions for the scientist to answer, what questions remained for philosophy and how were they to be approached?

The upshot of the scientific revolution for philosophy is this: Some questions, characteristically those of the natural and social sciences, can be settled by empirical methods, by hypothesis arising out of observation and observation confirming hypothesis. Other questions, characteristic of logical and mathematical subject matters, can be settled by calculation in accordance with settled rules of deduction. But there are a very large number of questions that do not seem to fall into either of these categories and among these are the traditional problems of philosophy, of ethics and of natural religion. But if such questions cannot be decided either by empirical or by purely deductive methods, how are they to be answered? This is the problem that has been set to philosophy by the success of natural science. Of course, we see it more clearly at the present day than did the philosophers of the seventeenth and eighteenth centuries since we have the advantage of profiting by their work. But it was well understood by most of them that the first problem for the philosopher had become the problem of finding a method. Descartes[4] and Spinoza, impressed by the certainty and efficiency of mathematical methods of proof, tried to prove philosophical conclusions as they proved problems in geometry, and actually set out part of their work in the axiomatic form of Euclid's *Elements of Geometry*. They were unsuccessful, as they misunderstood the nature of the axiomatic method that they were trying to use and overlooked the differences between mathematical symbolism and the language of philosophical arguments. Other philosophers, like Locke[5] and Kant,[6] did not raise the method so directly and preferred to ask: 'What are the limits of human knowledge?' They tried to outline a sort of programme of possible discoveries based upon our knowledge of the powers of the human mind. Instead of speculating about the nature of the universe and man's place in it, as the Greeks and the medievals had done, they wanted, in Locke's words, first 'to take a survey of our own understandings, examine our own powers and see to what things they were adapted'.

This examination of the powers of the mind proved just as difficult and controversial a matter as any of the traditional problems of philosophy. It served a useful purpose, indeed, in directing the attention of philosophers to what has been called 'the theory of knowledge', a group of important problems concerning the origin, nature and validity of human knowledge. Thus the moderate scepticism of the philosophers who tried in this way to solve the problem of philosophical method achieved only the incidental success of opening up a new field of enquiry. And as long as the problem of method was unsolved, this addition to the field of philosophy was rather like discovering new diseases without finding cures for the old ones. Nevertheless, though Locke's project of finding out the powers and limits of the human mind proved not to be the looked-for philosophical method, questions of this sort do offer a very good starting point for the search for such a method. Let us therefore look more closely at a variant of Locke's question: What kinds of problems can human reason solve for us? The key to problem-solving of all sorts is first to find the general method of solution for the kind of problem in question. How does this help us here?

---

[4] René Descartes (1596–1650), a French mathematician, philosopher and scientist.
[5] John Locke (1632–1704), an English philosopher.
[6] Immanuel Kant (1724–1804) was Professor of Philosophy in Königsberg.

A quite superficial acquaintance with the history of philosophy will show us that the general method used by philosophers in the past has been deduction from what appeared to be 'self-evident' premises. They believed, in other words, that it was possible to *prove* their conclusions about the existence of God, human destiny and the like by methods analogous to those used by mathematicians. The subject matter, to be sure, was very different from that of geometry but they supposed that the truth of their conclusions was guaranteed by the truth of the statements from which their arguments started and the logical validity of their deductions from these statements. This belief that philosophical discovery was essentially a process of proof took a long time to lose its plausibility even though none of the classical metaphysicians ever succeeded in proving anything and even though many of them did nevertheless make important philosophical discoveries. But these discoveries, like Columbus' discovery of America, were the by-product of a mistake. There can be no philosophical proofs because philosophy cannot proceed either by the axiomatic method of mathematics or by the experimental way of the scientist. And there are no other kinds of proof but formal deduction on the one hand and the establishment or refutation of hypotheses on the other. This is not to say that philosophy is not an exercise of reason; for reason does not consist only in giving proofs. But we are forced to conclude that questions which cannot be tackled by the deductive methods of mathematics or the observational and experimental methods of the natural and social sciences need a totally new method of approach. And we can get some sort of a lead to such a new approach by considering that scientists and mathematicians are relatively successful in their enquiries because they have a well-defined method of handling their problems. This means that they know in each case what evidence would settle the question that they are asking and that they usually know also how to set about collecting the evidence. Now this is just what we do not know in many questions relating to philosophy, morals, politics, religion and so on—all those questions that seem perennially controversial because there is no established, agreed and tested method of approaching them. The key question that we must ask is a preliminary to any sort of problem-solving procedure is this: What kind of evidence would have a bearing on this question?

If we have to admit, as well we may, that in some cases we simply do not know what the relevant evidence would be, then we should in all honesty admit that *for us* the question is not a meaningful one. This is a vitally important point for the proper use of reason. If you will consider for a moment some very simple examples of questions, you will see that they always presuppose some sort of knowledge about the answer. In other words, for a question to be a genuine one and capable of being answered, the questioner must have some idea of the terms in which the answer will be given. To take a trivial instance. If I say to someone: 'What's the time?' and he replies 'Tomorrow week' or 'Four yards square', I shall think that either he has misunderstood my question or that he is making a silly joke. I shall know not that the answer is *wrong* but that it is *irrelevant*. I shall know this because in asking questions, we ourselves set the framework within which the answer must fall. For an answer to be right or wrong, it must fall within the framework set by the question. And for a question to be a genuine one, it must have a framework that will determine in advance the form that the answer must take and the terms in which it will be made. We have such a framework for a question when we know the *sort* of evidence that will give us the answer but are ignorant of *exactly what* the evidence will be.

For this reason it is often said of questions, both scientific and philosophical, that a question well put is already half answered or that the secret of success lies in asking the right questions. Now asking the right questions means, among other things, putting questions that specify implicitly *the type of evidence* appropriate to their solution.

A meaningful question cannot be quite neutral as to the answer it invites. The most precise kind of question would be one which took the form: 'Which of these two answers is right, A_1, or A_2?' A vaguer question could be represented as asking: 'Which of these possible answers is right, A_1, A_2 . . . or A_n?' The larger the number n of possible alternative replies the more general will be the question. And where a question is so general as not even to imply a set of alternative answers, it loses its interrogative function. Thus the answer to a vague or woolly question is to say: What sort of evidence would you accept as relevant to the answer? If the questioner cannot tell you what sort of evidence would be relevant to his answer, his query is a mere pseudo-question, having the grammatical form of a question but not its interrogative function. For if the questioner does not know what sort of evidence would be relevant to his problem, he is in no position to distinguish a relevant from an irrelevant answer, still less a true answer from a false one.

We can propose then as a minimum safeguard against the abuse of reason the use of the following query whenever we are confronted with a problem: What kind of evidence would be relevant to the solution? But it is important to notice that there are two types of situation in which we might be unable to meet this challenge by specifying the sort of evidence that we should accept as relevant. (1) It might merely be that we personally did not know what kind of evidence would answer the question for us. (2) It might be that there was not and never could be any such evidence.

It has become obvious to philosophers in the past fifty years that a great many of the unprofitable controversies of the past can take on a new and enlightening aspect if we look at them from this point of view. The metaphysicians who debated about God, morality, human destiny and so on were assuming that these problems were similar to scientific questions at least in being clear questions about definite matters of fact to which answers were in principle possible. Yet it is obvious from the history of philosophy that equally honest, intelligent and well-informed men may have all the supposedly relevant facts at their disposal and still disagree profoundly about such matters. This indicates that the facts which they supposed to be relevant were not really relevant at all. If they had been, it is incredible that generally acceptable answers on these matters should not by now have been reached. For it is important to notice that facts are never relevant in philosophy in the way that they are in history or in science. Historians and scientists may, and often do, disagree on the way in which the available facts are to be interpreted. But these dis-agreements can, in principle, always be resolved by the discovery of *further* relevant facts; and no historical or scientific disagreement could outlive the knowledge of *all* the facts, if these were ever obtainable. Yet this can and does happen in metaphysical disputes. It is indeed one sure way by which we may recognize that the dispute is metaphysical.

There are two ways or proceeding from this point. We can say that questions and statements of this sort to which no generally acceptable evidence seems at all relevant, are simply meaningless or nonsensical, that they are grammatically correct forms of words which carry no meaning whatever of an informative kind. This was the view of the logical positivists, a pre-war school of philosophy which no longer survives in its original hard-shelled form. Under this ruling, only two kinds of statement retain any cognitive meaning, statements of empirical fact that can be confirmed by sensory observation and statements of logic and mathematics that can be checked by calculation. Every other kind of statement is ruled out as lacking any kind of cognitive content. This is clearly a very rough way of dealing with the statements of ethics, politics, religion and criticism of literature and the arts as well as the writings of the metaphysicians. And it shows perhaps a rather cavalier and unsympathetic attitude to matters which have excited men of ability and integrity since the beginning of history.

A more tolerant point of view which is not quite widely accepted among philosophers, may be expressed as follows: 'These statements are certainly mis-leading in looking grammatically like statements of observable fact. But perhaps we are being misled by their linguistic form. After all, language has many uses and fact-stating is only one of them. Let us consider all the other possible uses of lan-guage to see if we can re-interpret such apparently empty propositions in such a way that we can see what they are really asserting and so come to some agreed decision about their value.' This is one of the ways in which modern philosophers have come to be very interested in questions of language. And investigations of this kind have proved very fruitful in putting some of the oldest controversies of philosophy in quite a new light. Unfortunately, it is not easy to give in a summary way any adequate idea of the methods and results of the contemporary linguistic approach to philosophy. A general description of this work would be too vague to be informa-tive. It can be appreciated only by seeing it in action.

All I can usefully do here is to give in illustration one or two of the more im-portant discoveries about language and its workings that have been brought to light by these methods and show how they are philosophically enlightening. Perhaps the most basic of these notions (it is hardly recondite enough to be called a discovery) is a principle which derives chiefly from the work of G. E. Moore:[7] *The meaning of a word is created and controlled by the ways in which it is used.* To say this is merely to say that the relations between a word or phrase and its meaning is not a part of nature independent of human wishes but rests upon social conventions. Words and phrases have those powers of communication that their habitual modes of use have

[7] Professor G. E. Moore was Professor of Philosophy at Cambridge University from 1925 to 1939.

endowed them with, *and no more*. This fact, obvious enough though it is, has important consequences for philosophy.

It follows from this that many words, and among them most of the key terms of philosophy, must be both vague and ambiguous *and irremediably so*. For it is clear that the abstract and uncommon terms of philosophy will be used much less often and in much less concrete contexts than the words describing the common features of our everyday experience. They will thus be much vaguer since the precedents for their use in some contexts will not have been clearly established or, indeed, established at all. And they will be ambiguous when divergent or incompatible speech customs have directed the occasions of their use. The philosopher faced with these natural debilities of language is often in the position of an English judge who has to give a judgment in a common law case for which the relevant precedents are either conflicting or fail to cover the circumstances at issue. But whereas the judge knows that his judgment must contain some arbitrary element, the classical philosopher, blind to the nature of language, too often assumed that he had given the only right answer to his problem.

The modern philosopher who is sensitive to this natural feature of language often looks to the ways in which we remedy vagueness when it troubles us in everyday speech. We commonly do so by pointing to examples and especially to borderline examples. If someone asks, for instance, 'What colours do you include under the term "violet"?' you can show him a range of samples, both of the shades you are prepared to call 'violet' and also of those that are just too red or too blue to qualify for the term. Procedures of this kind will make your meaning much more precise, though still not perfectly so. In philosophy, the vagueness of such terms as 'mind', 'thought', 'God', 'free will', or 'cause' 'substance' is not so easily treated by this method. But where we can do something on these lines, the consequences may be important.

To take a concrete case, if we ask: 'What do you mean by "thinking"?', you might give a series of examples: I am thinking when I am daydreaming, when I am doing mathematics, when I am writing a letter, when I am playing chess, when I am talking with friends and so on. But are you thinking when you are dreaming as well as when you are daydreaming, when you are batting at cricket, as well as when you are playing chess, when you are playing the piano as well as when you are solving equations? And if you are thinking when you are solving your puzzles, does the rat think when he is solving his? Examples and counter-examples of this sort show how fuzzy this and similar concepts are round their edges and how there are no standard examples of them with a unitary set of properties that all genuine instances of the concept possess. Thinking is not an all-or-none affair but a matter of degree; and so too with the rest of those philosophical concepts whose vagueness can be elucidated in this way. The result of the elucidation is to show that these concepts are in no way like precise clear-cut technical terms. Thus a consideration of the workings of language has thrown new light on the nature of a concept and has gone a long way towards disposing of a philosophical problem that has been outstanding since Plato.

A secondary important discovery about language that is philosophically important is that language is not a picture or map of the world and, in consequence, no conclusions can be drawn from the nature of language to the nature of reality. This is a very large subject, and in its details, still a controversial one. But briefly the position is that many of the classical philosophers assumed that our thinking about the world mirrored what we found there, at least when our thinking was not mistaken and that our language mirrored our thinking. It was believed that thinking, correct or mistaken, was a sort of mapping of the universe and that the map was a good one when our thinking was true and a bad or distorted or even totally misleading one when our beliefs were false. Moreover, language was a sort of externalized model of our internal cogitations, the map, as it were, in its published form. This view was first stated in an embryonic form by Aristotle and was later canonized into what was called the Correspondence Theory of Truth. There is just enough in this kind of metaphor to make it easy for us to press it too far. The real harm of this three-level view of knowledge, thinking mirroring fact and language mirroring thinking, is not so much in the metaphor of the mirror or the map, though this is a misleading way of explaining even very elementary kinds of knowledge. The danger lies rather in the supposed split between thinking and its expression as if thinking is some sort of mysterious inner process that can proceed apart from language or from any other kind of symbolism whatever. Both the sources of this error and its consequences are too complicated to dwell on here. One of its most damaging results is to make us suppose that the actual grammatical and syntactical structures of natural languages are a key to the nature of reality. For language, on this view, is a picture of the world, or rather, a picture of a picture. And what we find in the structure of languages may fairly be supposed to correspond to the structure of the world. Thus to take one example, some metaphysicians seem to have taken the grammatical distinction between subject and predicate as evidence for the philosophical theory that the world consisted of a number of substances characterized by different properties.

I do not wish to suggest that traditional metaphysics must be rejected merely because of recent philosophical views about language. These views do indeed bring into focus some of the *reasons* for the failure of metaphysical speculation but the failure was obvious long before the attention of modern philosophers was directed to the nature of language. I suggested at the beginning that no system of traditional metaphysics has ever proved to be publicly testable by experts in the same field and coherent with the rest of established knowledge; and that this, in itself, refuted the claims of such systems to be taken seriously. If it is objected that this is an unfair criterion to use because it has been developed by application to factual disciplines like science and history, we have to ask: How else is the truth of any theory, historical, scientific, mathematical or philosophical, to be established? We learn to recognize truth in the future by seeing how it has come to be recognized in the past. Public recognition by experts, progressive corrigibility and coherence with established knowledge are not indeed *infallible* guarantees of true beliefs. For truth has no such hall marks. But they are the best guarantees we have. And it would be absurd to accept any belief which lacked them as more than a tentative hypothesis. We cannot indeed even regard it as a hypothesis unless we know (*a*) what consequences would follow if it were true; and (*b*) how these consequences are to be established. The basic weakness of metaphysics has been that its practitioners claimed objective truth for their conclusions without recognizing objective tests by which their claim could be verified.

No doubt there will be metaphysical systems in the future which will take account of the way in which language works and even of the need for criteria of proof. Such systems will have to be judged on their merits. But the present state of philosophical knowledge and its past history cannot encourage us to look on philosophy as more than a laborious piecemeal effort to criticize and clarify the foundations of our beliefs. Such successes as philosophers can claim have all been of this kind. And this means that in the present condition of human knowledge we cannot hope for more from philosophy than occasional and fragmentary glimpses of enlightenment along with a reasonable confidence that its continuous practice will keep our minds free of nonsense. But this is something very valuable that only philosophy can give us.

DOES PHILOSOPHY HAVE A FUTURE?

SIDNEY HOOK

In periods of world and national crisis, such as we are passing through, many individuals are wont to turn to philosophy and philosophers in hope of finding a faith to sustain them in time of troubles. If God is dead, is philosophy still alive? They usually discover that philosophers are not agreed on any particular faith, and that what they are commonly concerned with is the meaning of faith. Those who ask questions find that the answer which the philosopher gives them is an invitation to inquiry, not a conclusion or credo. Philosophy, they are sometimes told, is not so much an activity that offers definite answers to questions as one that questions answers. But surely philosophy does not question answers to anything or everything.

This failure to get a specific answer sometimes leads to frustration and to a series of other questions. What is philosophical inquiry as distinct from other forms? What is philosophy, after all? What has it to say? Why study it?

FROM *Saturday Review*, 50 (November 11, 1967): 21–23*ff.* Copyright by Sidney Hook, 1967. (Reprinted by permission of the publisher and the author.)

I propose to discuss briefly some of the uses of philosophy without offering a formal definition of it, because any definition presupposes some conception not likely to be shared by all philosophers. Further, it seems possible to convey a notion of what philosophy is by describing its common uses.

The first and most obvious use of the study of philosophy is that it helps us to understand the nature and history of our civilization. We cannot grasp the pattern of its events and the character of its institutions without some knowledge of the ideas of Plato, Aristotle, Plotinus, Aquinas, Kant, Hegel, and Marx. We cannot understand the political history of the United States without some appreciation of the philosophy of Locke. We cannot appreciate the recent history of Europe and Asia without a grasp of the social philosophy of Marx. I am not saying that the philosophical ideas of these thinkers alone are the forces which entered into the determination of history. Obviously, economic and national interests as well as outstanding personalities played a large role, too; but I am saying that philosophical conceptions of the nature of man, of the nature of justice, of social welfare, of human personality, of freedom, had some influence upon events, and that without reference to them we cannot explain the shape of the past.

Ideas—philosophical ideas—also have a direct relevance to present-day religious social, and political movements. They are not merely a part of the heritage of the West. They are the means by which we seek to preserve and defend the West. That is why ideas are among the most practical things in the world. Whoever wants to understand our world, and the world of the past out of which it grew, must therefore pay some attention to philosophical ideas. The study of philosophy, in other words, gives us a perspective upon our human history and our present-day experience. It reveals, in John Dewey's words, "the predicaments, the prospects, and aspirations of men."

But philosophy has an even more important use. It has a bearing not only on the shape of the past, but on the shape of things to come. To the extent that fundamental ideas determine our actions, they flow from our basic commitments. Philosophy is a mode of thought which analyzes our presuppositions and assumptions in every field of action and thought. It enables us to make explicit our allegiances to the ideals in behalf of which we are prepared to live, to fight, sometimes even to die. Its primary concern here is with meaning, not truth, and it aims to produce an awareness of what we are about. This awareness or self-consciousness is not easy to achieve. The fruit of ancient wisdom was expressed in the Greek injunction, "Know thyself," but this is a difficult task. Very few of us can answer the questions: "What do we really want?"; "What do we really mean by the large terms which play a role in human discourse?" We inherit a large mass—usually a mess—of traditional beliefs. Some of these we call first principles. Others, who do not share them, dub them prejudices. How do we sort them out?

This suggests the third use of philosophy. Awareness and self-consciousness do not come about by revelation. For the revelations—"the moments of truth," as the phrase goes—which overtake us are themselves in need of understanding. This can be reliably achieved only by the activity of logical analysis. A person may utter statements that are true or false and yet not be clear about their meaning or their justification or relevance. Whatever else philosophy is, it is an activity of logical analysis which seeks to locate issues in dispute and to help clarify them. When properly pursued, philosophy gives a methodological sophistication that can be achieved by no other discipline. It is not a mere matter of reasoning from premises to conclusion, as in mathematics or chess, because it scrutinizes the premises and basic terms which all subjects take for granted. It enables us to distinguish between statements of fact and disguised definitions, between hypotheses which may be true or false and resolutions which are adequate or inadequate. It is always prepared to consider alternatives to the familiar. William James actually defines philosophy as a quest for alternatives and their investigation. In summary, then, philosophy consists of an analysis of concepts and ideas in an attempt to cut through slogans to genuine issues and problems.

Let us consider a few simple illustrations:

1) The most fashionable slogan in intellectual and educational circles during recent years has been "Down with conformity and conformism." The conformist is the yes man, the man who agrees. He is at the bottom of the cultural ladder. But everyone who denounces conformism can be made to realize that one of the greatest nonconformists of the twentieth century was Adolf Hitler. Would that he had conformed to the accepted decencies of his time! To make a fetish of nonconformity won't do at all—especially when we run into a lunatic who refuses to conform to the traffic laws and rams our car, or a man who shortchanges us and tosses our complaint off with the observation that he is an arithmetical nonconformist. It is or should be obvious that conformism is a relational term. Conformity or non-conformity is no virtue in itself. Unless we know what we are conforming with or not conforming with, the term is meaningless. What we sometimes have in mind when we praise nonconformity is intellectual independence, the intelligence and courage to agree or disagree on the basis of evidence.

2) Another illustration is the slogan which originated in high places and which has been often repeated: "There are no alternatives to peace!" How many who mouth this sentence are aware that it commits them to unconditional surrender if an enemy threatens attack? What those who utter this sentence mean to say is that peace is desirable. The meaning of what they actually said is that peace at any price, even at the cost of freedom, is desirable. People who speak this way don't say what they really mean. More important—and this is not the same thing—they don't mean what they really say.

3) Another confusion is the belief that the equality or inequality of races necessarily has a bearing on the question of segregation or integration in housing, transportation, schooling. The view which condemns discrimination against human beings on the basis of religion or race is primarily a moral view. It flows from our belief in the validity of the democratic ideal which rests upon an equality of concern for all human beings to develop their personality to their highest potential. Some facts may have a bearing on this policy, but not the discovery that

there is a greater distribution of natural capacity in one race or group than another. Whatever be the facts about the distribution of capacity in group A or B, each member of that group is morally entitled to the rights and privileges which flow from the obligation of a democratic community to all its citizens.

Consider a family which has several children with varying natural capacities— very bright, normal, and dull. Would any responsible parent deprive any of these children of food, clothing, and shelter because of difference in their capacities? If the question of their schooling arose, their educational opportunities would be commensurate with their educational capacities. So with the educational opportunities for the children of members of different groups. The question is not whether the distribution of capacity is inherently the same or different among them, but whether they are to be given educational opportunities on the basis of their capacities or on the basis of their color. This would mean that children, white or nonwhite, Christian or Jewish, would find themselves in the same class in the same school if their educational capacities were the same. Once this analysis is made we can see where the issue lies. It lies in the field of social morality. It is not a question of physical anthropology at all, but rather of the extent to which we accept democracy.

I could have taken other illustrations for analysis from popular philosophy, such as the vulgar notion that because all human action is interested, everyone therefore acts for his own interests, that willy-nilly everyone is selfish. I wanted, however, to show how a little elementary logical analysis has relevance to practical affairs.

But a word about that old chestnut of adolescent cynicism—everyone is selfish, everyone acts for his own pleasure. If I say that all men have two eyes, I am saying something which is confirmed by universal observation. Were I to ask, however, under what possible circumstance one could show that this statement were false, you would be able to describe a state of affairs I could observe—the presence of only one natural eye or three; or, if the mother, when pregnant, had taken thalidomide, none. But suppose you could not describe any possible state of affairs which would invalidate your position; what meaning could be assigned to not having two eyes? Obviously, none. Now suppose I ask: Under what circumstances would you be prepared to say that a person is unselfish; how would he have to *behave* for you to count him as unselfish? As soon as you indicated the specifiable respects, observation of which would lead you to the conclusion, you could know what to do to put it to a test. But if you can't describe the behavior which you are prepared to describe as unselfish, then you are using the term "selfish" in such a way that it has no empirical meaning. You are claiming that the statement, "Everyone is selfish," is true no matter what the facts are or will be—and, therefore, you are not making a statement of fact at all.

4) There is a further use of philosophy. It concerns itself with the place of man in the universe from the point of view of certain large and perennial questions which all reflective men at some time or another ask. These questions are not raised or answered in any of the special sciences, but to answer them intelligently one must be familiar with the best science and theology of the day, and approach them

in a rational spirit. These are questions such as: In what sense, if any, does the universe show a design? Does this design imply a designer or a God or a Friend behind the phenomena? Is man a tenement of clay inhabited by an immortal soul or a handful of wonderful salts in a solution of water? Are human beings responsible for their actions? If they are, does this mean that they have free wills? If the will is free, does this mean that the will is uncaused? If the will is uncaused, does this mean that actions are a matter of chance, and if so, in what sense are men morally responsible for their conduct?

This leads on to all sorts of exacting and intricate questions. What do we mean by a cause? Can there be a first cause? Are these questions answerable? What is a genuine question anyhow? Does every sentence which has the form of a question possess the sense of one? Concerning these questions there is dogmatic belief and often dogmatic disbelief. Philosophy is the discipline which considers the fundamental questions in such a way that no matter what answers one makes to them, one can give reasons or grounds for belief or disbelief.

5) Finally, I come to what I regard as the most important use of philosophy, to which all the other uses of philosophy are ancillary—philosophy as the quest for wisdom. Everyone knows that there is a difference between knowledge and wisdom, but not everyone can tell in what this difference consists. We are aware that a man can have a great deal of knowledge about many things and still be a learned fool. We sometimes say he has been educated beyond his capacities. We also know there are wise men who are not encyclopedias of learning, and that wise men of the past often lacked the knowledge of present-day schoolboys. This has led some thinkers to contrast knowledge and wisdom as if they belonged to entirely different orders or dimensions of insight. But if we speak of a wise man, we are entitled to ask: "What is he wise about?" If he were ignorant of everything, he couldn't be wise.

Consequently, we must conclude that wisdom is a species of knowledge—it is knowledge of the origin, careers, interrelations, and reliabilities of human values in our experience. Wisdom is an affair of values, and of value judgments. It is intelligent conduct of human affairs. It is knowledge of what is of most worth in our experience, of the ends which we can justifiably pursue, of the good, the better, and the best, the bad, the worse, and the worst in those concrete situations in which, confronted by alternatives of policy or action, we ask: "What shall I do?"

This raises a very large question. How can we be wise or even rational about our values or our ends? What does it mean to be rational or reasonable about them? The term "rational," or "reasonable," has many meanings, but some eminent thinkers claim that they can all be reduced to variations of one meaning, viz, the appropriate or economical use of means to achieve ends. They assert that once we have an end we can be rational about the means of realizing it, but that it makes no sense to speak of ends being rational or reasonable. This suggests that ultimately all ends are on the same plane and that no good reason or rational ground can be given for accepting one or rejecting others. If one accepts Gandhi's ends, one can be rational about achieving them. If one accepts Hitler's ends, one can be rational about achieving them. But we cannot be rational in choosing between Gandhi's and Hitler's ends.

This is the position of Bertrand Russell, who says, "There is no such thing as an irrational end except one impossible of realization." Now, this is false on its face because in one sense there are many ends which are impossible of realization, but are not irrational to pursue because of the desirable consequences of our pursuit of them. Suppose I take all knowledge as my province. It is impossible to achieve literal mastery of the whole of knowledge, but it may not be irrational to pursue it as a goal, because I may thereby acquire more knowledge in this fashion than if I had taken a more restricted end. Or, suppose I take as my end kindness in all circumstances to everyone. This, too, given men as we know them, is impossible, but the world would be a far better place if I try to be invariably kind than if I take as my ideal a more restricted sort of kindness or an ideal of indifference.

One might retort that what Russell means is still valid, for in these cases what I am really taking as my end are those consequences which are realizable. The problem then is: How can you rationally decide concerning alternative ends, all of which are equally realizable?

The answer, it seems to me, is suggested by analyzing how we proceed in any concrete situation in which we must make a choice between ends. If we have only one end, we have no moral problem. It is only a question of means. But the obvious truth is that we always have more than one end—usually a cluster of ends or values —to which we are committed. Our problem is, which end should we commit ourselves to? Now, the answer I suggest is that we always proceed by checking the alternative possible ends in terms of the consequences of the means used to achieve them and in the light of all the other ends which, on the basis of past experience, we have accepted as having prima facie validity. Of course, every one of these other ends may itself be questioned. Every end in human experience is also a means to some other end. How do we test them? By the same process. But does this not set up an infinite regress? No, not if we take our problems one at a time.

Consider a simple example. A student comes to me in distress and wants to know whether he should remain in school or exploit some opportunity for remunerative employment. I point out the relative advantages and disadvantages of both, stressing the fact that in the modern world he is more likely to find a creative voca-tion through continuing his schooling. Now, this assumes that a creative vocation is a good thing to have. How do we know that? Suppose it is denied. Again, we point to the alternative uses of the concrete goals or possibilities of living. A creative vocation is a center around which to organize experience; it is a source of satisfac-tion and delight; it also provides occasions for companionship and friendship. But are *these* worthwhile? To which I reply that they enrich living. Yes, comes the rejoinder, but is life worthwhile? Now, at this point we can very well question the validity of the process. A student who wants to know whether to continue his schooling or discontinue it is not interested in knowing whether life is worth living. That is a legitimate question, too, in its context. But it is out of context here.

What I have been trying to illustrate is the general method by which we do, in fact, seek to answer specific moral questions. They are much more complicated, of course, when they concern other human beings. (I am not giving any answers here or claiming to be wise. A philosopher in his own life need be no more wise than a physician need be healthy.) I am particularly concerned to challenge the view that all our values are ultimate values that are inarbitrable. Indeed, I question whether it is true that any value in a specific context is an ultimate value rather than a penultimate one which is tested by its successive consequences. At any rate, I believe I have shown that we can be wise or foolish about the ends of action, that it makes good sense to undertake rational criticism of our ends, and that the originally desired end may sometimes appear in the light of our reflective analysis as undesirable.

Although the philosopher does not himself have to be a wise man, at his best he knows more than the methods and techniques by which the process of reflection is carried out. He has vision of possibilities. He is not only a critic but a seer. His vision is often expressed as a glimpse into what can make our society better for our time, into what can most enrich our life and give it abiding worth, an insight into human possibilities and how to realize them. When the philosopher is a man of vision, he leaves his mark upon the experience of others, whose ordinary life acquires new dimensions of significance.

Of such philosophers, Santayana says: "It is not easy for him to shout or to address a crowd; he must be silent for long periods; for he is watching stars that move slowly and in courses that it is possible though difficult to see; and he is crushing all things in his heart as in a winepress, until his life and their secret flow out together."

PART II
SOME HISTORICAL PERSPECTIVES

Times change, as the saying goes, and so do the issues of controversy in American education. The impetus for much philosophizing about education in this century, as John Brubacher indicates, was John Dewey's challenge to the traditional educational practices current at the turn of the century. It was a response to much more also—the social, religious, economic, and scientific tensions of a transitional age—but the focus for reform and a major center of interest in Dewey's thought was education. Previous ages have seen philosophical attention given to education, but in the twentieth century interest in educational philosophy became far more intensive. The initial conflicts between conservative and progressive educational practices set the stage for theorizing about the philosophical underpinnings of education. The first essay in this part undertakes to recount the main points of controversy between traditional and progressive education as well as the fundamental divergence of Dewey's philosophy from other positions. Brubacher concludes with a summary of issues in educational philosophy. Since this essay was written, new areas of concern have emerged, but no one assumes that these earlier pressing problems have ever been finally resolved.

Professor Phillips' contribution carries the story further in analyzing changing conceptions of the role of the educational philosopher in the shifting educational scene. He also helps to locate the intellectual place of Dewey and Kilpatrick in the development of contemporary educational philosophy. Probably the single most influential work in philosophy of education was Dewey's manifesto-like *Democracy and Education*. Its famous dictum that philosophy is the generalized theory of education, "the theory of education as a deliberately conducted practice," was nothing short of revolutionary. It would be unwise to view all of current educational philosophy against the subsequent explication of this claim in Dewey's thought,

59

particularly since a substantial portion of more recent philosophizing has borrowed from different traditions. Nonetheless, it is undeniable that pragmatism has influenced profoundly much that has been written in American philosophy of education.

William H. Kilpatrick was a leading interpreter and exponent of Dewey's educational philosophy. His essay, "The Relations of Philosophy and Science in the Study of Education," reflects closely Dewey's intimate association of philosophy and educational concerns as well as the pragmatist outlook on science. Lately, there has been a renewal of interest in the relation between philosophy and science; Kilpatrick's earlier thoughts on philosophy of education in this connection assumes new pertinence for contemporary theorists.

Viewed in the light of analytical and empiricist philosophy, George S. Counts' five criteria for judging a philosophy of education also seem worthy of note today. It is his insistence that an educational philosophy be empirically grounded, that it be relevant to the social needs of the time, and that it be "in essential harmony with the great social trends which characterize the age." Counts' views are echoed by many present-day philosophers of education who insist that educational theory addresses itself to matters of vital, living importance. His comments on the nature of philosophy of education reflect his basic conviction that education must be a socially reconstructive force in society, courageously facing the challenges of American life. In fact, it has been argued that Counts' philosophy seems more contemporary today in this respect than that of Dewey and Kilpatrick.

The concluding article in this section by Professor Kircher raises a perennially important point: the distinction between philosophy as a practical directive for human affairs as opposed to a liberal, enlightening discipline. The opposition is implicit in many of the contrasting views by authors writing on the aims of philosophy of education. Some will argue that educational controversy can be resolved by the adoption of a single philosophical position, thereby giving much-needed integration to American education. It is suggested that this aspiration moved many adherents of Dewey's philosophy of education. Kircher argues eloquently for an intellectual pluralism in American social life while pointing out the hazards of conceiving any one philosophy as uniquely qualified to shape and control education. At a time when voices are again being raised to lament doctrinal pluralism and to urge that philosophy of education "abandon its liberal status for a doctrinal status," the metaphor of the "philosophical cat" seems especially instructive.

THE CHALLENGE
TO PHILOSOPHIZE ABOUT
EDUCATION

JOHN S. BRUBACHER

EDUCATIONAL THEORY IN RELATION TO SOCIAL TENSIONS

The study of educational philosophy has flourished in the twentieth century as never before in the whole history of education. Earlier centuries, no doubt, produced a fair share of famous essays on education, but relatively few of these essays were philosophical in exposition and intent. Comenius' *Didactica Magna*, Locke's *Thoughts Concerning Education*, and Rousseau's *Émile* were notable publications, but none of the three was explicitly a philosophy of education. Perhaps a philosophy of education was implicit in these essays, but certainly none was systematically set forth. Philosophers like Aristotle, St. Thomas, Kant, and Hegel gave passing attention to education, but in no case did one of them give it rounded treatment. Herbart took education much more seriously, but even he limited himself to its moral and psychological aspects. Only Plato of pre-twentieth-century philosophers produced a notable philosophy of education (in his *Republic*). The twentieth century, by contrast, has produced almost a plethora of publications on philosophy of education, mostly American. It has produced not only one major philosophy of education, Dewey's *Democracy and Education*, but a dozen or more minor ones as well.[1]

What is the reason for this greatly augmented interest in educational philosophy? Perhaps the simplest answer is the rise of "progressive education" as a *cause célèbre*. At first, the newer educational procedures of this movement were a protest against the rather formal educational practices inherited from the nineteenth century. As the protest gained momentum, people began to see that the newer educational practices were not just an amendment to traditional practice but involved a fundamental departure from it. In the early phases of the movement,

---

FROM *Modern Philosophies and Education, Fifty-fourth Yearbook of the National Society for the Study of Education*, Chapter I. Chicago: University of Chicago Press, 1955, pp. 4–16. (Reprinted by permission of the National Society for the Study of Education.)

[1] For a bibliography of these writings, see John S. Brubacher's *Modern Philosophies of Education*, pp. 299n, 303n, 314n, 317n, 320n. New York: McGraw-Hill Book Co., 1950 (revised edition).

"progressive education" met no more opposition than the inertia of convention. While the progressive concepts had difficulty in overcoming this inertia in practice, the advocates of reform won easy victories over such opposition in the field of theory during the 1920's. As theoretical victories led to more and more victories in the field of practice, the defenders of traditional and conventional education finally took pen in hand to defend their own practices and even to go over to the offensive to attack progressive education during the 1930's. Then war intervened, causing an interlude in the strife of educational systems, and our whole energies were mobilized to resolve the international strife of political and economic ideologies. Now that there is an interlude after that war, we have returned to the conflict of educational ideologies again.

It is no doubt an oversimplification to ascribe the great interest of the twentieth century in educational philosophy to just the contest between progressive and traditional educational practices. The issue really lies much deeper. The experimental schools which made up progressive education were but the vanguard of that larger twentieth-century endeavor to assume more and more intentional control of the social process. Traditional methods of cultural transmission and renewal, once left to automatic processes, now became the object of conscious consideration. Progressive schools, for instance, deliberately fashioned their practices on scientific findings. As these often were in conflict with cherished traditional convictions there was an urgent demand for a fresh philosophical approach to resolve the conflict.

Thus, while traditional education has been based on a metaphysical psychology, "progressive education" has taken its cue from a psychology recently become scientific. Techniques of measurement devised by the new psychology have demanded a different conception of human nature, a conception which traditional education has often found repugnant to its metaphysical psychology. Again, the interpretation of biological findings, especially the theory of organic evolution, has widened the differences between traditional and "progressive" education. To attach the adjective "progressive" to education can mean quite different things depending on whether one uses an Aristotelian or a Darwinian conception of development. Further educational complications have arisen from a third scientific area, anthropological and sociological studies. The cultural relativity frequently espoused by these disciplines has stood in sharp contrast to fixed conceptions of the curriculum, especially in moral education, held by adherents of the old school. Underlying all these issues are conflicting assumptions which only careful and systematic philosophizing can clarify.

It must be remembered, too, that these disagreements over educational policy took place in the twentieth century in a matrix of political and economic upheaval. This century has witnessed a rising struggle for political power between varieties of autocracy—monarchic at first, fascistic later, and communistic currently—and varieties of democracy—laissez-faire individualism, benevolent paternal new-dealism, and a pragmatic liberalism strongly supported by many professional leaders of teachers. The resulting confusion over political ideals obviously has obscured the precise nature of citizenship as a dominating aim of education. The strife of political systems has been underscored by the further strife of economic systems, notably capitalism and communism. If, as some philosophers allege, the quality of education varies according to the way in which a man earns his bread, then the road ahead for education is anything but clear, for the rise of the working classes the world over is already making unprecedented demands for the reform of education.

The strife of political and economic ideologies has also greatly aggravated nationalistic rivalries. To the rational arguments which can be adduced for each ideology has been added the organized forces of national states. Consequently, national schools have taught these ideologies with patriotic fervor. The threat this provides to amicable settlement of international disagreements brings nearer the resulting danger of war. Just how to harness national resources to provide added educational opportunities and yet how at the same time to avoid irreconcilable rivalries is obviously another problem driving educators to philosophy. Their problem takes on complication as well as inspiration as they seek an educational policy to undergird the efforts of UNESCO, a policy which will respect diverse national, political, economic, and religious factors in education and yet will find a common denominator for them all.

Naturally, conflicts such as these have placed tremendous strain on the moral texture of twentieth-century culture. To teach children how to maintain moral integrity and integrated personalities in the face of all these conflicting demands is no simple task. The main trouble is that it is so difficult to tell in a period of accelerated social transition whether new departures in well-accepted customs are a weakening of former standards or a step toward new and better ones. It is even difficult to tell whether the ills which beset us presently are the result of changing social conditions or the changes brought about in the schools by "progressive education." On the assumption that it is the secularism of "progressive education" that is to blame, some in the twentieth century have demanded a renewed emphasis on religion in public education. This demand, of course, requires a re-examination of the nineteenth-century policy of the divorce of church and state in matters of education, to say nothing of rethinking the whole problem of religious and moral education in the light of the foregoing forces.

In view of the contradictory, often confusing, issues presented, it should not be surprising that men have resorted to philosophizing about education in this century as never before. This does not mean that it is anything new for men to be in a quandary about which direction education should take. Men have confronted many such crises in civilization's long history. Plato, for instance, wrote his *Republic* partly in response to the unstable social conditions of his day. Still, the present tensions seem more acute for education than previous ones. The principal difference between present and past eras seems to be that today education is consciously used as a tremendous instrument of public policy. Formerly, only the privileged classes benefited by an extended education. But today most states aim at universal education, the education of all classes. Consequently, alterations in educational direction caused by shifting configurations of tension among the forces mentioned above have a far greater outreach than ever before in the world's history.

PROGRESSIVE VERSUS TRADITIONAL AIMS IN EDUCATION

While aggravated tensions—political, economic, religious, scientific—are probably at the bottom of the proliferation of educational philosophies in the twentieth century, it should not escape notice that one philosophical endeavor to resolve these tensions is itself also a major cause of this proliferation. Except for the emergence of John Dewey and the persistent challenge of his pragmatism to every phase of contemporary education, it is unlikely that educational philosophy would have had anywhere near the rise to prominence it has had in this century. His writings were not only the inspiration for others who wrote in the same vein but, much more important for richness and breadth in professional literature, he provoked opponents of his view to make explicit a variety of philosophical defenses of traditional or conservative educational practices which had only been implicit thitherto. This was particularly true of the Catholic position.

Since Dewey's pragmatism has been the principal philosophical proponent of "progressive education" and since the launching of "progressive education" was the immediate, if not ultimate, cause of so much writing in educational philosophy, it may be well . . . to give some exposition of the nature of the attack that Dewey and pragmatism have made on conventional educational practices. Perhaps before doing that, however, we should take a look at the theory and practice of the sort of education which Dewey sought to reform when he inaugurated his experimental school at the University of Chicago.

Perhaps the briefest and at the same time the most accurate description of the conventional school of the late nineteenth and early twentieth centuries is to be found in the Lynds' *Middletown*.[2] "The school like the factory," ran their socio-logical description of Middletown, "is a thoroughly regimented world. Immovable seats in orderly rows fix the sphere of activity of each child. For all, from the timid six-year-old entering for the first time to the most assured high-school senior, the general routine is much the same. Bells divide the day into periods. For the six-year-olds the periods are short (fifteen to twenty-five minutes) and varied; in some they leave their seats, play games, and act out make-believe stories, although in 'recitation periods' all movement is prohibited. As they grow older the taboo upon physical activity becomes stricter, until by the third or fourth year practically all movement is forbidden except the marching from one set of seats to another between periods, a brief interval of prescribed exercise daily, and periods of manual training or home economics once or twice a week. There are 'study periods' in which children learn 'lessons' from 'textbooks' prescribed by the state and 'recitation periods' in which they tell an adult teacher what the book has said; one hears children reciting the battles of the Civil War in one recitation period, the

[2] R. S. Lynd and H. M. Lynd, *Middletown*, pp. 188–89. New York: Harcourt, Brace & Co., 1929.

rivers of Africa in another, the 'parts of speech' in a third; the method is much the same."

No one in the nineteenth century explicitly expounded the philosophy behind this practice. Yet an educational philosophy it surely had. The spirit of this school fairly breathes rigidity, formalism, and regimentation. These qualities may have been due to the shortcomings of unselected and poorly trained teachers of which there is an oversupply at any time. But over and above that, there were many educators, lay and professional people, who justified this formalism because it afforded a valuable discipline for children. By subduing their natural spontaneity and subjugating it to a fixed routine, to screwed-down seats and desks, to a logically organized subject matter, children learned to conform to the way things are. And things did exist in a definite order and fashion. This was particularly true in the moral order and the scientific order of nature. In this order, human nature was composed of faculties, and it was the role of the school to sharpen them by grinding them against the abrasive whetstone of the hard facts of life. If that seemed disagreeable, Mr. Dooley was at hand to humor critics by stating ironically that it did not really matter what children studied so long as they didn't like it. Consequently, interest was neglected and children were urged to put forth effort in the sheer performance of abstract duty. The teacher's authority, even for those so fortunate as to be trained along Herbartian lines, was omnipresent to enforce this duty.

At a little deeper level most thoughtful nineteenth-century educators, and many twentieth-century educators as well, whether Catholic or Protestant, subscribed to a humanistic theory of education. They held with Aristotle that the distinctive nature of man which set him off from other animals was his rationality. The principal function of education, therefore, was to develop this rationality. This was to be sought as a worth-while end in itself for, as Aristotle said, "The activity of God, which surpasses all others in blessedness, must be contemplative; and of human activities, therefore, that which is most akin to this must be most of the nature of happiness. . . . Happiness extends, then, just as far as contemplation does, and those to whom contemplation more fully belongs are more truly happy, not as a mere concomitant but in virtue of the contemplation; for this is itself precious."[3] Or, as Cardinal Newman put it centuries later with educational bearings more definitely in mind, "Surely it is very intelligible to say, and that is what I say here, that Liberal Education, viewed in itself, is simply the cultivation of the intellect as such, and its object is nothing more or less than intellectual excellence."[4]

The experimental schools of the twentieth century, of which Dewey's was merely one of the earlier and better known, made a definite departure from the type of education compositely described in *Middletown*. In these new schools the last thing school resembled was a factory. Instead of mechanical uniformity, school was characterized by flexibility and spontaneity. School furniture was movable and the length of periods was measured by the work in hand to be done. Pupil activity, far from being taboo, became the central feature of the progressive school. Indeed,

[3] Aristotle, *Politics*, Bk. X, chap. viii.
[4] J. H. Newman, *The Idea of a University*, p. 121. London: Longmans, Green & Co., 1919.

its curriculum became known as an "activity" curriculum. Children still dug subject matter out of texts but not isolated from life and for the mere formal purpose of reproducing it on examinations. On the contrary, they undertook projects in which they were interested and searched subject matter for suggestions for activities to be undertaken to insure the successful outcome of their projects.

Obviously, the spirit or philosophy of this school stood in marked contrast to that of *Middletown*. The features of this spirit which impressed observers most were its emphasis on pupil interest and pupil freedom in a school atmosphere where the teacher was less a task-master and more a friendly guide. Children were free to select tasks they were interested in and free to move about in search of resources from the library, laboratory, field, and shop which might promote the completion of what they had undertaken. Naturally, such a school had need to be rich in resources so that no side of child development would be neglected. If such a regime developed individuality, initiative, self-reliance, and a moral autonomy in its pupils, it was but the normal expectation.

Parenthically, it might be mentioned that this far even conservative and traditional educators had generally moved by the middle of the twentieth century. By that time, indeed, they had so absorbed many progressive practices that the Progressive Education Association had spent much of its driving protest force from the 1920's. Yet, while copying many progressive practices, conservatives and traditionalists still refused to support them theoretically with Dewey's pragmatism.

At a still more penetrating level, progressive educators themselves split on the theoretical underpinning of their practices. One group followed the lead of Rousseau and Froebel. They took the romantic view of natural development. Reverencing the essential goodness of child nature, they held it their duty as parents and educators to let nature express itself freely and to interfere with its laws as little as possible. Because they reverenced the unique in child nature as well as the universal, they insisted on giving a high priority to the individual interests of the child in organizing the school program. Romantic progressives derived further support for their theory from G. Stanley Hall and Sigmund Freud. Hall's theory, that the child must "recapitulate" racial experience just as his foetal development recapitulated organic evolution, led to the further theory of catharsis. According to this theory, if the child acts like a little savage when passing through and recapitulating the aboriginal stage of culture, adults must let him behave that way to get it out of his system. Even more recently the romantic progressives have leaned mistakenly on Freudian psychoanalysis to support their theory of freedom for child nature. From seeing the warped personalities which result from abnormal repression of natural drives, they have justified a system of education which encouraged uninhibited expression of native impulses.

The romantic wing of progressive education has attracted so much public attention, mostly unfavorable, that it has almost eclipsed the more sober and stable wing which drew its support largely from the leadership of John Dewey. Dewey, too, favored the activity program with its attendant pupil interest and freedom. But instead of grounding this program in a theory of child nature, he grounded it in his pragmatic theory of knowledge. Knowledge, he claimed, is the outcome of action. Confronted with a problem, an adult or child constructs in imagination a theory of hypothesis of how it might be solved. The truth or falsity of the proposed solution develops from whether or not the consequences of acting on the hypothesis corroborate it. Under such a regime freedom and interest are necessary conditions for selecting appropriate ends and means in solving the child's project. The progressive in contrast to the traditional school, then, according to Dewey, allows the child freedom to engage in interesting activities, not just because the child's active nature demands it (although that is important) but also because only by initiating activities and noting their consequences is an investigator or learner warranted in asserting when knowledge is true.

In Dewey's conception of the progressive school, the role of intelligence is clearly instrumental. Taking his cue from Darwinian evolution, he regards human intelligence as a relatively latecomer on the world scene. Consequently, the school cultivates intelligence as a tool to solve problems. This is very different from Aristotle and Newman, who would have education cultivate intelligence as an end in itself. For Dewey, taking his cue further from Darwinian evolution, there are no final educational ends in and of themselves. The ends of education are always subject to further reconstruction in the light of an uncertain and contingent future.

Not everyone has the talent, or what is more necessary, the economic leisure to join that stratum of society known as the intelligentsia which cultivates intelligence as an end in itself. Yet everyone can employ intelligence in the management of his daily affairs. In the one case, the cultivation of intelligence leads to the education of the few; and in the other, to the education of the many. Consequently, progressives claimed their educational philosophy to be more democratic than that of the traditionalists. Both philosophies, of course, supported the idea of education for all, but they differed on the quality of the education to be so given. Thus, progressives further claimed that their more pupil-centered practices were more democratic than the teacher-centered practices of the traditional school.

With the coming of the great economic depression of the 1930's, the romantic individualists in the "progressive-education" movement were severely taken to task for lack of a social orientation. Spurred on by the vital sense of direction fascist and communist education seemed to possess, many progressives turned social-planners and championed the notion that the school should take the initiative in bringing about a new social order cured of the defects of the present. The idea that progressive education should take a position in the van of social progress seemed entirely logical to many of its supporters. As a matter of fact, however, the left-wing group who captured "progressive education" for this cause received as much, if not more, unfavorable notice from the conservatively minded public as had the romantic individualists of the preceding decade. The traditional school considered itself the creature of the existing social order, not the creator of a new one!

Those who thought that the school should take a position of leadership in reconstructing the social order were in constant need of the protection of academic freedom. When the ship of state rocked violently to and fro during the depression,

conservatives were afraid that progressive educators might rock it just the bit
further which would cause it to founder. Loyalty oaths, designed at this time to
lessen the lurch by screening out "radical" teachers, became much more formidable
threats to schools after the war when the world settled down to the prolonged cold
war between the communist East and the democratic West.

CONTEMPORARY ISSUES IN AMERICAN EDUCATION

We have been at some pains to recount briefly the principal points of
the controversy between traditional and "progressive education"—all against
the twentieth-century background of world political, economic, religious, and
scientific tensions—not only to account for the great interest of this century in
educational philosophy but also to point up the main issues in contemporary
education.

Now to summarize and restate the issues.

1. *There is a current anxiety that modern education is adrift without rudder, chart, or
compass.* Is there a frame of reference by which we can defendably orient ourselves
and thus regain a sense of direction? It is all well and good to flatter ourselves that
in the twentieth century we are substituting conscious and deliberate transmission
and renewal of the culture for the automatic selection of the folkways. Yet we
could easily deceive ourselves without a reliable point of reference. For instance,
shall we make a monistic or pluralistic view of the culture we seek to screen and
renew? Can we detect any enduring structures in culture, or is culture quite
relativistic? By what standard of truth shall we judge our culture? Shall we teach
young people that there is just one standard or that there are several standards:
religious, metaphysical, and scientific?

2. *There is a current anxiety that, of the educational aims we have, too many are vague
or conflicting and too few generate strong loyalty.* By what standard can we validate our
aims and values? By the ordinances of some deity? By aptness to human nature?
By some subrational measure like "blood and soil"? By fitness to some particular
time and place? Of course learning involves the continual reconstruction of
experience but should that include a constant reconstruction of the aims of education as well? Or are there some aims of education which are not merely proximate
ends but ultimate and perennial? Without answers to questions such as these, how
can we tell which studies in the curriculum are the solid ones and which the fads and
frills? Are social studies, such as the college-preparatory ones, inherently and
intrinsically valuable while others, like vocational ones, are only instrumentally
valuable?

3. *There is a current anxiety that there has been a serious letdown in standards of
instruction as a result of modern educational procedures.* In part, this anxiety grows out of
an apprehension that too much attention is paid to the motivation of studies. All
agree that no learning takes place without some motivation or interest. But
should we go so far as to say that subjects in the curriculum derive their value

from being liked by children, or do subjects on occasion have values independently of being liked so that children can be told they ought to learn them even though they are not interested in them? Must standards necessarily fall unless we take this latter position? Is it good discipline to study what you do not like? Does such study result in greater force of moral character?

In part, the above anxiety grows out of the authority of instruction. How shall we regard the deposit of truth in the curriculum? Does the truth antedate instruction or is it the outcome of activities undertaken in the classroom, in school shops or laboratories, or on field trips? Is the problem-solving method, predicated on the scientific method, the best way of teaching and learning the truth? Would a student meet higher standards if his instruction depended on other methods as well, e.g., intuition, pure reasoning, or the acceptance of authority?

4. *There is a current anxiety that we are unsure of our democratic conception of education and that we have only fainthearted faith in it anyhow.* Just what does democratic regard for the individual mean? Does it mean a laissez-faire, almost romantic freedom for each student to design his own house of knowledge? Does it mean a benevolent paternalism wherein the school authorities determine what is best for children and then see that they get it? Or does it involve a situation in which children, together with adults and other children, learn to share decisions and their consequences even though this may mean testing out many things for themselves and sometimes reaching conclusions at variance with tradition? If the latter, should we expect the school to include controversial social issues in its curriculum? In that event, should the school take a neutral stand between the contending views, slant the outcome of instruction toward accepted democratic values, or encourage children to think in terms of a progressive reconstruction of the social order? This raises a question of the extent of our commitment to academic freedom as a preparation for the civil liberties of American life.

5. *There is a current anxiety that the social framework of the school accords the child too much freedom and does not subordinate him sufficiently to authority and control.* This statement stirs the inquiry whether parents and teachers yield children too much initiative and are too prone to assign priority to children's interests. Would it be better if children's interests were more frequently subordinated to those of adults, if adults would exert more control over children again? If more external control is restored in education, how at the same time shall we build initiative, self-reliance, and moral autonomy in children? And if the authority of the adult regains some of its former importance, how at the same time shall we preserve education from becoming authoritarian and undemocratic?

6. *There is a current anxiety that the public schools, overanxious to avoid sectarianism, are neglecting religion and becoming too secular.* Is there a religious dimension to education which is being neglected? Would more attention to such a dimension give current education a much-needed stability and sense of direction? Will more attention to religion in the public school confuse the proper spheres of God and Caesar? Should we re-examine the nineteenth-century tradition of the divorce of church and state in the field of public education?

THE ROLE OF PHILOSOPHY IN EDUCATIONAL PROGRESS

No doubt, as already stated, more issues could be listed. No doubt, too, the issues listed could have been drawn up under different categories. In terms of where we are in the twentieth century, however, the foregoing seem to be the areas in which the major contemporary issues lie. The issues have been stated largely in educational rather than bald philosophical terms. But the underlying philosophical issues are not far to seek. The usual problems of philosophy lie just beneath the surface of these educational terms. The nature of knowledge, of value, of man, of society, and of the world must each be met before a satisfactory conclusion can be formed of what to do next in our present predicament.

VARIOUS CONCEPTIONS OF THE ROLE OF THE EDUCATIONAL PHILOSOPHER

GENE D. PHILLIPS

In any age there has been a constant need to re-appraise the proper role of any given group in society. This has been true of the doctor, lawyer, teacher, theologian, among others. Inasmuch as there exists this seemingly perennial activity, though often there is not adequate time provided for it, it might be fitting to examine here and now the proper role of the educational philosopher in an era of extreme cultural anxiety.

It has been said recently by a visiting Japanese educator, who had visited here in the 1920's, that he had sensed a feeling of direction where education was concerned. The motivation for this direction, he felt, was not always accepted, since it largely emanated from the thinking and writing of John Dewey and his disciples; however, he felt some sense of direction was present. Upon his recent visit he sensed that even this much direction was lacking.

Whether or not this could be accepted as truly reflective of our age is not the point; rather, it serves as a point of dramatic emphasis. Though Dewey's role was

FROM *Journal of Education* (Boston University), 141 (October, 1958): 2–6. (Reprinted by permission.)

not primarily that of educational philosopher, his persistent interest in effecting a more deliberate interaction on the part of school and society was never ending. The educational enterprise was waiting for direction for the first half of the twentieth century just as is the second half. At the present time, no apparent consensus seems to stand which could put this direction in motion.

Alternatives are being posed constantly which might offer education a possible course to follow. Panaceas for education's ills appear without due consideration of their consequences for the future. The alternatives and panaceas are often compromises of past educational activity, and lack the vigor or reasonableness of bold experimentation. Their proposed content lacks any mild adventure or real excitement. Those who hearken to the virtues of the past are not willing to verify their worth by making their choices consistent with the most rigorous empirical tests; those who insist that the perpetually tentative present is foremost often fail to provide the method which makes such a condition flourish; those who speak glowingly about a predictive future need to educate us in the ways of finding security in uncertainty.

Educational and philosophical literature abounds in extolling the worth of each of these and many more genuine alternatives; therefore, it will not be the intent here to do likewise. It might be adequate enough to point out merely that the educational philosopher needs precise skills, information, and talents which would make each of these intelligible to him. He is committed to make a choice amongst these or others. Once he has done this, then a particular kind of behavior will ensue. His choice will necessarily involve him in a fuller or lesser use of science and its methods. He will either become more or less interested in human arrangements which can make men free to create new patterns of beauty, goodwill, love, and thoughtfulness. These concerns to be followed to their logical conclusions would involve only the most thoughtful efforts, notwithstanding the fact that our society does not find its members so arranged as to permit this specialized kind of inquiry. Since the teacher, the parent, as purveyors of this kind of education often feel the need for direction, there has been an increasing use made of the educational philosopher.

The professional philosopher has been omitted too often in this communication scheme. The reasons for this are many. Often his talents have not cared, nor have been free because of disposition, conventions, or training to deal with such affairs. As will be pointed out by various contributors to this issue, philosophers have been concerned deeply about education and its proper functions—whether it be to preserve the best in the culture, or to involve everyone in conscious activity and participation in the ongoing affairs of everyday life, or to prepare people for a more knowing tomorrow. This point can be further elaborated upon in the case of Plato.

His political ideals, in order to be implemented, had to take education into account very early lest they never be realized. Aristotle's recognition of the importance of the aims of education raised an issue still being pondered by all, whether the moral or the intellectual virtue is to receive prior or equal attention from the teacher. And so on does the progression of interest develop for relating educational practice and theory. Many factors—social, cultural, political—quickened the conscience of the masses for education's necessity. Education in the twentieth century became an imperative, not a luxury or a gift if chance permitted. The urgings of many have made this necessity more nearly realizable.

Universal education was launched as a vast experiment—the findings and the conclusions of which have not yet been fully revealed because the conceptions of its nature, its purposes, its methods, its goals, its proper maintenance have not been agreed upon. Its importance has known greatness and mildness as our culture moves through periods of economic depression and plentitude, of hot and cold wars, of a rising nationalistic superiority in some parts of the world.

The content of education, what is being emphasized or de-emphasized, can almost certainly reflect the trend of the times. Apparently respected aims of one period can be forgotten completely if a cultural vicissitude of the moment over-powers it. Must the course of education be so easily upset? If a society's cultural perspective included in it some agreement concerning its values, then might such a directionless situation be altered for the better? It might be well then for the educational philosopher to maintain closer communication with values which have created confusion in the conduct of educating, as well as those which seem to offer hope for new direction and order. Such sensitivity might well be developed.

If such a development is needed, in what ways can it be done? The educational philosopher can place his faith in the past which allegedly contains respected values; he could prefer to get them from the solution of problems of the present; he might prefer to ascertain their conduct from the findings of the social, cultural, and behavioral sciences; still further, he might create language and symbols for new values. As in the first case, he might seek religious authority for this derivation process; in the second case, he might well make active and conscious use of the methods of science or the democratic ethic; in the third case, he might make use of scientific progress in all of man's creative activities; lastly, he might employ the techniques of the contributors to philosophical analysis. In any event, the human community awaits those values which can lead it to a plan insuring continuance and survival.

Many educational philosophers are conceiving their role to be many sided. Some feel that it is not necessary for them to provide another system or educational doctrine, nor to compare various systems; rather, it is their task to question pervasive conceptual problems. This would involve extended conversations between philosopher and educator. Just as philosophers are divided by their countless "ists" and "isms," so are educators. The hearty suspicions held by each side could be expressed here; rather, it might be said that both are brandishing the other less and less with epithets hardly becoming to men of learning.

Morton White [1] indicates that a substantial portion of recent philosophy has been critical, scientific, and analytic in temper. If such were accepted as an appropriate

[1] M. White, *The Age of Analysis*. New York: The New American Library of World Literature, Inc., 1955.

function of the educational philosopher, he might function in the way that has been so significantly stated:[2]

. . . when he conceives his function to be neither the spinning out of implications from general doctrines nor the authoritative pronouncement of basic and intermediate values for the guidance of schools. . . . He can try to clarify our fundamental ways of thinking about education: the concepts we employ, the inferences we make, and the choices we express. He can render explicit the criteria of judgment we use in reaching educational decisions. He can test our common assumptions indirectly by striving for a systematic picture that will embrace them all. He can analyze the major positions taken on issues of educational policy by exposing their premises, consequences, and alternatives. In sum, he can improve our understanding of educational contexts and the problems they generate. . . .

The vigor of this conception of the educational philosopher would rest with his use of language and symbolism. Needless to say, he would need to make a fuller scientific study of language.

The philosopher of education, assuming this role, would find such concerns as these to be uppermost in his thinking: education and the science of education; the scientist's role and the aims of education; moral philosophy and education; decisions of principle; knowing how and knowing that; the methods of science: what are they? can they be taught?; is the teaching of the scientific method a significant educational objective; tradition and the traditionalist; reasons in art criticism; modern education and its critics.[3] Such a listing clearly indicates that these are all issues within a wider range of educational indeterminancy. Energy must be given to the solving of these issues, else the course of education anywhere in the world will not be smooth.

Going from this particular view of the role and the tasks carved out for the philosopher of education, one might look to the conception of philosophy as a vision. This was particularly held by Dewey. His constant reiteration that man must have faith in the worth of human experience gives additional credence to this thought. All values, he felt, were not necessarily restricted to those ascertained by experimental procedures. Because of this visionary perceptiveness, he brought us to appreciate more forcibly the morality of democracy; the experimental method and its relevance for helping the young to develop fully; the nature of experience; another view of mind; the lost individual; broader concepts of method; the public and its problems involving social, cultural, industrial, political, and economic issues. This raises the question, can this same perceptiveness have relevance in the work of the educational philosopher today? Must he leave this thinking, and forge ahead to new ideas not yet conceived, or must he be fearful of leaving them behind?

It has been said that Dewey's primary concern was not that of an educational philosopher, but it can be said otherwise for William H. Kilpatrick. He did much to identify his role as an educational philosopher. In turn, this has influenced the conduct and direction of many who came under his guidance. He raises some questions that require very diligent thinking: what is the philosophy of education?

[2] I. Scheffler, *Modern Readings, Philosophy and Education.* Boston: Allyn and Bacon, Inc., 1958, p. 5.
[3] *Op. cit.*, p. 2, vii–ix.

what does it teach us? what does it tell us about education that we cannot otherwise find out? can it help us, practically, to run a schoolroom? or a school system? can it help parents rear their children?[4]

After Kilpatrick worked through such questions with his students, his public, he would look to such concerns as the life process itself, the social nature of man, institutions, concepts of change, the culture, the individual and society, morality as a social necessity, respect for personality, democracy, the life good to live, the problem of progress, the philosophy of thinking, modern theories of learning, the building of interests, character building, the aesthetic life in education, and countless others. These were not vacuous topics unrelated to the thousands of teachers who studied with him; rather, they were ones with which they become intimately involved through rigorous debate, discussion, and experimentation.

Kilpatrick further helped his students come by a method of analysis: is the point of view defensible; has it been judged for its consistency; has it been judged for its inclusiveness; and has it been judged on the basis of the values it upholds and acts upon?[5]

And Kilpatrick goes on to say,

... Do these criteria mean that most people cannot have a philosophy, that 'only professional' philosophers can have one? The answer is no; any person who is willing to question his present point of view, who is open to critical examination of his own views and those of others, who is earnest in his search for deeper, finer, more defensible values, can build a philosophy. ...[6]

Many philosophers could take exception to this attitude toward philosophizing, but this in effect, is largely what the philosopher of education is attempting at all times in his teaching.

[4] W. H. Kilpatrick, *Philosophy of Education.* New York: The Macmillan Company, 1951, pp. ix–x.
[5] *Ibid.*, pp. 7–8.
[6] *Op. cit.*, p. 8.

PHILOSOPHY AS THE GENERAL THEORY OF EDUCATION

JOHN DEWEY

Philosophy has generally been defined in ways which imply a certain totality, generality, and ultimateness of both subject matter and method. With respect to

FROM John Dewey, *Democracy and Education.* New York: Macmillan Company, 1963, pp. 324–332. Copyright by The Macmillan Company, 1916. (Reprinted by permission.)

subject matter, philosophy is an attempt to *comprehend*—that is, to gather together the varied details of the world and of life into a single inclusive whole, which shall either be a unity, or, as in the dualistic systems, shall reduce the plural details to a small number of ultimate principles. On the side of the attitude of the philosopher and of those who accept his conclusions, there is the endeavor to attain as unified, consistent, and complete an outlook upon experience as is possible. This aspect is expressed in the word "philosophy"—love of wisdom. Whenever philosophy has been taken seriously, it has always been assumed that it signified achieving a wisdom which would influence the conduct of life. Witness the fact that almost all ancient schools of philosophy were also organized ways of living, those who accepted their tenets being committed to certain distinctive modes of conduct; witness the intimate connection of philosophy with the theology of the Roman church in the Middle Ages, its frequent association with religious interests, and, at national crises, its association with political struggles.

This direct and intimate connection of philosophy with an outlook upon life obviously differentiates philosophy from science. Particular facts and laws of science evidently influence conduct. They suggest things to do and not do, and provide means of execution. When science denotes not simply a report of the particular facts discovered about the world but a *general attitude* toward it—as distinct from special things to do—it merges into philosophy. For an underlying disposition represents an attitude not to this and that thing nor even to the aggregate of known things, but to the considerations which govern conduct.

Hence philosophy cannot be defined simply from the side of subject matter. For this reason, the definition of such conceptions as generality, totality, and ultimateness is most readily reached from the side of the disposition toward the world which they connote. In any literal and quantitative sense, these terms do not apply to the subject matter of knowledge, for completeness and finality are out of the question. The very nature of experience as an ongoing, changing process forbids. In a less rigid sense, they apply to *science* rather than to philosophy. For obviously it is to mathematics, physics, chemistry, biology, anthropology, history, etc. that we must go, not to philosophy, to find out the facts of the world. It is for the sciences to say what generalizations are tenable about the world and what they specifically are. But when we ask what *sort* of permanent disposition of action toward the world the scientific disclosures exact of us we are raising a philosophic question.

From this point of view, "totality" does not mean the hopeless task of a quantitative summation. It means rather *consistency* of mode of response in reference to the plurality of events which occur. Consistency does not mean literal identity; for since the same thing does not happen twice, an exact repetition of a reaction involves some maladjustment. Totality means continuity—the carrying on of a former habit of action with the readaptation necessary to keep it alive and growing. Instead of signifying a ready-made complete scheme of action, it means keeping the balance in a multitude of diverse actions, so that each borrows and gives significance to every other. Any person who is open-minded and sensitive to new perceptions, and who has concentration and responsibility in connecting them has, in so far, a philosophic disposition. One of the popular senses of philosophy is calm and endurance in the face of difficulty and loss; it is even supposed to be a power to bear pain without complaint. This meaning is a tribute to the influence of the Stoic philosophy rather than an attribute of philosophy in general. But in so far as it suggests that the wholeness characteristic of philosophy is a power to learn, or to extract meaning, from even the unpleasant vicissitudes of experience and to embody what is learned in an ability to go on learning, it is justified in any scheme. An analogous interpretation applies to the generality and ultimateness of philosophy. Taken literally, they are absurd pretensions; they indicate insanity. Finality does not mean, however, that experience is ended and exhausted, but means the disposition to penetrate to deeper levels of meaning—to go below the surface and find out the connections of any event or object, and to keep at it. In like manner the philosophic attitude is general in the sense that it is averse to taking anything as isolated; it tries to place an act in its context—which constitutes its significance.

It is of assistance to connect philosophy with thinking in its distinction from knowledge. Knowledge, grounded knowledge, is science; it represents objects which have been settled, ordered, disposed of rationally. Thinking, on the other hand, is prospective in reference. It is occasioned by an *un*settlement and it aims at overcoming a disturbance. Philosophy is thinking what the known demands of us —what responsive attitude it exacts. It is an idea of what is possible, not a record of accomplished fact. Hence it is hypothetical, like all thinking. It presents an assignment of something to be done—something to be tried. Its value lies not in furnishing solutions (which can be achieved only in action) but in defining difficulties and suggesting methods for dealing with them. Philosophy might almost be described as thinking which has become conscious of itself—which has generalized its place, function, and value in experience.

More specifically, the demand for a "total" attitude arises because there is the need of integration in action of the conflicting various interests in life. Where interests are so superficial that they glide readily into one another, or where they are not sufficiently organized to come into conflict with one another, the need for philosophy is not perceptible. But when the scientific interest conflicts with, say, the religious, or the economic with the scientific or æsthetic, or when the conservative concern for order is at odds with the progressive interest in freedom, or when institutionalism clashes with individuality, there is a stimulus to discover some more comprehensive point of view from which the divergencies may be brought together, and consistency or continuity of experience recovered. Often these clashes may be settled by an individual for himself; the area of the struggle of aims is limited and a person works out his own rough accommodations. Such homespun philosophies are genuine and often adequate. But they do not result in systems of philosophy. These arise when the discrepant claims of different ideals of conduct affect the community as a whole, and the need for readjustment is general.

These traits explain some things which are often brought as objections against philosophies, such as the part played in them by individual speculation, and their controversial diversity, as well as the fact that philosophy seems to be repeatedly occupied with much the same questions differently stated. Without doubt, all these things characterize historic philosophies more or less. But they are not objections to philosophy so much as they are to human nature, and even to the world in which human nature is set. If there are genuine uncertainties in life, philosophies must reflect that uncertainty. If there are different diagnoses of the cause of a difficulty, and different proposals for dealing with it; if, that is, the conflict of interests is more or less embodied in different sets of persons, there must be divergent competing philosophies. With respect to what has happened, sufficient evidence is all that is needed to bring agreement and certainty. The thing itself is sure. But with reference to what it is wise to do in a complicated situation, discussion is inevitable precisely because the thing itself is still indeterminate. One would not expect a ruling class living at ease to have the same philosophy of life as those who were having a hard struggle for existence. If the possessing and the dispossessed had the same fundamental disposition toward the world, it would argue either insincerity or lack of seriousness. A community devoted to industrial pursuits, active in business and commerce, is not likely to see the needs and possibilities of life in the same way as a country with high æsthetic culture and little enterprise in turning the energies of nature to mechanical account. A social group with a fairly continuous history will respond mentally to a crisis in a very different way from one which has felt the shock of abrupt breaks. Even if the same data were present, they would be evaluated differently. But the different sorts of experience attending different types of life prevent just the same data from presenting themselves, as well as lead to a different scheme of values. As for the similarity of problems, this is often more a matter of appearance than of fact, due to old discussions being translated into the terms of contemporary perplexities. But in certain fundamental respects the same predicaments of life recur from time to time with only such changes as are due to change of social context, including the growth of sciences.

The fact that philosophic problems arise because of widespread and widely felt difficulties in social practice is disguised because philosophers become a specialized class which uses a technical language, unlike the vocabulary in which the direct difficulties are stated. But where a system becomes influential, its connection with a conflict of interests calling for some program of social adjustment may always be discovered. At this point, the intimate connection between philosophy and education appears. In fact, education offers a vantage ground from which to penetrate to the human, as distinct from the technical, significance of philosophic discussions. The student of philosophy "in itself" is always in danger of taking it as so much nimble or severe intellectual exercise—as something said by philosophers and concerning them alone. But when philosophic issues are approached from the side of the kind of mental disposition to which they correspond, or the differences in educational practice they make when acted upon, the life-situations which they formulate can never be far from view. If a theory makes no difference in educational endeavor, it must be artificial. The educational point of view enables one to envisage the philosophic problems where they arise and thrive, where they are at home, and where acceptance or rejection makes a difference in practice.

If we are willing to conceive education as the process of forming fundamental dispositions, intellectual and emotional, toward nature and fellow men, philosophy may even be defined *as the general theory of education.* Unless a philosophy is to remain symbolic—or verbal—or a sentimental indulgence for a few, or else mere arbitrary dogma, its auditing of past experience and its program of values must take effect in conduct. Public agitation, propaganda, legislative and administrative action are effective in producing the change of disposition which a philosophy indicates as desirable, but only in the degree in which they are educative—that is to say, in the degree in which they modify mental and moral attitudes. And at the best, such methods are compromised by the fact they are used with those whose habits are already largely set, while education of youth has a fairer and freer field of operation. On the other side, the business of schooling tends to become a routine empirical affair unless its aims and methods are animated by such a broad and sympathetic survey of its place in contemporary life as it is the business of philosophy to provide.

Positive science always implies *practically* the ends which the community is concerned to achieve. Isolated from such ends, it is matter of indifference whether its disclosures are used to cure disease or to spread it; to increase the means of sustenance of life or to manufacture war material to wipe life out. If society is interested in one of these things rather than another, science shows the way of attainment. Philosophy thus has a double task: that of criticizing existing aims with respect to the existing state of science, pointing out values which have become obsolete with the command of new resources, showing what values are merely sentimental because there are no means for their realization; and also that of inter- preting the results of specialized science in their bearing on future social endeavor. It is impossible that it should have any success in these tasks without educa- tional equivalents as to what to do and what not to do. For philosophic theory has no Aladdin's lamp to summon into immediate existence the values which it intellectually constructs. In the mechanical arts, the sciences become methods of managing things so as to utilize their energies for recognized aims. By the educative arts philosophy may generate methods of utilizing the energies of human beings in accord with serious and thoughtful conceptions of life. Education is the laboratory in which philosophic distinctions become concrete and are tested.

It is suggestive that European philosophy originated (among the Athenians) under the direct pressure of educational questions. The earlier history of philosophy, developed by the Greeks in Asia Minor and Italy, so far as its range of topics is concerned, is mainly a chapter in the history of science rather than of philosophy as that word is understood to-day. It had nature for its subject, and speculated as to how things are made and changed. Later the traveling teachers, known as the Sophists, began to apply the results and the methods of the natural philosophers to human conduct.

When the Sophists, the first body of professional educators in Europe, instructed the youth in virtue, the political arts, and the management of city and household, philosophy began to deal with the relation of the individual to the universal, to some comprehensive class, or to some group; the relation of man and nature, of tradition and reflection, of knowledge and action. Can virtue, approved excellence in any line, be learned, they asked? What is learning? It has to do with knowledge. What, then, is knowledge? How is it achieved? Through the senses, or by apprenticeship in some form of doing, or by reason that has undergone a preliminary logical discipline? Since learning is *coming* to know, it involves a passage from ignorance to wisdom, from privation to fullness from defect to perfection, from non-being to being, in the Greek way of putting it. How is such a transition possible? Is change, becoming, development really possible and if so, how? And supposing such questions answered, what is the relation of instruction, of knowledge, to virtue?

This last question led to opening the problem of the relation of reason to action, of theory to practice, since virtue clearly dwelt in action. Was not knowing, the activity of reason, the noblest attribute of man? And consequently was not purely intellectual activity itself the highest of all excellences, compared with which the virtues of neighborliness and the citizen's life were secondary? Or, on the other hand, was the vaunted intellectual knowledge more than empty and vain pretense, demoralizing to character and destructive of the social ties that bound men together in their community life? Was not the only true, because the only moral, life gained through obedient habituation to the customary practices of the community? And was not the new education an enemy to good citizenship, because it set up a rival standard to the established traditions of the community?

In the course of two or three generations such questions were cut loose from their original practical bearing upon education and were discussed on their own account; that is, as matters of philosophy as an independent branch of inquiry. But the fact that the stream of European philosophical thought arose as a theory of educational procedure remains an eloquent witness to the intimate connection of philosophy and education. "Philosophy of education" is not an external application of ready-made ideas to a system of practice having a radically different origin and purpose: it is only an explicit formulation of the problems of the formation of right mental and moral habitudes in respect to the difficulties of contemporary social life. The most penetrating definition of philosophy which can be given is, then, that it is the theory of education in its most general phases.

The reconstruction of philosophy, of education, and of social ideals and methods thus go hand in hand. If there is especial need of educational reconstruction at the present time, if this need makes urgent a reconsideration of the basic ideas of traditional philosophic systems, it is because of the thoroughgoing change in social life accompanying the advance of science, the industrial revolution, and the development of democracy. Such practical changes cannot take place without demanding an educational reformation to meet them, and without leading men to ask what ideas and ideals are implicit in these social changes, and what revisions they require of the ideas and ideals which are inherited from older and unlike cultures.

SUMMARY

After a review designed to bring out the philosophic issues implicit in the previous discussions, philosophy was defined as the generalized theory of education. Philosophy was stated to be a form of thinking, which, like all thinking, finds its origin in what is uncertain in the subject matter of experience, which aims to locate the nature of the perplexity and to frame hypotheses for its clearing up to be tested in action. Philosophic thinking has for its differentia the fact that the uncertainties with which it deals are found in widespread social conditions and aims, consisting in a conflict of organized interests and institutional claims. Since the only way of bringing about a harmonious readjustment of the opposed tendencies is through a modification of emotional and intellectual disposition, philosophy is at once an explicit formulation of the various interests of life and a propounding of points of view and methods through which a better balance of interests may be effected. Since education is the process through which the needed transformation may be accomplished and not remain a mere hypothesis as to what is desirable, we reach a justification of the statement that philosophy is the theory of education as a deliberately conducted practice.

THE RELATIONS OF PHILOSOPHY AND SCIENCE IN THE STUDY OF EDUCATION

WILLIAM H. KILPATRICK

I shall understand the term philosophy in the sense that I myself use and teach it in its bearing on education. Science I shall understand in what I take to be its currently accepted sense as the effort to apply the methods of "exact science" to the study of education. It need hardly be said that there are other definitions of both philosophy and science. For myself, I prefer a broader definition of science than merely the processes of exact science, but I am counting that it is "a condition and not a theory" which confronts. We are to consider the actual situation of greater or less conflict between these two approaches in the study of education. I shall maintain

FROM *School and Society*, 30 (July 13, 1929): 39–48. (Reprinted by permission.)

that there is no proper conflict between the two, and that any existing conflict results either from a misconception of the function of one or both or from an unwarranted extension of conclusions beyond the conditions on which the conclusions were reached.

Let us first try to clear up the different provinces of "philosophy" and "science" as defined above.

It appears that the methods of exact science have arisen by refinement out of the methods of common sense, and that in this development physics, for obvious reasons, led the way. To see the original against which the refinement is to be contrasted let us imagine the case of an old farmer who has lately installed in his home his first water system. The work was badly done and a cold spell has frozen a pipe. The farmer wishes to thaw it out but hesitates, asking, "If I pour hot water on it, what will happen?" His wife urges caution. They discuss their past experience of vessels that have burst in connection with freezing and thawing.

What now this farmer asks and answers at best haphazardly—"If I do this, what will happen?"—a scientific procedure would undertake more carefully with all the known precautions in order to obtain as reliable resulting knowledge as possible. In general we may say that science relies fundamentally upon hypothesis and testing. It will use the principles of the separation of variables and of control group procedures. In particular it will work with all possible care, and will especially seek to prevent any personal bias from entering as a factor in the determination of the outcome.

Science is thus the most careful possible way of finding and stating how a given quantity varies under named conditions. "If I do this, what will happen?" may be taken as a popular way of stating the problem which science undertakes most carefully to answer.

In analogous fashion philosophy too may be said to have originated by refinement out of a common-sense type of problem. For illustration let us go back to the farmer and his wife as they were beforehand considering whether or not to install the water system. The alternative was to allow their daughter to go to college. Available funds did not suffice for both. A choice had apparently to be made. We can hear the old fellow say: "We *need* the water works. Mary don't need to go to college. It's only she's set her mind on it." "If she goes to college, she'll want to go off somewhere else to live. I want to see her married and settled close by. In another year I hope she'll marry Jeff Smith and be settled for life." "Yes, and if she goes to college I'm afraid she'll lose her religion, the same as Trudy van Landingham did, a-saying the Bible is wrong in spots. To my way of thinking Mary's safer at home."

Again we have common-sense with its easy-to-hand answers as opposed to the possibility of a more carefully considered weighing of what is involved. Some of the matters involved in this instance readily present themselves.

What does "need" mean? When is a thing needed? It is such questions as these which arise if we look more closely into the character of the desirable life than the farmer seemed inclined to do. Water in the home and the development of life's possibilities for Mary seem fairly disparate, difficult of comparison, but they must somehow be weighed against each other if the farmer and his wife are to decide more adequately the question as to what they shall do.

There is further involved the relations of the different persons to each other. Are the parents the ones to decide whether Mary shall "marry Jeff Smith" and "settle down"? Kant's problem seems here involved as to whether Mary is to be used as means or as end. In this again is involved life in its deepest sense and meaning. Still further we have the question of authority in religion and still again whether parents have the right to settle such matters for their children. The old farmer was ready to count all these questions settled. Others of us think them worthy of far more consideration.

All such questions as those raised just above seem to concern life as such, life as consummation, life as an intermingled aggregate of values which do in fact affect each other in much the same way as do the parts that make up a whole. Analysis will help to study the problem, but no separate study of the values involved will as a rule suffice. The solution seems to lie along the line of integrating all the factors into a whole, into one course of procedure that shall somehow best save and serve as far as possible all the values. And this still holds true in spite of the fact that values and factors taken analytically often seem disparate, even radically incommensurable, with respect to each other.

Philosophy, or better, philosophizing, is thus conceived as "an unusually stubborn effort" to settle such problems as the foregoing with as full consideration as possible of what is involved. It is the problem of determining what to do in a specific case in the light of all the warring values involved.

To make clearer the contrast between science and philosophy as these are here thus defined and illustrated it may be well to consider more fully certain contrasting elements involved.

1. As to type of problem. Science is concerned with facts. Its effort is to find and establish uniformities. Following its typical method it isolates each instance of such and then undertakes to find and state the relations which hold between varying conditions of the matter under consideration and the respective corresponding results. Its question (in substance) is, "If I do this, what will happen? Or perhaps better, "when these conditions hold, what follows?" If no answer to the question is forthcoming, science must say so and wait. As to what use will be made of the facts so determined, that is for others to say.

Philosophy in contrast faces a situation of necessary action. It says, "The case is doubtful. There is apparent conflict of values. Any course seems likely to bring both good and evil. What shall I do?" Note that any such situation confronting is actual and must be met, and that any choice or course whatever, including refusal to act, is *an* answer which carries with it its appropriate harvest of consequences. Philosophy then asks, "In the light of all this what shall I do?"

2. As to type of consequence considered. As implied above, exact science seeks to isolate each variable involved, subject it to assigned varying treatments and ascertain the corresponding changes that ensue as the treatment is changed. To the scientist, for the matter at hand, no value attaches to one change over another. That a certain

diagnosis foretells death to the patient can in no wise enter into the determination of the diagnosis. It is the excellence of scientific method that these consequences are rigidly excluded.

For philosophy, on the other hand, consequences of value and import are integral in its purview. It is just the consequences that follow because people see and feel that most of all constitute the data which concern philosophy.

Science concerns itself with results that follow in terms of "causation." Philosophy must know and use these, but its final concern is with consequences that follow because these things have *meanings* for the people variously concerned.

3. As to bias or wish or interest.[1] Science, in the degree that it can effect it, must eliminate all bias or wish or interest in one specific result over another, at least so far as allowing such bias to affect the result. Philosophy, on the other hand, must deal exactly and precisely with interest, wish and preference. These constitute its primary subject-matter. All such, both immediate and remote, must be brought out into the open and there weighed, related, considered, each in its varied bearings, all to the end not of eliminating preference or preventing it from affecting the result but precisely to give to each such preference as far as possible its own sway and to grant to it its greatest possible part in determining the result. Greatest possible part, that is, in relation to all the other preferences or interests or values involved. The effort is, as far as may be possible, to find a course of action which will save all the interests, which will integrate all into one course of action that best saves all.

4. As to dealing with parts or with whole. Science (in the degree that it is "exact") proceeds by analysis and the separation of variables. It abstracts part from a total setting and seeks to find relations thus existing in this condition of abstractedness. Thus in any statistical treatment of people, as, for example, in life insurance discussions, the age may be the sole factor considered. For such purposes all men forty years old are exactly alike, precisely interchangeable, each one exactly and identically equal to each other one. Clearly this treatment involves a high degree of abstractedness.

Philosophy, on the contrary, must deal with "whole" situations, that is, with the parts as they are actually related and conflicting in the existing total situation. It will analyze but must always reach its conclusion only after the abstracted element has been put back into the actual total working relationship along with all the other elements that are in fact involved. It is hardly possible to overstress this difference of procedure between "philosophy" and "exact science" in its treatment of the part-whole relationship.

5. As to the time element involved.[2] Science deals with things that are at hand here and now. On no other basis can it measure or weight or count. Philosophy in addition to things that are now in existence must deal also with what is not yet in

---

[1] Here I wish to acknowledge my indebtedness to my colleague, Professor R. B. Raup. For a fuller discussion of this point see his article, "Limitations of the Scientific Method," in the *Teachers College Record*, 30: 212–26, December, 1928. It is worthy of remark that Dr. Raup chose to conduct his discussion without using the term philosophy. I believe, however, that I am here doing no injustice to his position.

[2] For this point I am indebted to an unpublished lecture by Professor Dewey.

existence but might or could be and perhaps should be. It must somehow weigh such as these against each other and in the end decide that what now is not shall come to be.

It is probably wise before taking up the more controversial matters to consider next some of the interrelations between "science" and "philosophy," how the two more or less overlap and interact.

(1) Both science and philosophy (as herein defined) use the procedure of hypothesis and testing. Both appeal equally to the facts of experience as the final test of the validity of an hypothesis. The testing is likely to be different. It is also true that "science" may at times refuse to decide; it can wait. Philosophy, however, can not wait. To decide to wait constitutes both for life and for philosophy an answer. But having answered, philosophy awaits the outcome to test the validity of its answer as truly as does science.

(2) Philosophy must respect facts as definitely as does science. And it will properly get its facts from science. Many so-called facts, however, are so suffused with interpretation as to be questionable from the point of view of other interpretation. Philosophy stands peculiarly ready to re-question all such interpretation-facts.

(3) Scientific findings may affect "philosophy" by changing the data upon which its conclusions had hitherto been based. Such change of data may upset an old conclusion, or it may remove doubt at a certain point and so abolish an old problem, or it may create new problems.

It is probably in connection with this point that there has arisen the opinion, widely held in certain circles, that the advance of science, having thus at times cleared up doubt and so abolished old philosophic problems, will, given time enough, clear up all such problems and so, as it were, "push philosophy off the map." The contention—or hope—might be more tenable if we lived in a finite world, with nothing new happening in it. In such a world there may, for aught I know, be a finite number of problems with the possibility of solving at least some of them so that they would stay solved. So far as we can yet tell, however, our world is not finite, but has infinite possibilities for new problems. In fact, each significant advance of science, in general, adds more problems for philosophy than it subtracts, and besides makes many an old problem still more tangled. For instance, man in his philosophizing has not yet digested the doctrine of evolution, and now comes the new physics with the promise of enough problems to keep us busy for generations to come. In a smaller way, the testing movement in education has added to the number of problems facing the philosophy of education. Testing has helped to solve some problems in education, but it has added more than it had settled.

As long as the world remains infinite and science will oblige us by continuing to grow, philosophy has no fears of running out of problems. To think of it is to laugh.

(4) "Philosophy" often, perhaps generally, gives to "science" its basic assumptions. This is to say nothing more than that the men of any time think the thoughts of that time. The trouble about it is, as another has said, that theories often continue

to live after their brains have been knocked out. Old assumptions hang on after they should be discarded. One such hang-over probably lies back of the conflict we face here to-day. Medieval theology through its influence on Descartes (in spite of his wish to start afresh) gave to modern exact science its most hurtful assumption, the body-mind dualism. Physics, accepting the dualism and restricting itself to matter and motion, worked wonders. Thus arose the wide-spread tendency to restrict careful inquiry to the measurable aspects of life, with the more or less definite tendency to deny validity or worth to all else. We see some of the results of this dualism when one writer objects that another "has made up his windpipe that there is no mind." It is the same dualism but from the other side when a writer admits habit in lower responses but denies it a place in "the higher processes." Even Eddington in presenting the most astonishing and revolutionary aboutface of modern physics can not stand outside his surrounding dualistic atmosphere as he tries to state the new position. In this particular case in spite of this limitation we get, however, in his words a breath from a new world:

Recognizing that the physical world is entirely abstract and without "actuality" apart from its linkage to consciousness, we restore consciousness to its fundamental position instead of representing it as an essential complication occasionally found in the midst of inorganic nature at a late stage of evolutionary history.[3]

The body-mind dualism with its unwarranted emphasis on measuring is not the only hurtful assumption currently made in scientific circles. A fixed-in-advance universe is another. In an astonishing degree the less careful upholders of the subject-matter basis of education assume (apparently without knowing it) that the universe is fixed and change a negligible factor, thus helping to perpetuate certain concepts which were originally devised or at least promulgated in defense of feudalism and medieval religion. If change as an actual factor in our world were given its rightful place in educational thought, many current emphases in the discussion of learning would undergo great transformation. The need for the continual criticism of current thought assumptions in the light of their wider bearings would of itself, apart from all other considerations, suffice to give to philosophizing a permanent place among the higher services of thought to man. That such criticism is painful to all varieties of fundamentalists is only additional reason for demanding its continuance.

We now have before us the more significant distinctions in meaning and interrelations in fact between science and philosophy as upheld in this discussion. Let us next ask whether there are situations in education which especially demand the kind of treatment here reserved for philosophy. It appears that there are such and that for their adequate treatment the methods of exact science will (so far as yet appears) be forever insufficient. To clarify ideas only clear-cut instances will be used, where significant values conflict and decisions must be made. It is freely admitted that such situations of doubt shade off by degrees into those too trivial or too familiar to present problems of interest in the field of our discussion.

[3] A. S. Eddington, "The Nature of the Physical World," Macmillan, 1928, p. 332.

Four such situations are here presented as peculiarly the province of philosophizing.

First, *wherever there is indecision or doubt or dispute regarding the "good life," that is, the life that we shall approve and seek.* This will manifest itself clearly in (a) the problem of the curriculum content. Shall these pupils study French? Science in some of its departments may supply valuable data to be considered in attempting the problem. The solution, however, is essentially that of budgeting French and the time and effort spent on it with other constituents and factors in life. Everything pertinent to the life of the pupils, actual or potential, is involved. Merely to study the effects of French could not suffice. The separation of variables and control group procedures are not sufficient where the *whole of life* is contemplated. If the question were whether a stenographer working under such and such conditions should give so many hours of preparation to learning French for use as a stenographer and the judgments were to be made in terms of contrasted money returns, then something could be said for an exact scientific determination of the problem as stated. But the curriculum problem is not a limited problem. It involves all of life for these pupils and for all whom they will influence. There is no claim that "philosophy" has a method or an answer adequate to the problem. The claim is that anything less than an actual facing of what is in fact involved and of all that is involved, such as philosophizing accepts as its task, is not even a reasonable attempt at solving the problem. One whose sole method is that of "exact science" is by that very fact shut out from even facing the curriculum problem as a whole.

And along with the curriculum problem (as a whole) go also (b) all method procedures in dispute. These for their final evaluation must be judged by their effect on character and life. On no other basis can we adequately compare or weigh contrasted method effects. It is increasingly recognized that the organism responds as a whole, which means that indefinitely many learning effects accompany any significant responding. Any proposed weighing of contrasted results must include and weigh all these and in their varied consequential effects. But such weighing as a whole is beyond the separate-analytic processes of exact science. Method accordingly is in any adequate sense beyond it.

With method of course goes (c) all valuation of teaching procedures. The analytic method can tell which procedure will best give, other things being equal, any precisely specified outcome; but this is no adequate evaluation of a procedure that, like method in general, entails an innumerable host of attendant learnings. So also in general (d) any administrative procedure that significantly affects learning outcomes can not be adequately evaluated by the analytic methods of exact science. In this is involved problems of class size, apportionment of supplies, the examination system, platoon school procedure, etc., etc. All such require that relating of part to whole which "exact" science by its very analytic processes is inadequate to deal with.

We thus conclude that curriculum, method, teaching and administrative procedures of all kinds in so far as they affect life and character present problems which while admitting also countless "scientific" inquiries, will none the less forever, require the outlook and effort herein called philosophic. And even if we could ever once get the problems solved they would not stay solved; for our world is a changing world and as such constantly introduces novelty in such way as to shift from time to time the factors in our problems and consequently to upset the solutions. Philosophizing is, as far as concerns these problems, forever and continuously inherent in the study of education.

A second situation which calls for philosophizing in education is to be found *wherever the school must make a choice among persons or in the relation of person to person.* The considerations here practically repeat the preceding. Shall we have separate vocational high schools or keep all secondary people together? Whatever may be the proper solution in any given case, it can not be reached without a consideration of life as a whole, as a whole in respect of each person involved and as a whole in respect of the total group life. For vocational segregation has its effect on life's outlooks. Similarly with segregation by ability. Similarly with any proposition to limit secondary education facilities to those of certain ability standards. So also with regard to any proposed use of the facts of individual differences. In all such, life and its outlooks are involved, so that philosophizing becomes involved. If any were disposed to doubt that philosophizing is involved it is only necessary to study history and see how the different philosophies (inclusive assumptions, inclusive points of view) have returned different answers as to how to treat individuals in all such regards.

A third and very far-reaching type of situation calling for philosophizing is *where a principle, or even fact, established in respect to abstracted data is sought to be applied in general.* The contention here made is that what is proved with abstracted data may or may not remain valid when applied in a total (non-abstracted) situation, and in education only a "philosophizing" attack can tell in general whether it is applicable. For instance, in mathematics the whole is equal to the sum of its parts and a whole may be constructed from the requisite parts. But in biology it is not true. The biologic whole is more than the sum of its parts. So also is an esthetic whole, and likewise a social whole. It may be that this third principle is but the generalization of the other two. An experimenter studies "motivation." (This term is, by the way, interesting as carrying with it the implicit assumption that subject-matter shall first be selected and then taught, an assumption which I for one more than question.) He concludes from his study that one type of "motivation" is superior to certain others in that the pupils of the one group make consistently higher scores on a standardized test than do those of the other groups. If the work is properly done, we must admit that when the like conditions are repeated the like results will follow. But it does not follow from this alone that schools should therefore follow the type of "motivation" thus approved, and this for at least two reasons. One, that there are other attendant results which were not measured by the tests. These may be some good and some bad—good for one type of "motivation" and bad for the other. When these are properly weighed in with the test results, superiority may be shifted. The second reason for holding up the conclusion is that best results by test are not necessarily best in life. To learn in the sense of being able to stand an examination is not the same thing as to learn in the sense of use in life. Ability may be present but disposition lacking; or ability may be present for one set of cues but absent for a different set of cues. Life's dispositions and cues are different from those of the examination room.

It may be rejoined—and quite properly—that adequate scientific criticism would point out these same limitations at least to the degree of indicating the conditions beyond which the conclusions do not necessarily hold. To this two replies may be made. First, it appears by actual observation that those not sensitive to the wider values jeopardized by these unwarranted extensions are often correspondingly insensitive to the bad science involved. The studies that have been published regarding optimum class size furnish a flagrant example of this unwarranted extension, and it can not be claimed that the sponsors—at any rate—are inconspicuous in scientific research. Meanwhile it has been left to the "philosophizing" interest to urge the limitations. The second reply is that any final judgment as to range of application is impossible apart from the process and outlook herein called philosophizing.

This principle denying the right of general validity to conclusions reached under abstracted conditions, if it be allowed to stand, queries all unconsidered applications of strictly scientific findings, for such findings are as a rule made on abstracted data. Laboratory conditions need not be life conditions; and, more generally, measurement of one type of outcome does not *ipso facto* measure all the attendant outcomes. And this limitation when applied is often severe.

The fourth and final situation calling for philosophizing has to do with *questioning assumptions*. It was pointed out above that many assumptions of science have been given by outworn philosophies. Whitehead says in connection:

> There will be some fundamental assumptions which adherents of all the variant systems within the epoch unconsciously presuppose. Such assumptions appear so obvious that people do not know what they are assuming because no other way of putting things has ever occurred to them.[4]

Questioning assumptions is always a possibility. We never know when it will be successfully done. And progress of a very definite kind lies here, probably the most strategic kind of progress. Whitehead elsewhere,[5] speaking of an analogous revision of our working body of abstractions, says:

> It is here that philosophy finds its niche as essential to the healthy progress of society. It is the critic of abstractions. A civilization which can not burst through its current abstractions is doomed to sterility after a very limited period of progress.

Speaking for myself I feel compelled to question the common notion of the educative process. Its assumptions seem to be unfounded. This common notion in effect seems to assume among other things (a) that analytic learning should come first, to be followed at quite a distance by synthetic; (b) that, as has already been

[4] A. N. Whitehead, "Science and the Modern World," Macmillan, 1925, p. 69.
[5] *Ibid.*, p. 82 f.

pointed out, only one thing is learned at a time; (*c*) that life so far as learning is concerned is both fixed and knowable in advance, without significant admixture of the precarious; (*d*) that learning as fixing in habit will suffice (that is, to the virtual exclusion of any creative aspect of learning), and (*e*) that learning to give back on demand is sufficient for education purposes. Each of these I should wish to deny and with them the customary school procedure based on them. I wish accordingly to revise most terms as used in educational discussion, such as subject-matter, study, learn, teach, educational objectives, minimum essentials. If all these terms as currently used do in fact commit us to indefensible assumptions, then it behooves us to examine into the matter. And I should myself wish, moreover, to claim that such far-reaching assumptions as these implicate us with life and its values in such way that the examination can not be adequate till again the philosophizing outlook has been invoked.

It may in connection be worth while to call attention to two limitations found in much of current psychology which result, it seems fair to assert, from unwarranted philosophical assumptions. First of these is the evident shunning by many writers of such words as thinking, meaning, idea, ideal and consciousness (in any of its derivatives). It seems practically certain that this has been brought about by the Cartesian dualism already referred to and the definite wish to explain "mind" away or to reduce it to a terminology suited to "body." There is at times a definite disposition to teach that such things do not function in experience. One of my students last summer thus objected to me that I seemed to think that "ideas" really function, apparently not realizing that he was attacking an "idea" with "ideas" he had gained from an author who seemed to him to prove that "ideas" can not function. If these writers who are squeamish about "consciousness," thinking, ideas, and the like could but get rid of the old dualism, they could then see how unwarranted is their effort at denying what after all is their own chief stock in trade, as it is of all who are trying by thinking to improve affairs. Revision of certain current conceptions of "consciousness," yes—there are many unwarranted conceptions in connection, and all resulting, it appears, from this same dualism denial of any and all validity to conscious action, idea, intention or purpose, no— without these we can not live as humans.

A second warping of psychology due to bad assumption is found in the failure to discuss psychology and education in terms of doubtful or hazardous life situations. The old curriculum was limited to content where the teacher knew "the answer." The pupil might be in doubt, but no good teacher could fail to know. The (apparently) unconscious assumption was twofold: one that education is for the immature only and is concerned only and exactly with what competent elders already know is true and right; the other that the world of affairs and finally the universe itself contains nothing essentially unknown or precarious. Most who have not thought seriously of the point—and most have not—hardly see the point or bearing of the matter. The result is that for most people a curriculum is necessarily matter-set-out-to-be-learned and we-who-are-expert at any rate know the answers. This is the starting point of most educational psychology—and sadder still the ending point. If contrariwise we could but get it clearly in mind that—so far as we can tell—the actual universe includes, along with dependable uniformities, much inherent precariousness and uncertainty, and that both elements are inextricably interwoven in life as such with its efforts, then we should see the need for a different emphasis in education and a correlative development of psychology to take care of it. The more one thinks of it the more astonishing it appears that so little note has been taken of this so obvious precariousness. It with the dependable uniformities must supply the two legs which together are absolutely necessary if life and thought are to go forward in effective fashion.

And thus we reach the end. "Philosophizing" and the processes of "exact" sciences appear as complementary. Both are needed if life and education are successfully to face their problems. Neither can take the place of the other. Nor if properly used can they conflict. And I should myself like further to conclude that education can never become a science. Within education science will extend itself more and more and will render greater and greater service; but always—so long as this world stands—will there be problems, nay regions of problems, with which the processes of "exact" science are insufficient to cope. With such what is here called philosophizing is forever essential.

CRITERIA FOR
JUDGING A PHILOSOPHY
OF EDUCATION

GEORGE S. COUNTS

The evaluation of philosophies is one of the oldest of human sports. Moreover, even though a maker of psychological tests would no doubt regard *armchair* as the appropriate associative response to the stimulus *philosopher*, this particular sport has not always belonged to the indoor variety. In fact, if my history is not greatly at fault, the process of evaluating philosophies has not infrequently been attended by the breaking of heads. I am even of the opinion that the Crusades of the Middle Ages, the horrors of the French Revolution and the bitter struggle between reds and whites in contemporary Russia, not to mention our own domestic troubles in the sixties of the last century, represent at least in part efforts to evaluate philosophies. Indeed, we might regard these sanguinary episodes in history as illustrative

FROM *School and Society*, 30 (July 27, 1929): 103–107. (Reprinted by permission.)

of nature's method of approaching the subject which we are to consider . . ..
Let us hope, however, that we shall be able to avoid the more extreme forms
which the process tends to take. Perhaps we may succeed in doing this if, following
the tradition of college professors, we keep the discussion in the field of abstractions
and rather far removed from the world of concrete things and human passions.

There is, however, another policy which we might pursue with a reasonable
expectation of maintaining a general condition of amity and good feeling. The
basic cause of conflict, I think, is found in the fatal human liking for absolutes.
Every individual or group tends to regard its own peculiar philosophy as altogether
good and true and right. Although in the modern age of swiftly moving events one
may change philosophies half a dozen times in a lifetime, most of us are inclined to
regard the particular philosophy to which we hold for the moment as partaking of
the nature of divine revelation—fixed, unchanging, eternal. As a consequence the
usual attempt to evaluate educational philosophies is almost certain to be fruitless:
one philosophy is judged in terms of another. As a mental exercise this is of course
easy enough, but, since any philosophy worthy of the name is prepared to meet
attacks from practically every quarter, such a procedure is without practical
outcome. The very existence of different philosophies would seem to presuppose
the existence of different systems of value—systems of value for which there is no
common denominator. Obviously, to set up one as a standard against which all
others are to be measured is to beg the question at the outset. It can only precipitate
a trial of personal strength between the champions of the opposing philosophies.

Is there then any possibility of setting up criteria, which are not entirely subjective
in quality, for passing judgment on a given philosophy of education? To this
question an affirmative answer can, I think, be given; but the task is fraught with
very great difficulty. For an individual to get outside his own system of values is
almost impossible, however honestly he may strive to do so; and while failing
utterly to achieve this goal he may think that he has succeeded. It is, therefore, with
no little trepidation that I propose my own solution to the problem. The thought,
however, that the great majority of us in this room have been reared on practically
the same mental pabulum comforts me somewhat. While we differ among ourselves on minor matters, we have for the most part the same fundamental biases
and prejudices. If I beheld before me an audience of Hindoo yogis, Russian communists, Melanesian shamans, Italian Fascists and Confucian scholars, I would feel
much less certain about my criteria; but as I look at you and see the familiar faces
of citizens of the American democracy and hereditary members of the Methodist,
Baptist, Presbyterian and other Christian, but preponderantly Protestant Christian,
sects, I take courage and suggest that a defensible philosophy of education should
conform to at least five requirements: it should be systematically empirical in its
foundations; it should be comprehensive in its outlook; it should be consistent in
its several departments; it should be practicable in its provisions, and it should be
satisfying to its adherents. Let us now proceed to put a bit of content into each of
these criteria.

Our first criterion is that a philosophy of education should be systematically empirical in its foundations. This means first of all that it should be derived from experience. There is, of course, nothing radical in this proposal, for, if my theology is sound, there is no other possible ultimate source of derivation. Even the most highly speculative and abstract systems of thought must rest in the last analysis on some sort of empirical basis. That basis may be very narrow and altogether inadequate to support the superstructure reared upon it, but the connection between philosophy and experience, however tenuous, must always exist. Our contention, however, is not merely that a defensible philosophy of education should have an empirical foundation but rather that it should represent a *systematic* exploration of human experience. In the degree that it fails to take into account all departments of that experience it must be inadequate and lacking in authority.

This means in particular that the educational philosopher can not disregard that most refined body of human experience which we call science. Especially must his formulations embrace the results of investigation in the realms of biology, psychology and sociology. Indeed, one of his major tasks should be that of providing a synthesis for educational purposes of knowledge drawn from these sciences. To the extent that he is unfamiliar with the discoveries of the scientist his conclusions and pronouncements will be unsound. Since the complete assimilation of existing knowledge is probably beyond the power of a single mind and since that knowledge itself will always be partial, we may assume that every philosophy of education must fall short of the ideal.

Science, however, does not embrace the whole of human experience. Even in his efforts to free himself from intellectual error, man must have recourse to methods other than the methods of science. That these methods may lack reliability does not destroy the fact that there are vast areas in which no other methods can be employed. Thus the metaphysician, standing on the findings of science, pursues the search for truth in those spheres of being which lie beyond the domain of science. Although some of us may be satisfied with the world as revealed through eyes, ears and nose, the great masses of mankind, I fear, will always demand a more integrated and comprehensive view of the universe. While metaphysics may seem very remote from the concerns of education, it can not be wholly disregarded in the construction of educational theory. At any rate, every great educational philosophy with which I am familiar rests upon some metaphysical foundation.

But human experience possesses more than a single dimension. It is more than intellect; it is more than physics and metaphysics. An educational philosophy might be free from intellectual error and yet be woefully inadequate. It might be essentially true as measured by intellectual standards and yet lack those elements of warmth and color which after all give meaning and significance to life. An educational philosophy, therefore, in addition to having the dimension which separates truth from error, should have a second dimension which divides right from wrong, and a third which distinguishes beauty from ugliness. In other words, it should comprehend and bring into a synthesis, not only science and metaphysics, but ethics and esthetics as well. I, of course, do not mean to say that morals and art can not or should not be investigated by the scientific method. This is entirely possible and desirable, but certainly no more so than that the findings of science, before they are set to practical purposes, should be evaluated in terms of the canons of ethics and esthetics. An educational philosophy which is concerned only with what is true and is wholly insensitive to what is good or what is beautiful would be as cold and barren as the ice fields lying within the Arctic circle.

Our second criterion is that a philosophy of education should be comprehensive in its outlook. It must not only derive its substance from the whole range of human experience, but it must also face squarely and with some sense of proportion all the problems of education. In particular it should strike a careful balance between the demands of the individual and the demands of society, between the demands of childhood and the demands of maturity; it should take into account all the qualities, traits and powers of the learner, all the elements of the social heritage, all the groups, classes and sects of society and all the processes and functions of the social order; it should recognize the existence of the various educational agencies and should develop some theory regarding the educational responsibilities of each; it should in particular isolate the tasks of the school and provide for the sound coordination of pupil, teacher and curriculum. In a word, an educational philosophy should bring into comprehensive synthesis a theory of the nature of the individual, a theory of the learning and educative process, a theory of the growth of personality, a theory of the special function of the school, a theory of the structure and processes of society and a theory of the meaning of life. Perhaps we should also say that an educational philosophy should be a philosophy of life. It is in its one-sidedness that much of current educational theory is at fault. Because of some peculiar bias of character or training each of us tends to emphasize some one aspect of the problem to the neglect of others which are of equal importance.

Our third criterion is that a philosophy of education should be consistent in its several departments. It is clear, I think, that in the field of educational theory the right hand often "knoweth not what the left hand doeth." Thus at one place we seem to adopt a purely mechanistic psychology and reduce all learning to a process of establishing connections between stimuli and responses, while at another without any apparent sense of contradiction we speak of the giving of insights and of the conscious control of conduct. There is also a very common conflict between our aims and our methods. We say that our children should be trained for life in a democracy and then we place them in schools which are autocratically managed from the board of education to the pupil in the classroom; we say that our children should learn the lessons of cooperation and then we subject them to an educational regimen of marks, certificates and degrees which places a premium upon individual competition and self-aggrandizement; we say that our children should be taught to love music and literature and then place them in learning situations which engender feelings of distaste and boredom; we say that our children should be led to an understanding of the present complex and bewildering industrial order and then place them under the tutelage of teachers who are scarcely aware that a radically new civilization is rapidly spreading throughout the world.

Our fourth criterion is that a philosophy of education should be practicable in its provisions. It should be adapted to a particular time and a particular place. There is no philosophy, unless it is couched in the most general terms imaginable, that could possess universal validity. An educational philosophy for twentieth century America must take into account the existing conditions of life and civilization. In my judgment this criterion is of unusual significance to-day because of the extraordinary social changes which are sweeping through American society. The old agrarian order which produced our distinctive traits and institutions is crumbling before the advances of industrialism; the age of rural simplicity and neighborliness is giving way to an age of machines and impersonal social relationships. Those to whom this new order is repugnant, and there are many of them, would organize the forces of formal education and endeavor to stem the tide of industrial change. They would even use those forces to create a society with quite different foundations. However praiseworthy such efforts may appear in the abstract, they are certain to be futile. Industrial civilization, at least in its broad outlines, is here to stay for a period, and the civilization to which it will give birth in the course of the years defies prediction. If our educational philosophy is to be effective it must be in essential harmony with the great social trends which characterize the age. Whatever may be its ultimate goals it must articulate with the world as it is.

Our fifth and last criterion is that a philosophy of education should be satisfying to its adherents. After full allowance has been made for those elements which are objective in quality and determined by the external situation, there will always remain something of a more intimate and personal nature. In its essence a philosophy is the reaction of a particular individual or group upon experience; it will therefore always carry a personal flavor; it will always be the expression of personality. Thus in its composition an educational philosophy is not unlike a work of art: it reveals the personality of its creator. Moreover, if it finds favor in the eyes of other persons, then it has met one of the most important tests which may be applied to any philosophy. And if it is not pleasing to others, if it does not appear true to them, if it strikes no responsive chord in them, then at least for the time and the place it is inadequate. Unless it fits experience as the glove fits the hand, it will be acceptable to no individual or group.

In conclusion I wish to call attention again to the difficulty of setting up criteria for evaluating a philosophy of education. No doubt the analysis which I have presented contains certain elements with which many of you do not agree. Moreover, some of you perhaps would like to add criteria which I have disregarded or overlooked. Towards all such differences in point of view I would, of course, be thoroughly tolerant. There is one general position, however, upon which I would like to insist with peculiar emphasis. There are many philosophies of education, as there are many philosophies of life, which in my judgment are excellent, and in a sense, true. For a given time and place the number is, of course, much reduced. But even for our industrial civilization I am convinced that a number of educational philosophies, all of them possessing considerable merit, are available. Just as the same theme may be variously treated by different artists, and perhaps with equally satisfactory results, so our society to-day may give rise to various educational philosophies at the hands of different philosophers. And the effective judgment on these philosophies will be passed not by you and me but by the American people.

PHILOSOPHY OF EDUCATION—DIRECTIVE DOCTRINE OR LIBERAL DISCIPLINE?

EVERETT J. KIRCHER

Like most cultures, American democracy has evolved to its present state without benefit of any single formal system of philosophy. This is not to deny that the philosophic mind has been present nor that the general character of our culture has benefited at one time or another from a rich diversity of both formal and informal philosophies. It is rather to deny that our culture has been self-consciously constructed along the lines of any one comprehensive system of thought which was first theoretically formulated and subsequently actualized into a whole way of life. In other words we have not built our American democracy deliberately according to any pre-selected system of philosophy. Conversely, modern Russia is an example of a culture in which it was belatedly decided to do just this.

Marx was a philosopher with a disposition toward philosophy which has become more and more popular throughout the world. He was a philosopher who inclined to the notion his disciples wholly embraced that the discipline of philosophy could recover itself only if it largely abandoned its role as one of the liberal disciplines and became literally directive of human affairs. Since the teaching of philosophy, like other of the liberal studies, has often been unimaginative and sterile and has failed to function as an intellectual leaven in our common culture, it was easy for him to conclude along with many another in other systems of thought that philosophy fell into either one of two categories. Either it was ivory tower and irrelevant to the moving concerns of men or it was an ultimate commitment, doctrinally conceived, and effectively directive of the practical affairs of the market place. Faced with these two alternatives, he concluded that philosophy

FROM *Educational Theory*, 5 (October, 1955): 220–229. (Reprinted by permission of the publisher and author.)

should be changed from its esoteric status and be made to bake bread. Such a proposal was not only congenial to the Marxist reformers who followed him, it has been congenial to the academic reformer in America. The idea has intrigued us. Pre-planned systems in the large, theoretically formulated world views, inspire the imagination with a high hope. And reformers respond to the notion that a system of philosophy can be used as a reliable referent in the conduct of the confusing, inconsistent and conflicting forces of the human enterprise.

One in this mood looks at the social scene and asks what it adds up to other than over-all, meaningless and incoherent confusion. One sees only a welter of disparate and conflicting social forces in the fields of religion, economics, and politics. One senses that the gods looking down from Olympus see us running helterskelter like ants at cross purposes with one another in a state of endless frustration and conflict. What any culture and finally the world desperately needs, we are then told, is an over-all system of thought, an integrating world-view, which would establish a common purpose for mankind and mutually consistent subordinate goals. Some all-comprehending philosophy within whose generous circumference men could find themselves at peace; a common way of life in which social forces were harmonized and the culture convincingly integrated is what is required. Then men would enjoy a community of mind and spirit, social harmony would be approximated and the brotherhood of man would become a reality on this earth. Such is the philosopher's dream, and all it would take to realize this cultural millenium would be the long-sought discovery of the philosopher's stone.

This is a noble dream which the over-agitated and the over-eager recurrently discover that they are destined to fulfill in reality. In other words, men who seek the philosopher's stone too expectantly soon find it. There is a compulsion in their quest which guarantees its premature discovery. And upon such an occasion they look down upon struggling man and know what he must do. This is where Hegel finally stood. It is where Marx stood. And it is where every philosopher-reformer is destined to stand who lays claim to the exclusive adequacy of his philosophy for any culture or for the world. This evil role in which knowledgeable man succumbs to the temptation to play God because he is surrounded by men without sufficient knowledge to controvert his system of thought does not pertain only to philosophies we have come to look upon as evil. It pertains alike to those philosophies we have come to look upon as good. The evil and the suffering ultimately entailed derives from misrepresentation on the grand scale. Philosophic man presumes to an adequacy of systematic knowledge that he does not have, and other men follow in an unwarranted faith eternally destined to disaster.

Yet men in the large hold themselves perennially prepared to believe again that the philosopher's stone has been found. Consequently there is a social climate conductive to the notion that a philosophy of freedom has been found, a philosophy that is inherently not susceptible of subversion to evil ends. What is so alien to our thought is that the very claim to have found such a philosophy makes that philosophy inimical to human freedom. To claim that one has found the true or the ultimately adequate philosophy is to claim that one has found the philosophy of philosophies, that the philosophic quest in the large has been completed. The philosophy of Marx speculatively projected and creatively entertained would not have jeopardized the philosophic enterprise nor human freedom on this earth. The Communist institutionalization of this system of philosophy as a wholly adequate world doctrine is the point at which the philosophic enterprise and all human freedom was cast into jeopardy. The evil is not inherently in the speculative system but in the disposition of those who would universalize it. It is therefore unfortunate that so many of us have been so preoccupied with the notion that the Russian error was in the selection of a wrong philosophy that we have neglected to note their more fundamental error; namely, that they embraced the inhumanity of attempting to integrate their social order, and finally the world, in accordance with some one pre-planned and elaborately conceived philosophy. Their fatal error in judgment revealed itself in their uncompromising conviction that a distinguished system of thought could be made so logically adequate that it could be put into practice without fundamental modification. Their error did not seem greater to them than ours does to us when we also incline to the notion that a comprehensive and carefully conceived theory could be made reliably adequate to the conduct of human affairs. We too indulge, from time to time, in the unwarranted faith that the academic mind at its best is equal to the task of providing a system of philosophy that will prove itself adequate to the complex exigencies of fact. And the systematic academic mind is understandably susceptible of this persuasion whenever reforming zeal runs high. Conversely, the creative and dedicated scholar is uniquely impervious to this profane presumption himself and always suspicious of it in the many varied forms it takes in others.

EDUCATION AND THE ONE PHILOSOPHY

There have been many theorists and some formal philosophers in the history of American culture who have periodically proposed to involve us in the same error. It is the common aspiration of theorists, and their recurring presumption, to have worked out a system of ideas that would adequately harmonize and integrate the American social order. It is to the credit of our own culture that it has largely resisted persuasion in this matter up to the present time. Not only in the culture at large have we resisted the temptation to be wholly logical according to some one system of logic, we have largely resisted this temptation in the public school systems of the state. Consequently, our educational program shows neither the theoretical benefit nor the actual deterioration which would result from the adoption of the central doctrine of a one-philosophy state. In other words, public education in the United States is not, and never has been, conducted according to any one system of philosophy. *It is significant to note, however, that it has become the prevailing mode of our time to lament this fact.* The past generation of educational theorists have been at great pains to show that this has been unfortunate in the past and promises to be disastrous in the future. We are told that the welter of prevailing philosophies and theories in conflict can logically result only in general confusion, cultural dis-integration and the ultimate frustration of both the American teacher and the rising generation. To many academic minds intent upon effecting logical coherence and cultural integration, this is self-evident.

Since it is the primary function of the intellectual to knit the disparate and dis-arrayed tag ends of things into clear and consistent meaningful wholes in every area of learning, nothing could be more natural than for each to envision the whole as finally organized, integrated and explained in terms of the generalized insights of his own distinctive philosophy, religion or academic discipline. Not only is this natural, to a certain degree it is inevitable, and there is a sense in which it is proper. It is proper as forever unfinished aspiration.

The social and educational theorist is faced in a more dramatic way with the same paradox which faces every man and every culture. For his own sanity, he must hold to the somehow rightness of his own personal-intellectual point of view. He cannot be forever qualifying, denying and doubting himself. And yet, in any free society, and in the world at large, every man's carefully intellectualized outlook on life is in fact qualified, denied or doubted by men and cultures of equal intellec-tual equipment and equal intellectual integrity. To believe in one's self and yet to honor the person and the thinking of those who find it necessary to deny one's own beliefs, presents finite and inevitably biased man with a dilemma he does not have the cosmic mind finally to resolve. All extant theories for the resolution of this problem end in one more theory which attempts to persuade man that he actually is intellectually competent to resolve this dilemma after all. And the native pre-sumption of men is always prepared to rise once more and to believe again that a new device has been created that will allow him to transcend those limits of his finitude that it is not reasonable to believe he can surmount with any distinctive point of view or any unique system of logic. Indeed, to be distinctive and to be unique is to be *other than* other forms of distinction and uniqueness that forever rise to confound the intellectual resolution of uniqueness.

One must grant that there is no more adequate evidence of learning and personal culture than the progressive enlarging of one's own understanding of the world from his own unique perspective. One's coherent distinctiveness is doubtless the greatest contribution one has to make to the world. But the all too human tendency to universalize this uniqueness and presume to assimilate all relevant diversity into one inclusive perspective, the fatal end toward which all systematic rationality inclines, fails to recognize the strategic limits of intellection and robs a diversity of men of the only real freedom in the world, the freedom to engage life with integrity each on his own terms.

GROWTH OF ANY ONE PHILOSOPHY

There is no open-minded philosophy in the sense that each often boasts that it is. No philosophy is open to other than its own assumptions, its own methods, its own distinctive pattern of meanings and, above all, its own ultimate propagation.

No philosophy frees a man in all directions for any or all assumptions or values. Every philosophy releases man into the full and generous arena of the only universe there is—the materialistic, the idea-istic, the realistic or the empirical—but the only universe there really is; and it is designed to explain all the others away. If there is anything characteristic of any system of philosophy, it is that it is sufficient unto itself. Of all the things it logically does not need in the world, it is the conflicting and denying assumptions and propositions of other philosophical systems. Or if it does need these, it needs them as the materials for its own assimilation and development. It needs them as the negative to its own positive, the error to demonstrate its own truth. It needs them as food upon which to feed, a process which results in the disintegration of the food and its assimilation into a growing body of thought which is designed to prevail through the disintegration of its opposition.

In a sense, a system of philosophy is like a cat in the forest. It grows by what it feeds upon and by transforming what it feeds upon into itself. It has no way of doing justice to other forms of life except from its own point of view. And from this point of view, other forms of life look like a means of growth and development for itself. Its promise of the good life to what it regards as lesser forms is a promise to assimilate them into a nobler structure that is more glorious in the sight of gods or men. Sometimes they are promised that this will be a painless transformation. Sometimes they are promised a special place of residence that will not do violence to their own distinctive form. And yet it seems to be the fact with both the organic system of the cat and the organic system of a philosophy that undigested foreign matter must ultimately be assimilated or be passed off, and this on pain of death. Regardless of high promises on the part of any system of thought to protect the distinctiveness of other organic forms within its own system, we would do well to recall that no matter how many birds a compassionate cat may eat, it never becomes more birdlike. Rather, it becomes a bigger cat. A philosophy lives upon the assimilation into its own organic system of the facts of life, the problems of men and the relevant aspects of all other philosophies. It is modified in this process but not in a way congenial to the forms assimilated.

There is a fundamental sense in which all philosophies are, therefore, philosophies of growth. Each struggles to grow into a state of universal explanation of the only real world it acknowledges. Anything not yet assimilated into the organic structure of any philosophy leaves it still hungry and growing. Philosophies which would distinguish themselves as philosophies of growth have a doubtful distinction for they are as ungenerous in the large as any other philosophy. They are always characterized by growth toward their own fulfillment through a disintegration of other logical forms and by a digestive process distinctively designed to this end. It is consequently the dilemma of all systematic intellection that it is carried on in such a way as to perpetuate its own distinctive form and proceed from its own perspective whereas it aspires to enfold a variety of forms and it wishes to appear inclusive of a wide diversity of perspectives. The implicit denial of this which occurs when any philosophy aspires to universalization and to becoming directive of a whole way of life sounds the knell of philosophic thought, makes a mockery of the liberal university and introduces into any culture the rational conditions for the denial of freedom to all who choose to define it differently from the prevailing rationale.

In simple point of fact, a philosophy can no more afford to assimilate the total complex of life into its own system than a cat can afford to assimilate the total complex of forest life into its own system. For a philosophy to explain the world, and finally all other philosophies, a not uncommon presumption of comprehensive world-views, is literally to embrace self-extinction. The ongoing life of both philosophies and cats depends upon the continuing existence of other organic forms. In the case of the cat, these other forms must be both an abundance of birds and other cats. No matter how many of the former are consumed and the latter bred or killed in combat, cats die from this earth when they assimilate into themselves all that they prey upon, fertilize or engage in mortal combat.

Remarkably similar observations can be made of integral and organic systems of philosophy. In order to keep healthy, vital and growing, they need what they commonly hasten to deny; they need an abundance of as yet unexplained problems, aspects of the natural world and of the human enterprise that they have as yet been unable to assimilate into their own organic structure. Moreover, they need cross-fertilization with other systems of philosophy which they commonly attack with the intention of annihilation. The perennial claim of exclusive adequacy for any philosophy is the expression of an unwitting presumption calling for the abandonment of the philosophic enterprise. Contests of explanation among the philosophies and creative engagements over the problems that beset us result both in health and procreation of a rich diversity of philosophies. But the determination, once and for all to win the field results in a declaration of war. The philosophic temper and intention is abandoned; and if the war is successful, the winner will have devastated the field in which he was wont to forage. Yet there are educational philosophers reminiscent of such cats, for they leave the survival of the philosophic enterprise not to intention but to chance. Like the forest tom, many a philosophy would have annihilated the condition of its being except that it was not able to assimilate the whole field.

We must conclude, therefore, that no system of philosophy, not even the presumed right one should be allowed to gain the uncontested status of being the exclusively adequate philosophy of free men. Freedom resides not in a system of philosophy but in the acceptance of a state of consciously maintained diversity which thereupon becomes a state of ethical diversity. In saying this, we have dealt only with the ought; no philosophy ought to aspire to universal and exclusive adequacy. We may go on to say that any philosophy uniquely designed to guarantee freedom among men not only ought not be universally adopted, it probably cannot be universally adopted. The complex enormity of the world appears to protect the philosophic enterprise from self-annihilation. There is just too much in the world for any one organic structure to assimilate. Even in Soviet Russia the original Marxist philosophy has not only been grossly modified in process of Communist application but there is reason to believe that large and silent sectors of the people have never accommodated themselves to its fundamental assumptions.

In the attempt to translate any one system of philosophy into a whole way of life, we are therefore confronted with an aspiration that not only ought not but cannot finally be realized. A very real evil and much suffering results from the attempt and the partial success that is attained.

It is probably safe, then, to say that no philosophy has ever fully realized itself in any culture without fundamental compromise. Moreover, it is probably true that no formal system of philosophy has ever taken up unqualified residence in the life of any single man. A man, like a culture, is forever more than any theory about him. Each encompasses not only a logic but a mystery beyond the logic. Consequently, while it is apparently possible for both a man and a culture to identify themselves with some comprehensive rational theory, it is not possible for them to conduct their lives strictly in accordance with any such theory. The whole man is never encompassed by any rational theory but suffers unaccountable modification and growth out of the mysterious heart of him. Whether the intellectual system is Christian, Marxist or pragmatist, it appears impossible to fulfill the theorist's dream and strategically or forcefully to actualize any formal theory either in the free society or in the totalitarian state.

There is, of course, some basis for believing that the integration of a social order in terms of some one philosophy of life can be more fully attained in the totalitarian state. Certainly this is widely assumed. Yet there is reason to doubt that the overt conformity to the state philosophy is expressive of the vital and living principles of that philosophy. It is doubtful if the philosophy lives as philosophy in the hearts and minds of those it appears to motivate and direct. Perhaps in such seemingly monolithic states philosophy is largely dead and only the philosophic skeleton remains to give the appearance of philosophic structure to the social body. In such cases, conventions, ritual, habit and formal directives take the place of action enlightened by philosophic principles. However this may be, no one philosophy can endure indefinitely in any culture without stimulating alternative and conflicting systems of thought. The formal regulation of life according to some rational system cannot finally bring about the stultification of the human spirit. It would therefore behoove us in all of modern culture, but in the schools of the state particularly, to ask ourselves whether or not we are incorporating into our teacher training the assumption that one of the formal systems of philosophy in our time holds the promise of freedom for the human spirit. In other words, we must ask whether we are openly or subtly imparting the notion that there is one wholly adequate philosophy of democracy.

DEVELOPMENT OF DISCIPLESHIP

There is reason to believe that creative philosophers themselves tend to divide on this issue even though the great majority of them have long made the assumption that the freedom and vitality of the philosophic enterprise depended, among other things, upon a rich diversity in philosophic speculation. Yet it appears that some philosophers are more content than others simply to bring into being a new perspective on life for the general enlightenment of men. Others incline to the notion that they have conceived a theoretical formulation of such adequacy that it merits universal acquiescence. Santayana was typical of the former and therefore finds it natural to say in the preface to his *Skepticism and Animal Faith*,

> Here is one more system of philosophy. If the reader is inclined to smile, I can assure him that I smile with him. . . . I think that common sense, in a rough dogged way, is technically sounder than the special schools of philosophy, each of which squints and overlooks half the facts and half the difficulties in its eagerness to find in some detail the key to the whole.[1]

Conversely, Friedrich Hegel is widely known to have grown congenial to the notion that his dialectical system of thought finally led to the possibility of an ultimate synthesis on its own terms in the German state of his time.

Between these two extremes there rests the great majority of philosophic minds about whose location on the scale we may only speculate. This much may be said however; the character of some systems of philosophy appear to solicit followership in ways almost too subtle to define. Others seem to effect the conditions which make discipleship next to impossible. Of the former, the disciples are characteristically unphilosophic and essentially doctrinal in their thinking. And one of the hidden sources of their power and of their cruelty is that they are oblivious to this fact. The doctrinal mind of the disciple who is following the authority of a pre-fabricated system of thought finds what he calls freedom in this enterprise, and he would like to enroll as many others as possible into this kind of freedom. In speaking of his commitment he often refers to it as the philosophy of freedom. But the genuinely philosophic mind is of an entirely different order. It finds its freedom in creating distinctive modes of thought out of the philosophic heritage and the occasion of its time. Former systems of thought are reconstructed rather than simply followed, implemented and applied. Any philosopher worthy the name is therefore the beneficiary of the philosophies of the past but never the victim of any one of them.

The transition from the creative thinking which results in a system of philosophy to a doctrinal acceptance of the system is very subtle. One lives through the creative process with the original mind, knows the delight of an unfolding organization of thought and discovers life more richly meaningful than he had known it before. In this state of intellectual excitement it is a very great temptation to identify one's self with the master and with his system of thought, envision one's self as a co-partner in the evolution and the extension of his ideas and become a champion of his views. If one's distinguished mentor is living, it is common to be desirous of his public approval and deeply enthralled by his expression of endorsement and affection. The long struggle to be worthy of discipleship then follows. The rewards for acceptance are very great, for the disciple himself becomes an authority through his identification with an undeniable authority. Competition for favor among the disciples always sets in and much bitterness attends every followership. Among such disciples every face is turned toward the central philosophy; their

---

[1] George Santayana, *Skepticism and Animal Faith* (New York: Scribner Sons, 1923), p. V.

teaching and discussion centers upon philosophy; they are primarily concerned with philosophy—and yet natively philosophic minds look upon them in wonderment, for the philosophic enterprise has mysteriously been abandoned. A cult has developed, and the cult struggles in vain to fill the philosophic vacuity left by a great and seminal mind.

Much good work is done by disciples and much necessary work but much evil ensues from the very deception that they are philosophers who have inherited the authority that originally attached to an intellectual enterprise of great scope and integrity. They do not know how to wear the authority, for their power stems from their commitment and their commitment denies them the privilege of fundamentally reconstructing the philosophic source of their authority. Yet it was this privilege that kept the original philosopher free and philosophic. He was free to abandon or rebuild anything he constructed; he was free to indulge in doubt about his most fundamental premises; he was free to wonder about the adequacy of his system. Consequently, he was free to listen to other competing and conflicting philosophies and, across the bridge of his wonderment and his doubt, meet other philosophic minds also stepping out to the precarious edge of their thought. He was free to join in the transcendent community known to all philosophic minds of integrity, the key to which is the qualified commitment to what one has rationally proved to be true and necessary. The qualified commitment to one's own rational system and an unqualified faith in an undiscovered future or an unknown God that transcends systematic rationality—these are the conditions of the philosophers' community of mind in the midst of their inevitably diverse rational systems. Yet these freedoms and this transcendence are characteristically what the disciple abandons. He is, therefore, not only a philosopher, he is not free. He is the victim of his appropriated system and he is the uncompromising enemy of those systems of thought which are in conflict with his own. With him literal rationality takes precedence over the philosophic temper and the philosophic quest. He cannot say with Whitehead that at its best all philosophy becomes poetry. Refusing to admit poetic transcendence over literal rationality at the higher levels of insight, he wages unremitting war over literal and exact differences in doctrine. This is the common fate of the man who goes through life on the ultimate authority of another. And it is thus that he makes the transition from freedom to slavery through a philosophy of freedom.

DEWEY'S PHILOSOPHY OF FREEDOM

One is constrained to believe that this is essentially the transition that has taken place between John Dewey, the philosopher, and many of his disciples. Their native presumption in the face of other social, religious and academic philosophies must derive from an essentially unqualified commitment to their naturalistic empiricism. Their arbitrary denials of other philosophies of life can hardly mean other than that they really believe Dewey found the philosopher's stone and passed it on to them. This allows them the presumption that their philosophy is different in the sense that it is the only truly democratic, the only truly adequate philosophy of freedom. Over the last generation unnumbered students have been given to believe that this philosophy is so exclusively adequate, in this sense so universally true, that a democratic society has no need to sponsor and teach other conflicting systems of philosophy. Consequently, in a largely Christian-Hebraic culture, this nontheistic philosophy is commonly spoken of as THE democratic philosophy. It implies, we have been told, a whole *Weltanschauung* waiting for explicit realization which may properly be thought of as the only adequate conception of the democratic way of life. Yet what this turns out to be is the implementation of the formal philosophy of Dewey-pragmatism as a whole American way of life. Bode's *Democracy as a Way of Life*[2] turns out to be naturalistic empiricism as a way of life. Such indirection on the part of one of the many formal systems of philosophy in American culture may be strategic and persuasive among American teachers who are not philosophically oriented, but to many professional philosophers in the last generation it has appeared unwarranted and unwise. Indeed, it has appeared inimical to freedom in the name of freedom because the literal identification of freedom with one system of thought violates the most fundamental faith of free men; namely, that no one system of philosophy finally defines freedom in a culture which is dedicated to being inclusive of a diversity of philosophies speculatively entertained.

Progressive education is the educational counterpart of the naturalistic philosophy of John Dewey, and probably William Heard Kilpatrick has been its most celebrated exponent. Gentle, patient and persuasive, Professor Kilpatrick oriented himself steadfastly to this one philosophy of life and in a lovable, temperate, and compromising approach to all his teaching inclined untold thousands of teachers in our time toward a philosophy of life whose fundamental principles he has not compromised. The comprehensive statement of his position in his later years[3] reveals his steadfastness, his dedication and his uncompromising philosophic commitment. The American teacher to whom the book is largely addressed is gently dissuaded from believing in other less adequate philosophical views with an artfulness and sincerity that can hardly offend them even when they wonderingly differ. But the philosophically astute who hold self-consciously to a Christian, idealist, or other system of philosophy may be offended by what they properly take to be caricatures of their philosophical positions. To them, this gentle man is an unfair partisan, and many of them are as gentle and liberal in the entertainment of their views as he. Most of them are also unconditionally committed. And here we are confronted with the human dilemma again. How is a committed man to make good his boast of impartiality in the presentation of views contrary to the truth as he sees it?

Some hold to the proposition, herein denied, that it is the distinguishing character of a certain system of philosophy that it is uniquely impartial toward all philosophies. Some hold that their philosophy is inevitably biased toward all others but

---

[2] Boyd H. Bode, *Democracy As a Way of Life* (New York: The Macmillan Co., 1939.)
[3] William Heard Kilpatrick, *Philosophy of Education* (New York: The Macmillan Co., 1951.)

that they have the capacity to stand outside of their philosophy and present all the rest as sympathetically as their own representatives would. Still others incline to the notion that teachers in training can only get a fair presentation by the representatives of each position. There may be one more alternative. From time to time, there are teachers of history, and literature and of philosophy in the tradition of the liberal university who have no ultimate commitment relative to systems of thought. Such men present a variety of philosophies with the kind of sympathy which comes from genuine indebtedness to each and genuine reservations with respect to each. Such a teacher's faith may be of another order. It is the faith of the pilgrim rather than the disciple. It is the commitment to the unending quest in which one's way is enlightened by all systems of thought but not finally directed by any one of them. It is the commitment of the doctrinally uncommitted scholar. It is the faith of liberal learning in which the teacher knows more but learns with his students in a distinctive sense. For about one thing he does not finally know. He does not finally know what really is the best rationalized ultimate commitment for mankind even though he does know more than his students do about what man's ultimate commitments have been and more of the arguments for and against them. In other words, he has much more knowledge than his students do, but his knowledge has led him not to an ultimate dogma but to wisdom. And in a state of wisdom he discovers that, in all his knowledge, he does not finally know. It is the students' sense of this fact, when it is a fact that sets them at one with their teacher in ultimate wonderment. It is this fact that sets them free. And it is dedicated inquiry in this state of disciplined freedom through knowledge in which the liberal university at its best puts its final faith. Qualified commitment at all levels of knowledge may very well be the condition of ethical community in the free society. If so, such teaching would tend to extend it by example and by contagion.

In contrast to the basic motivation of such men, there are those who incline to the conviction that a social order must be integrated along the lines of a comprehensively coherent system of thought. They ask that a philosophy be actualized into a whole way of life, that it become practical and directive of the human enterprise rather than merely enlightening of it. They ask that philosophy abandon its sterile role as one of the liberal disciplines, that it take up residence in the market place and that it become self-consciously the ideological center of reference for the culture. They are asking, in deference to practicality and their highest partisan hope, that philosophy abandon its liberal status for a doctrinal status. This has been the fundamental error of the pragmatist-progressive school of thought; namely, that they would rescue human freedom by substituting one philosophy of freedom for another, in this case the philosophy in which Dewey found his freedom. But they have forgotten to note that he found his freedom both negatively and positively—negatively, by not commiting himself to any extant philosophy in his heritage, positively, by constructing his own system of thought out of this heritage and the occasion of his time. His is the kind of freedom we honor and he took the only sure pathway to it. Thus must each philosophic mind and each generation hew its own freedom from the raw rock of life.

PART III

WHAT IS PHILOSOPHY OF EDUCATION?

Almost two decades ago, the Philosophy of Education Society mounted a special committee to consider the problems of defining the nature and function of philosophy of education. From the outset, the committee found it impossible to frame a single description of what philosophy of education is and what educational philosophers do. No single definition sufficed to encompass the variety of approaches that can be taken nor the diversity of conceptions that can be held. Rather, the committee settled for a statement of the formal criteria for determining the content of a philosophy of education. The final statement distinguished three interrelated phases of philosophic thought as they apply to education. The conditions were (1) the descriptive-analytical phase, (2) the critical-evaluative phase, and (3) the speculative phase. This short document provides a fitting starting point for examination. In diverse ways, the writers in this section all make reference to one or more of these aspects of philosophical thought. Some authors tend to emphasize one to the virtual exclusion of the others. It becomes apparent that the position taken by a writer is a function of which aspect is considered most important in general philosophy. Although any classification system is likely to oversimplify, the following considerations largely shape the particular position taken:

1. What is philosophy? Is its primary function analytical, evaluative, or speculative?
2. What is the most important, relevant way of looking at education from a philosophical perspective? In other words, ought the philosopher to focus

107

attention on education considered as a set of instructional techniques? as a
set of theories which purport to justify and explain teaching and learning
processes? as a set of values and ideals embodied and expressed in the objectives of teaching? as a social institution in society?

3. What is the fundamental intent of philosophy of education? To criticize
existing practices and theories? to frame alternative directions, goals, or
objectives? to improve teaching practice directly? to assist in the construction
of educational theories?

Obviously, different answers to these questions will produce different
answers. The possible combinations of alternatives are enormous but not
quite infinite. Thus, certain points are repeated, similar arguments and
counter-arguments advanced, similar perspectives proposed. Yet each writer
chosen for inclusion here has something distinctive to offer. The emphasis
may differ as different questions are raised: Is there or can there be a distinctive
discipline of education? What is educational theory? How is philosophy
related to theory in education? What are the roles of an educational philosopher? What should be the aims and content of a philosophy of education?
The underlying theme throughout is the movement toward a definition of
philosophy of education. Some insights are unique. And finally, it may not
be meaningful to conclude that there can be any single "correct" answer as
to what is philosophy of education. Instead, the range of alternatives set
forth may provide the stimulus for informed but original thinking. Ultimately, this may be the most valuable consideration. At the very least, the
importance of making an idea one's very own is a value stressed in the best
tradition of philosophers.

The articles by Professors Broudy and Price are the springboards for much
of the subsequent discussion. These two papers were originally delivered at a
meeting of the American Philosophical Association and later served to
stimulate the editors of *The Harvard Educational Review* to devote an issue
to a discussion of the issues raised. Several papers of the respondents are
reproduced here. Many of the distinguished philosophers make explicit
reference to the Broudy and Price presentations.

Various ways of building philosophical theory relating to education are
examined by Broudy. The philosopher may offer his own observations in
those problematical areas of educational controversy where knowledge of
the relevant facts does not suffice to produce clear-cut solutions. Or the
philosopher may turn to what was earlier termed the "systems," or "school
of thought," approach to educational philosophy. A cogent analysis of the
strengths and defects inherent in this strategy is presented. Finally, another
task of educational philosophy is to criticize rather than to construct theory.

Broudy indicates how this process of analysis and evaluation typically proceeds.

Price's discussion constitutes an "exploration of the territory" within philosophy of education. He distinguishes between the factual and the recommending parts of education and between philosophy as an activity of analysis and as an activity of constructing certain kinds of metaphysical, axiological, epistemological, and aesthetic theories. Although his particular formulation of the domains of philosophical activity do not command universal assent, those unfamiliar with the terminology of the traditional subdivisions of philosophy may find this plan of organization helpful.

The offerings of Kandel, Morris, Hook, and Ducasse, which follow the Broudy and Price selections, are essentially criticisms and clarifications of the points raised. As a matter of historical interest, it should be noted that Hook's criticism of philosophies of education derived from philosophic positions such as existentialism, realism, or pragmatism as "garrulous absurdities" has often been quoted in the literature of educational philosophy. Of special interest also is the striking disagreement between Hook and Morris on the place of epistemology in philosophy of education.

The article of Abraham Edel has as its focus the contribution of philosophy in the analysis and evaluation of various types of educational theories. With eloquence and wit (rare enough commodities among philosophers) Edel illustrates how theories in special fields such as education can be scrutinized in the light of different world perspectives and the categories these outlooks provide. In the "philosophical workshop" the implicit values assumptions, the view of human nature presumed, and the hidden prescriptions embedded in a particular educational theory are uncovered and laid bare. Otto Krash seems to reach similar conclusions in his plea for an educational philosophy that puts human reason to work upon significant problems in education. He calls attention to the fact that philosophers may have to move out of their traditional frames of reference in order to perform this service effectively.

The fact remains however that any philosophical inquiry commences from within *some* frame of reference or point of perspective. James Feibleman poses the reminder that to get into a frame of mind from which a presupposition-less standpoint would appear attractive is a most difficult task. Nonetheless, ideally speaking, the *sine qua non* for philosophy of education is to examine educational problems without benefit of any *a priori* assumptions or beliefs. In other words, the philosopher of education ought to exhibit the range of choices confronting educators, but to do this fairly he must not have his own axes to grind. Susanne Langer, on the other hand, notes that much ambiguity and confusion in educational thought may be the result of lack of a *Weltan-schauung* viable in the changing world of today. Perhaps a coherent philosophy for education cannot emerge until an analysis of pedagogical ideas can be articulated within a frame of reference that makes sense for modern man. Newsome's observations go a long way toward clarifying the fundamental difference between Langer's position and that of Feibleman.

It was noted earlier that the way one defines philosophy and its relation to education shapes one's understanding of what philosophy of education can do. Paul Hirst undertakes to examine this relationship and concludes that there is no direct relation between the two. Rather than supposing that philosophical beliefs form some of the premises for deducing educational principles one can nonetheless make a case that the former provide "reasons" for the educational judgments that are made. This in turn leads Hirst to explore what we mean when we talk about an "educational theory" and an autonomous "discipline" of education. He rejects the orthodox scientific model as an adequate pattern for assessing educational theories while stressing the unique and distinctive function of philosophy in theory construction and evaluation. McNaught's article, which follows, suggests some problems in the development of a philosophy of education such as Hirst seems to envision.

The selection by Millard and Pertocci and the article by Taylor serve as summaries of much that has gone before. The former review the challenges that make a unification of philosophy and education imperative for the responsible conduct of educational practice. The latter effort seeks to derive a definition of philosophy of education that designates rather than denotes or stipulates. It remains open to further question whether Taylor has succeeded in this ambition or whether, in defining philosophy of education purely as process rather than as a body of knowledge, he too has laid out a Procrustean bed which might cramp some philosophical approaches to education.

The question raised by Gowin whether educational theory can guide practice represents an extension of Hirst's discussion on the nature and function of educational theory. It also provides an excellent transition to the points made by Brameld in the last offering in this section. In the final analysis, one must ask how philosophy of education can count for something. Brameld sketches briefly the roles of the educational philosopher as an integral part of a cooperative endeavor to improve existing educational practice. He claims that as resource person, as interdisciplinarian, as co-researcher, and as policy shaper, the educational philosopher has valuable contributions to make. The crucial question for our time is whether in fact the philosopher of education can and will fulfill these responsibilities.

THE DISTINCTIVE
NATURE OF THE DISCIPLINE
OF THE PHILOSOPHY
OF EDUCATION

A STATEMENT BY A COMMITTEE
OF THE PHILOSOPHY OF EDUCATION SOCIETY[1]

We make a distinction between disciplines or modes of inquiry such as psychology, sociology, administration, engineering and philosophy, and the persons who utilize these disciplines. Our attention is to the disciplines persons employ rather than to the persons who employ the disciplines.

What philosophy of education ought to be and do is a highly debatable matter insofar as differing answers come from differing philosophical positions. This statement, therefore, attempts only to delineate the basic, common, or minimal characteristics of the discipline within which we find these differing answers and positions.

A. The various philosophies—philosophy of education, art, science, politics, religion and history among them—share three characteristics which help distinguish philosophy from other fields of endeavor:

(1) Unique theoretical tools consisting of hypotheses, concepts and categories (such as meaning, truth, value, method).

(2) The employment of these tools in the examination of the criteria, assumptions and/or reasons which guide assessments, judgments and choices.

(3) A scholarly acquaintance with events, practices, circumstances, and/or ideas relevant to that which the philosophy is *of* (that is, education, art, politics, science or religion).

FROM *Educational Theory*, 4 (January, 1954): 1–3. (Reprinted by permission.)

[1] This statement was prepared by the Committee on the Nature and Function of the Discipline of the Philosophy of Education, of the Philosophy of Education Society, composed of the following members: Nathaniel Champlin, Chairman, Brooklyn College; David Adams, New York University; Otto Krash, State University of New York; Robert Mason, Western Reserve University; and Francis Villemain, New York University. The statement was included as part of the report of the Committee to the Philosophy of Education Society in its meeting in the spring of 1953. The report of the Committee was adopted by the Society.

When this critical examination is directed to the criteria and the conceptual tools of the different philosophies we have what some would call "pure" or "general" philosophy, and what others would call the philosophy of philosophy.

The philosophy of education, art, science, religion and history may then be viewed as distinctive philosophic disciplines which achieve their distinctiveness by virtue of that to which they direct their critical and reflective attention. All are philosophies, or philosophy, because of the kinds of conceptual tools and skills employed. Each is a distinctive philosophy because of the domain, subject matter, problem area, or activity about which it theorizes and speculates. Moreover, the theorizing and speculating of one philosophy, say, the philosophy of education or the philosophy of art, may provide conceptions and ideas which act to modify the theorizing of another, say, the philosophy of history or, even possibly, "pure" philosophy. Each philosophy may be considered a resource for others.

We may, through contrast and comparison, locate differences within philosophy. Some have used the terms *realism*, *idealism* and *experimentalism* to note these differences. Called philosophic positions or "families," they have been differentiated further. Realism, for example, may include such differences as are noted with the terms *sense-realism*, *materialist realism* and *classical realism*. Idealism and experimentalism also admit of family differences. In the case of the latter we hear of *logical empiricism*, *bio-social instrumentalism* and *Peircian pragmatism*. This is to say that the philosophy of education, art, science, history, or politics may be qualified by such terms as *realist*, *idealist*, or *experimentalist* philosophy of education, art, science, history or politics. Such terms (others have been suggested) are used to distinguish the different criteria and grounds used in establishing philosophical concepts, hypotheses and categories.

B. The term *education* may refer to any deliberate effort to nurture, modify, change and/or develop human conduct or behavior; or it may refer to organized schooling. For purposes of consensus we adopt the latter (institutionalized schooling).

Wherever education, thus defined, is taking place we find:

(1) Preferences for certain procedures, resources and goals (methods, means and ends) implicit or explicit in the undertaking.

(2) The employment of criteria, guides or reasons with which procedures, resources and goals are determined and established.

This is to say that teachers, administrators and others caught up in the educational enterprise, are making choices for desirable procedures, resources and goals in terms of implicit or explicit, critical or uncritical, criteria or reasons. When, prior to choosing, educators delineate and examine alternative criteria and grounds for the selection and rejection of these procedures, resources and goals, they are being critical about the choices they make.

The criteria guiding educational choices and policies may be consistent with the theories and concepts of one philosophical position (e.g., idealism, realism or experimentalism), or with some combination from the alternative positions. Therefore, in order that educational choices and policies be *philosophically* critical they must be made in view of the delineation and examination of alternative philosophical criteria: and anyone, thus oriented, is working within an area that is included in the subject matter of the discipline of the philosophy of education.

Putting it another way: when we (1) single out and examine the criteria and assumptions guiding the choices being made in education, and (2) conduct our examination in terms of the concepts and categories of philosophy, we are working within the discipline of the philosophy of education. This discipline is alternative to other educational disciplines such as administration, psychology, and pedagogy. (This is not to say that competence in one discipline precludes competence in one or more other disciplines.)

C. Three interrelated phases of philosophic thought devoted to education are to be noted. These phases may be viewed as conditions for establishing the "content" of the discipline of the philosophy of education.

(1) The *descriptive-analytical* task of the philosopher of education may be in the articulation of (making explicit) the criteria which, in fact, guide the choices made in educational circles. This task may include relating these criteria to philosophic positions, and examining them in terms of consistency, meaning, expectation, and method.

(2) The *critical-evaluative* task of the philosopher of education may be in the framing of alternative criteria provided by the philosophy of education. This task may include locating criteria for assessing these alternatives for purposes of determining the more adequate and/or "reasonable" criteria.

(3) The *speculative* task of the philosopher of education may be in the forging or framing of new alternatives for use in philosophy, education, and/or the discipline of the philosophy of education.

D. In those institutions having courses in the philosophy of education, we should have provision for the study of, and the gaining of skills in, the conceptual materials (content) peculiar to the discipline. The teaching personnel should be equipped with, and trained in, the conceptual tools and skills peculiar to the discipline.

In those institutions having no place for the philosophy of education, we have, nevertheless, philosophically oriented conceptions and theories "hidden" in, or screened by, policies (administrative-curriculum), and other courses (educational psychology, pedagogy, "methods," and "principles"). Unless these philosophic materials are singled out for special examination they are uncritically assumed and fostered.

HOW PHILOSOPHICAL
CAN PHILOSOPHY OF
EDUCATION BE?

HARRY S. BROUDY

At a time when sovereignty over all domains both spiritual and terrestrial is so fiercely contested, it is surprising to find intellectual territories of doubtful owner-ship and ambiguous borders. These are the lands of "philosophies of": philosophy of law, science, history, and education; the very areas in which concepts, theories, and systems meet their existential kin, often for the first time. Frequently these meetings are uncomfortable affairs for both participants. But if, as Hegel insisted, essence must appear, then "philosophies of" are not merely desirable confronta-tions of essence and existence; they are inevitable and indispensable.

The purpose of this paper is not, however, to defend "philosophies of." It is rather to investigate the more specific question: How philosophical can a philosophy of education be? Inevitably, albeit not so extensively, the complementary question: How educational can a philosophy of education be? will also be examined. Obvi-ously, neither question would have point if there were not a substantial doubt that philosophy of education could be philosophically genuine or educationally helpful.

Accordingly, the first task is to ascertain why this doubt exists; the second is to ask what would make philosophy of education philosophically adequate and respectable; and the third, to indicate how such a discipline could be actualized, and the advantages of such a realization.

I

In the context of common language usage, neither of the above questions is amenable to precise or even sensible discussion. This is so because philosophy can denote anything from the logic of modern physics to a reflective mood about life. Education, for its part, is used to name anything from the reciting of nursery

FROM a paper presented in a symposium on "Philosophy of Education" at the meeting of the American Philosophical Association, Eastern Division, December 27, 1955, published in *The Journal of Philosophy*, 52 (October 27, 1955): 612–622. (Reprinted by permission of the publisher and the author.)

rhymes to the taking of a university degree. Philosophy of education compounds two welters of meaning into a sea in which all meaning is drowned.

It is proposed, therefore, to use the terms "philosophy," "education," and "philosophy of education" throughout this discussion in their narrow sense of academic disciplines. These terms are intended to denote what is taught or what might be taught in courses bearing these titles in college and university catalogues. By philosophers and educators are meant persons who exercise a professional interest in these disciplines.

It is not intended by this limitation of terms to beg the question as to whether the philosophy of education is or can be an academic discipline in its own right. The answer to this question will depend on the degree to which one can specify a content or method sufficiently distinctive to earn for it a separate room in the academic mansion. The limitations are made imperative, however, by the tendency of professional philosophers and educators to take a logical holiday the moment they step out of their professional roles.

Educators discoursing about philosophy of education are likely to equate it with a set of goals, principles, or values to which they are accustomed to pay intellectual and emotional homage. Philosophers—with some very notable exceptions, of course—are rarely disposed to be precise, rigorous, or systematic when talking their "philosophy of education." Much of what Kant, for example, says about education (E. F. Buchner, *The Educational Theory of Immanuel Kant*, Philadelphia, J. B. Lippincott Company, 1904) is wise and humane, but one would hardly suspect that he was reading another Kantian Critique. And something quite analogous might be said about the philosophical and educational writings of Bertrand Russell (*Education and the Modern World*, New York, W. W. Norton & Co., Inc., 1932).

As a result, the philosophy of education in the hands of both educators and philosophers boils down to a set of general and not very illuminating statements about the good life and what, in the light of their own experience and preferences, the schools ought to be doing about it. Such a body of assertions and exhortations does no particular harm, but it scarcely qualifies as an academic discipline, and certainly not as a philosophical one.

II

In keeping with the very limited meaning given in this paper to the term philosophy, it will be sufficient to answer the question of its proper content by pointing to logic, epistemology, metaphysics, aesthetics, ethics, and value theory in general. The problems taken up in these disciplines are philosophical problems. This means that a philosophy of education to be genuinely philosophical must at one stage or another study, talk about, or refer to these problems as they are formulated in the philosophical disciplines. It will not be enough to show that some relation between an educational problem and a philosophical one *could* be made

explicit. We shall see shortly that there are a number of ways in which this requirement can be met, and some ways are more productive and less artificial than others.
The important point to be reiterated here is that this requirement—which entails a
rather thorough competence in philosophy—cannot be evaded.

Although we have excused ourselves from discussing or defining the content of
philosophy, this much perhaps needs to be said. It is that philosophical activity has
two phases: theory-building and theory-evaluation or theory-criticism. The force
of this remark lies as much in what it excludes as in what it intends to assert.
Philosophical activity is not a search for true statements about matters of fact.
However difficult it may be to distinguish philosophical method from scientific
method, there is little doubt that their respective outcomes are quite different.
However theoretical and even metaphysical the involvements of the empirical
sciences may be, their ideal is to discover or predict states of affairs that give
preponderant evidence in favor of one theory over its rivals. On the other hand,
no matter how frequently and sincerely philosophy pledges its loyalty to empirical
fact and scientific method, it does not rely on new facts to abolish philosophical
controversy. Although philosophers do plead with each other to look at the facts,
there is apparently no way of agreeing what the relevant facts are and no way of
insuring that all observers "see" what they are urged to "look at." Educational
philosophy to qualify as philosophical will also have to be essentially theoretical in
its activity, but not an activity that has as its primary objective the discovery of fact.
It should not, therefore, be confused with history of education, educational
psychology, sociology, and educational tests and measurements.

The distinction between theory-building and theory-criticism is a distinction *in
mente* merely, but it does help to differentiate types of philosophical activity and
types of philosophers. For, although to build a theory one usually begins by
criticizing an existing theory, and to evaluate a theory one needs a theory of his
own to serve as a criterion, it is nevertheless true that some philosophers construct
theories to account for a wide range of philosophical problems, while others do
not. There is a sense in which Plato, Aristotle, Kant, Hegel, Whitehead, and Dewey
were predominantly theory-builders, and Sextus Empiricus, Hume, and some of
our current analytical philosophers are predominantly critics of theory.

Language and concept analysis, the search for presuppositions and consistency,
and testing for the presence or absence of meaning are characteristic of theory
evaluation, while speculative creativity and synthesis are more essential to theory
building. We shall consider educational philosophy in each of these phases
separately.

THEORY-BUILDING

Theory-building in the philosophy of education is incited by controversies that
seem to be beyond the help of empirical science but which one would like to argue
on the basis of human reason. A few sample controversies are:

Shall college education be universal or restricted to those who can qualify on some such criterion as intelligence?

Shall religion be taught as part of general education?

Shall the policy of the public schools be fashioned by educational experts or by those who provide the funds for their support?

While these questions could involve matters of fact, the facts would become relevant only when agreement on norms and objectives had been achieved. Thus, whether or not there are reliable tests of intelligence, and whether they are prognostic of certain achievements, are or could be matters of fact. But they would become relevant to the controversy only if the parties could agree that the achievements requiring intelligence are valuable or more valuable than some other sort of achievement. And when such agreement has been achieved has not the philosophical dimension of the problem been erased?

It is dangerous to assert that any given class of problems are safe from scientific solution. If, for example, psychology should establish as a fact that valuable achievement—on whatever value criteria the controversialists happen to be maintaining—is directly correlated with the kind of achievement requiring intelligence and stimulated by college education, then this particular issue would cease to be philosophically controversial and become a quarrel over means to a generally accepted goal.

Accordingly, one cannot rule out the possibility that the philosophy of education could be deprived of all its controversies by a maturing set of social sciences. This possibility remains remote, however, until science discovers a set of facts that indubitably validates one set of value norms and invalidates all alternative sets. But should this come to pass, not only would the philosophy of education find itself out of business, but even philosophy as such would have to seek a new excuse for being.

However, in the present state of knowledge, the controversy about college education cannot be decided by the facts. If, therefore, the controversy is to continue in rational fashion, both parties will have to take to higher ground. Each position will have to be justified in terms of value schemata, which, in turn, lean on epistemological, ethical, and metaphysical theory. Thus, although the starting point of the discussion was an educational problem and its terminus, it is to be hoped, will be an educational solution, the discussion itself both in content and in method will be throughout philosophical.

Similarly, the issue as to whether religion should or should not be a part of general education can be stated in economic, sociological, political, and psychological terms to begin with, but sooner or later it has to be fought out on epistemological grounds. Either the religious categories have truth value or they do not. Likewise the question as to whether education as a social institution has autonomy with respect to certain educational matters has to be argued out in the epistemological arena, for unless the educator can have superior knowledge in these matters, his claim to autonomy and authority is empty.

In analogous fashion, all problems of curriculum, organization, standards, and methodology, when persistent and serious, force the controversy into philosophical waters and to a considerable depth.

The educational philosopher is impelled to build educational theories which will satisfy both parties to the controversy while avoiding inconsistency or the creation of new difficulties. A theory that purported to solve all educational problems would constitute a systematic philosophy of education. It would provide a terminology (set of concepts) in which to state or to restate the issues and a set of arguments designed to defend one statement against alternative statements. The Platonic theory of education is a classic example of a systematic philosophy of education.

Educational philosophers are often motivated by a sense of social mission that impels them to devise educational schemes for reforming man and society. Rousseau, Pestalozzi, Froebel, and Dewey come to mind as examples. None of these—nor Plato, for that matter—cold-bloodedly "applied" a theoretical system to education. The point to be emphasized is that they took their departure from educational problems and tried to solve them by constructing an educational theory—more or less adequately grounded in philosophy.

In studying the philosophy of education by this problem approach, students learn the standard gambits of dealing with a well-defined set of educational problems. They practice these attacks and defenses on each other and on anyone else willing to engage them in argument. All of which bears a strong resemblance to what students and teachers of philosophy have always done.

Another and more common method of building a philosophy of education is to derive it from some philosophic position such as Idealism, Realism, Thomism, Pragmatism, or Existentialism. This approach asks the question: What does a given position imply for education?

Philosophical points of view may imply much or little for education. Every position implies at least the value of studying and stating that position, and to that extent would favor an education that would encourage such study and statement. Unless a view is fairly explicit about its value theory and incorporates it into some sort of philosophical anthropology, it is rather difficult to derive educational principles and practices from it. Logically, it may even be impossible to make anything more than plausible guesses because educational theory takes into account existential factors that have the brutishness of particulars and do not necessarily follow from any principle. Thus Thomist educators do not agree on which methods or even which type of curriculum would be implied by a Thomist philosophy. Rather diverse methods and curricula seem to be compatible with that philosophy.

Dewey's Instrumentalism comes off best in this type of derivation because Dewey's activistic theory of knowing is at the same time a theory of learning, reflective thinking, ethical thought, and democratic process. Perhaps this is not so much a process of derivation as of identification.[1]

---

[1] A systematic attempt to derive philosophies of education from standard philosophical schools was made in The National Society for the Study of Education 41st Yearbook, Part I, *Philosophies of Education*, 1942. This symposium volume was prepared by educational philosophers (with the possible exception of

This derivative approach encourages the labeling of views—a necessary albeit universally deplored activity of philosophers. In the philosophy of education one finds today a tendency to make this labeling and classifying almost an end in itself. Perhaps this tendency can be both understood and forgiven, if it is realized that as an academic discipline philosophy of education is still very young—and in many institutions still embryonic.

Whatever difficulties and shortcomings the derivative method of theory-building may harbor, to carry it on as a student or teacher demands a high order of technical competence both in philosophy and in education. The mental processes used in effecting the derivation, moreover, are indistinguishable from those used by philosophers *qua* philosophers.

So far, two types of theory-building in philozophizing about education have been discussed. First is the devising of a theory to solve an educational problem or a set of them. This leads to logic, epistemology, metaphysics, ethics, and general value theory as a source of concepts and arguments. The second method is to "apply" a general philosophical position such as Idealism to educational problems. This has been called the derivative method. Whatever the merits of these methods, the contention of this paper is that they can qualify as philosophical both with respect to content and method.

THEORY-EVALUATION

The two modes of theory-building indicate how one may proceed to evaluate theory. A theory that proposes to solve educational problems can be judged with respect to its success. Logical analysis is instituted to test the explanatory power of a theory—its adequacy to relevant factors, and its merits as compared to rival theories.

As with other types of criticism, logic will carry the critic far, but not all of the way. Certain considerations about adequacy are a matter of knowledge and experience and not of logic. Insofar as this is so, the educational philosopher as a critic needs a double armament. Hence his formal training will be required to make him literate and even facile in two literatures—of education and philosophy— although perhaps not to precisely the same degree nor simultaneously.

The criticism of the translation of a position in general philosophy into an educational theory or the milking of a philosophic position for its educational implications also entails a mastery of logic and a familiarity with fact. The critic begins by checking the deductions made by the translator for logical rigor. After that, his knowledge of the philosophical position enables him to point out errors of interpretation (if any) and to suggest deductions that escaped the translator. If his

Mortimer Adler). In the Society's 54th Yearbook, entitled *Modern Philosophies and Education*, "pure" philosophers—John Wild, Jacques Maritain, Theodore M. Greene, George R. Geiger, Robert S. Cohen, Ralph Harper, Kenneth Burke, Herbert Feigl, and James K. Feibleman—were asked to state the import of their views for education.

knowledge of education is adequate, he can direct the criticism from this perspective as well. One could elaborate the description of these critical processes, but enough has probably been said to enable philosophers to recognize their own mode of activity in them.

One special mode of criticism should be noted: the linguistic and conceptual analysis currently so popular. Whether the claim that this type of analysis alone is philosophy in the disillusioned meaning of this term is anything more than a claim or not, there is no doubt that semantic dissection is philosophically useful; and particularly so in educational philosophy where slogans and clichés carry so heavy a burden of communication.

Consider one example of semantic chaos: the familiar concept of adjustment. Educators heeding the *dicta* of the psychologists and social scientists use this concept as a value standard. Where adjustment can be given an operational meaning, there is little difficulty with it; for example, "The body makes temperature adjustments," or "The store made a price adjustment on the stove with the cracked enamel."

But suppose a child, being very shy, adjusts by developing an overactive imagination with the result that he habitually tells tall stories—even for the purpose of avoiding punishment. Psychologists, teachers, and moralists agree that this is not a good adjustment, but would they agree as to why it is not?

The statistical concept of normality when used as a measure of adjustment is clear enough, but its adoption as a *desideratum* would condemn all behavior that was more vivid, more interesting, and even more productive than what the middle 68 percent of the population happens to exhibit. Consider now the awkward situation that results when the statistical concept of adjustment is confronted by the "creative development of the personality," a notion no less dear to certain segments of the educational profession than adjustment.

"Interest," "need," "learning," and many other concepts cry out for the kind of semantic purgation that so many philosophical concepts have undergone in recent decades. The cry has been heeded, especially by the more recent Ph.D. aspirants in the philosophy of education who are eager to try out the analytical tools of logic and linguistics.

Some of this analysis, it may be surmised, will be of the puppy-dog-tearing-the-house-apart variety, serving primarily as an outlet for philosophical vigor and enthusiasm. But there will be more solid results also. In educational philosophy clarity and precision are more than the craving of an intellectual fastidiousness because theory is here so close to practice. Inasmuch as educational practice is a resultant of many vectors, its rationale gravitates toward the syncretic, apologetic, and the hortative. The shock of astringent semantic treatment is, therefore, almost always beneficial to the educational enterprise. The problem is all the more urgent because teaching personnel are not notably sophisticated either in the method or the content of philosophy. If they are to become more so, both philosophy and philosophy of education will have to occupy a much more important position in their formal preparation than they now do.

III

It would be a waste of time to argue that sound theory is a *desideratum* in education, were it not for the fact that so many educators and philosophers do not believe it. To some educational administrators education has become equivalent to budgets, school board meetings, building programs, and the hiring and firing of faculty. The "big time" educators in our time are more likely to resemble a "big time" manager or promoter than an intellectual of any stripe. Such men hold theory of any kind suspect unless it leads to immediate results in terms of budget, enrolments, salaries, and similar marks of institutional prosperity.

Other educators are more hospitable to theory, provided it is scientific theory. Although they may not agree on which disciplines to honor by the name of science, they usually agree that philosophy only complicates the already complicated business of running a school.

On the other hand, there are philosophers who likewise tend to regard education, especially in its institutional forms, as a collection of empirical procedures designed or stumbled upon in specific situations. That this so often is the case with educational procedures does not, of course, mean that it cannot be otherwise, and that it should not be otherwise. To put it bluntly, the theorist of education looks to the philosopher as his most important ally, but too often the philosopher has looked the other way.

At this point it seems pertinent to raise the following questions: Do we need educational philosophers? Do we need educational philosophy as a distinct discipline on the graduate level of study? What kind of training should the specialist in philosophy of education have? We shall concentrate on the last question and thereby touch on the others.

If philosophy of education represents the kind of activity described in this paper, then candidates for the higher degrees in the philosophy of education need professional training in both philosophy and education. Being a professional in one area and an intelligent layman in the other will not do. A student at the master's level with a flair for philosophy and a zeal for education is the ideal candidate for the doctorate in the philosophy of education. He is to be found with about equal frequency in a department of education or in a department of philosophy.

As to the need for specialists in this area, it so happens that in a large number of institutions there is a course, and perhaps more than one, called philosophy of education. Many of these courses are being taught by men who cannot even by courtesy be called philosophers or philosophers of education. The course, therefore, becomes what its teacher can manage to make of it with whatever resources he happens to have. Once, however, persons trained in the philosophy of education are available, the discipline will become better defined and thus more formidable to many who now are not abashed by the prospect of teaching it.

Granting that advanced training in educational philosophy is justifiable, and that individuals with appropriate gifts and zeal are attracted to this field, there still remains an important nest of questions that can arise in the mind of the philosophic-ally inclined graduate student. Am I abandoning philosophy? Will I be giving up the kind of activity I have enjoyed so much in the courses, seminars, and books labeled philosophy? Will I be caught up in social movements, community involve-ments, so that I cease to be a thinker?

These are important questions because they are most likely to come from just those men and women who might also make the very best philosophers of educa-tion. The answer is one that this paper has tried to indicate, viz., that one need not and, indeed, that one cannot leave philosophy and still be a philosopher of educa-tion. And the proof is rather simple. Whoever has doubts about this matter need only devote some time and honest effort to thinking rigorously about any of the current problems of education. It will not be long before he will realize that he is engaged in an enterprise of no mean philosophical order and of unsurpassed human significance.

IS A PHILOSOPHY OF EDUCATION NECESSARY?

KINGSLEY PRICE

In these times, the school is an institution of great importance. In our country, and probably in others, public controversy abounds concerning it. Should it be used to further, to preserve, or to dissipate the form of society which fosters it? To what degree, and by what procedures, should it receive public support? Should it provide moral, political, or religious training? Should its actions be controlled from without by private groups or public agencies; or should it be free to serve the community as it sees fit? From these and from related questions pours an anxious torrent of words; and many of those concerned feel that it cannot be contained by any wall but one which is raised upon a philosophy of education.[1]

I write this essay in an effort to show the way in which a philosophy of education might be useful in channelizing the flood. And this effort will be advanced by showing what a philosophy of education is.

FROM a paper presented in a symposium on "Philosophy of Education" at the meeting of the American Philosophical Association, Eastern Division, December 27, 1955, published in *The Journal of Philosophy*, 52 (October 27, 1955): 622–633. (Reprinted by permission of the publisher and the author.)

[1] Cf., e.g., Theodore Brameld, *Philosophies of Education in Cultural Perspective*, The Dryden Press, New York, 1955, p. 15.

I

I shall use the word "education" to refer to the academic discipline which treats of all those activities through which the arts and sciences are transmitted from one generation to another as well as those by which they are fostered and advanced. Many accomplish this transmission and fostering with no knowledge of how to do so. But there is, at present, a tremendous current of academic activity which treats of that subject; and it is for reference to this discipline that I here use the term.

Education concerns itself with three different aspects of transmitting and fostering the arts and sciences: instruction, administration of schools, and guidance of students into those professions and occupations which are best suited to them. With respect to each of these kinds of activity, it makes statements of fact and recommendations. For the making of statements of the former kind, it draws upon a great number of different sources. History, sociology, psychology, anthropology, and common sense—all of these and many other areas as well may be gleaned for information concerning instruction, administration, and guidance. And this information is embodied in statements of the form: If people of a certain sort are dealt with in a certain way, then a certain kind of result will follow. We should notice that this rummaging of common sense and science for information concerning the consequences of instructing, administering, and guiding in certain ways may now give very little reliable information to the factual part of education. It is, nonetheless, the discovery of such information which motivates the academician who is genuinely interested in the factual part of education; and to this idealized discipline, the word is here used to refer.

To the three subordinate areas of the factual part of education correspond three kinds of statement in the recommending part. The factual part informs us that a certain method will suffice to instruct students of a certain sort in a certain subject, that organizing a school in a certain way will, under certain conditions, maintain it as a going concern; and that guiding persons of a certain kind into a certain area of life will satisfy them adequately. But in no case do whatever reliable statements there may be concerning those subjects tell us that instructors, administrators, and counselors ought to act in the ways described. The recommending part of education involves, therefore, some consideration other than that of facts; and consists of statements which recommend that instructors adopt certain teaching methods, that administrators employ certain administrative techniques, and that counselors use certain principles for the professional and vocational direction of their charges.

The factual and the recommending parts of education are thought to be related in a certain way. The factual part is, in all cases, conceived of as a support or justification for the doctrines of the recommending part. It is in view of facts concerning particular kinds of students, schools, and guidance problems that certain teaching methods, administrative procedures, and guidance principles are recommended; and the facts which education seeks are thought to provide a basis for inference to its recommendations.

Education as an academic discipline is the activity of gathering facts which will justify certain instructional, administrative, and guidance procedures. And this elucidation of the sense of the word "education" must be followed by a brief statement of the concept of philosophy appropriate to the question "Is a philosophy of education necessary?"

"Philosophy" is a word which refers to two distinct kinds of activity. One of them is analysis. This is a process motivated by a desire to understand words, to clarify ideas, and to comprehend concepts clearly and distinctly. There is no way in which its scope may be limited a priori; for there is no way of knowing, a priori, what words, ideas, or concepts require clarification. But it suffices for our purposes to describe it in this general way.

The second kind of activity may be more precisely delimited. It need not exclude analysis, but does differ from it. It is the activity of arriving at certain theories, those of metaphysics, ethics, epistemology, aesthetics, and logic.

All metaphysical theories declare that the observable world is a manifestation of reality, but each ascribes to reality a different nature. Idealism declares that reality is spiritual; materialism, that it is material; and dualism, that it is somehow both. However they differ, each urges that its reality lies behind, not in, the observable world. That world is described by common sense and science. And since reality is found nowhere in that world, common sense and science can never profess to account for it; nor metaphysics, for common sense and science. If idealism is true, human beings are really spirits; if materialism, they are really matter in motion; if dualism, they are in some way really both. But whatever metaphysical theory be true, or even if none should be, the truth or probability of statements in psychology remains. And so, for all the statements of common sense and science. They are logically independent of any metaphysical theory.

Ethical theories attempt to answer the questions "What things are good and right?" and "What is the nature of goodness and rightness?" With respect to the first question, their answers must, in general, coincide. They must recognize a common body of moral statements; for, as Kant pointed out, no ethical theory can create a new obligation or moral principle. Each must show why these moral statements are correct; and in this endeavor, each must make clear the moral traits which these moral statements express; and from divergent directions of this endeavor, divergent answers to the second question arise. Some ethical theories hold that moral goodness is a trait accessible only to reason; others, that it is some quality like pleasantness, the possession of which is open to empirical verification; and others still, that it properly characterizes nothing, being, like love or rage, a human response to things, although subtly different from these. And similar statements might be made concerning the varying treatments of moral rightness.

The answers which an ethical theory provides for its first and second questions are related to each other in a way different from the way in which statements in common sense and science are related to metaphysical theories. Common sense and science are indifferent to metaphysics. But in the answer to its second question, ethics professes to clarify and analyze the very traits which everyday moral statements express. If moral goodness is pleasantness, and rightness is conduciveness thereto, then pain can never be good, and actions which make for it never right. And any moral agent who makes either assertion must be mistaken. We might know, in some sense of that word, what is good or right independently of a theory of ethical value; but this is cognitive independence at best. And answers to the first and second questions of ethics are not logically independent of each other. A complete catalogue of what is genuinely good and right would, at once, test every theory as to the nature of goodness and rightness, and show which are true and which false. For a theory of ethical value requires that certain things be good and right, and precludes the possibility that others are.

Epistemology endeavors to answer two questions: "What is knowledge?" and "What are the methods by which it is secured?"; but a list of the statements known and a set of descriptions of the ways in which they come to be so would not answer these questions. The former task is that of a remarkable encyclopedist; the latter would be performed by psychology were it sufficiently developed. The first question asks, rather, for an exhibition of the constituents of knowledge, and for a statement of the relation it requires between the knower and the known. The second asks for a reconstruction of the methods which serve to secure knowledge such that the critic may be assured that it is not vitiated by errors in the procedures through which it was achieved.

The philosophy of education may be understood with relation to the definitions of "philosophy" and "education" made out above. "Philosophy of education," as the phrase is employed here, means an analytical treatment of education together with an attempt to relate it in a certain way to metaphysics, ethics, and epistemology. It should be noted that this way of understanding the phrase conforms to the practice, if not to the explicit formulation, recorded in the literature.[2] And it should be noted also that logic and aesthetics are not called upon to provide subdivisions of philosophy of education; the reason is that the literature with which we are concerned does not provide any clear basis for such classifications.

In its first subdivision, analysis, philosophy of education is the activity of clarifying our understanding of those terms in education which need it. In its second subdivision, philosophy of education attempts to show that there is a metaphysical explanation for the factual part of education, and a certain supplement for it. In its third subdivision, ethics provides a justification and clarification of the recommendations which education includes. In its fourth subdivision, the philosophy of education endeavors to provide a theory of learning derived from epistemology. I shall now explain this view of philosophy of education in a little more detail.

II

It is not necessary to add anything in elucidation of the first subdivision of education, its analysis; this theme will be resumed in the third section of this essay.

[2] Cf., e.g., *ibid.*, p. 27; and *Modern Philosophies and Education*, edited by Nelson B. Henry, The University of Chicago Press, Chicago, 1955, p. 16.

The metaphysics of education attempts to explain the facts which education states. A statement of fact is one belief in whose truth or probability demands only observation of the fact it asserts or of some fact appropriately connected with it; and it is often said that no such statement can explain any other. "That adolescents are rebellious" may truly assert a fact about them; but why they are so the statement itself, of course, cannot explain. Nor can any other statement of fact explain this one adequately; for about every statement of fact, a similar demand for explanation may be made. Indeed, were there a statement which truly asserted all observable facts, one might still ask why this particular statement was true, and not some other. And so, it might be argued, while common sense and science give education its facts, a theory of reality is necessary as their ultimate guarantee.

Besides explaining the facts of education, metaphysical theories also would supplement them in a certain way. Orthodox metaphysical theology throughout Christendom asserts immortality; and orthodox materialism, wherever it occurs, denies it. The assertion of neither theory is a statement of fact in the sense of the phrase employed here; for belief in them need not, and perhaps cannot, depend upon observation. But they are statements which, nevertheless, supplement the information which common sense and science provide for education. Most metaphysical theories would add to the statements of fact in education some similar statement concerning the persons and things involved in instruction, administration, and guidance.

The ethics of education concerns itself with the recommendations which education makes concerning those persons and things. These recommendations are of two sorts: those which advocate the existence of certain social orders and personal characters, and those which advocate the means by which those orders and characters are realized. Within education, there is an attempt to justify both the goal recommendations as well as those subordinate to them by statements of fact which education includes. Dewey, for example, endeavors to justify democracy as a goal for the activity of schools by many statements of fact drawn from social psychology and evolutionary biology, and his recommendation that the moving force of learning be allowed to issue from the student, from other statements of fact and from its being a subordinate means to democracy. The ethics of education is a check upon the justification which education offers for its own recommendations. It provides a general theory of what a justification for an ethical statement is; and consists, in part, in an application of this theory to the justifications which education gives for its recommendations. In this way, the question "What things are right and good?" has its counterpart in the ethics of education; for, if we did not know that a recommendation was properly justified, we might not know that the state of affairs recommended was good or right.

The other question of ethics is also reflected in the ethics of education. Suppose we were convinced that the realization and preservation of democracy was the goal toward which the activity of schools should be directed, and that certain instructional and other techniques were the channels through which it could be most easily reached. Suppose further that the justification of this goal and of its subordinate recommendations proved valid upon ethical reflection. It is clear that our conviction might, nonetheless, be mistaken. If we did not know what it is to be good, our belief might attribute this character to democracy by mistake, and thus, the goal recommendations and those subordinate to it would be vitiated. The justification of both recommendations would be correct provided democracy is good; but not knowing the nature of this attribute, the proviso might well be false. And an ethics of education should uncover the nature of the goodness and rightness of the things education recommends as well as that of their justification. The ethics of education is simply a consideration of its recommendations, in the light of ethical theory.

Of the two parts of epistemology, only one, to my knowledge, has been thought to have any particular bearing on education. A considerable number of philosophers from Locke to Dewey if not farther have endeavored to make use of their answers to the question "What are the methods by which knowledge may be secured?" for educational purposes. Locke argued that knowledge results from inscription of experience upon a *tabula rasa*; and, accordingly, held that instruction must be a matter of imposing habits upon the student, and confronting him with real things, so far as possible, rather than with verbal descriptions of them. Dewey believed that all knowledge is achieved by engaging in the "scientific method"—apparently the hypothetico-deductive procedure with which we are all familiar; and he contended, accordingly, that instructing and learning must follow that course. The epistemology of education consists in an attempt to derive from an epistemological study of the method of knowledge a description of the procedures by which learning may be furthered, and a consequent recommendation that such courses be pursued in the schools.

III

With this view of the philosophy of education in mind, let us ask why a philosophy of education is necessary, i.e., what the use might be of an analysis, a metaphysics, an ethics, and an epistemology of education.

The necessity of an analysis of education need scarcely be mentioned to be agreed to. Many of the key terms of the discipline are covered with obscurity. Consider, for example, such terms as "experience," "participation," "citizenship," "loyalty," and "democracy." Many persons, in this country at least, hope that democracy may be achieved through the schools; and they endeavor both to point out the paths by which it may be reached and to recommend those paths, by use of terms such as those listed above. One author, with this intention, writes: "Events become experiences through participation, and learning is the process of experiencing. Without effective participation there cannot be effective learning. ... Learning experiences, to be effective, can seldom be arranged in serial order because the organism does not mature serially. Experiences need to be built on experiences, and behavior patterns on behavior patterns." It is difficult to see how the use of these principles in the schools would further democracy; for, putting aside the obscurity which gathers around the last term, the dark of their expression makes it difficult to know what those principles are.

The book from which this passage is taken was selected at random, but, although it is more intelligible than many, one who has read a few books of education cannot doubt that the obscurity of the words, ideas, and concepts it employs is typical of the literature. Terms such as "experience" and "participation" possess no settled significance; and a moment's reflection will suffice to bring in question many an initial agreement or disagreement felt by the reader. Much discussion in education, as it is presently conducted, fails to secure mutual understanding for want of a clear analysis of the words, ideas, and concepts in which it is embodied; and until this is forthcoming, we shall know neither what an educational theory is saying, nor whether, consequently, its statements of fact are true and its recommendations legitimate. An analysis of education is necessary in order to provide clear terms, in whatever context they are required, for the description of the facts of education, and for the statement of its recommendations.

It is often supposed that a metaphysics of education is necessary as an explanation for the factual statements of that discipline. It has been supposed, further, that in performing this function, a metaphysics of education exercised a second good office, that of guaranteeing the recommendations which education makes. For, since these recommendations are derived from education's statements of fact, a guarantee of the latter amounts to a strengthening of the former. Let us ask whether these two functions of the metaphysics of education are really necessary.

It is not necessary that metaphysics should explain the statements of fact in education; and it is not, because it is impossible. If it did do so, some metaphysical theory would be a basis from which the statements of fact in education could be derived by logical procedures; but we have seen that all such statements are logically independent of any metaphysical theory. The factual statements of education like all others are shown to be true or probable by scientific procedures or by those of common sense. The explanation of their truth or probability consists in the discovery that observation and inference from it strengthen the evidence for them. If metaphysics did explain them, either metaphysics would be about the observable world as well as reality, or some statements of fact would transcend that world; and both these alternatives are impossible.

It is a simple conclusion that the second good office of the metaphysics of education is also not necessary. The recommendations of education should, of course, in some way depend upon its facts. If it is true that adolescent children are likely to be rebellious, instructors, administrators, and guidance experts ought to treat them in certain ways, and ought not to treat them in certain others. But if metaphysics does not explain the statements of fact in education, it cannot support its recommendations by that explanation; and it is not necessary that it should.[3]

[3] In support of the need for metaphysics of education, cf. (e.g., realism) Rupert C. Lodge, *Philosophy of Education*, Harper and Brothers, New York, London, Revised Edition, 1947, p. 78; (e.g., idealism) J. Donald Butler, *Four Philosophies and Their Practice in Education and Religion*, Harper and Brothers, New York, London, 1951, pp. 211–212. I do not attribute, by virtue of these citations, the metaphysical theories mentioned to these authors.

There is another function which the metaphysics of education may claim. We saw, earlier, that metaphysical theories yield a kind of statement supplementary to statements of fact. That God exists, that the person survives death, that he does not survive it, these are all statements of the kind I have in mind. If they can be shown to be true, metaphysics will provide for education the basis for a considerable number of recommendations. For none can be rendered probable or improbable by scientific procedures; and consequently education's statements of fact cannot include them. Yet, if they are true, they tell us of things about which it is extraordinarily important to urge certain courses of action. And many of those concerned with education have proceeded, consequently to one or other of these metaphysical statements, to lay down as the chief goal recommendation of their education the glorification of God, the salvation of the soul, diligent efforts at material progress, etc.

If this metaphysical supplementation of the information of science and common sense is possible, it is eminently desirable that the metaphysics of education should be practiced. If we could know any statement of the kind I have in mind to be true, it would be the height of folly to fail to draw from metaphysics whatever statements one can that might be relevant to deciding the goals that education should seek, or the courses subordinate to their realization. But it must be noted that, in the present state of things, two preliminary tasks must be accomplished. Metaphysics must first make its supplementary statements clear. "The existence of God," "personal survival," etc., leave much to be desired in this particular. After they are understood, the metaphysics of education must show that they are true. Once these tasks are accomplished, metaphysics of education will be of the greatest importance for education itself. It is unfortunate that they have not yet been executed.

It might be supposed that the ethics of education is in the same case with its explanatory metaphysics, i.e., not, in its present state, necessary to education at all. This would be a mistake. The reason for the inability of metaphysics to explain statements of fact lies in the metaphysical supposition that reality cannot be found by common sense and science, that it is always behind what we can experience. It is precisely this assumption which renders statements of fact logically independent of the metaphysical theories which would explain them. The ethics of education is not logically independent of its concrete recommendations. The ethics of that subject consists of an analysis of the ethical terms it employs, and of a list of educational recommendations shown to be valid. In its latter part, it requires that education incorporate those recommendations included in its list, and exclude all others. In its former part, the ethics of education includes all the theories there are of the nature of ethical goodness and rightness; and we may not know which of these is correct. But if any is, then the truth of that theory, were it known, would show that many things are not good and right, i.e., those which do not exhibit the features into which goodness and rightness are resolved; and that many others must be good and right, i.e., the ones which possess those features. Thus, for example, the recommendation now often made that the schools be a channel to democracy is not logically independent of an ethics of education. For, if it is valid, it will be an item in the list of those recommendations shown to be so by the ethics of education; and if it is a valid recommendation, a theory of ethical value which is true will require us to make it. The recommendations of education, thus, are not indifferent to either part of the ethics of education as its statements of fact are to metaphysics.

Ethics of education is necessary for a second reason. The goal recommendations and those subordinate to them which education makes are in need of justification; and ethics, as we have seen, can provide a theory in terms of which a justification may be understood and worked out. Such a justification is partly a tracing out of causal relations. That a given course of action will, in fact, make for a certain goal is a causal judgment; as such it is a part of the justification of the subordinate recommendation of that course of action. But the business of justifying any concrete recommendation, is not merely a matter of knowing its causal relatives, but one of sifting and weighing all of the consequences to make sure that arriving at the goal which is recommended will not be offset by the badness of its accompaniments or of its intermediate collateral ancestors. What the accompanying consequences, and what the intermediate collateral effects of treating children in a relaxed progressive way may be, for example, is a matter which those who have advocated the latter have inquired into too little, and whether the comprehensive result of this treatment of them is a good one is something which those who recommend the happiness and "creativity" of the child's school day have too little concerned themselves with. The conclusion is that an ethics of education is necessary to clarify, to justify, and to correct the recommendations both of goals and subordinate means thereto which education makes.

In our discussion of the epistemology of education, it was pointed out that some philosophers of the subject have supposed that an epistemological study of the methods of knowledge would yield factual statements which might be recommended as principles for instruction. This view is, I think, mistaken. The description of the ways we come to know falls to the authority of psychology; the analysis of the procedures necessary if knowledge is to be secured is within the province of epistemology. The latter consists in a reconstruction of procedures which shows us the criteria which any method must meet if it is to yield knowledge; it provides no actual path. The reason the epistemology of education has been thought necessary lies in the identification of an idealized method of knowledge with those which are actually employed; and this identification seems to have been required because those who make it fail to distinguish epistemology from psychology. The latter science may afford laws of learning which education may recommend, but epistemology proffers only the criteria of the knowledge learned.

The philosophy of education is necessary to that discipline; for it provides an analysis of its obscure terms, a metaphysical supplement to its statements of fact, and a clarification, justification, and correction of its moral recommendations. The present controversy over the relation of the schools to society, the manner of their support, the kind of training they should provide, and the amount of freedom from external control they should possess, is reflected in education by divergent and incompatible recommendations as to the aims and methods of instruction, administration, and guidance. A philosophy of education could now certainly help to settle this controversy by an analysis of educational terms; this procedure would, at least, aid in arriving at an understanding of the differences between opposing views. But before the metaphysics of education can succor that discipline by supplementing its statements of fact, the supplementation must be made clear and shown true. And the aid that an ethics of education could provide must wait upon warranted agreement on ethical theory at large. It is to be hoped that a philosophy of education, in the sense in which it is necessary, may be arrived at; this will not be soon. But if philosophers will work at the philosophy of education, little by little and step by step, the analysis may be successful, the ethical help may be realized, and the metaphysical supplementation at least understood.

PHILOSOPHY
OF EDUCATION

I. L. KANDEL

American education has been the poorer in the last four decades not so much because the philosophy of education has been neglected but because it was derivative and dominated by one philosophical approach to the neglect of all other possible approaches. It is true that a number of books have appeared on philosophies of education, but only one of these philosophies pre-empted the field and was pursued almost as a theological cult. This particular philosophy of education had an appeal because it was simplicist and superficial in the American tradition. Further, the philosophy which inspired it isolated itself from preoccupation with a large number of questions which in other philosophies have been considered essential. There was a tendency to regard it as self-contained and able to answer all problems that might arise in education. A kind of sanctity surrounded this theory of education; all other theories and their professors came to be regarded almost as profane. Students passed their novitiate in mastering the dominant philosophy of education and in most cases eschewed the study of any other. Criticism of it was classed almost as blasphemy and critics were damned as traditionalists, perennialists, or essentialists, or even as out of touch with the American ethos.

In the meantime, as a result in part of the prevailing attitude among educators to

FROM I. L. Kandel, "Philosophy of Education," *Harvard Educational Review*, 26, Spring, 1956, 134–136. Copyright © 1956 by President and Fellows of Harvard College. (Reprinted by permission.)

philosophy in general and in part for other reasons which are more familiar, the street between academe and the education departments or teachers colleges came to be described as the widest in the world. Critics of the public schools are considered to be enemies of public education; it is not realized that the revolt of the public or of its vocal elements may be traced back to a certain dissatisfaction, whether implicit or overt, with this domination of education by a cult.

It is for these reasons that the papers by Broudy [1] and by Price [2] are encouraging signs that a different and more comprehensive approach to the subject is to be made. This approach does not seek to isolate the study of philosophy of education from that of philosophy in general, but promises to enrich the consideration of the problems of education by reference to the ways in which similar problems are handled in metaphysics, epistemology, ethics, logic, and value theories, to which Broudy adds aesthetics.

Both writers are concerned that theory-building should be accompanied by theory-evaluation or criticism. To this end both seem to advocate an analytical approach of logical or linguistic (semantic) analysis current in general philosophy. To the few examples of terms cited in the papers as needing analysis a number of others could be added which have in recent years been used indiscriminately—the child, society, growth, learn by doing, curriculum, subject, character, personality, adjustment, and so on. Useful as analysis may be, however, as a contribution to clarity, there is some danger that it may become an end in itself with a consequent inability to put the pieces together again into a synthetic, systematic whole. Educational psychology, for example, was once defined as analogous to the art of taking a watch apart without being able to put it together again.

The contribution that could be made to a sound philosophy of education by drawing on the various aspects of general philosophy are illimitable in determining the nature of ends, content and methods; in defining the meaning and place of knowledge and learning; in exploring the nature of values and the values to be aimed at. It would raise education above the earthy notion of growth as its own end, of problem-solving as the only stimulus and method for thinking, and of "mere" knowledge as unworthy of pursuit.

It would, however, be shortsighted to claim that a comprehensive philosophy of education can be developed by reference only to the disciplines envisaged by Broudy and Price. They admit that educational administrators do not appear to have any use for philosophy of education. The reason may be found in the failure of such philosophy to consider those aspects of education which the administrator must take into account. They are concerned with relations of the school to the public that supports it, of the school to society, of education to political theory in general, as well as with the details of educational administration and organization —the cost of education or even school buildings may be affected by certain philoso-

[1] Harry S. Broudy, "How Philosophical Can Philosophy of Education Be?" *The Journal of Philosophy* LII (October 27, 1955), 612–622.

[2] Kingsley Price, "Is a Philosophy of Education Necessary?" *The Journal of Philosophy* LII (October 27, 1955), 622–633.

phical points of view. Accordingly the study of political and social philosophy cannot be evaded, for political and social ends are among the strongest determinants of education, particularly at a time when the war of ideas and ideologies is being waged everywhere, and the influence of aggressive nationalism is stronger today than ever. It is precisely because these determining forces have been neglected in the study of educational philosophy that public education has encountered many of its recent difficulties and that so many conflicts have arisen on academic freedom, controversial issues, and social change through education.

While some of these issues pertinent to a philosophy of education may not have been given the emphasis they deserve, there is one that is not even hinted at. There is always a real danger that those who have the responsibility of preparing teachers talk *ex cathedra* and not from practical experience; or their practical experience in the classroom may be so remote in time that they have become insensitive to its realities. It would be well in formulating a theory to take into account also the cultural patterns that affect the pupils and may in turn influence reactions to education on their part and on the part of the public.

In a reappraisal of philosophy of education, it would also seem to be sound to evaluate theory in the light of practice and its potentialities. Nor can the lessons of the history of education or of comparative education be ignored. Above all it is important to bear in mind that a philosophy of education, if it is to serve the education profession, can neither be speculative nor wedded to one source from which all its wisdom is professedly derived.

THE PHILOSOPHY OF EDUCATION: A QUALITY OF ITS OWN

RICHARD KNOWLES MORRIS

In the comments of Harry S. Broudy[1] and Kingsley Price[2] considerable doubt is cast on the legitimacy of the philosophy of education as an acadeimc discipline. Where their views represent a soul-searching critique, the effect is ameliorative.

FROM R. K. Morris, "The Philosophy of Education: A Quality of Its Own," *Harvard Educational Review*, 26, Spring, 1956, 142–144. Copyright © 1956 by President and Fellows of Harvard College. (Reprinted by permission.)

[1] "How Philosophical Can Philosophy of Education Be?" *The Journal of Philosophy* LII (October 27, 1955), 612–622.
[2] "Is a Philosophy of Education Necessary?" *The Journal of Philosophy* LII (October 27, 1955), 622–633.

Where and to the extent that their views imply that the philosophy of education has not yet "arrived," they proffer a challenge. Those who have identified themselves with the subject, who have accepted its pursuit as a discipline worthy of their devotion, cannot long refuse to take up the gauntlet.

What makes a subject "adequate and respectable"? Whether or not the philosophy of education is, or can be, an academic discipline will, says Broudy, " depend on the degree to which one can specify a content or method sufficiently distinctive to earn for it a separate room in the academic mansion." [3] This admirable conclusion suggests a need for greater specificity of the subject matter than was actually presented by either author. They do not for a moment question the adequacy and respectability of philosophy. They even admit that it is quite proper to philosophize about education, no doubt because Plato, Aristotle, Aquinas, Herbart, and Dewey were among those who lent dignity to the practice. But since Locke, Kant, Whitehead and Russell, who might have succeeded in such an enterprise, failed to derive significant educational positions from their own philosophical systems, Broudy and Price seem to hold suspect the claim that the philosophy of education can possess an independent and distinctive quality of its own.

The degree of success in the demonstration of the existence of a specific body of knowledge, with its own methodology, appears proportional to its acceptability within the academic curriculum. Once having scaled the well-nigh impregnable fortress, with its ivy walls and cellular interior, a block is found for it within which it may exercise some measure of autonomy, real or apparent. Only at this moment is it a discipline that will be permitted to inform an outside world. If the subject is a fledgling, like the philosophy of education, and if it has the further drawback of a need to seek access to other compartments for nourishment, then its first hundred years will be the hardest.

But levity aside, the task remains. One can philosophize about education all he likes, in journals and out, but if he fails to exhibit a structure for his subject, if he cannot succeed in finding for it a niche in the academic wall, then it may be lost to the world as a discipline. Only by a continuous and concerted effort can such a goal be achieved, assuming that it is desirable in the first place. Certainly the effort is beyond the possibility of any one paper. However, it may not be too presumptuous to set forth one observer's view of the basic ingredients of a course in the philosophy of education. It should not be overlooked, as a practical consideration, that membership in such a course is likely to comprise prospective and in-service teachers whose backgrounds in the history of thought will be highly diversified and, in a few cases, negligible.

1. Epistemology is the *sine qua non* of educational philosophy.[4] The student of the philosophy of education would do well to begin here, whether he is absorbed in "theory-building" or "theory-evaluation." Problems of knowledge are at the heart of the educative process. If one accepts the pragmatic position that knowledge is instrumental to the future, then he has already catapulted himself into value

---

[3] Broudy, *op. cit.*, p. 613.
[4] See J. S. Brubacher, *Modern Philosophy of Education* (New York: McGraw-Hill, 1950), p. 71.

theory. In any case, epistemology is to be treated as rigorously as it is in the parent discipline, and apart from its educational implications. This latter precaution prevents final educational theory from carrying too many latent assumptions.[5] It provides justification for a thorough study of "theory-evaluation" before "theory-building." It rules out Price's conclusion that logic is not a sub-division of the philosophy of education.[6] Since psychology has been unable to formulate a single, all-embracing, scientifically verifiable theory of learning, the educator must still concern himself with the method of knowledge as well as its criteria.[7] And the method of knowledge is so closely interwoven with the content of knowledge that curriculum considerations are pregnant in all such inquiries. So it is that epistemology sheds light on more than classroom procedures.[8]

2. Metaphysics is to be treated in a fashion similar to that followed in epistemology. Rigor again demands the postponement of educational implications until one is trained to isolate and appraise the principles upon which the implications are to be based. Failure to heed this rule has done much to discredit the academic status of the subject. The educational theorist can no more avoid problems in cosmology, teleology, mind, and freedom than can the philosopher. From his conclusions regarding these problems, he may deduce his views of ends and means, the nature of the child and society, the role of the rational, and his theory of discipline.

3. The early divisions of the course are necessary preparation for the final stage. Here the student will establish the relations between what Price so aptly calls "the factual parts" and "the recommending parts" of education.[9] Here the search for "the ethics of education" culminates. In fact, philosophy's ethical and aesthetic inquiries are replaced by strictly educational ones: the aims, values, methods, and practices of education which are consistent with one's findings in stages one and two. Once again, theory-criticism serves to inform the student. His final assignment will be to build his own theory. He need no longer travel the epistemological and metaphysical blind alleys of the past. He may, of course, find his own dead ends, or in his explorations uncover some new avenue leading to brighter vistas for education. If he is a teacher, he should return to his classroom and pupils a wiser, less naïve, man—more sober perhaps, but no longer content to conceal the assumptions which lie behind his practices.

It is this sharp and final focusing of the mind on the third stage that gives the philosophy of education adequacy, respectability, a *raison d'être*, and a quality of its own.

---

[5] See J. S. Butler, *Four Philosophies* (New York: Harper & Bros., 1951), p. 485.
[6] Price, *op. cit.*, p. 626.
[7] For the contrary view, see *ibid.*, p. 632.
[8] Also, contrary, see *ibid.*, p. 628.
[9] *Ibid.*, p. 623.

THE SCOPE OF PHILOSOPHY
OF EDUCATION

SIDNEY HOOK

There is a great deal of nonsense talked about philosophy of education. This is particularly true of claims that a metaphysical or epistemological position has logical implications for educational theory and practice. Any two philosophers who share a common philosophical position whether it be objective idealism or pragmatism—or even Thomism—may still disagree with each other about specific educational objectives and techniques. And educators who agree about the desirability of certain educational aims and methods may disagree profoundly in their world outlook.

The notion that the resolution of educational problems, whether it be the place of the project method or the role of vocational courses in a liberal arts curriculum, depends upon one's "theory of reality" is almost comical if it suggests that we cannot as educators achieve a sensible agreement about the first unless we agree about the second. If that were true, then since there is no likelihood that we will agree about theories of reality, our prospects of ever agreeing about educational matters would be remote, indeed. Nonetheless there are many educational questions on which substantial agreement has been reached, for example, the importance of motivation, the use of visual aids in instruction, the integration of cognate subject matters, by educators, who are at odds with each other in their metaphysics and epistemology. The specific educational problems about which they differ, like, say, the different methods of teaching reading, they hope to settle as a rule through continued empirical inquiry. And as I understand empirical inquiry it includes here investigation of value proposals in the light of our common value commitments and of the consequences of acting on the proposals.

But surely, it will be objected, *some* metaphysical or theological beliefs entail some educational corollaries if only in the way of what should be taught. For example, does it not follow that if one believes in the existence of God, religion should be taught in the public schools? I do not see that it follows logically at all. As a matter of fact many religious people who do believe in God do not believe

FROM S. Hook, "The Scope of Philosophy of Education," *Harvard Educational Review*, 26 (Spring, 1956): 145–148. Copyright 1956 by Sidney Hook. (Reprinted by permission of the author.)

that religion should be taught in public schools. And it is perfectly conceivable that some who do *not* believe in the existence of God or in any religious doctrines should nonetheless believe it desirable that religion constitute part of the curriculum. A number of statesmen and their advisers known for their personal religious skepticism have held that it was desirable to give religious instruction in state schools in order to strengthen the foundations of peace and order.

The phrase "a philosophy of education" is an ambiguous expression which designates two related types of inquiry. We may ask questions like: (a) what role does education play in the organization of society and the transmission of culture? How are individual needs and interests affected by community traditions and institutions? Or—and this is the chief concern of a philosophy of education—we may ask questions like: (b) what are the *ends* of education? What kind of society can best further these ends? And having answered them tentatively we go on to inquire: What knowledge, skills and techniques, shall we impart, what habits and values and powers shall we encourage, in order to achieve these desirable interrelated personal and social ends?

It is apparent at once that the philosophy of education is primarily concerned with questions of value, with issues of ethics and social philosophy. Insofar as philosophy can be distinguished from science, where science is broadly regarded as ordered, grounded knowledge including its language and principles of organization, philosophy is the study of desirable ways of life. Its end is wisdom. It is in this sense that Dewey writes: "If we are willing to conceive education as the process of forming fundamental dispositions, intellectual and emotional, toward nature and fellow men, philosophy may even be defined as *the general theory of education.*"

The philosophy of education, more conventionally understood, is inquiry into the attitudes and dispositions which formal schooling should aim to develop in students. But does not this in turn depend upon metaphysics or epistemology? The answer seems to me to be clearly no. No ethical statement can be deduced from a metaphysical one except where we are dealing with disguised value judgments in the form of metaphysical expressions. If our values depend upon our metaphysics or theologies we should be at one another's throats all the time. We are more convinced of the validity of our moral judgments, for example, that it is wrong to inflict pain upon another for the mere sport of it, than we are of *any* alleged metaphysical or theological justification of our ethical judgment. This does not commit us to ethical intuitionism. Although there are many statements of fact which if they turned out to be false might affect the validity of our moral judgments, I cannot see what differential bearing statements like "Being Is One" or "Being Is Many" or "God Created the World," or their denials, have on such statements as "Sharing is better than stealing," or "Actions performed voluntarily are nobler than those done under compulsion."

The derivation of the ends or objectives of the educational process is no easy task. It involves detailed study of the biological, psychological and historical nature of human beings, their culture and traditions and focal problems, in short of anything which is *relevant* to settling the questions: what is of worth in human life? What knowledge and power are necessary to discover it and to make it part of the texture of human experience?

But surely, it might be objected, does not the relation between progressive education and pragmatism show that the foregoing is false? Is not progressive education specifically related to the pragmatic or experimental philosophy of Dewey either as conclusion to premise, or as corollary to conclusion, or as a particular application of a general principle? To make any such affirmation is to fall into a profound misapprehension of the character both of progressive education and Dewey's philosophy. This misapprehension is very widespread and accounts for the fanatical and hasty criticism of modern or progressive education, not on the grounds of empirical evidence, drawn from concrete educational experience, but on grounds of antecedent opposition to Dewey's naturalism and his theory of meaning, truth and experience.

There is considerable historical evidence to show that Dewey reached his characteristic educational insights *before* he elaborated his characteristic philosophical views. Aside from the historical evidence, Dewey himself has often maintained that what is called progressive or modern education is the result of the verified findings of scientific psychology applied to the processes of learning and teaching, and of the introduction of democratic ideals and procedures wherever relevant in the classroom and school experience of the student. (Let us recall that even student self-government, commonplace as it is today, would have been incomprehensible to most educators at the turn of the century.) The refusal to follow the lead of scientific method in developing new approaches and techniques in learning, or to adopt democratic values in classroom experience reflect moral differences, not metaphysical or epistemological ones. It is perfectly possible, however, to accept the findings of scientific psychology about the learning process and to believe in democracy in education and still reject the pragmatic philosophy as in the case with Felix Adler and Bertrand Russell, men as far apart from each other as each is from Dewey. Dewey would argue, however, that what they accepted on the plane of practical and moral experience made their characteristic philosophic doctrines implausible.

Dewey believes his theory of experience is more adequate to account for the way in which we learn effectively than any other theory of experience just as he believes that his theory of inquiry does greater justice to the way in which human beings actually solve their concrete problems than do conventional theories of meaning and truth. His theories of experience and inquiry come focally into play when difficulties arise in teaching and learning or when puzzles and paradoxes arise in investigation. In this sense, Dewey believes that his philosophy is better grounded in the facts of scientific inquiry, of education, law, art, and practical experience, when these have satisfactory or prosperous issue, than are other philosophies. Dewey is convinced that "Education is the laboratory in which philosophic distinctions become concrete and are tested" because it is a preeminent area in which moral attitudes are developed and understood in relation to knowledge of facts of different kind and degrees of warrant. He invites philosophers to formulate their theories and distinctions in such a fashion that they can be squared with what actually happens in the serious activities of the school, court, marketplace and scientific laboratories. Otherwise their theories may be consistent but incredible and their distinctions subtle and yet irrelevant.

To encourage philosophers as Mr. Broudy does "to derive (a philosophy of education) from some philosophic position such as Idealism, Realism, Thomism, Pragmatism or Existentialism,"[1] is to encourage them to perpetrate garrulous absurdities. Philosophers would do better to test their philosophic positions by first familiarizing themselves with what takes place in the educational (legal, artistic, scientific, social) process. Similarly, when Mr. Price writes that "The epistemology of educators consists in an attempt to derive from an epistemological study of the method of knowledge a description of the procedures by which learning may be furthered, and a consequent recommendation that such courses be pursued in the schools,"[2] he has put the cart before the horse. Epistemology is bad enough in its confusions of logic and psychology: epistemology of education is worse. No one ever derived a single item of new knowledge about learning either from epistemology or epistemology of education. What we know about reliable procedures by which learning may be furthered, we know through scientific or empirical psychology without benefit of epistemology or metaphysics. Similarly a recommendation that certain courses, whether of method or content, be pursued does not depend in the least upon epistemology but upon our conception of the ends of education and the best way of achieving them. We should look to education and psychology and other concrete fields in which knowledge is gained in order to see whether our theories of knowledge make sense. Philosophers should not presume to determine whether the specific results won in these fields make sense in the light of their abstract and general theories of knowledge. What is true of "the epistemology of education" is true also of "the metaphysics of education,"[3] only more so.

A philosophy of education, worthy of consideration, will not develop as a result of philosophers *applying* their philosophy to questions of education. It will develop when philosophers and educators, as well as other intelligent citizens, concern themselves with questions of education, explore their bearing on conflicting value commitments and seek some comprehensive theory of human values to guide us in the resolution of conflicts.

[1] Harry S. Broudy, "How Philosophical Can Philosophy of Education Be?" *The Journal of Philosophy* LII (October 27, 1955), p. 617.
[2] Kingsley Price, "Is a Philosophy of Education Necessary?" *The Journal of Philosophy* LII (October 27, 1955), p. 628.
[3] *Ibid.*, p. 631.

WHAT SHOULD BE THE AIMS AND CONTENT OF A PHILOSOPHY OF EDUCATION?

ABRAHAM EDEL

I

The operating capital of philosophers, as I see it, consists in a sensitive logical-critical methodology, and in an historical accumulation of different world-perspectives— from Plato and Aquinas and Spinoza to Dewey and Whitehead—integrating broad descriptive vistas with analytic refinements and basic valuations. Whatever be their individual merits, they constitute the most momentous efforts at comprehensive whole-world outlooks that rational man has ever undertaken. At the very least, then, philosophy runs a speculative workshop equipped with logical machinery, to which theories in special fields may be brought for processing. In this processing, an educational theory, for example, can have its concepts taken apart and their structure articulated; its presuppositions dug out and scrubbed, so that factual components can be tested on machinery imported from the natural, psychological and social sciences, and its value assumptions tuned up to a desired degree of scope and sensitivity. Then comes the problem; for the whole thing has to be reassembled according to some selected model. Now the workshop has many models, some dusty on the shelves, some on active display in the window. And which is selected is not just a matter of decoration; it will tend to determine the range of the theory and its selective reception—whether, for example, it will be black and white or receptive of many shades of difference, whether it will move in established grooves or be capable of ranging widely, whether it will operate on orders from outside or impose its own quality on its environment.

Perhaps I ought also to add that there are at present two kinds of workshops of this sort. One is run by philosophers who do not know too much about the local

FROM A. Edel, "What Should Be the Aims and Content of a Philosophy of Education?" *Harvard Educational Review*, 26, Spring, 1956, 119–126. Copyright © 1956 by President and Fellows of Harvard College. (Reprinted by permission.)

conditions where the products are to be used. The other is a do-it-yourself service shop, where educators reach for whatever tools look serviceable. The ideal establishment would be at least a partnership.

Let us take an indirect approach to the aims and content of a philosophy of education by exploring two examples of the shop at work. Let us see how an apparently scientific question—the underlying assumptions about the nature of the human material which is being educated—and an apparently normative question—the examining of goals in education—might be processed.

II

When an educational theory is brought into the philosophical workshop, one of the first parts to be unpacked is its implicit theory of human nature. This is diagnosed and sorted. Does it look upon the student as a bundle of inherent drives destined for a determinate pattern of growth and expression as they receive the proper nourishment? Then it is probably a *teleological* model. Does it look upon the child as neutral raw material to be stamped into an assigned design (or variantly as a wax tablet or blank sheet of paper to be inscribed)? Then it is obviously a *mechanistic* (behaviorist or Lockean-type) model. Does it see the child as a bundle of energy seeking liberation or growth in the succession of problem-situations in which he finds himself? Here is the familiar *pragmatist* model. Is the child's nature seen as a constantly interactive product of the historical conflicts of society? If so, we have probably some type of *dialectical* model. Similarly, there are *positivist* models, *existentialist* models, *naturalist* models, and numerous others. And within each of these, there are specific variants.

These diagnoses are not performed merely from the use of terms in the educational theory, nor from its general attitudes. For the same term may turn out to have different meanings in different models, as "growth" or "development of creative powers" do in such philosophers as John Dewey and Martin Buber. And even the same general attitude, such as a readiness to conserve what is best in tradition, obviously admits of very wide practical and conceptual variation. Diagnosis of the underlying human nature model therefore involves a realistic conclusion about the actual mode of functioning of the educational theory in the institutional and social milieu in which it operates.

What then is the point in attaching a hard-working educational structure to a philosophical model? It is not merely to give it an honorific title or to condemn it by philosophical association. Indeed such glib ascriptions tend to be misleading and dangerous. The point is rather that in each of the models the philosophical tradition has explored and analyzed the underlying concepts, refined the underlying problems, posed fundamental criticisms and developed alternative answers or at least paths of solution. To see the philosophical character of the educational theory is therefore to bring it to fuller consciousness in some of its fundamental dimensions.

Perhaps it will be felt that the examination of the implicit conceptions of human nature in the educational theories is a strictly scientific business pertaining to psychology, just as the question of window size and room height relative to floor space is a question of cooperative medical-engineering inquiry. And so it is in part. But at least in our time it remains true that the various theories of psychology themselves embody different philosophical approaches, perhaps inextricably combined with their scientific content, and usually at those precise points at which their opposition may involve quite different educational potentials. Thus the difference between a behavioristic theory with its emphasis on conditioning, and a Gestalt theory with its emphasis on insight, is a difference in philosophic conception of mind, and points to a different stress in the educational task of intellectual development. Similarly, a struggle between a Freudian and a neo-Freudian psychology, which may involve different consequences about desirable procedures in nursery school, carries us back to theories about the relation of the cultural and the biological in the fashioning of personality, and so to the whole philosophy of man.

I am not saying that philosophy will provide authoritative answers to the question of human nature insofar as it is relevant for educational processes. Far from it. This requires the active cooperation of philosophy, the human sciences, and education itself as furnishing experience of teaching and learning processes. What I am saying is simply that both educational theories and scientific theories of man seem to involve implicit use of some model which ties in with a whole philosophic outlook. Accordingly, to see the relation of the human nature theory to that whole outlook reveals more profoundly its structure and problems. Philosophy, in its systematic and historical studies of the different outlooks and in its elaboration of criteria for evaluating them, thus contains a gold-mine by resort to which the full scope and relations of education theory can be brought sharply to critical consciousness.

III

Let us turn to our second example—the goals of education. The complaint is often found that the goals of education are in a scrambled heap. If only they were clear, it is said, then the educators could go about their business of finding the proper means to achieve them. For they are masters of educational techniques and the theory of techniques—witness the hosts of books and courses on educational method—but a little more professional touch is needed in the treatment of goals. Hence send the educational theories to the philosophical workshop to have the goals put in order. For after all, are not order and system, values and goals, the business of the philosopher? Let us then look at the problem as it is seen in the process of such attempted servicing.

First the philosopher heaves a very deep sigh. This has happened before. Every so often when things get tangled in society and people turn to the scientists in specialized fields they meet with the answer, "We're objective scientists, we make no value judgments; tell us the goals and we'll give you or try to give you the best means." And when the customer asks where the goals are to be found, he is referred to the Philosopher as the Keeper of the Good. (Two other possibilities are a referral to Religion as Custodian of traditional Spiritual Values, and the Customer himself

on the assumption that it's up to him what he wants, and after all this is a Democratic Society. But usually the customer goes to the philosopher, because he feels
that his own problems are special and modern while the religious objectives are
broad and ancient, and as for deciding for himself, that's the last thing he feels he
can do. He is ready, so to speak, to judge the taste of the meal, but not whether the
meal is "really good" for him.) And so philosophers have been asked by government sociologists to specify the goals of rural life, and by political scientists to
analyze the value principles of democracy, and so on. Sometimes philosophers have
thought of setting up a value-servicing department right next to every science
dealing with human life! Certainly there are university courses along all these
lines. Only perhaps next to psychology is business bad, because the psychologist
using the concept of mental health seems to get along without outside help and
doesn't worry whether it's good to aim at a happy child if he finds that a happy
child is a healthier child. But everyone knows that the psychologist is smuggling
in value judgments under the concept of health, and really ought to get them
processed!

   Now the philosopher is usually an obliging chap. But if he is busy, he is likely to
ship over such conceptions of the good as the greater glory of God, or the greatest
happiness of the greatest number, or something similar that he finds nearest to
hand, or that is going slow in his inventory. But obviously he ought at least to send
directions in small print on how to contribute to the greater glory or how to find
the greatest happiness. And to do this seriously involves knowing at least the conditions under which the advice will be applied, what problems and what pressures
and what intermediate ends will arise. Otherwise it would be like shipping the goal
of speed, with the substantiating hypothesis that any human being will get a thrill
out of it, in the form of a high-powered car to a region that has only cow-paths; a
jeep will do even the speed job better.

   A serious servicing job therefore starts by examining the goals that are already
built into the educational theory and the practice to which it is addressed. It is
precisely here that we have to uncover stratum after stratum and trace their interaction. For example, we can see how powerful objectives come in at special times
reflecting the changes and demands of the social milieu: during a depression, down
go the "fads and frills"; when expansion is needed, let the schools produce more
mathematics and science students. We can trace the havoc wrought by the demand
that the schools be instruments of "national policy" geared to the demands of a
cold war that it is felt will last some generations—havoc not in terms of external
criteria but in terms of goals previously built into the system, such as some measure
of independent critical attitude, seeing both sides of a social issue, and so on. We can
trace minimal goals of keeping the children out of the way so their parents can go
to work; teach them at least to read and write because nowadays you can't be even
a soldier without that, much less steer your way round a job; specific instrumentality
themes such as teach the elementary school child about safety in the home and make
him carry out an inspection, or teach the high school child how to drive a car
because the accident rate may go down; persistent goal themes such as teach the

child to think for himself, but, watered down by, make sure that he doesn't get subversive ideas; perennial character themes such as teach the child to have the virtues of sportsmanship and to be law-abiding in spirit—so at least the delinquency rate will go down; goal themes that cut a broad swath through educational theory but have only an occasional influence on practice, such as the progressive education ideal of the growth of the child in terms of inner needs and individual scheduling; organizing goal themes such as educating for freedom, or educating for a world of change in which the directions will be chosen not by us but by the future.

Suppose the various strands have been unraveled, the major and minor objectives sorted, the conflicts located. Again, the reassembling, with its responsibilities about what to refashion, what to omit, how to integrate, poses the most serious philosophical—in this phase, ethical—problems. No philosopher at this point is without his own recommendation, his own conception of the human good in the human predicament. Here will be found his most mature conclusions about what men can and ought to aim at, what methods they can rely upon in directing their conduct to the achievement of their ideals, what the typical obstacles will be, and how men are to meet them. And because the pattern of educational objectives reflects this wider picture—in its selection and integration of goals, in its forging of methods, in its structuring of human relationships in the educational institutions, in its interrelation of school and society—no educational theory can avoid some basic philosophical choices and commitments.

Thus it may happen that a picture of the human good cast in terms of a specific ideal of character will subordinate everything else to turning out a certain type of person, whether it be the pious obedient type or the self-assertive warlike type. A picture cast in terms of a dominant social goal, say personal success, will move towards a familiar vocationalism, treating as a dispensable luxury or even as an obstacle the imaginative play of the intellect. A picture focusing on a ruling intellectual élite will move towards a limited and selective educational system, restricting large masses of the student body to a narrow practical or hurried capsule education. These remarks obviously over-simplify a complex subject, for there is no time to enter into the relation of major theme and basic motifs forced on any educational system in the interplay of social forces in the modern world. Our attention is directed primarily at the kind of role a philosophical conception of the human good can play in integrating and guiding educational objectives. Perhaps this would be best illustrated if I took my own outlook in ethical theory and suggested what its educational implications might be or at least what kind of questions it would give rise to about educational objectives.

In ethical theory I believe that it is possible to develop and stabilize what may be called a *valuational base* for evaluating moralities, institutions and social outlooks and practices generally.[1] This is not a full inventory of the good to be mechanically applied with a built-in solution to every question, but a basis for critical judgment,

---

[1] Cf. my *Ethical Judgment: The Use of Science in Ethics* (Glencoe, Illinois: Free Press, 1955) esp. pp. 297f.

a common-human framework embodying major decisions of policy supported by an interlocking structure of human knowledge and human striving. It is not to be identified simply with the basic values held in a given culture, but with value conclusions embodying the fullest knowledge about man's aspirations and conditions. In securing this knowledge, it is expected that the human sciences will play an increasing role. As our knowledge grows and changes, the valuational base undergoes refinement and modification; similarly as human problems take new historical forms and human aspirations are altered in specific directions, the valuational base may be rationally reconstructed. It is no substitute for the creativity that human valuation involves, but constitutes a guide for it. Its constituents include such categories as: universal human needs, the perennial aspirations and major goals of mankind, central necessary conditions for their expression and achievement, and critical contingent factors to be coped with in a given age. A theory of educational goals would therefore have to face questions arising along all these lines. Let us briefly examine each in a contemporary context, both as actually operative in educational policy and, as providing a dimension of necessary inquiry.

On universal needs, think of the changes brought about in educational theory, especially on the earlier levels, by the psychological discovery of the need for warmth, affection, or belonging, as contrasted with the assumption of an inherent aggressiveness to be kept in check by stern discipline. What changes have followed, and what are still required, in educational attitude, in the structuring of the teaching situation and the classroom, in the content of instruction, or even, for that matter, in the administrative-teacher relationship by working toward the fulfillment of this need?

On perennial aspirations and major goals of mankind—once a human aim is certified as clearly among these, can an educational system really resist the injunction to do what is in its power to help men work towards it? Or at least can it avoid measuring its own fitness by its contribution to their success? Take such different aims as the desire for systematic knowledge, the love of beauty, and the desire to have a home. What can and should education undertake with respect to these? Should it strive only so far as is instrumentally useful, as systematic knowledge is for technology, or so far as to show how basically satisfying these can be to human beings? Has it not at least the basic responsibility for awakening the inquiring mind? Similar responsibilities are likely in a field such as art that can greatly enhance the human joy of living. Again, in a society in which the character of home and family has undergone considerable transformation, some educational responsibility in this realm is unavoidable. Decision on all such questions, once the ethical goals are accepted, requires a careful examination of what the school can do in comparison with other social institutions and agencies. It involves an evaluation in detail, not merely acceptance or rejection. Thus, if it is not enough just to impart knowledge in relation to specific socially useful jobs, then at what point in the educational level should the concept of systematic knowledge be introduced, as contrasted with simply problem-solving techniques? If art is not a dispensable luxury to be cut on budgetary grounds, then is it enough to develop minimal appreciation, or else a taste for creation? And should not the school assume responsibility for discovering and assuring that there be no loss of artistic talent, just as scientists are now urging in the case of mathematical and scientific talent? In all these the establishment of a major aspiration or goal imposes responsibilities, raises questions, and articulates a standard of judgment.

On central necessary conditions, take the clear acceptance of an industrial technology as required in the modern world. This imposes on the schools the need not merely for transmitting the corresponding theoretical and technical education, but also for cultivating attitudes of precision, caution, punctuality, empirical-mindedness, sense of causal order, that are appropriate to such a technology. But does it not also impose on the schools the clear discrimination of what is really involved and what is separable—for example, maintaining a sharp distinction between the technological processes and their demands on the one hand, and the cultural organization and business organization which are separable on the other? Again, take as a central necessary condition of social organization in the modern world some democratic form which opens the way for political participation by the mass of people. Has not education then the responsibility for imparting a clarified concept of democracy which teaches non-discriminatory equality and human dignity (whatever be the philosophical bases, whether religious or secular or both) and embodies it in its institutions; and yet refrains from identifying a common human concept of democracy with the particular cultural forms of a specialized political organization?

Finally, to illustrate a critical contingent factor of the particular age, take the general agreement that the achievement of a permanent peace is the basic problem of our time. Has not education then the responsibility for looking through its content, methods and attitudes, to see whether it can contribute both directly and indirectly to the achievement of peace? For example, if peace requires a global-mindedness, should we not ask whether we are teaching a too narrow national perspective? In geography, would the globe literally provide a supplementary corrective to the flat one-hemisphere map? Are anthropological materials being used and in such a way as to make sense of cultural differences? Is the history of other countries being taught so as to show the aspirations of their people as well as the mistakes of their governments? Has language instruction become a live instrument rather than exhibition of an alien tongue? And so on, in questions that any group of teachers can multiply indefinitely.

I do not mean to suggest that there can be an itemized inventory of objectives—for each will raise wider problems of content and relation. But I do believe that nothing is more powerful or stimulating in the inquiry about objectives than a philosophical principle or a broad purpose, in bringing down conventional barriers, in reaching into inmost corners, in relating curricular content and institutional practice from areas that are far apart, and in providing a sense of unified purpose in the self-inquiry that pressure for the clarification of objectives inevitably brings.

IV

What then should be the aims and content of a philosophy of education? There can be no simple answer. An authoritative picture of human nature will not come back from the philosophical workshop, nor will the educational theory return with a neat bundle of educational objectives.

One reason why there can be no definitive description of the philosophy of education is that there cannot be a definitive description of philosophy. Philosophers disagree about the nature and tasks of philosophy because philosophizing is a highly refined act of consciousness; because the nature of consciousness and its relation to reality is part of the content of a philosophy; and so because the answer to the question what is philosophy is therefore in part a function of the philosophical results which themselves vary. This is not necessarily an evil; it means that there are different hypotheses to explore with respect to the areas and significant features of human life and its world setting.

Another reason, clearly involved in the examples given, is that there has to be a greater two-way give-and-take than there has been between philosophers and educators. In the long run it does not matter whether educators become philosophers or philosophers become educators or both work out methods of mutual creativity. Perhaps one of the foundations might subsidize a substantial experiment in which major courses in the philosophy of education, whether in liberal arts schools or schools of education, would be given jointly by a professor of education and a professor of philosophy.

And yet, even if a specific inventory of aims and content be at present unavailable, philosophy of education is important today. For, as Whitehead pointed out, we are living in a time when change occurs rapidly and in the lives of one generation. Hence neither rules of action nor even methods seem to me to be enough. We are driven back to fundamental outlooks, that is to philosophy. And while there is not a body of certified truths which philosophy can hand over to education, educational theory very much needs the imaginative-speculative sense of alternatives, the comprehensive-integrative sense of wide relationship to the whole of life and culture, and the critical sense of responsibility in probing for its own presuppositions and testing objectives, that the philosophical tradition has developed and sharpened.

HOW DO PHILOSOPHERS
KNOW WHAT THEY
ARE DOING?

OTTO KRASH

If philosophers are not clear about what they are doing, this is not unusual. Men were engaged in thought for many centuries before they began to think about thinking. And it was not until the advent of science that men could claim with any reasonable degree of accuracy that what they were thinking was either true or false.

Recently, a group of teachers met to consider the relation of philosophy to the normative dimension of education. The participants were *reasoning about* the problem area and were doing an excellent job of being reasonable. But if knowing what you are doing necessitates *an accurate report*, then the participants in our conference did not know what they were doing .The problem of ethical re-evaluation was being confronted with reason (with alternative conceptions of reason, of course), yet those engaged in the reasoning did not recognize that they were, in fact, actually, *being* reasonable.

Norman Cameron, Professor of Psychology and Psychiatry at the University of Wisconsin, underscores the significance of the conference theme when he states;

One of the gravest problems that great social change presents to any human society is one of deciding which of its ethical formulations are proving ineffectual, and what procedures shall be adopted in modifying these, or in developing new ones.

He goes on to say that,

To a considerable degree this is exactly what is happening in contemporary American life even though *some of the persons most earnestly engaged in ethical re-evaluation are often reluctant to recognize what it is that they are doing.*[1]

FROM *Educational Theory*, 5 (July, 1955): 167–171. (Reprinted by permission of the publisher and the author.)

[1] Norman Cameron, "A Biosocial Approach to Ethics," in Frederick Burkhardt, ed., *The Cleavage in Our Culture; Studies in Scientific Humanism in Honor of Max Otto* (Boston, Beacon Press, 1952), pp. 122–3. Italics mine.

THE FUNCTION OF EDUCATIONAL PHILOSOPHY

What *is* philosophy of education? What are we, who identify ourselves as professors of philosophy of education, in effect, doing? How can we forward what it is that we are doing into other disciplines? Is this enterprise worth forwarding: forwarding into other areas of human experience? Into education? Or is philosophy of education like Bertrand Russell's definition of mathematics—a science in which we do not know what we are talking about and whether what we are saying is true or false.

We seem to have no difficulty in recognizing what some have called our "internal" problems. Meaning by that, our several alternative conceptions of reason, what those alternatives are, how those alternatives are made more precise and more systematic, how we attempt to cut the grounds of reasonableness out from underneath positions that are different from our own, how to extend respect to an opponent in argument when we, in fact, hate his ideas, or even worse, when we cannot understand what he is saying. What is it that we prize in all this? Are we not, in thus extending respect and designating an alternative philosophy of education as worthy of analysis, witnessing the point at which an alternative view gains acceptance as an alternative?

Now, it is proper to extend great respect toward those who have displayed competence in philosophizing. Indeed, it is also fitting to become humble before those who by their grasp and breadth of reasoning have enlisted our efforts in behalf of the great enterprise of attacking problems of education philosophically. But when will some recognize what they are doing? Assessing reasons alternative to their own in order that they may sharpen or dull their own reasoning against the formidable, systematic thought of others. Is this what it means to think philosophically? If this is the way in which philosophers of education are reasonable— accepting alternative views as worthy, as systematic developments of human thought, *worthy*, because precise, organized and funded in the greatest of resources —human reason; then this is our discipline and we have a proposal to make to other dimensions of human experience and to education.

We believe that this great achievement of thinking about thinking (philosophizing) was begun and nurtured by the Greeks. There are those among the scientists, however, who disparage philosophy and label the discipline with the derogatory name of "classicism", thereby meaning that philosophy makes no significant difference in the human situation. Those who are of this mind in the sciences have reasons for believing thusly, and those "reasons" have, in great measure, been supplied by the philosophers themselves. For many philosophers have been content to sharpen their tools of criticism and analysis endlessly without any perceptible gain save a continuous sharpening of their tools of analysis into even sharper, thinner, and smaller tools. They have been content to sharpen their tools without submitting them to any test of substance or significance. These technical operations, directed "internally" toward the "tools of the trade", or the problems within philosophy, are to be rejected as the sole function for the philosopher of education. Philosophy of education must adopt the notion that philosophizing ought to make a difference in the educational scene. The tools of philosophy must be put to work on the problems of men wherein philosophizing may achieve significance for men.

If we put philosophy to work upon significant human problems, then we have problems that are "external" to the discipline, as well as the internecine problems that have absorbed the energies of countless "classic" and contemporary philosophers. The challenge of science to philosophy comes in the charge of insignificance in the affairs of men. The challenge of education is identical with that of science: of what significance is philosophy to education?

What does philosophy and philosophizing mean in terms of the following significant educational problems:

1. Freedom and free inquiry (censorship and indoctrination).
2. An adequate education for a democratic society—the "needs" of the child, the "needs" of the society, the "needs" of the student teacher.
3. The Church-State issue—Federal aid to education.
4. The requirements that private schools must meet in order that they be permitted as alternatives to, or substitutes for, the public schools and public education.
5. Theories of thinking and learning.
6. Theories of method—the method of science; where that method is applicable and where it isn't.
7. Higher or university education—its role in the cultural-educational picture: the vocational-liberal arts split.
8. The communist teacher.
9. Curriculum construction (place and role of the descriptive sciences, philosophy, art).
10. Education altering other institutions; and the alterings of education by other institutions.
11. Educational policy—the place and function of the discipline of philosophy of education.

Kardiner of Columbia University states that:

It is a sign of the times that philosophers who are moved by the contemporary scene must abandon their traditional frames of reference and enter upon that of the sciences of human behavior with which they are less familiar.[2]

THE CHARGE OF DETACHMENT

Many philosophers have refused to abandon their traditional frames of reference and have refused to accept the concept of continuity that undergirds modern science. Therefore, scientists as scientists who have occasionally taken philosophy seriously, seeking guides in systems of reasonableness, have rejected what they call "classicism" as constituting belief in static truths that are derived dialectically from other than human-natural sources. Scientists must reject any philosophy that refuses to recognize the basic grounds of scientific method: namely, the concepts

[2] A. Kardiner, in a review of H. A. Overstreet, "The Great Enterprise: Relating Ourselves to Our World," (W. W. Norton & Co., 1952) in *The Annals of the American Academy of Political and Social Science*, Vol. 286, March, 1953, p. 206.

of continuity and change in the experiences of man in nature. The charge of "classicism" is justified to the degree that philosophers refuse to recognize these two ground conceptions.

Why is the charge of "classicism" a just charge? For the reason that a rejection of continuity and change sets up arbitrary, *a priori*, criteria of truth and falsity. Rejection automatically blocks further inquiry. Inquiry is blocked when final truths become unattached to those conditions in which those truths are testable. The religionists who posit the arbitrary division of the spiritual and the "practical" prevent inquiry from attending a genuine search for the problems of significance in the lives of men. Such a position defeats inquiry at the start, inasmuch as the problems in the relation of the "practical" to the "spiritual" are the "more significant" problems, no matter how much intellectual effort is extended in the "practical" affairs of men.

Those who reject continuity and change (the notion that values emerge in, through, and out of human experience) are, therefore, prevented from making free inquiries into such problem areas as the relation of Church and State, Federal aid to education, private schools, and ultimately inquiry into alternative theories of intelligence, because they are committed *a priori* to the extension of their spiritual-practical division of experience where the concepts of continuity and change cannot become the test of significance. Ultimately they cannot examine into alternative theories of intelligence—unless having to arrive at the conclusion held at the beginning of inquiry constitutes freedom!

The charge of "classicism" holds for some experimentalists in philosophy of education—witness a statement by a committee of the Philosophy of Education Society.[3] For the "truths" of the religious dogmatist in philosophy of education are no different from such concepts as "freedom of inquiry," "free speech", and their attendant "rights", if these too become established as "eternal truths". Let Boyd H. Bode offer the challenge and charge to the experimentalists when he says:

> It is presumably obvious that such concepts as liberty, democracy, equality, and the public good do not come to us with a set of directions to show how they are to be interpreted and applied.[4]

We make no significant contribution to American education and the idea of free inquiry unless we accept the intellectual responsibility required for "spelling out" those conditions in education wherein "intellectual freedom" achieves significance in the lives of American children and their teachers.

Reinhold Niebuhr states that:

> No intellectual life, worthy of the name, can be at ease with the massive spiritual, moral, and cultural crudities, which make themselves normative in a civilization.[5]

---

[3] Committee on Freedom of Inquiry, "The Right to Intellectual Freedom," *Educational Theory*, Vol. 3, (April, 1953), pp. 185–6.

[4] Boyd H. Bode, "The Cleavage in Our Culture," in Frederick Burkhardt, ed., *op. cit.*, p. 8.

[5] Reinhold Niebuhr, *America and the Intellectuals* (Partisan Review Series; New York City, No. 4, 1953), p. 81.

The intellectual life of philosophy of education ought not to rest at ease with the greatest of cultural crudities of our time—blocking inquiry into the split between "the spiritual life and practical life" that is supported by Niebuhr himself. A professional society blocks inquiry and retreats from reason when it embraces those who affirm, *a priori*, the spiritual-practical division of human experience and who reject, *a priori*, continuity and continuous change in human experience wherein dialectic achieves significance in the lives of men.

ALTERNATIVE PHILOSOPHICAL PERSPECTIVES

Are we representing alternative philosophies, criticizing others? Do the legitimate and historic categories of Realism, Idealism, and Experimentalism mean anything? Are there any real differences among us? Are we, honestly, criticizing representatives of other positions? Is this an exhibition of human reason at work? Is this cross-criticism an office, an enterprise, of human reason? If this be accepted as the significant theory of human intelligence, it becomes a definition of education. And if this be education, those who reject it must be identified and exposed as enemies of education.

To hold any single metaphysical outlook as the single authority, and to reject other alternatives as non-genuine or false is to block inquiry and impose thought control. The rejection of alternatives as genuine eliminates the possibility of free choice and subjects truth to a predestined conclusion. Are there genuine alternatives to the experimentalist philosophy? Yes, and significant alternatives are to be found in all philosophic views that accept the concepts of continuity and change. Without too great a digression, there is an intellectual responsibility to be met and performed in a *research* into the three historic philosophic positions. And this task must be a continuing one if the factor of free choice is to retain its significance for this conception of human intelligence. Where are these genuine alternatives to the philosophy of experimentalism to be found? For example, Dewey states that:

The term 'naturalistic' has many meanings. As (he employs it) it means on the one side, that there is no breach of continuity between operations of inquiry and biological operations and physical operations. 'Continuity' on the other side, means that rational operations *grow out* of organic activities, without being identical with that from which they emerge.[6]

Kaufmann finds Cassirer stating: "Somewhere in the process of knowledge we must acknowledge a genuine 'mutation' which leads to something new and independent." And again that; "The unity of knowledge must be discovered in the progress of knowledge from its primary and primitive stages to 'pure' knowledge."[7] We find Dewey citing Whitehead;

The living organ of experience is the living body as a whole. Every instability of any part of it—be it chemical, physical, or molar—imposes an activity of readjustment throughout

[6] John Dewey, *Logic—The Theory of Inquiry* (New York: Henry Holt and Co., 1938), p. 18f.
[7] Felix Kaufman, "Cassirer's Theory of Scientific Knowledge," in Paul Arthur Schilpp, ed., *The Philosophy of Ernst Cassirer* (The Library of Living Philosophers; Evanston, Illinois, 1949), pp. 197, 188 respectively.

the whole organism. In the course of such physical activities human experience has its origin. The plausible interpretation of such experience is that it is one of the natural activities involved in the functioning of such a high grade organism. *The actualities of nature . . . must be explanatory of this fact. . . .*[8]

It is in these alternative philosophic views that we may locate and create genuine alternative perspectives. A profound problem remaining is to see to it that these alternatives find their significance in the affairs of human experience. These three historic philosophies represented by Dewey, Cassirer, and Whitehead accept continuity and change. And they can be turned to account and become significant if submitted to the problems of men.

Does the philosophy of education have a mission in the contemporary scene? Does philosophy of education have problems of significance? Yes. The problems of philosophy of education can be of significance *to men* if they advance and extend the course of reason *in* human experience. If this be the distinctive function of philosophy of education, will philosophers of education accept the responsibility? Will they know what they are doing?

If they do, they may make significant contributions in American education and perhaps may serve as gadflies to general philosophers.

[8] John Dewey, "The Philosophy of Whitehead," in Paul Arthur Schilpp, ed., *The Philosophy of Alfred North Whitehead*, 2d ed. (The Library of Living Philosophers; New York, Tudor Publishing Co., 1951), p. 644. Italics are Dewey's.

ON THE RELATIONS BETWEEN PHILOSOPHY AND EDUCATION

SUSANNE K. LANGER

Philosophy is the establishment of coherent meanings in the whole domain of thought. The domain of thought varies, of course, with the scope of people's factual knowledge and the range of their imagination. It may be predominantly factual; then its core is likely to be economic and practical thought, and its further reaches, hypothetical propositions, progressively verified and welded into the system of facts we call "science." Or, in some time and place, people's thought may center on personal and social values; then its core will be moral reflection, and its

FROM S. K. Langer, "On the Relations between Philosophy and Education," *Harvard Educational Review*, 26, Spring, 1956, 139–141. Copyright © by President and Fellows of Harvard College. (Reprinted by permission.)

widest sweep the other-worldly speculations of religious consciousness, sifted and settled into the tenets of a theology.

The establishment of coherent meanings is not a simple process, for which one could prescribe a clean-cut method, such as logical analysis and selection of premises for a system which may thereupon be expected to follow deductively, and to be both consistent, and adequate for direct application. Analysis, as a rule, only reveals a most amazing inconsistency of notions that were pragmatically acceptable for short-term theory, and an equally surprising inadequacy of such premises as could be made consistent. There is no set of premises to be got out of common sense, simply by analysis and selection. Analysis of commonsense notions is only a first step. After that, philosophy is the logical construction of basic concepts, a process of giving words adequate meanings; and that can be done only with a constant eye on the subject matter to which the new concepts will have to be adequate.

For this reason, a philosophical thinker has to know the field from which he takes his departure; and no philosophical construction is absolutely final. It is, at its best, sufficient. The sign of its sufficiency is that its concepts can be progressively elaborated to articulate more and more detailed problems. A philosophy invented *in vacuo* does not furnish such basic concepts; it allows one only to translate any previously posed questions and their previously given answers into a new, more satisfying language. All too many attempts to make psychology, sociology, or the special field of education scientific have yielded no more than such a translation into the language of some "ism"—empiricism, pragmatism, behaviorism, operationalism. An "ism" denotes an attitude, at best a set of conventions; but what is to be stated under those conventions remains essentially what was stated in commonsense descriptions, if not in loose metaphorical terms, before.

Scientists do far more philosophical work than they themselves realize. If a science grows suddenly, its facts fall into clear lines and its special problems proliferate so it seems to spread out in all directions, then its concepts are consistent and adequate; the philosophical work, at least for the time being, is done. But it may not be done for more than the scientist's purposes; outside his sphere it may prove utterly inconclusive. The extension of conceptual systems by more and more abstract formulation, until they become relevant to quite distant realms of thought and elastic enough to yield new structures there, different from those of the original content, is not work for scientists, but for professional philosophers. It is reflective, comparative work, not incidentally but essentially philosophical. It may illuminate other sciences, arts, morals, religions. It may lead into metaphysics, and then use the new metaphysical propositions in its own business.[1]

---

[1] I cannot agee with Dr. Price on the nature of metaphysics. ["Is a Philosophy of Education Necessary?" *The Journal of Philosophy* LII (October 27, 1955), 622–633.] Whitehead once defined a metaphysical statement as "the most general kind of statement we can make about reality." Such generality, ultimate for the time being, does not properly involve the relegation of the sensible world to a sphere of unreality, even if it does, as Prof. D. M. McKinnon says, "suggest the reality (and perhaps the greater dignity) of entities which lie beyond the limits of sensible experience and are regarded as in some sense conditioning the character of that experience." The "greater dignity" is a gratuitous factor imported into philosophy from religion, but it is what links the proper use of 'metaphysics' with another which Prof. McKinnon also adduces—"to refer to certain types of speculation to which philosophers, including some who would

A philosophical idea is like a stone dropped into water: its influence goes out in rings, over the whole domain if it is strong, or else until it becomes negligible. The center from which it spreads is the special problem, or complex of problems, which its proponent tried to clarify and had to recast, or even replace by altogether new questions.

There is, consequently, no topic unfit for philosophy, and no pre-eminent starting point. All the great philosophers started from some special interest, and developed, in its service, powerful ideas which carried far beyond the problems that first invoked them. Aristotle's greatest thought was what, today, we would call a philosophy of science—more precisely, of biology. His teleology, his doctrine of form and matter, his theory of mind bear the imprint of his central mediations on life, growth, proliferation, and the continuity of species. Plato's thought has a different stamp, for, as Prof. Broudy [2] remarked, it began in a philosophy of education. Yet both Plato and Aristotle, in the end, take in most of the intellectual issues that Greek religion, science, art, and political life had created.

The question of what should be the content of a philosophy of education is not answerable. Socrates began with a philosophical problem of education: What is teaching? His answer—not lightly proposed, but based on deep reflection—that teaching is a process of eliciting knowledge which is dormant in the pupil's mind, and bringing his own insights to birth—required for its further explanation the whole Platonic doctrine of the soul and its relation to the eternal verities. What, then, is the content of his philosophy of education? Where does that central sphere end and a wider sphere of metaphysics take over? And where does that metaphysical sphere, to which the speculative doctrine of Reality belongs, yield to the still wider one of the philosophy of value that contains the ultimate concepts of the Good, the Divine, the standards of beauty and life and truth? One may judge where the philosophical work on a confused discipline had best begin, but what it will ultimately draw into its domain and make its content is beyond anybody's ken.

Let us, then, ask the more practical questions: What are the sources of the vagueness, emptiness and incoherence that mark our discourse in the realm of Education [3] today? What do we mean by Education? The answers may be long and involved; but once we decide precisely what we mean by Education we should be in a position to judge such issues as Professor Broudy raised, e.g.: "Should religion be taught in the schools?" The definition of Education could probably not be given without some implication of its aims; and, as Professor Price said, it makes a great difference whether its ultimate aim be the glorification of God or the successful negotiation of a strictly terrestial life. Similarly it makes a difference in purely secular terms whether its aim is to develop each individual mind as fully as possible, or to favor

---

be called empiricists, are prone when they misconceive the character of those discoveries which they have . . . made." ["What is a metaphysical Statement?" Proceedings of the Aristotelian Society, N. S. XLI (1940–1941), 1–26. See p. 14.] To use an important term like "metaphysics" only to denote an intellectual foible is surely not good professional practice.

[2] "How Philosophical Can Philosophy of Education Be?" *The Journal of Philosophy* LII (October 27, 1955), 612–622.

[3] As this word was defined by Professors Broudy and Price in their respective essays.

special abilities that would be immediately useful to society, letting youthful interests, secondary talents, and idle curiosity die the natural death they usually meet after adolescence if they are not fostered; or even to ignore the personal equation altogether and build a strong nation of soldiers, as alike as possible in feeling, ideology, ambition and taste, who will take satisfaction in the advance of a "cause"—the power of their state, the fulfillment of a prophecy, the spread of a "way of life" or what not.

To determine the aims of education is probably the most urgent philosophical problem in the whole pedagogical field today; and it cannot but draw in vast further questions of the aims of human societies, the ultimate values that set up these aims, our basic ideals of society and individual life. Seriously pursued it may lead to entirely new definitions of "society," "life," "individual," "purpose," "action," and other terms, to some unpredictable number and perhaps in startling ways—until we find ourselves involved in a new formulation of our whole modern *Weltanschauung*, which is vague and dark at present, in this stormy age of transition to some new world that no one can yet foresee. Then it may well appear that this branch of philosophical study, the analysis of pedagogical ideas, is not a branch of a greater discipline at all, but a source, as every beginning from realistic problems is: that, indeed, philosophy of Education is simply Philosophy.

SOME PROBLEMS IN THE PHILOSOPHY OF EDUCATION

JAMES K. FEIBLEMAN

Philosophy is a field in which it is difficult to discover what the problems are, and education is in the same case; and so when we complicate the matter by raising the question of the philosophy of education we are in genuine trouble.

These statements need some elaboration.

A survey of the history of philosophy reveals at least this, that the problems change from time to time and the methods of solving them do, too. Such problems are rarely if ever solved; they are merely dropped in favor of other problems. At the present time, despite frantic efforts to free ourselves from this apparently frustrating situation, things are no better. It would be difficult and may even be impossible to set forth a single proposition about which all contemporary philoso-

FROM J. K. Feibleman, "Some Problems in the Philosophy of Education," *Harvard Educational Review*, 26, Spring, 1956, 150–153. Copyright © by President and Fellows of Harvard College. (Reprinted by permission.)

phers would be willing to declare themselves in agreement. Under these circumstances it seems fair to ask, why, then, continue philosophy? Here, again, there would be a division. Some would say, yes, why indeed! Others would observe, however, that while philosophers fail to find the ultimate answers they do submit proposals; and although professionally they regard each other's answers as interesting (or uninteresting) failures, other institutions latch on to such failures and raise them to the status of unalterable dogmas. The Roman Catholic Church has adopted the philosophy of Thomas Aquinas as official, for instance, while the Soviet Union has done the same thing with the philosophy of Marx and Engels. So the efforts of philosophers, you might say, have not exactly gone unnoticed, and others are more satisfied from time to time than the philosophers themselves. For while each serious philosopher has an answer, none has the final answer, no one answer, at least, that satisfies continued inquiry on all sides.

If we find the situation in philosophy confused, things are no better in the field of education. Empirical fields always seem more down-to-earth because in them things are *done*. But since what is done is changed from time to time in accordance with the theory of what ought to be done, we must not take this too seriously. What do we teach, and why; and what ought we to teach, and how? Ought we to teach didactic knowledge: theories and facts concerning what we have agreed upon, or rather ought we to teach how little is known and how to go about acquiring more of such tentative knowledge as we may? In either case, what we teach, we may be sure, will be superseded by what others who come after us have found to be better and more preferable, "better" for what, or for whom, and in what ways, again to be decided in terms of criteria which are not yet to be found among us.

When we put together the two fields of philosophy and education, then, we have the problem of the philosophy of education, and the situation which was before merely confused now becomes desperate. We began, let us say, with an elementary situation, for philosophy is necessarily elementary, and moved on to an advanced standpoint. No matter how elementary the contents of education may be, the presentation of it is bound to be complex; but now we have the further complexity confronting us of interpreting a complex situation from an elementary standpoint. And what do we get as a result? Singly-motivated structures. A metaphysical dogmatism advocated because it is metaphysical, or an established inquisitiveness advocated because it is not. We observe no effort to investigate a field of inquiry, only a determination to defend a corner, and the same monotonous determination whatever the corner. In the end, all absolutists hold inquisitions and prohibit more than they permit.

Executive action of an impulsive kind may be necessary so far as brute exigency is concerned, though even that much is to be doubted. Life situations can be handled with a great deal more tentativeness, with more subtlety and delicacy, than one might ordinarily suppose. Less than full belief may be required to act with less than positive firmness; and it is the open door with respect to as much of what we hold to be the case as possible that we want, if we do not want certain results in all instances as badly as we want steps toward the truth. But in speculative theory, deliberate forthrightness will not do. One wonders sometimes whether a speculative field is not empty after all, since those who ought to be exploring it are at war for its possession. We wish more to expand our boundaries than to investigate the whole area in which we have staked out a freehold. Before we can decide what position is best, ought we not to ask what positions are known? The investigation of ranges could precede rather than replace the selection of preferences.

We must ask the philosophers to inform us, then, what philosophies there are, and, so far as they can tell, what philosophies there could be, for not every position has yet been held nor every corner defended. Then we must ask the educators to perform something like the same task, to explore what teaching methods there have been and what there could be, what contents education has and what possibly it could have. And finally we must ask a special group, the philosophers of education, to engage in some sort of theory of matching, for the problem is so complex that we shall need some kind of logical guide to help us in putting together the proposed philosophical theories and the proposed educational practices; for the theory of the unity of theory and practice is a theory and not a practice, and requires a theory to precede the practice as in all cases of deliberate conduct.

Here, then, is the problem which confronts the philosophy of education considered as a speculative field. As a prerequisite for it, one particular condition has to be fulfilled. It is necessary to get into the frame of mind from which a presuppositionless standpoint would appear attractive. Freeing oneself from any and all positions in philosophy and in education requires a tremendous self-discipline to approach (for approach is all, since it can never be absolutely reached). It would be necessary first off to discover what positions one already implicitly held—an enormously difficult discipline. And then to get rid of them—an often impossible assignment. Philosophy, regarded in this way, requires almost complete devotion and almost continuous thinking. It is no mere exercise, like writing a book on a summer vacation. Getting rid of undesirable beliefs which may intrude themselves between the investigator and his problem—and absolutely any beliefs except the belief in the desirability of investigating the problem may come under this category when his problem is as fundamental as philosophical problems are apt to be—means getting rid of all beliefs, at least for this purpose and for the time being; and this in turn requires the anterior effort of discovering what these beliefs are.

The philosophy of education is a new field, and if we have attempted to set forth the ideal method for examining its problems in somewhat rigorous terms, this may be considered a theoretical ideal and as such a limiting case. Other interim possibilities exist and might be recited more briefly.

The fear of false knowledge is the beginning of wisdom. Most young persons begin their education by incorporating errors and half-truths as part of their standard equipment. Then education reassures the ignorant by intensifying the ignorance. The less we know, the more positively do we impart it to others. The result is not knowledge, for we do not in most cases trouble to furnish the evidence, but absolute beliefs. The awareness of ignorance ought to be part of the beginner's equipment, and this ought to be replaced gradually with evidence for the limitations of knowledge. We ought to learn what Socrates said constituted his most sage possession: how much we do not know. The half-way stage of partial but guaranteed knowledge with which we replace the unacknowledged ignorance of the unlearned is a limbo between ignorance and knowledge.

So much for theory; now what about practice? Here we find the same distressing situation. Gone are the trained senses of the outdoor workers, of the farmers and the fishermen; and in most cases these remain unreplaced by the ability to move easily among the abstractions, which the mathematicians, for instance, have. Instead, the preparation is for living in a half world prepared by the advertising copy writers under instructions from public relations counsels on the basis of what they have gauged a public to be prepared to accept, a world of formulas, of prejudices, of slick repetitions, in which the facts, and the theories concerning the facts (since we rarely know "the facts"), are either turned aside or deliberately ignored. This is what we might call the practical side of education: preparation for accepting more of what is as though it were what ought to be.

The results obtained by current methods are well known, but the problems which stand in the path of improvements are not for that reason easily solved. We have the problem, for instance, of mass higher education. Everyone knows how to read —and so reads the yellow press and the comic books; everyone learns something of what has been accepted of what has been thought—and nobody learns how to think. The result is a scarcity of original work in the arts, the sciences and philosophy. We develop our own educators but we have fallen into the habit of expecting to import our geniuses. We hold the line for the world, but fail to advance it ourselves. It is an achievement, but is it enough of an achievement? Not if the deepest of satisfactions are indications, for they are wanting.

We need to overhaul our profoundest decisions, to open every area to inquiry, to welcome self-criticism for its constructive aspects, to give over complacency, to put the positive values on the search for the answers and not on the answers themselves, to adopt facilitative principles, such as that nothing is known for the last time, to regard no reason as final and every practice as temporary. And where are these actions to be initiated? In the schools, yes, but also in the open forum. The possibilities of education are not confined to the young or to the formal methods of "adult education," though it is chiefly there that we need to hold theories explicitly and to make practices felt. There are no isolated fronts, where the battle against false knowledge is concerned, and no persons in whom the awareness of ignorance could not be inculcated with advantage.

At the same time we shall have to make sure that the errors of the past are not to be repeated in the future. The psychologists are at the present moment very much concerned with learning theory; memory awaits physiological analysis, and nobody studies belief. Learning is the method by which beliefs are acquired, memory is the technique by which they are retained, and conviction is the process by which they are held. And they are held in various degrees of strength. How do the aims of education get involved in this series of steps? By choosing what is to be learned, by judging what is to be remembered, by deciding how firmly to believe? At these points we encounter again the strongholds of philosophy; since value judgments are required, logical analyses are called for, and system-building is demanded.

And so we have come full circle to the topic of the relations between philosophy and education with which we began. Practice cannot be improved in any progressive fashion, in the complex cultures to which the modern world is committed, without some investment in the long look which the philosophers of education must hold to be their special even though not their exclusive province.

EDUCATIONAL PHILOSOPHY AND THE EDUCATIONAL PHILOSOPHER

GEORGE L. NEWSOME, JR.

Considerable attention has been given by educators, educational philosophers, and philosophers to a definition of the term "philosophy of education." Writers of texts on the subject, teachers of educational philosophy and related studies, and philosophers have all sought to define philosophy of education, state its peculiar aims, subject matter, scope, and the like, or to advocate in its place some autonomous discipline of education. Indeed, the numerous articles dealing with some phase of this problem which have appeared in *Educational Theory* in the past five years indicate the concern shown by educational theorists for the problem. The fifty-fourth yearbook of the National Society for the Study of Education entitled *Modern Philosophies and Education* reveals the interest of professional teachers of philosophy for educational philosophy. More recently papers presented at the meeting of the American Philosophical Association December 27, 1955 by Professors Harry S. Broudy and Kingsley Price [1] posed the problem of educational philosophy for more direct consideration by philosophers. The spring issue of the *Harvard Educational Review* followed up this issue by a symposium on the aims and content of philosophy of education.

Needless to say, various conceptions of educational philosophy which can be found in these many sources show that philosophy and educational philosophy can be, and in fact have been, defined in different ways. Philosophers, who have not

FROM *Educational Theory*, 9 (April, 1959): 97–104. Reprinted by permission of the publisher and author.
[1] See, H. S. Broudy, "How Philosophical can Philosophy of Education Be?" *Journal of Philosophy*, LII (Oct. 27, 1955), 612–622; and Kingsley Price, "Is a Philosophy of Education Necessary?" *Journal of Philosophy*, LII (October 27, 1955), 622–633.

yet defined their own discipline except to their own personal satisfaction, nevertheless, do not hesitate to try to define educational philosophy. This situation, however, is probably to be expected and, on the whole, might prove valuable in that
it might highlight areas of agreement and disagreement and bring forth new and
valuable ideas.

Philosophy of education, no doubt, has something to do with philosophy, since
the term "philosophy" is used. Philosophers, as we know, have not yet reached
agreement upon a definition of philosophy. Such statements as "philosophy is an
attempt to comprehend reality," "philosophy is an attempt to rationalize experience," or "philosophy is an attempt to see reality steadily and see it whole" all
depend upon what one means by "reality," "experience," or "wholeness."
Similarly, attempts to define philosophy in terms of its subject matter have failed.
Philosophers select their own subject matter and treat it as they see fit. Philosophers,
it seems, hold different opinions regarding the particular characteristics of philosophy as a branch of knowledge, although they seem generally to agree that it is not
a special form of activity apart from human problems.[2] In short, about all that
philosophers can agree upon concerning philosophy as a discipline is that it has
something to do with the problems of men. Educational philosophers might possibly
reach a similar agreement concerning educational philosophy.

Educational philosophy, no doubt, pertains to education. Education, like philosophy, is a term that is difficult to define. It can be defined in many ways, from the
narrowness of formal schooling to the generality of life. The indications are that
philosophers and educators have not yet come to any very general agreement upon
a definition of education.

If definitions of philosophy and of education can not generally be arrived at,
then any attempt to define philosophy of education in terms of them is hopeless.
Even if definitions of philosophy and of education were established it seems doubtful
that philosophy of education could be defined by mechanical linking of the two
definitions with an "and" or "of." Such a mechanical linkage would presuppose
two separate subject matters, two fields of endeavor, two sets of problems, and the
like. Secondly, it is presupposed that two such fields linked together would give
the field of educational philosophy in which the educational philosopher finds the
problems of his concern. It is highly doubtful that this is actually the case. The idea
of defining educational philosophy in terms of a definition of philosophy on one
hand and a definition of education on the other is a gross oversimplification of the
problem.

COMMON APPROACHES TO DEFINING EDUCATIONAL
PHILOSOPHY

How can the problem be effectively approached? First, let us look at several
alternative approaches. Some of the more common approaches may be classified
as follows:

[2] UNESCO, *The Teaching of Philosophy: an International Inquiry*, p. 185.

1. Regard educational philosophy as a point of view toward education.
2. Regard educational philosophy as the application of philosophy to education.
3. Regard philosophy as the generalized theory of education.

Under each of these generalized classifications there are various differences that should be noted, especially in the case of the second classification.

The first approach to educational philosophy seems to range from the common sense notions of "practical" schoolmen to systematic philosophies. Sometimes one hears or reads statements about educational philosophy that suggest that it is more or less one's own personal outlook and uncritical beliefs about education. For example, an elementary school principal expressed her philosophy of education by singing a little song called "Let's all Get Together." One often hears such expressions as "my philosophy of audio-visual aids is . . . ," or "my philosophy of lunchroom management . . . ," and the like which also suggest common sense notions.

In a similar manner one frequently encounters ideas concerning educational philosophy which suggest that people are by nature idealistic, realistic, and the like. These natural inclinations, however, need to be developed by formal study of "rival and conflicting" systems of philosophy. Such formal study will enable one, it is implied, to find their "philosophical home" and enable them better to formulate a "philosophy of life." Educational philosophy, then, becomes a study of philosophical systems in connection with education. Most of those texts in educational philosophy which set forth system by system such classical positions as idealism, realism, and the like seem to make these assumptions and imply this view of educational philosophy.[3]

The second approach to educational philosophy is probably the most common approach of all. The idea of applying philosophy to education does not mean that there is agreement as to how philosophy is to be applied, nor what is to be applied. Philosophy might be applied by applying the answers philosophers have given to various questions that might be of concern to education. Philosophy might also be applied to education by utilizing the methods, tools, techniques, and such of philosophy in investigating problems of formal schooling.[4] Philosophy can be applied to education in yet another way. One might utilize "world frames," systems of philosophy, and the like to explain or interpret education.[5] Finally, one can apply philosophy to education by deducing educational implications from systematic philosophies.[6]

The view that educational philosophy is an applied discipline in the sense that it

[3] For example, see, Rupert C. Lodge, *Philosophy of Education* (New York: Harper and Brothers, 1947), p. 1; and John T. Wahlquist, *The Philosophy of American Education* (New York: The Ronald Press Company, 1942) p. 12.

[4] "The Distinctive Nature of the Discipline of Philosophy of Education," *Educational Theory*, January 1954, p. 1.

[5] For example, see, The National Society For the Study of Education, Forty-First Yearbook, Part I. *Philosophies of Education.*

[6] For example, James N. Brown, *Educational Implications of Four Conceptions of Human Nature* (The Catholic University of America Press, 1940).

is the application of "unique theoretical tools" to problems of formal schooling[7] warrants further consideration. This view was apparently one that emerged from efforts of educational philosophers to make their field of study academically respectable. They, no doubt, wished to show that it possessed a "distinctive nature," and this distinctiveness was found in the "unique theoretical tools" employed and in what the philosophy was *of*. The theoretical tools named in the report of the committee could hardly be called unique to philosophy of education, nor for that matter even to philosophy. Sciences both natural and social utilize hypotheses, concepts and categories, and ideas of meaning, truth, value and method which were termed "unique theoretical tools." They also employ these tools in much the same manner as the report suggested. The idea of defining a field of study or work in terms of "unique tools" falls short of expectations. Carpentry, plumbing, auto mechanics, or any other activity can not be defined in terms of its tools alone. The artisan must also be considered. The committee, however, refused to consider the person using the tools. If they employed a person alleged to be a carpenter on this basis, they might be most disappointed in the results of his work, even though it is often recognized that a workman can be judged by the *condition* of his tools. Finally, in limiting educational philosophy to problems of formal schooling, the committee seems to have sawed off the limb that they were sitting on. How can one effectively deal with problems of education in isolation from the other activities of life?

The third approach to educational philosophy is probably one that has not received much attention. As Professor Axtelle has said, ". . . Dewey's conception of philosophy as the general theory of education is not only one of his most profound insights, but one of the most profound insights in the history of thought."[8] The insight, however, does not seem to have occurred to very many educators and educational philosophers. Indeed, it might well have never been evident to any except Dewey himself. Just what does this insight mean? What is implied in the idea that philosophy is the generalized theory of education?

Dewey thought that philosophy might be described in terms of the problems of social life;[9] that it *could not* be defined in terms of subject matter;[10] that it was reflective thinking which had generalized its place, value, and function in experience;[11] and that it was the general theory of education.[12] Such reflective thinking, however, required freedom to think and to inquire with no prior guarantee of the outcomes. He said:[13]

Freedom of thought denotes freedom of thinking; specific doubting, inquiring, suspense, creating and cultivating of tentative hypotheses, trials or experimentatings that are

[7] This is the view represented in a statement by a committee of the Philosophy of Education Society, "The Distinctive Nature of the Discipline of the Philosophy of Education," *Educational Theory* (4 : 1–3) January, 1954.
[8] George E. Axtelle, "Philosophy in American Education," *Harvard Educational Review* (26 : 184–189, Spring, 1956), p. 187.
[9] John Dewey, *Democracy and Education*, p. 378.
[10] *Ibid.*, p. 379.
[11] *Ibid.*, p. 381.
[12] *Ibid.*, p. 383.
[13] John Dewey, *Experience and Nature*, p. 222.

unguaranteed and that involve risks of waste, loss, and error. Let us admit the case of the conservative; if we once start thinking no one can guarantee where we shall come out, except that many objects, ends, and institutions are surely doomed. Every thinker puts some portion of an apparently stable world in peril and no one can wholly predict what will emerge in its place.

Dewey also thought that philosophy was not concerned with furnishing solutions to so-called practical and immediate problems, but rather in locating significant problems and devising methods for dealing with them, or as he stated it: [14]

Philosophy is thinking what the known demands of us—what responsive attitude it exacts. It is an idea of what is possible, not a record of accomplished fact. Hence it is hypothetical, like all thinking. It presents an assignment of something to be done—something to be tried. Its value lies not in furnishing solutions (which can be achieved only in action) but in defining difficulties and suggesting methods for dealing with them.

The fact that philosophy was hypothetical in character did not lead Dewey, however, to think that it was in any way a special discipline, or that it was in any way unrelated to the world of men and things. In fact, he urged that: [15]

Unless philosophy is to remain symbolic—or verbal—or a sentimental indulgence for a few, or else mere arbitrary dogma, its auditing of past experience and its program of values must take effect in conduct.

All of these conceptions of educational philosophy suggest a role for the educational philosopher. That is, the way in which one conceives of educational philosophy indicates the functions of the educational philosopher. If educational philosophy be thought of as a common sense view of education, then the educational philosopher functions at the common sense level. If educational philosophy is the study of "conflicting philosophies" or systems with a view of helping students find a comfortable philosophical home, then the educational philosopher is concerned with demonstrating conflicting systems and guiding students into consoling and personally satisfying positions. Where educational philosophy is conceived as an applied discipline, the educational philosopher is half philosopher and half educator whose chief function is to take what philosophy may give him and apply it as he can to education. The chances are that he is not a philosopher in his own right, but rather one who borrows from philosophy. As a borrower he borrows ideas, conceptual tools, methods, and the like from philosophy, or he borrows systems which might be milked for educational implications. When the educational philosopher becomes a borrower he is expected to return what he borrows, and, in some cases, pay interest on the loan as well. In any case, the borrower is servant to the lender. On the other hand, if philosophy is viewed as the general theory of education, the educational philosopher must be a philosopher in his own right.

THE EDUCATIONAL PHILOSOPHER AS A PHILOSOPHER

What does it mean to say that the educational philosopher should be a philosopher in his own right? First of all, it does not mean that he has to be a teacher of those

[14] John Dewey, *Democracy and Education*, p. 381.
[15] *Ibid.*, p. 383.

studies usually found in philosophy departments, nor that he has to be a member of group, faculty, or department labelled "philosophy." It does mean, however, that he must engage in philosophical activity, exercise the functions of a philosopher, and think and act philosophically. To do these things, he must think reflectively, think freely, doubt, inquire, cultivate hypotheses, infer consequences, think what the known demands, analyze, synthesize, and project ideas. Secondly, to be a philosopher does not mean that such thinking need be done apart from education nor that it be restricted to education. The philosopher does not just think, he, must think about something. What he thinks about are problems of men, what the known objects and events of life demand, what seems possible; in short, human experience and nature. Education, then, if it be life, or related to life, must be a concern of the philosopher. The philosopher can not effectively deal with education alone, however, for he can not treat education separately from the rest of experience. In short, he can not explain education merely in terms of education.

Were educational philosophers more concerned with defining philosophy in terms of philosophizing instead of in terms of distinctiveness of knowledge, their efforts might be more fruitful. The first two views of philosophy of education have notable shortcomings. They either fall into the trap of common sense or lead to what Sidney Hook called the "garulous absurdities" of supposing that an educational philosophy might be deduced from some systematic cosmology.[16] Let it be admitted that such educational philosophies can, and have, been deduced, but to suppose that they are more than symbolic and verbal is yet to be seen. It might be well to ask such philosophers how they know what they are doing.[17] Both of the first two views of educational philosophy seem to tend toward the formation of what has been termed useless theories of education. Foster McMurray has said:[18]

> While educational philosophers engage at second hand controversies of systematic philosophy and in finding implications for education, practical educators with no training in theory proceed with their own task of constructing and changing school programs.

Unfortunately for educational philosophers who hold the first two positions concerning educational philosophy, McMurray's statement can not be easily dismissed, nor well refuted in the light of factual evidence.

The alternative to the present dilemma is to stop thinking of educational philosophy as a self-contained discipline and begin to show concern for the functions of educational philosophers as philosophers. Disciplines suggest disciples, not philosophers. What can educational philosophy offer in this age of anxiety, conservatism, and transition? Could the answer be philosophical thinking rather

[16] Sidney Hook, "The Scope of Philosophy of Education," *Harvard Educational Review* (26 : 145–148) Spring, 1956, p. 148.
[17] For example, see, Otto Krash, "How Do Philosophers Know What They are Doing ?" *Educational Theory* (5 : 167–171, July, 1955). Krash suggests that failure to accept the principles of change and continuity leads to dogmatism and *a priori* reasoning. Are philosophers doing this when they seek to deduce educational theories from fixed systems?
[18] Foster McMurray, "Preface to an Autonomous Discipline of Education," *Educational Theory* (5: 129–140, July, 1955), p. 131.

than stories about philosophies, and ghosts from the philosophical cemetery? The challenge of philosophy seems to be to press forward, not regress; to philosophize, not merely talk about philosophy; and to seek to make students philosophers, not merely disciples. It is not the mission of philosophy to console the timid and faint-hearted, nor to defend vested interests, nor to publicize current practice. The aim of philosophy is criticism and vision, not complacency and hindsight. The means are critical and reflective thinking. The instrument is the educational philosopher upon whom so much depends.

If this conception of educational philosophy were accepted, the educational philosopher might come to feel less like a second-hand dealer in philosophy operating a shabby establishment on the lower end of academic avenue. Instead, he might come to think of himself as a philosopher and educator, a critic of the total culture, and as a thinker capable of developing new alternatives to present problems. He would not need to limit his activities to problems of institutions labelled schools. The school and its problems would be viewed in the total life situation of our times. The educational philosopher would not allow any subject matter boundary lines to prevent him from examining issues that were of living significance, for such issues could not be foreign to education formal or informal.

Although educational philosophers do not seem to have taken so radical and comprehensive a view of their field of scholarship, there now seem to be indications that a growing number of them are working in this direction. For example, Myron Leiberman (*Education As A Profession*) and L. G. Thomas (*The Occupational Structure and Education*) indicate that educational philosophers are bringing philosophy to bear upon real problems that heretofore have been outside the customary domain of educational philosophy. Theodore Brameld, in seeking to develop a reconstructed philosophy of education, has drawn upon many fields of scholarship and dealt with a number of pressing problems. Recent periodical literature also seems to reveal that there are a growing number of philosophers in education who are philosophizing about real and pressing social and educational problems. Finally, the quality of recent philosophizing in education seems to be of a high order. These trends point to the maturing of educational philosophy as a significant field of scholarship.

With the maturing of educational philosophy it might be expected that philosophers will give more attention to their own activity. They are likely to become more critical of what they do when they philosophize, and also more concerned about their role as philosophers. In so doing, they might become more concerned with the *how* of philosophizing and theory building. Just how do philosophers philosophize and build theories? Educational philosophers seek also to explain education. Explaining is one of the chief tasks of the philosopher; it is the foundation of his theories, or probably what his theories are designed to do. Questions of how philosophers explain and theorize raise questions concerning the use of categories, and classification, language form, definition, models, logic of inquiry and explanation, and ideas of systematic methods of explaining such as concepts of description and causation. More careful inquiry into questions of this sort might well help educational philosophers explain education in a more effective manner, and help them to build theories that can not be labelled "useless." Such inquiry might also help overcome a situation which has been described as follows:[19]

> The need for perspective and direction in such a critical area as education is plainly evident and to this end the discipline of history and philosophy of education can make increasingly significant contributions. One must add, however, that rigorous and scholarly research of high excellence in the discipline is conspicuously lacking.... There is great assiduity in accumulating knowledge about things educational, but disconcerting lack of systematic, integrating theory which would give meaning and significance to our efforts.... The fragmentary and ragbag character of a great deal of current educational research indicates slight evidence of the construction of such a theoretical framework.

[19] Frederick E. Ellis, "Historical and Philosophical Aspects of Education," *Review of Educational Research* (25: 5–11, February, 1955), pp. 5–6.

ON THE FUNCTION AND NATURE OF THE PHILOSOPHY OF EDUCATION

C. J. DUCASSE

Each of the two papers—by Professors H. S. Broudy[1] and Kingsley Price[2]—in the American Philosophical Association symposium of December, 1955, seems to me to answer satisfactorily in essentials the question to which it addresses itself. Only two minor criticisms, both concerning Professor Broudy's paper, occur to me.

1. *Professor Broudy's distinction between "philosophy" and "philosophy of."* The first criticism relates to the distinction, with which he introduces his discussion, between "philosophy"—meaning "logic, epistemology, metaphysics, aesthetics, ethics, and value theory in general" (p. 614)—and the various "philosophies of ..."; for example, "philosophy of law, science, history, and education." (p. 612)

This distinction, I believe, tends to obscure rather than clarify the nature and utility of philosophy in general and of the philosophy of education in particular, and is anyway artificial; for *all* philosophy is "philosophy of" something or other: logic is the philosophy of inference; epistemology, the philosophy of knowledge; metaphysics, the philosophy of reality; aesthetics, the philosophy of beauty

FROM C. J. Ducasse, "On the Function and Nature of the Philosophy of Education," *Harvard Educational Review*, 26, Spring, 1956, 103–111. Copyright © 1956 by President and Fellows of Harvard College. (Reprinted by permission.)

[1] "How Philosophical Can Philosophy of Education Be?" *The Journal of Philosophy* LII (October 27, 1955), 612–622.
[2] "Is a Philosophy of Education Necessary?" *The Journal of Philosophy* LII (October 27, 1955), 622–633.

and of art; ethics, the philosophy of conduct; value-theory, the philosophy of appraisals. Indeed, there is also the philosophy of philosophy—philosophical reflection concerning the nature, the content, and the utility of the philosophizing activity, whether in general, or as directed upon some special subject, such as education. And the true relation between *these* "philosophies of", and the more special "philosophies of" to which Professor Broudy refers, is that the issues with which the latter are directly concerned always ultimately turn on those to which the former directly address themselves. This dependence, indeed, is emphasized by Professor Broudy, and I am sure he would readily agree that it remains even if, as just contended, *all* philosophy is "philosophy of" something or other.

2. *Science, philosophy, and scientific method in philosophy.* My second criticism, which is also minor, concerns a statement Professor Broudy makes, and which I would myself make as positively as he does, but on very different grounds. The statement in view is that "it is dangerous to assert that any given class of problems are safe from scientific solution." (p. 616)

Professor Broudy interprets this as implying the possibility that science might so progress as eventually to do better than philosophy what the latter undertakes; so that science would then have put philosophy out of a job. I, on the other hand, do not think that is a possibility because the tasks to which philosophy on the one hand, and the natural or social sciences on the other, address themselves are as distinct as, for example, those of the carpenters and those of the plumbers who work on a house—although, of course, I do not mean that philosophy is analogous to carpentry and the sciences to plumbing, or the converse!

The sense in which I think the quoted statement is on the contrary true is that there is no reason why philosophy cannot, and every reason why it should, attack its problems in a scientific manner. For a scientific manner or method, no matter in what field of inquiry, is any method there capable of yielding knowledge properly so called, as distinguished from groundless or ill-grounded opinions, wishful beliefs, irresponsible speculations, or dogmatic assertions. Knowledge, in contrast with all of these, consists of beliefs based on evidence sufficient to prove or to render positively probable that the beliefs concerned are true. And I conceive that philosophy, since it commonly offers reasons—however often unfortunately flimsy and poor—for its assertions, purports to be seeking knowledge properly so-called, about the matters it occupies itself with.

Centuries elapsed before the practitioners of the natural sciences acquired a grasp on the particular forms which the general principles of scientific method have to take as applied to the problems of those sciences. Before that, irresponsible speculation was in large part the procedure there, as it has been and still is in philosophy, whose problems are far more elusive, and where the form scientific method has to take as applied to them has been correspondingly more difficult to discern. But in the last fifty years, philosophers have become rather less prone to write as if they were God's press-representatives passing out authoritative information from cosmic headquarters. Instead, they have concerned themselves increasingly both with the philosophy of science, and with the philosophy of philosophy; and with the question of what form scientific method must take as applied to philosophical subject-matter.

3. *Questions about the philosophy of education are metaphilosophical.* Leaving now these brief comments on the two papers mentioned, I shall next attempt to define the roles which, in attainment of wise solutions of practical educational problems, belong respectively to the philosophy of education and to empirical observation or experiment.

As we prepare for this task, however, it is of some importance to realize that it is not one of the tasks of the philosophy of education itself, but is a metaphilosophical task. For the question as to the nature, content, and utility of the philosophy of education, and as to the relation of the philosophy of education to empirical observation, does not arise *within*, but is *about*, the philosophy of education. Calling therefore as it does for philosophical reflection *not on education itself* but *on the philosophy of education*, that task belongs to the metaphilosophy of education; that is, to the philosophy *of the philosophy of education.*

That task, I believe, can best be approached by considering, in terms of a concrete educational problem taken as example, how man spontaneously comes to philosophize concerning educational matters, what his philosophizing then consists in, and what utility it has.

4. *How philosophical reflection naturally arises.* Philosophical reflection is not a mere spectator sport indulged in by idler contemplating human affairs without participating in them. Rather, it is something to which almost every man finds himself driven when he faces practical problems of a certain type, which I shall first illustrate by an example from the field of education, and then define in general terms. The example is as follows:

Some years ago in a Western city, the mother of a child of school age said to me that the public school to which he had been going for some time adhered to the theories of so-called Progressive Education, and apparently interpreted them in so irresponsible a manner that the boy was learning nothing. She had looked about for another and more efficient school, and the only one so located that it would be practicable for the boy to attend it was a denominational school. It had the reputation of doing a good job of teaching the regular school subjects, but it also indoctrinated its pupils with religious beliefs which diverged radically from those of herself and her husband. In this situation, she found herself unable to tell what would be the wise course to adopt.

Now, obviously, any reasons that happened to suggest themselves to her or to her advisers for choosing one rather than another of the alternatives actually open to her constituted the embryo of a philosophy of education. If those reasons had been developed, critically examined, generalized, and purged of inconsistencies, irrelevancies, and ambiguities, then, as thus systematized, they would have constituted a comprehensive philosophy of education. It would have made clear two things: (a) the nature of the various values that are at stake in educational decisions and that must therefore be taken into account, and (b) the various kinds of objective facts that have to be ascertained by observation or experiment, if one is to be in position to answer in a responsible manner puzzling educational questions that resemble in certain respects the question used above as example.

The point, however, which I now wish to emphasize is that *to make clear* what various kinds of objective facts are relevant to the decision to be made and have to be ascertained by observation or experiment is *one task*; and that *actually to make those observations and experiments is a different task.* The latter is not a philosophical task and therefore does not belong to the philosophy of education, but to objective observational or experimental inquiry whether at the lay or the scientific level. The former task, on the contrary, is one of the two essential tasks of the philosophy of education, namely, *to make clear* matters (a) and (b) described above.

5. *Features of the questions that give rise to the need for a philosophy of education.* The questions which give rise to the need for a philosophy of education are marked off from others by the following features:

i) They are questions, of course, that *concern education.*

ii) They are *practical questions;* that is, they concern a *choice to be made* between two or more alternatives.

iii) The choice is either as between *alternative means* available to a given end; or/and as between *alternative ends* attainable with the means possessed.

iv) They are questions as to which of the alternatives open to choice it would be *wisest* to choose.

v) They are questions which common judgment finds itself unable to answer responsibly with confidence; i.e., they are questions in whose case *doubt or dispute* actually exists, and where a responsible not an arbitrary answer is desired.

6. *The root problem of the philosophy of education.* We have now reached the point where we can descend from the metaphilosophy to the philosophy itself, of education. The root problem of the latter is of the same form as the root problem of each of the other "philosophies of." Just as the root problems of the philosophy of knowledge, of the philosophy of art, of the philosophy of morality, etc., are, respectively, What is knowledge? What is art? What is morality? etc. so the root problem of the philosophy of education is What is education?

The first part of the answer to this question is that education is a purposive activity; and the second part consists of an account of what differentiates education from the other species of purposive activity. Such an account is what will make clear the kinds of objective facts that are relevant to educational decisions. Before we attempt to supply it, however, we must pause to borrow from the philosophy of action an analysis of the nature of purposive activity in general, and of its several levels, for, without this, the statement that education is a purposive activity means very little.

7. *The nature and levels of purposive activity.* A simple instance of purposive activity would be that of a boy's shaking an apple tree in order to get the apples he desires. We have here a causal sequence, of which the successive steps are as follows. Assuming that the boy sees the apples and that the sight of them arouses in him the desire for them, we may take this desire as the first step in the causal sequence. The desire then immediately arouses from latency in the boy's mind his previously

acquired knowledge that shaking an apple tree causes apples to fall. Consciousness of this fact, together with desire for the apples, then causes the next step in the causal chain, namely, the act of shaking the tree; and the motion thus caused in the tree finally causes apples to fall. The boy's purpose of getting them is then attained.

The only essential difference between instances of *purposive* causation such as this, and instances of so-called *mechanical* causation, is that, in the former, a certain sort of psychological state, namely, a desire, or more broadly, a craving, constitutes the first event of the causal sequence; whereas in cases of "mechanical" causation, craving or desire does not enter.

The instance analyzed, however, was one where the activity was not only purposive, but *consciously* purposive—i.e., the agent knew what it was he craved —and not only consciously purposive but in addition *skilled*. This is the level of purposive activity most commonly in view when purposive activity is thought of; but it is not the only level nor the only important one there is; and, if our notion of purposive activity is to be comprehensive, its typical levels must be described briefly.

The first necessary remark is that "desire" is the name applied to a craving that not only is felt, but in whose case the person feeling it is in addition *aware of what would satisfy it;* for a craving may be felt but not be accompanied by such awareness. In such a case, it is a "blind" craving. Those of a new-born infant would be examples of this.

The next point to note is that the activity induced in a person by a blind craving may be either "autotelic" or "heterotelic." It is *autotelic* in cases where the particular form of activity which satisfies the craving is *innately* tied to the craving. Examples would be sneezing, coughing, etc. In such cases, what satisfies the craving is the very *performing* of the activity tied to it, not some ulterior event caused in turn by the activity.

The activities, however, that are commonly in view when one speaks of purposive activities are *heterotelic;* that is, what in their case satisfies the craving is not the activity itself, but some occurrence distinct from it, usually but not necessarily caused by the activity. In the boy's case, for example, what satisfied his desire was not the tree-shaking activity itself, which the desire induced, but the effect of that activity upon the apples—to wit, their fall within his reach.

The *lowest* level of heterotelic activity, however, is that where the craving is "blind" (in the sense that the agent is not aware of what would satisfy it), and where it causes a variety of more or less random acts. An example would be, in the case of a baby, the craving connected with itching.

If, however, a certain sort of perceived occurrence, e.g., that a certain skin area is getting scratched, turns out more or less regularly to satisfy the craving, then— whether that occurrence resulted from some one of the random acts stimulated in agent by his craving, or from some agency distinct from his own—the idea of an occurrence of that particular kind becomes associated in him with that particular sort of craving—this being what constitutes *awareness* on his part of what specifically he craves, and what therefore gives his craving the status of "desire" as distinguished from that of "blind" craving.

When the craving which instigates the activity is thus coupled with awareness of what would satisfy it, the activity may be termed *consciously* purposive. If it is of the tentative, "trial and error" kind, then it is consciously purposive but *exploratory*. This constitutes the *second* level of heterotelic activity.

The *third* level is that where the agent not only knows what it is he craves, but also "*knows how*" to obtain it, i.e., knows what sort of activity on his part would directly or indirectly cause the kind of state of affairs that would satisfy his desire. His activity is then not only consciously purposive, but in addition *skilled*—i.e., exactly adapted to bring about what will satisfy his desire—instead of exploratory.

The *fourth* level is similar to the third, except that at the fourth level the knowledge which shapes the activity and makes it successful consists of "information" in the sense of *conceptualized rules* of appropriate action, instead of (or in addition to) knowledge in the sense of "know how," i.e., of skill. At the fourth level, the activity is not only consciously purposive, but in addition *informed*.

Summarily, then, in heterotelic activity the agent may be:

1) blindly purposive and his activity then *random*; or
2) consciously purposive but his activity *exploratory* ("trial and error"); or
3) consciously purposive and his activity *skilled*; or
4) consciously purposive and his activity *informed*.

In the light of the preceding analysis of purposive activity, we may now examine the purposive activity called Education.

8. *The purposive activity called Education.* Evidently, education is a purposive activity at the conscious and in various degrees skilled or informed levels. In this connection, it should be noted that the "exploratory" status of a given would-be-educational activity constitutes no part of the description of that activity itself. That the activity happens to be one of the several "trials" contemplated in a "trial-and-error" program is plainly a fact external to and independent of the activity's own nature.

This being clear, we may now proceed to specify the features which differentiate education from other consciously purposive skilled or informed activities. Those features are as follows.

Education is activity of one or another particular kind A, by a person T (teacher); activity A being motivated by T's desire to cause in a person P (pupil)—who may or may not be the same person as T—a response of kind R, which T believes will immediately or eventually result in acquisition by P of some capacity C which T desires P to acquire; activity A being shaped by T's belief (i) that the existing circumstances are of a certain kind S; and (ii) that, under circumstances of kind S, activity of kind A by T would more or less probably cause or contribute to cause directly or indirectly in P acquisition of the desiderated capacity C.

9. *The objective facts, causal laws, and values relevant to wise educational decisions.*

The preceding analysis of the general nature of educational activity entails that in educational matters the following factors enter:

1) The educator or teacher, T
2) The educand or pupil, P
3) The educational activity A by T
4) The educational response R in P
5) The capacity C, which T desires P should acquire
6) The kind of circumstances S (AR) under which activity A by T would cause response R in P
7) The kind of circumstances S (RC) under which response R by P would generate capacity C in P
8) The values, positive or negative, intrinsic or instrumental, of various kinds, which (i) the *process* of acquisition of C by P, (ii) the *possession* of C by P, and (iii) the *exercise* of C by P, would have on the one hand for P, and on the other for such other persons Q as would be directly or indirectly affected by the process of acquisition, or the possession, or the exercise, of C by P.

The eighth item in this list calls for a few words concerning a distinction often overlooked when purposive activities are considered. If we agree to call the "target" of consciously purposive activity the occurrence which would fulfil the desire which caused the agent to engage in the activity concerned, then we have to distinguish between *satisfaction of his desire*—e.g., the boy's getting the apples he desires to get—and the *satisfactoriness of the object* which he desired to get and has got. Should the apples turn out to be "Dead Sea apples," uneatably bitter, the boy's desire for the apples he saw, though satisfied, would then be judged by him to have been *unjustified, unwise*; for they were desired for the sake of a value they were assumed to have but in fact did not have. Thus, what the *target* is, which a consciously purposive activity aims at, is one thing; the *value of hitting* that target is another thing; and the *value of the target itself* that has been hit is still another thing. As some of the men who have succeeded in winning the lady they wooed discover, the fact that something is desired and striven after does not insure that it is worth *having*, even if success in *getting* it has a certain worth.

As the business of the philosophy of education was described in earlier sections, it consists in *making clear* what diverse factors educational decisions must take into account if they are to be wise decisions. This is what the preceding list of eight factors purports to do. The first seven of these factors, and certain parts of the eighth, consist, in the case of any given educational decision, of what the concrete, objective facts and the objective causal relationships, of the listed kinds, actually happen to be. To ascertain them, empirical observation and experimentation are called for; but, as stated earlier, to *make* the necessary observations or experiments is *not* the business of the philosopher of education. More specifically, it is not his business for instance to investigate the character, intelligence, technical preparation, etc., of a given teacher; but only to make clear what kinds of positive or negative qualifications in him would be relevant to what particular kinds of educational tasks. Similar remarks would, of course, apply in the case of a given pupil. Again, it is not the business of the philosopher of education to make the objective inquiries which would be necessary to ascertain whether or not T's activity A in fact will or probably will cause response R in P; nor, if it does, whether response R will eventuate in acquisition of capacity C by P. These objective inquiries are the task of the psychologist, not of the philosopher, of education. Nor is it the latter's task to ascertain what the existing circumstances—physical, psychological, sociological, or other—actually are in the given case; nor how the process of acquisition, the possession, or the exercise of a given capacity C by P would affect such other persons Q as would be affected thereby.

On the other hand, it *is* part of the business of the philosopher—and in educational matters, of the philosopher of education—to make clearer than it commonly is what constitutes "moral" value; or "aesthetic," or "epistemic," or "practical," or "religious," or other particular kinds of *value*, which acquisition, possession, or exercise of a given capacity C by a person P, may have; and for the sake of which the educational process by which that capacity is developed in P is undertaken. And it is also part of the philosopher's business to make clear what the value called Wisdom consists in and depends on.

10. *Wisdom, and its factors in educational decisions.* A few words on this subject will now bring this paper to a close.

Wisdom is knowledge of what, *in given circumstances*, it would *on the whole* be best to do. This definition implicitly presents wisdom as what emerges out of knowledge of three different things together.

One is knowledge of the concrete, objective circumstances that exist in the particular case concerned, and that are relevant to the choice to be made of a course of action. Knowledge of those circumstances is gained by observation of them.

The second factor of wisdom is knowledge of such relations of causes to effects as are relevant to the choices of ends and of means one is called upon to make, under the circumstances which exist in the case concerned. More specifically, this means knowledge of the diverse effects which, in those circumstances, could be brought about by employment of such means as happen to be at one's command; and knowledge of what diverse means, among those at one's command, would alike be capable of bringing about a particular effect. Such knowledge of what in fact would cause what is gained inductively from experiments.

The third factor of wisdom consists in awareness of all the diverse values, positive and negative, intrinsic and instrumental, that would result from adoption, respectively of the alternative courses of action open to choice in the particular case; and in perception of which particular one of those courses would, all things considered, yield the greatest total of value.

This perception is bound to be somewhat different in different persons, since what one person values highly may have little value in another's judgment. This means that the final judgment as to what, for the person whose choice of a course of action is concerned, is the wise, i.e., the best, course to choose cannot be made for him by another. What another may be able to do for him is only to *enlighten* his judgment by pointing out to him particular existing circumstances, or particular probable objective consequences of one or another possible choice, or particular kinds of value those choices or their consequences would have, of which the person called upon to choose a course of action *was not aware*. But, once this person has been made aware of all these relevant matters, the final judgment has to be his own. He may, of course, later come to judge it to have been foolish instead of wise; but this is the judgment of the then different and wiser person he has become. The most that can be said for the contention that there is such a thing as objective, super-personal wisdom is that the more the judgments of different persons as to the wise course in a given case get *enlightened* in the sense just described, the less divergent will those judgments probably become.

PHILOSOPHY AND EDUCATIONAL THEORY

PAUL H. HIRST

Philosophers have not infrequently written on education and their ideas, until the recent spate of works by psychologists and sociologists, have exerted considerable influence in this field. The impact of empirical studies however, together with contemporary radical questionings about the nature of philosophy itself, has of late made educationists uncertain of the function of philosophy in educational discussion. Clarification here is urgently needed.

There are three particular views of the relationship between philosophy and education which I wish to discuss.

(a) The traditional view that from philosophy there follow directly certain implications for educational practice.

(b) The view that there is an autonomous discipline of education which draws to some extent on philosophical beliefs.

(c) The more analytical view that philosophy has a purely critical and clarificatory function for educational discussion.

I

It is often taken for granted, though rarely explicitly asserted, that from a set of philosophical beliefs there follow directly and necessarily certain clear explicit

FROM *British Journal of Educational Studies*, 12 (November, 1963): 51–64. (Reprinted by permission of Faber & Faber Ltd.)

implications for educational practice.[1] After all, is it not rather obvious that if people differ about the nature of ultimate reality they must differ in judging what is important in the school curriculum? Must not a religious person think religious education absolutely essential and an atheist think it thoroughly undesirable? Must not a western liberal democrat, because he holds different ethical doctrines, necessarily disagree with a communist on at least some issues in moral education? And must it not therefore be true that philosophical beliefs do determine clear educational principles which must be put into practice if obvious inconsistencies are to be avoided?

Certainly few people would wish to deny that a system of metaphysical, epistemological and ethical beliefs that provides a theory of what is ultimately real and ultimately important in life must have some significant contribution to make to educational ideas and practice. But whilst it is perhaps obvious that there is *some* connection between philosophy and education, the traditional view takes this to be one of direct implication assuming that thoroughly valid principles for determining educational practice can be readily inferred straight from philosophical beliefs. Even if we accept the view that philosophy is a body of beliefs of this kind, what is here said about its connection with education seems to me not only far from obvious but in fact quite untenable for two major reasons.

First I would suggest that the account is far too simple and that it thereby gives a seriously misleading picture of what is involved in making judgements on educational issues. It is too simple because it implies that on philosophical grounds alone we can satisfactorily answer certain questions about educational practice. This, however, is not so. By their very nature all such questions are necessarily complex and any answers based on philosophical beliefs only must therefore be regarded as ill-considered. No matter what one's ethical views may be, to ignore in issues of moral education what is known of the psychological development of moral understanding is bound to result in irresponsible judgements. Similarly to decide matters of curriculum content without due regard to social and psychological as well as philosophical considerations is quite indefensible. Whether we are thinking about particular practical decisions made whilst teaching or, as here, about the formation of general principles that state what ought to be done in practice, there are many diverse aspects to the issues that must be taken into account. The philosophical alone can never be sufficient for the task. I am not wanting to deny that on the basis of certain philosophical beliefs alone some valuable general statements about education can be made and that these have an important place in educational discussion. But I am wanting to deny what the traditional view implies, that such statements are adequately formed principles that ought to be allowed to determine our educational practice.

If this is so, it means that responsible educational principles need to be formed by a serious attempt to build together whatever knowledge, values and beliefs are relevant to the practical issues. And further, it means that between philosophical

[1] For a statement and criticism of this position, see H. W. Burns: The Logic of the 'Educational Implication,' in *Educational Theory*, Vol. XII, No. 1, 1962.

beliefs themselves and educational practice we must envisage a domain of theoretical discussion and investigation concerned with forming these principles. To this domain, which I shall refer to as educational theory, philosophical beliefs make their own distinctive contribution alongside social theory, psychological theory and so on. The traditional view that there is a direct connection between philosophy and educational practice either totally ignores, or heavily underestimates, the significance of educational theory in this sense. It fails to recognize the important truth that unless philosophical beliefs are to influence educational practice in a distorting manner, they must influence it indirectly through the medium of educational theory where they are considered conjointly with many other elements before any particular principles for educational practice are explicitly formulated.

In reply to this a traditionalist might argue that if the term philosophical beliefs is interpreted broadly enough it will embrace all the considerations that could possibly be relevant to judgements of educational principle. In this case, it would be true to say, after all, that educational principles do follow directly from philosophical beliefs. But this reply simply covers up the problem by a blanketing use of the term 'philosophy'. If the term is to be used so as to include psychology, sociology, and all else that is significant for education, then by definition the traditionalist is right. One can only protest at the refusal to recognize important distinctions and point out that without them we must give up all hope of distinguishing the role of philosophy in educational affairs from that of psychology, sociology, etc. For a purely verbal victory one must pay a very high price.

But secondly the traditional view is not only too simple in that it fails to recognize the many different elements that must go into the making of educational principles. It also suggests that these principles can be and ought to be formally deduced from our beliefs. And even if it is granted that philosophical beliefs are not of themselves adequate to the task, it might still be maintained that given all the necessary understanding whatever its nature, educational principles ought to be derived in much the same way as we can derive the theorems in Euclidean geometry from the axioms. This I think mistaken.

The process of deduction depends entirely on the formal manipulation of statements and the conclusions to which it leads are therefore based solely on what is actually and literally expressed in the premises. The process must begin with statements that cover quite explicitly all the considerations that are involved in the issues. What is more, all the concepts and terms that are used must be fully related to each other so that no gaps appear in the chains of argument. Deduction can never be used unless we can start with premises equal to the task, covering all the necessary facts and beliefs and relating these so that the conclusions are reached in a purely formal manner.

Can we then set out our beliefs and knowledge in series of statements so that from them we can work out deductively what our educational principles must be? There are several reasons why in general this is impossible. Sometimes when an issue is clear cut and the factors on which it depends are limited, deduction may be used, and small pieces of deduction may well occur too as part of some larger argument. But in general the complexity of practical issues is so great that it is quite impossible to set out explicitly all the facts and beliefs which must be taken into account. Nor is this difficulty simply one of time and space for the job. Many of the terms in which we express the knowledge and beliefs that are vital for educational issues are not exact and precise but vague and ill-defined. Terms expressing personal relations and moral values are notoriously lacking in the quite clear constant meaning that the deductive use of statements assumes. Again much of our relevant understanding is not expressible in literal terms but depends on metaphor, analogy and even paradox. Deductive arguments using, or rather misusing, such statements are quite valueless even when they make sense. In addition, to evolve educational principles by deduction certainly means using, amongst other statements, a set of moral principles, and whilst these can be used formally in this way, if they are, it means that morally speaking educational judgements are being produced by rule. Yet moral principles are never once for all rules whose formal implications should be invariably accepted. They need perpetual reconsideration and re-interpretation in the light of experience. If they are used formally to produce educational principles they are likely to be as destructive of what is good in educational practice as mechanical living is in everyday affairs. Finally, it is difficult to see how conclusions that depend on the putting together of considerations from practical experience, from psychology, social theory and philosophy, weighing them up, estimating their relative importance, could possibly be reached in an uninterrupted chain of deduction. The process that is employed generally is far removed from the formal manipulation of accepted statements, being rather a form of judgement based on as comprehensive a view of the issues as it is possible to get.

Once again I am not wishing to deny that from statements of our knowledge and beliefs we can by a process of deduction come to make some valuable statements for education. It is the adequacy of these as principles for practice that I am again questioning. For the reasons given above deduction seems to be a far too limited and in some respects far too dangerously perverting a method for us to work by it uncritically in this field. It follows from the nature of adequate educational principles that in general they cannot and ought not to be formed in this way. We need to think in terms of a much looser and much more open process of judgement to which philosophical beliefs, psychological and social theory, etc. contribute in their appropriate ways. Beliefs, knowledge of facts and values provide the grounds on which judgements of educational principle are made and it is by reference to these that we give the reasons for what we advocate. But this does not mean that there is some logically necessary connection between the knowledge and beliefs on the one hand and the educational principles on the other. It is not that we work out formally our conclusions from explicit statements which are the complete and necessary grounds for the resulting principles. It is rather that in the midst of a complex network of understanding which cannot be adequately and formally expressed, we form our judgements and in the statements which we use to express our reasons, draw attention to the major considerations which have influenced us. This being so, it is not at all surprising that people who agree to certain statements of their beliefs do often in fact advocate quite different educational principles. It is not at all uncommon, for instance, to find Christians who favour a secular school system and not a few atheists judge there to be good reasons for having universal religious instruction. Contrary to the crude assumption mentioned earlier, it appears on closer inspection that educational principles that are adequate for directing practice do not follow by simple deduction from philosophical beliefs. This is borne out by the fact that philosophical agreement is no guarantee of educational agreement and fortunately many educational principles are acceptable to the holders of very diverse philosophical views. This does not mean that philosophical beliefs are unimportant for educational theory, it means simply that the part they play is not that of axioms in a deductive system. Their role is highly influential but much more subtle than that envisaged by traditionalists, being part of a broad over-all understanding that lies behind all educational judgements. A philosophical system of considerable generality may of course greatly determine a set of educational principles even when other factors have been taken into account. It is then tempting to speak loosely of the principles as derived or even deduced from the system. This is however most misleading and it would be better to describe the principles as constructed so as to be consistent with the system. Consistency between beliefs and principles denotes nothing more than the absence of any contradiction between the two. This there must be, but it by no means follows that there must also be an explicit deductive chain that leads from the one to the other.

From this brief discussion of the traditional view, I suggest that in seeking to be clear about the connection between philosophy and education we must

(i) reject the idea of a direct relationship and instead recognize the importance of a field of educational theory concerned with the formation of educational principles, and

(ii) reject the idea that philosophical beliefs form some of the premisses for deducing educational principles and instead think of them as providing some of the reasons for the educational judgements we make.

II

If the traditionalist view underestimates the importance of what I have called educational theory, the second view I wish to comment on swings radically to the opposite extreme. There is here the impressive claim that the theory of education is an autonomous discipline. Philosophical beliefs and other branches of knowledge are said to contribute to this discipline but their contributions are assessed by criteria that arise within the theory itself. Educational principles are thus formed within a theoretical framework that is in some genuine sense free from, independent of, all other disciplines, including philosophy.[2]

[2] See F. McMurray: Preface to an Autonomous Discipline of Education, in *Educational Theory*, Vol. V, No. 3, 1955. Quoted and discussed in G. F. Kneller: Philosophy, Education and Separatism, in *Educational Theory*, Vol. XII, No. 1, 1962.

But what are the features of an 'autonomous discipline' and are these the features that characterize educational theory? Disciplines may be demarcated from one another in more than one way. Physics, for instance, may be demarcated from chemistry because it deals with a different range of related physical properties and in so doing develops techniques peculiar to itself. The two studies have distinguishable subject matters. Yet they have many points of contact and are not in any final sense separable from each other. What is more they share the same theoretical or logical structure and both rest firmly on empirical tests. They cannot be distinguished from each other in terms of any particular types of judgement that they use, only in terms of the particular subjects with which they deal. On the other hand it is maintained by some that physics and history, though they too have many points of contact can be distinguished not only in their subject matters but also in terms of their logical forms. Historical explanation is said to involve a type of judgement which the natural sciences, including physics, do not employ.[3] To explain why Hitler invaded the U.S.S.R. in 1941 depends on the use of evidence and the putting together of many strands of knowledge and conjecture in a way that has no parallel in the explanation of why it is a stick looks bent when standing at an angle in water. It is in fact in terms of distinctive types of judgement that disciplines are usually said to be autonomous. It can be claimed that history is just such an autonomous discipline. It is not claimed that there is no use of other forms of knowledge and judgement here, indeed historical explanation usually depends on a great deal of scientific investigation. But historical knowledge is said to be not entirely dependent on the forms of judgement that are used elsewhere, in some important respects historical explanations are sui generis and unique in character. Perhaps the most frequent claim of this kind is made for the autonomous character of moral judgements. These may depend on many facts and much experience, but the judgements themselves are unique in kind, clearly distinguishable from all others, for instance, those of an aesthetic or factual kind.

What then about educational theory, does it contain any unique forms of judgement? As we cannot lay down a priori that this is or is not impossible the only way for the question to be decided is for those who claim there are such to produce examples of these judgements. As far as I am aware no judgements of quite this exclusive character have been shown to occur and it is therefore difficult to accept the claim in this extreme form. The formation of educational principles does certainly involve particular acts of judgement and these do not seem to be of a kind that occurs in the pursuit of theoretical knowledge in say the sciences or history. These are in fact practical judgements as to what ought to be done in education made on the basis of much knowledge and experience. In this way educational theory draws on a great variety of specialist disciplines, but consists of much more than a collection of isolated pieces of knowledge. A building together of these elements occurs when in the judgements rational educational principles are formed. Practical judgements are, however, not unique to educational theory for

[3] See W. Dray: Laws and Explanation in History, O.U.P. 1957 especially chapters II and V.

in everyday affairs and in political and social theory, for example, the same process is to be found. I would suggest that educational theory is one of a group of related theories each concerned with making similar forms of judgement, much in the same way as the various physical sciences form a related group. It is their concern to answer questions about intentional practical activities by making practical judgements that distinguishes this group of theories from other groups. And within the group it is the particular constellation of activities we label 'educational' that determines in the first place the scope of educational theory.

Because of the nature of the questions with which it deals educational theory is dependent on a particularly wide range of knowledge and experience. It does not however seem to me correct to speak of the theory as developing criteria of its own for assessing the knowledge and beliefs on which it draws. These forms of under-standing are valid in their own rights and must therefore be accepted into the theory as they are. As their function is to provide a wider knowledge of what is involved in educational practice and so promote more responsible judgements, it is difficult to see how the knowledge itself can be assessed by criteria within the theory. The theorist has to recognize or discover the relevance of other specialist studies for education, taking these into account when he forms his principles.

If then educational theory is not in the strictest sense an autonomous discipline, it is nevertheless a distinctive theoretical pursuit which

(i) is distinguishable like all other disciplines by the particular questions which it seeks to answer, in this case questions about a certain group of practical activities, and

(ii) is dependent on many branches of learning, including philosophy, the understanding thus drawn on being the basis of practical judgements.

III

Though both the views I have commented on are quite widely held in educational circles, neither of them has been expounded or criticized at any length in recent British writings. The third view I wish to discuss has, however, received fairly detailed treatment by Professor D. J. O'Connor in his book 'An Introduction to the Philosophy of Education'. Early in this volume the author makes it clear that in his view 'philosophy is not in the ordinary sense of the phrase a body of knowledge, but rather an activity of criticism or clarification' that 'can be exercised on any subject matter at all, including our present concern, the problems of educational theory'. This analytical activity is not 'a kind of superior science' which can 'be expected to answer difficult and important questions about human life, and man's place and prospects in the universe' by using special techniques.[4] It is better understood as an attempt to answer questions where the meaning of terms and their relations to each other have produced complex and far reaching difficulties in

4 D. J. O'Connor: *An Introduction to the Philosophy of Education*, Routledge and Kegan Paul, 1957, p. 4.

our understanding. Problems of this kind certainly arise when we are trying to formulate educational principles and philosophy has thus a distinctive contribution to make to educational debate. Quite clearly O'Connor assumes the distinction between philosophy and educational theory that I have previously urged, but his elaboration of the relationship between the two is largely a consequence of his idea of educational theory. Whilst in general his view of the nature of philosophy seems to me acceptable as far as it goes (and to this I will return), his account of educational theory is, I think, open to serious criticism. Indeed there are good reasons for thinking his account unsatisfactory whatever one's attitude to his philosophical position may be.

Professing to look for the 'job an educational theory is supposed to do',[5] O'Connor first distinguishes four main senses of the word 'theory', two of which seem to be important in educational contexts. In one of these, theory is contrasted with practice and here the word refers to 'a set or system of rules or a collection of precepts which guide or control actions of various kinds. . . . Educational theory would then consist of those parts of psychology concerned with perception, learning, concept formation, motivation and so on which directly concern the work of the teacher.'[6] In the other, the word 'theory' is used as it occurs in the natural sciences where it refers to a single hypothesis or a logically interconnected set of hypotheses that have been confirmed by observation. It is this sense of the word that is said to provide us with 'standards by which we can assess the value and use of any claimant to the title of "theory". In particular this sense of the word will enable us to judge the value of the various (and often conflicting) theories that are put forward by writers on education.'[7]

Judged by these standards, a great deal of educational theory certainly comes off rather badly. For as O'Connor himself states, educational discussions are not usually entirely empirical in character but include as well value judgements and appeals to metaphysical beliefs. These other two elements differ quite radically from the first as his earlier analysis of them has shown. Of metaphysical statements it is said that we have no way of confirming what they assert and that we cannot even be sure that they have any cognitive meaning at all. Their contribution to educational theory is therefore of very doubtful value. The importance of value judgements in this field is not questioned and O'Connor's chief concern is that we should recognize them for what they are so that we do not get into muddles by confusing them with assertions of fact. Nevertheless he concludes:

We can summarize this discussion by saying that the word "theory" as it is used in educational contexts is generally a courtesy title. It is justified only where we are applying well established experimental findings in psychology or sociology to the practice of education. And even here we should be aware that the conjectural gap between our theories and the facts on which they rest is sufficiently wide to make our logical consciences uneasy. We

[5] *Ibid.*, p. 74.
[6] *Ibid.*, p. 75.
[7] *Ibid.*, p. 76.

can hope that the future development of the social sciences will narrow this gap and this hope gives an incentive for developing these sciences.[8]

The first thing that must be said about this account is that O'Connor has singularly failed to do what he set out to do—to discover the job educational theory performs. If in fact he had begun to discover this a very different picture of the theory would certainly have emerged. In addition, because of his obsession with scientific theory as a paradigm for all theories, he totally misjudges the importance of the non-scientific elements that he himself diagnoses in educational discussions. In the last analysis metaphysical statements and value judgements are dismissed as not being elements that fundamentally characterize this field of discourse.

If we accept O'Connor's classification of the two main senses of the word 'theory' that are important for education, it is surely the first of these that gives the primary meaning here, not the second as he suggests. Educational theory is in the first place to be understood as the essential background to rational educational practice, not as a limited would-be scientific pursuit. Even when O'Connor momentarily recognizes this, he nevertheless fails to realize the complex kind of theory that is necessary to determine a whole range of practical activities. He therefore falls back on his scientific paradigm maintaining that the theory must be simply a collection of pieces of psychology.

Yet the theories of science and the theories of practical activities are radically different in character because they perform quite different functions, they are constructed to do different jobs. In the case of the empirical sciences, a theory is a body of statements that have been subjected to empirical tests and which express our understanding of certain aspects of the physical world. Such tested theories are the objects, the end products of scientific investigation, they are the conclusions of the pursuit of knowledge. Where, however, a practical activity like education is concerned, the place of the theory is totally different. It is not the end product of the pursuit, but rather is constructed to determine and guide the activity. The function of the theory is to determine precisely what shall and what shall not be done, say in education. The distinction I am drawing between scientific theory and say educational theory is the traditional distinction between knowledge that is organized for the pursuit of knowledge and the understanding of our experience, and knowledge that is organized for determining some practical activity. To try to understand the nature and pattern of some practical discourse in terms of the nature and pattern of some purely theoretical discourse can only result in its being radically misconceived.

If the theories of theoretical knowledge must be clearly distinguished from the theories of practical knowledge because they fulfil quite different functions, we must also recognize that practical theories will differ considerably amongst themselves because of the very different kinds of practical activity with which they are concerned. In some cases, as for instance in engineering, the theory is largely a reorganization of scientific theory. In the case of medicine, other elements includ-

[8] *Ibid.*, p. 110.

ing certain moral values are involved. Education being the kind of activity it is, the theory must range right across and draw from many kinds of knowledge, value judgements and beliefs including the metaphysical, the epistemological and the religious. All these must contribute to the peculiar character of the theory.[9]

At the beginning of his book, O'Connor gives the impression that philosophy, even of the strictest analytical variety, has some genuine contribution to make to educational theory. As the work proceeds, greater and greater importance is attached to the scientific ideal for that theory, and the contribution that philosophy can make seems to grow less and less. The final impression that is left is that philosophy is no more than an accessory to the theory, useful only when difficulties of a logical or conceptual kind arise. If we reject the scientific model as thoroughly false and artificial, with it there can go too the idea that philosophy is of only peripheral significance, even if by philosophy we still mean an analytical activity.

From this contemporary point of view, philosophy does not directly lead to knowledge about the world or about ourselves, it is in fact a study of the meanings of the terms in which such knowledge is formed. If the sciences and humanities are said to be first order subjects because they seek to describe and explain the world, philosophy can be said to be a second order subject because it seeks to describe and explain the way in which first order subjects do their job.[10] In this double-decker system, lower deck activities are concerned with understanding the world, upper deck activities with understanding what goes on on the lower deck. Seen in this way, philosophy has a contribution to make to educational theory wherever second order understanding is necessary, wherever we need to know about the nature of human knowledge, about the meaning of particular concepts and so on. If educational theory is thought of as scientific in character, then this kind of understanding may well seem of only fringe significance. If however the theory is as complex as has been suggested above, it may well be of quite central importance after all.

I suggest therefore,

(i) that to think of educational theory after the pattern of scientific theory is to fail to understand the function it performs as a background to educational practice and therefore to misconceive its nature, and

(ii) that if philosophy is understood as a second order activity, there is no a priori reason to think that it has little or no significance for education; what is needed is a thorough investigation of the ways in which understanding of this kind enters into a theory concerned with the making of practical judgements.

IV

On the basis of what has already been said about the nature of educational theory and about philosophy as a second order subject, I should like to add a few very tentative comments about the relationship between the two.

[9] For a fuller discussion see L. A. Reid: *Philosophy and Education*, Heinemann, 1962, ch. VI.
[10] See A. J. Ayer: Philosophy and Language, an Inaugural Lecture, O.U.P. 1960.

By the nature of the case, philosophy will be related to educational theory in the formal sense in which it is related to other fields of discourse. It is second order to this theory in the same way as it is second order to scientific theory, legal theory and so on. Because of this, philosophy is of value whenever difficulties arise about the meaning of terms in educational discussion. 'Equality of opportunity', 'subject-mindedness', 'the education of character' are examples of phrases of uncertain meaning which cause genuine difficulties in educational debate. They are all in need of careful philosophical clarification. But clarification of this sort does not contribute to the basic first order knowledge that the theory draws on. The philosopher is doing a formal job, clearing the lines of understanding, helping to make plain what the fundamental issues are. In a similar way philosophy can be of use to the sciences, for though it can contribute nothing of substance to them, it can contribute in this formal way when problems of meaning arise. Yet the significance of philosophical work in these two fields is very different. Generally speaking the sciences depend little on this kind of clarification for it is part of the scientific pursuit itself to construct and refine the concepts used so that they clearly express what is understood about the world. This they do directly against the empirical evidence. As has been repeatedly stated, educational theory is not developed in this monolithic manner, but depends upon the bringing together of many diverse elements of understanding to form a composite theory in which practical judgements are made. In such a complex activity, serious problems of meaning frequently occur and in particular a failure to understand the relations between different fields of discourse befogs many educational issues. Behind certain questions of planning there lies the difficulty of knowing what we mean by this concept 'equality of opportunity' and how we are to reconcile it with an equally difficult notion, that of 'the freedom of the individual'. In dealing with questions of moral education we must be able to relate together all the relevant understanding that we have from moral insight, religious beliefs and accounts of psychological development, etc. The formal contribution that philosophy makes to educational theory in cases of this sort is surely of major importance. If philosophy is an accessory to the theory then it would seem to be rather like some crucial tool without which it is hard to see how the various bits of the machine can be put together.

But besides this formal contribution to educational theory, philosophy does also seem to contribute to its 'substance'. Philosophical analyses are themselves part of the basic evidence on which certain judgements of educational principle are made. They constitute one of the diverse elements that are brought together as the material out of which educational theory is built. To take again the example of moral education, it is not enough when dealing with questions in this area to have moral insight, psychological knowledge and religious beliefs and be able to relate all this understanding. We must also know what moral judgements are, how they differ from other judgements and how they are justified. Only with knowledge of this kind can we be aware of a great deal of what moral education is about. Similarly in discussing the place of the physical sciences in education and the content of courses in them, an understanding of the nature and scope of these sciences is

indispensable as well as much scientific knowledge, a grasp of the psychology of
scientific understanding, an awareness of society's scientific needs and so on.
Educational theory needs then the aid of philosophy in a 'substantial' sense for it
needs understanding which only philosophical investigation can provide. It would
seem that the analytical philosopher can after all be said to contribute philosophical
beliefs to educational theory, but because of their particular second order character
he would wish to distinguish them from other beliefs, say religious and moral,
which the theory will include.

In an attempt to make out an exclusive field for philosophy of education, it
might be maintained that only the formal function of philosophy for the theory is
strictly speaking its concern, moral philosophy, philosophy of science and other
branches being able to make the 'substantial' contribution. Such a distinction is, I
think, unfortunate. In practice the distinction between the two functions is almost
impossible to draw, for the 'substantial' contribution of some piece of philosophical
analysis to the theory is likely to provide help in formal clarification too. In addition many of the problems of formal significance have been discussed by philosophers in other contexts so that philosophy of education in this sense would not be
unique in its subject matter. What is important is not any dispute over labels, but a
recognition of the distinctive character of the contribution that philosophy makes
to the theory and an awareness of the extent to which it is necessary.

V

From this discussion the following conclusions about the relationship between
philosophy and education can be drawn.

1. A satisfactory account of the relationship turns on
(a) the recognition of a distinctive body of theory whose function is the determination of educational practice, and
(b) the clarification of the distinctive contribution that philosophy makes to
educational theory.

2. Educational theory is thoroughly composite in character and is not on the
one hand describable after the pattern of some other theory, but neither is it on the
other hand in a strict sense autonomous. Such misunderstandings of its nature only
serve to distort any attempt to clarify its relationship to philosophy.

3. Educational theory is distinctive because of the particular questions with
which it is concerned, questions about a range of intentional activities. It is the
theory which in practical judgements determines what ought to be and what ought
not to be done in educational practice.

4. Understood as a second order activity, philosophy contributes both formally
and in a 'substantial' sense to educational theory. This contribution is in part one
of second order, or philosophical, beliefs.

5. Though educational theory must be built so as to be consistent with some set
of philosophical and other beliefs, it is not in general deduced from these and there

is no logically necessary relationship between the two. As in addition the theory is by no means entirely philosophical in character but radically complex, 'educational theory' seems to me a much less misleading term for it than the more traditional phrase 'a philosophy of education'.

6. The term 'philosophy of education' is perhaps best used to refer to the comprehensive contribution of distinctively philosophical methods of investigation to the discussion of problems that occur within educational theory.

These conclusions are of more than theoretical interest. There is a marked tendency for those involved in the work and teaching of philosophy of education to look at things from a firmly traditional angle, seeing educational theory as largely determined by philosophy. The result is frequently a very superficial consideration of the vast field of philosophy in general and an attempt to draw some educational principles from this without serious appeal to other fields of knowledge. It has here been contended that the function of philosophy for educational theory is more rightly understood and better exercised by working in the opposite direction. This means starting with questions about educational practice that occur within the theory, philosophical clarification and understanding being directly brought to bear on the principles that these involve. Educational theory is primarily concerned with making practical judgements in answer to practical questions and it looks to philosophy and other studies for the particular forms of help they can provide. But educational practice brooks no delay and it often seems that whilst philosophers are busy debating the possible implications of certain beliefs for education, the philosophical contribution that educational theory really needs goes by default. There is indeed a pressing need for the development of philosophically informed educational principles but these can only be achieved if those engaged in the work and teaching of philosophy of education direct their attention to philosophical questions that arise from specific educational issues.

TOWARDS A PHILOSOPHY OF EDUCATION

PETER C. McNAUGHT

Questions regarding the origin and status of a philosophy of education are accepted as perennial. Yet recent discussions emerge clearly as more than the products of a natural desire for intellectual satisfaction. They express a fundamental hunger for

FROM *International Review of Education*, 10 (1964): 257–262. (Reprinted by permission of the publisher and the author.)

well-founded theory arising from the recognition, more widespread than ever before, that education devoid of a philosophy may become simply "a bag of tricks".

G. H. Bantock [1] has recently pointed out that although societies change and so do systems of education, it is invalid to assume a necessary connection between these events, and from this to argue a moral obligation on the part of education today to respond to what the author terms "vacillating social pressures". We have to ask ourselves again what we take to be the distinctive features of a philosophy of education properly so-called.

The word "philosophy" has itself fallen into a measure of disrepute. Professional philosophers are disinclined to the construction of systems: analysis rather than synthesis is often taken to be the mark of philosophic maturity as the contrast between Wittgenstein's earlier and later work clearly shows.

If we further exclude the case where the phrase *philosophy of education* is employed simply as a more pretentious way of stating an opinion, we come to the crux of the problem. People do, by reflection, arrive at a series of what they believe to be *desirable goals* which imply certain curricula and particular class-room methods. Implicit in this kind of thinking is the idea that *desirable* is to mean more than that something could, as a matter of fact, be desired. To establish compulsively, bindingly, the obligatoriness of these aims, one must have recourse to the possibility of deducing one's educational philosophy A) from a logically prior system or B) according to an intrinsic discipline. I shall now examine the first possibility.

A

The deducibility of a social ethic from the study of history has exercised an irresistible attraction upon several philosophers. The detection of a real direction in human events would, it was thought, permit the deduction of particular courses of action from general truths.

In this sense, a philosophy of history could claim a universality of relevance to all aspects of the human condition. In this sense, too, it might hope to press the categorical right to inform one's thinking in the field of education.

The basis of this claim, whether urged by St. Augustine or Hegel, has never been a rigid Determinism. Such an account of the history of man might render certain principles intelligible only at the expense of abolishing the possibility of choice and hence the idea of moral obligation.

The intention has been to dissolve the problem by underlining the secondary influence of human agency. In K. R. Popper's [2] words: "It (historicism) does not teach that nothing can be brought about, it only predicts that neither your dreams nor what your reason constructs will ever be brought about according to plan. Only such plans as fit in with the main current of history can be effective." The wise will be those who discern and perform their role as "social midwives".

[1] Bantock, G. H., "Education and Society." *The Educational Review* 1963, vol. XV, no. 3.
[2] Popper, K. R., *The Poverty of Historicism.* London: Routledge 1961, p. 49.

It would not be too difficult to show the basic philosophic difficulties in such a position. Even if an account of history remarks only general characteristics and thus preserves the case for human libertarianism, it is hard to see how an ethical obligation is to be derived from a series of general statements about the relatively small part of the past which is known to us.

This general defect in historicism is aggravated in the hands of certain of its classic exponents. Having surveyed the Hegelian premises and conclusions, Jacques Maritain[3] rejects them as the work of "a kind of philosopher-God re-creating not only history but the whole universe". Other critics have concentrated on Hegel's imprecision in language, the chauvinism of his predictions, the conniving at unpalatable fact. The only significant refutation however, of Hegel or of the historicist position in general, is the criticism that to apply to history a selectivity demanded by a theory which is itself selectively derived, is doubly invalid.

It is true that present-day philosophers of history such as Toynbee and Maritain reject such approaches but their avoidance of rigidity relies on qualifications for every short step taken. One feels their caution rather than conviction. They provide a properly academic corrective rather than a doctrinal basis for a philosophy of education.

The basic inadequacies of "millennium" theories, Hegelian, Marxian or otherwise have always been obscured by their emotional contagion, their remarkable power of presenting life as a clear challenge in which all the mental and physical energies of man are to be harnessed now to create a new society. I think it wrong to argue that this fervour of creation, of experimentation, is an illusory emotional accompaniment to such a plan. It is a tertiary quality always experienced by man as system-builder, creator of a new order. It is the thrill of entering into an understanding, an obligation, a purpose. This is the lesson which even an authoritarian system clearly teaches. The real nature of things is thus revealed by action and realisation rather than by reflection alone. Yet, paradoxically enough, the nature of future events is already prescribed by the Marxist logic of history. The details are unknown but, on this view, one always knows their ontological structure.

If history has a meaning which is within our grasp, it seems unlikely that it would take the form of a final solution to all problems. Only an authoritarian system would claim to have distilled the meaning of events so clearly that a philosophy of education could or should be derived from it. Undeniably a *logically prior system* is made available. Those who reject the price demanded must look elsewhere.

The second possible source of a valid philosophy of education is a complete system of philosophy—an epistemological and ethical interpretation of the real nature of things. This could fairly claim to be regarded as a *logically prior system*. Yet this is precisely what philosophy, particularly in the West, has not produced. It is not sufficient to say that a fragmentation of society, undermining of traditional class systems naturally leads to a drying up of progressive theory. On the contrary, periods of rapid social change such as the Renaissance, the Reformation, the French and American Revolutions all produced a rethinking of the meaning and

[3] Maritain, Jacques, *On the Philosophy of History*. London: Geoffrey Bles 1959.

purpose of life, a re-definition consequent upon this of the nature of government and community, social right and obligation.

Philosophy today claims essentially to be a method, a series of recommendations and caveats about the use of language. It has been preoccupied with the role of clearing up the errors of previous philosophy and rejecting their pretensions to system-building. All that is now certain is the history of philosophy. The powerful influence of Hume is everywhere as if the last word had been said. What are the grounds for rejecting one set of beliefs in favour of another? It depends, we are told, on what you want to do. This is, of course, no help with the only real question of what we *should* do. Even if we accept Dewey's[4] tenet that the teacher is not in the classroom "to impose certain ideas or form certain habits", he is still left with the problem of choice: what to teach and why, if he is to "select the influences which shall affect the child".

Concern of this kind is the beginning of philosophy in that it seeks to establish some order from transient fact, some significant form in which can be reconciled one's most persistent and pervasive intuitions about the meaning and purpose of education.

It may be that it will fall to the "plain man" so frequently the target of professional philosophical articles, to lead philosophy back to a proper estimate of its capabilities. It is well-known that contemporary practice in logic and ethics has been a reaction to the "cosiness" of philosophical systems such as those of T. H. Green and F. G. Bradley. Self-Realisation and the Absolute may or may not have been refuted, but system-building itself has not.

B

A. N. Whitehead in a famous passage[5] associated himself with both attack and defence when he wrote: "Philosophy is not a mere collection of noble sentiments but . . . . at once general and concrete, critical and appreciative of direct intuition." He is concerned to warn that man cannot afford to be prodigal with intuition. Its flashes are rare and require collation, comparison and reference to the raw material of daily life in which they are ultimately grounded. The continuing discovery of ourselves is dependent upon this.

Thus the kind of system which could be genuinely philosophical and specifically educational must arise out of practice itself. Precepts are general, but the individual is real. The philosophy of education must work with instinctive reactions and problems arising from the incompatibility of common beliefs, but the statement of these in a disciplined manner is only the preface to, and not the entire limit of, philosophical enquiry. We are committed to system-building whether we like it or not because the only reason for rejecting one instinctive belief in favour of another, must be that it clashes with a system. Even the rejected Bradleian Idealism succeeded in showing that the process of thinking necessarily implies the attempt to create novel unities from diversity. The rejection of one reason for another is always made in terms of a contemplated theoretical unity. In science, we still proceed on the

---

[4] Dewey, John, *Education Today*, p. 8.
[5] Whitehead, A. N., *Adventures of Ideas*. Cambridge Univ. Press 1933.

assumption that the demands of reason are themselves reasonable though these are unverifiable. Few present-day scientists would exclude insight and intuition from their proper place in man's greatest discoveries. Are we then to exclude them from man's examination of his own society?

Philosophy was once described by Bertrand Russell[6] as the task of "showing us the hierarchy of our instinctive beliefs". This is exactly the task of a philosophy of education. So often the main problem in education is getting our priorities right. It is not hard to see that we must learn to distinguish between those opinions which arouse a vague feeling of moral approval in us and those which take the form of imperatives.

The test of such a system would be its internal coherence with reason and intuition as defined above discharging complementary and not opposed functions. The old philosophical tradition certainly made too much play of reason and intuition as two wholly disparate entities. The fullest refutation of this view is to be found in Chapter XI of "Subjects and Objects" in Whitehead's *Adventures of Ideas*, but it is not necessary to agree with Whitehead's view of the relatedness of reason and intuition to rehabilitate system-building. It is enough to recognise the falsity of the dichotomy drawn between these two functions of the mind. The cognitive aspect of each must be acknowledged and used if we are to scrutinise philosophically our assumptions in education.

What we retain or discard among these assumptions should be based on a well-founded criterion. Whitehead himself has suggested[7] that "an assumption is justifiable only when it can be shown that it is a presupposition fundamental to the framing of a necessary system in terms of which all experience can be interpreted." It is in this prescription that the possibility of system-building in philosophy, and the philosophy of education in particular, seems principally to reside.

We have to advance from the "collection of noble sentiments" of which we approve but which neither form a coherent whole nor individually move us to action.

We have also, as Professor Macmurray[8] warns us, to remember that "a logical system of true propositions does not in itself constitute a body of knowledge. To constitute knowledge, it must be believed by someone." He insists that although philosophy ‘is necessarily theoretical and must have the appropriate theoretical strictness, "it does not follow that we must theorise from the standpoint of theory." Action is the real inclusive situation. Only the Cartesian *cogito* insists on an inflexible dualism between theory and practice.

It is not possible here to give such a classic problem even a fraction of the consideration it deserves. It is obvious, however, that of all philosophers, the man engaged in education is most in need of a solution to the problem of the relation of theory and practice.

Nonetheless, he is better equipped than a cloistered colleague to provide a solution. Indeed he already provides a tentative answer every day and every session, for

[6] Russell, Bertrand, *The Problems of Philosophy*. Oxford Univ. Press p. 38.
[7] Whitehead, A. N., *Adventures of Ideas*. Cambridge Univ. Press 1933.
[8] Macmurray, John, *The Self as Agent*. London: Faber & Faber 1954, p. 78, 85.

teaching is at all times declaratory of one's personal attempts to sense and express the meaning and purpose of life.

The conception of philosophy of education implied in all this would be the result of an intrinsic discipline to the extent, as H. P. Rickman[9] has recently argued, that it was "based on a comprehensive view of life and alert to the factual contributions of the studies concerned with man". It would embody in this search the traditional aims of both speculative and analytic philosophy "self-knowledge and a growth of critical awareness of one's own presuppositions."

The borrowing days of educational philosophy are gone forever. Theory propped up by Church or State acquires little allegiance, less integrity and no sense of witnessing the facts as they now are. A whole new range of responses and emotional awareness have arisen in every branch of learning. Theology and political theory themselves are suddenly involved in a radical re-thinking of their own premises. This is not evidence of error or insubstantiality but of enlightenment, of a desire to come to terms with many new areas of human enquiry and endeavour. Can we refuse to do less in education?

It may be that the quest for a consistent self-sufficient system will mean the abandoning of preconceptions, watchwords and other legacies of the past. It may also entail a deeper and more diverse study of theory and practice than educationists have previously contemplated. Even those out of sympathy with the idea of a philosophy of education will surely not quarrel with that.

There remains the objection that it is only an article of faith that such an enquiry will ever yield a workable philosophy of education. Though this cannot be refuted in advance, it is an argument which applies to most areas of speculation and its real destructive power is to paralyse original thinking both good and bad. If we really believe in what we are doing, in what, in the best sense of the word, we "profess," we cannot refuse the contest.

[9] Rickman, H. P., "Dilthey and the Philosophy of Education." *International Review of Education*, vol. VIII 1963, no. 3/4, p. 336.

PHILOSOPHY AND PHILOSOPHY OF EDUCATION

RICHARD M. MILLARD, JR.
PETER A. BERTOCCI

To talk about the relation between philosophy and philosophy of education or educational theory as though one were talking about two totally different disciplines

FROM *Journal of Education* (Boston University), 141 (October, 1958): 7–13. (Reprinted by permission.)

or areas of investigation is to confuse issues at the outset and to perpetuate a
relatively recent divorce which the authors feel should never have occurred. When
in 1954 a joint committee of the Boston University graduate department of philosophy and the department of Social Foundations in the School of Education began
discussion of the possibility of a program for a doctorate of philosophy in philosophy
of education we found that only eleven institutions in the country offered such a
degree and that of these only two required any specific course work in the field of
philosophy as such. To many members of the American Philosophical Association
philosophy of education has tended to be an unrecognized stepchild. The inclusion
of a symposium on philosophy of education at the fifty-second meeting of the
Eastern Division held at Boston University in 1955 caused more than a few raised
eyebrows.

This indifference of men in the general field of philosophy to philosophy of
education has had its counterpart in an almost equal indifference to philosophy of
education by professional educators. Far too frequently philosophy of education
disappeared from education curricula altogether or, if it did appear, as former Dean
Kandel has so strongly pointed out,[1] it too often was offered by persons with little
or no philosophic training who had little to present in terms of philosophic content.
This is not to say that through the second quarter of our century there were not
exceedingly able men working in the area of philosophy of education, but it is to
suggest that far too frequently these men were voices in the wilderness spurned
both by "technical" educators and those who would call themselves "technical"
philosophers.

And yet we would insist that not only philosophy and philosophy of education
but also education in general are inseparably linked. The failure to recognize the
inseparability of the link constitutes a peculiar sort of professional myopia on
the part of all concerned. At the point at which communication among any of the
three breaks down all three tend to be the losers. This is not to claim that all three
are identical, nor is it to agree with Max Black that "in practice, philosophy of
education becomes nothing less than philosophy, without qualification or restriction."[2] It is, however, to insist that each necessarily involves the other to a greater
or lesser degree.

Our task at this point cannot be an exhaustive analysis of the relations among the
three. Such an analysis would involve not only developing a complete philosophy
of education but a detailed philosophy about philosophy of education. But we can
at least suggest some of the major areas of mutual involvement and some of the
dangers of misunderstanding the character of these involvements, as they appear
from at least one philosophical perspective.

If philosophy is conceived of not as an oracular deliverance of Olympian insights
but as the persistent, critical, and systematic attempt to discover and consistently
formulate in relation to each other the basic characteristics, meanings, and values
of our experience in its widest perspectives, then a person engaged in philosophic

[1] I. J. Kandel " Philosophy of Education," *Harvard Educational Review*, 26 (1956), pp. 134–136.
[2] Max Black, "A Note on 'Philosophy of Education'," *Harvard Educational Review*, 26 (1956), p. 155.

investigation, of all persons, can least afford to overlook or fail to think critically about educational experience. From Plato to Dewey and Whitehead recognition of the central relation of educational philosophy to other specialized areas of philosophic investigation has characterized western thought.

It is exactly in the educational process that the problems of knowledge, of value, of what constitutes the good life or lives, of the kind of world we live in and what we can do about it become most crucial. Philosophically one is concerned with drawing out and making explicit presuppositions and meanings, and developing tools for critically evaluating these presuppositions and meanings in relation to each other and all available additional areas of experience. To a large extent it was the practical business of education and the need for clarification of what education is about that gave rise to the typical areas of philosophical investigation and not vice versa. It is no accident culturally or logically that the sophists (Greek educational practitioners) preceded and set the stage for Socrates, Plato, and Aristotle. Nor was it an accident that Plato's central work, *The Republic*, is basically a philosophy of education for the good society and the good life.

To put the matter in a slightly different way, philosophic investigation is not something that does or can occur in a cultural or personal vacuum. Of all disciplines it can least afford to remain indifferent to any pervasive area of human experience, for to do so is to deprive it of its content. The major philosophic positions, as Professor Brameld has suggested,[3] may well be described as critical "interpretations of cultural experience and hence, of the pervasive human problems always indigenous with that experience or "as the articulated effort of any culture to give maximum meaning to itself." To this it must be added that few of the major philosophic positions are intentionally culturally exclusive, for, ideally at least, each of them must deal with cross-cultural reference and criteria of cross-cultural or intercultural as well as intracultural judgments. Nevertheless, insofar as education (not conceived of as restricted to the schools alone) is "the supreme human activity whereby any organized group seeks to perpetuate and modify its own way of life,"[4] education provides some of the most important data areas for philosophic investigation on the one hand, and philosophic investigation becomes a prerequisite to critical and directed as opposed to non-reflective and accidental education and educational planning on the other. A philosopher who is not willing to listen to and learn from the educator may be a linguistic technician in some restricted area but hardly a philosopher. An educator who is not philosophically literate in relation to his aims and presuppositions educationally may be an educational technician but he is operating blindly. The philosopher of education whose function it is to keep the vital discussion alive by bringing the resources of philosophy to bear on educational problems and the results of educational practice and discovery to bear on philosophic investigation needs to be particularly well grounded both theoretically and practically in both areas.

[3] Theodore Brameld, "Philosophy, Education, and the Human Sciences," *Harvard Educational Review*, 26 (1956), p. 137.
[4] *Ibid.*

Every educational system or body of educational practices does involve some set of ends or aims felt to be of sufficient importance or value to be perpetuated, or strengthened, or created in individuals and the community by the particular processes of education as such. Without these no education would, in fact, occur. Quite apart from "schooling," the primitive father who teaches his child to fish and hunt does so for some end which he feels is of vital importance for the child, for himself, and for the community. This would seem to be obvious, and yet, what may not seem quite so obvious is that education is thus in its root conception purposive in character. As such, it inevitably involves a theory of value, including both a general theory of value or criteriology of values and an ethics and social philosophy (conceptions of the life and the community worth attaining). Today, for example, someone needs to face such questions as the following: Are we to educate for self-realization in community or efficiency in industrial production? Is communal adjustment more important than individual initiative? Is education for conformity or for creativity of prime importance?

The particular theory of value involved in a particular educational system or set of educational practices may be implicit or explicit, may be critically adopted in the light of thought through value criteria and awareness of the problems of value criteria or uncritically adopted via tradition, authority, inertia, or hasty judgment induced by crisis. In the light of present post-sputnik proposals, someone needs to ask: Is a crash program in the physical sciences with de-emphasis on the social sciences and humanities the most adequate way to meet the challenge of the "space age"? What kind of scientists and society would such a program produce? Are we willing to educate for security at any price?

In addition to a theory of value, every educational system or body of educational practices involves an epistemology, that is, a series of hypotheses or assumptions or presuppositions which constitute, when made explicit, a theory of knowledge. Such a theory of knowledge includes assumptions about the possibility and limits of knowledge, a conception of truth, and a criterion or criteria determining when truth is obtained or approached and how one goes about obtaining it. The form and techniques an educational system utilizes will be and have been rather strikingly different in a society in which it is assumed that the final court of appeal for truth and falsity lies in some one institution or document as contrasted with a society in which truth or the approach to it is considered to be determined by rational weighing of evidence.

Further, every educational system or body of educational practices involves at least some metaphysical presuppositions, that is, some conception of the nature of man and his place in the universe in the light of one's conception of the kind of universe this is. The segregationist and the desegregationist in actual practice hold quite different conceptions of what men really are. Somewhere this issue of what men in fact are needs to be faced. Such assumptions as the following lead to quite different educational practices and conceptions of the nature of education itself: All men are selfish; all men are altruistic; all men are economically determined; all men are only physiological organisms determined by stimulus-response patterns and conditioning; all men are children of God. The social sciences may help throw light on the accuracy of such assumptions but even this help may be limited. In some cases at least, particular schools within the social sciences make such assumptions at the outset themselves and to appeal to these for proof is to beg the question. Again, in the educational process, these and other assumptions may be more or less explicit, more or less complete, and more or less critically assumed. Those who guide the educational processes may or may not have some explicit criteria or criterion of what constitutes reality. And yet the unavoidability of metaphysical assumptions is strikingly demonstrated by the fact that even those contemporary thinkers who would deny that a metaphysics is possible are asserting something about the amenability of the universe to human intelligence and thus are making metaphysical statements.

The function of a philosophy of education may be conceived in two ways—ways which are not mutually exclusive. On the one hand an educational philosopher may be concerned primarily with a critique of the philosophic assumptions of existing educational systems and practices. On this level his task is primarily analytic, that is, he is concerned with making explicit the implicit assumptions in any particular educational system and looking at them from the standpoint of their compatibility, consistency, and adequacy in the light of the growing body of knowledge in the social and physical sciences as well as the humanities and philosophic disciplines. He is concerned with developing critical acumen and purging discussion of fogginess, meaninglessness, and inconsistency. He is the educator become self-aware and self-critical. We have heard a great deal, for example, about education for democracy, but what kind of democracy are we educating for? Mussolini, Stalin, and Dewey agreed (surprisingly enough) that we should educate for "true" democracy, but each one's conception of "true" democracy was three worlds apart and so was each one's conception of education. To talk about education for democracy without clarification of terms is to compound confusion under cover of a warm feeling.

On the other hand, an educational philosopher may be primarily concerned not with a critique of existing educational systems so much as with developing a philosophy of education, that is, a positive conception of what education ought to be in the light of as much information about man, society, and the universe as he can muster from all available areas of experience and knowledge. This has been essentially the concern of educational thinkers such as Plato and Dewey. Contemporaneously, one question of such an order raised on the level of a United Nations Commission as well as in more restricted philosophic and educational circles, is that of whether or not there are any basic human rights that apply to all men as men and, if there are any such, what do these mean in terms of education? Is the right to education one such right? If so, what kind of education? It is not difficult to see that the first, what we called the analytic function, and the second, what we shall call the theoretical function, of educational philosophy are intimately related. One can hardly carry the critical function very far without developing critical norms nor can one carry out the theoretical function with any hope of relevance unless he relates it critically to existing educational systems and practices.

Each function, however, critical or theoretical, is apt to be truncated if the investigator is philosophically naive or if he lacks adequate background in the practices and sciences of education. If for no other reason than to avoid past blind alleys and to keep one's critical tools sharp the continuing conversation between educators and those in the general field of philosophy via the educational philosopher or philosophical educator is of vital importance.

But if such cooperative endeavor is vital then why the seeming divorce between the two areas of philosophy and education we noted above? Is it apt to be permanent or is a reconciliation likely? A number of factors might be suggested in answer to the first question. High on the list would have to be placed the indifference of many persons in the field of philosophy to educational problems. Part of this indifference has been due to the intense concern in philosophical circles in the second quarter of this century with the problems of philosophy of science and linguistic analysis and has not been due to any basic antagonism to educational questions.

A second factor has been the dominance in educational circles of one major philosophic position which, not in terms of its founder or leading proponents in the field of education but in some educational quarters, has seemed on theoretical grounds to disparage the importance of theory in favor of an almost exclusive emphasis on practice.[5] This in practice has tended to give rise to what might be described as a naive empiricism which has forgotten its theoretical foundations and the fact that it is not self-evident or self-justifying. Still another factor in educational circles has been the rapid development of the sciences of education with a resulting preoccupation with these to the exclusion of seeing these sciences in the perspective of the total educational process, its aims and goals. This growth of the sciences of education, while temporarily shifting attention from theoretical questions, has and will continue to have a salutary effect on rethinking the foundations of education. If for no other reason, it will do so because of the tremendous increase in data which these sciences plus the social sciences in general have made available for the task, data which call for assimilation in educational theory.

One other deterrent to effective communication in the past and not wholly absent today has been the assumption on the part of some educators (not without some justification) and some philosophers (though few philosophers like to admit it) that once the philosopher has his foot in the door he will proceed to legislate what education must be from some privileged pinnacle. It must be admitted that some men in the field of philosophy have attempted to deduce philosophies of education with little regard for the demands of educational practice. But nothing less befits a person in the field of philosophy than intellectual pride. Two things must be said to the contrary: It is not the business of the philosopher to tell the educator or anyone else what he must do. There is a legitimate place for developing

[5] An instance to the contrary that advances the role of unifying theory in the education of the teacher is: Theodore Brameld, *Cultural Foundations of Education*. New York: Harper & Brothers Publishers, 1957, Chapter XIII, "The Study of Culture in Teacher Education," with particular reference to pp. 269–273.

the educational implications of major philosophic positions. This is particularly desirable insofar as the philosophic positions themselves form part of the cultural context in which and for which education occurs. But even when the philosopher, educational or otherwise, is so engaged, his function is not dictation. Rather the function he may be able to perform is that of opening up new vistas and suggesting aspects of experience that may previously have been overlooked or underestimated. This is exactly the kind of a task in relation to education that John Dewey, for example, helped to perform. But a philosopher who under such circumstances failed to work closely with the professional educator or who did not grasp the practical problems of education would undermine the relevancy and the effectiveness of his work.

But far more basically the philosopher may serve as a resources person: one who can in cooperation with the educator bring the methodology and alternatives of philosophic investigation to bear upon common educational-philosophic problems. One might put the matter another way: The educator, whether he realizes it or not is, as we have suggested earlier, inevitably involved on a day to day basis with philosophic problems and issues. To perform his educational task as effectively as possible, he needs enough philosophic sophistication to recognize the problems for what they are in their historical context and the alternatives available. Here the philosopher may be of direct aid in the common task of helping human beings become as fully aware as possible of what is involved in evaluating the direction of their experiences with a view to the fullest and most worthwhile life possible.

Fundamentally, the contention of the authors is not that those who are called professional philosophers ought to be called in on every educational problem. This would be nonsense. Rather our contention is threefold: (1) that the lines of communication be kept open for the mutual enrichment of both areas, (2) that those persons who specialize in the field of philosophy of education have the opportunity to develop competence in philosophy commensurate with their competence in education or vice versa, and (3) that all persons who intend to teach should have some acquaintance with the aims, presuppositions, and alternatives in educational theory through work in philosophy of education offered by persons competent in both fields.

In a period of shifting values, of national and international cultural crises such as our own, the educational philosopher stands in a peculiarly responsible and sensitive spot, for his task is the articulation and development of the aims and presuppositions of the educational processes. To a remarkable degree failure to keep educational philosophy vital and to translate it into educational process can mean the demise of a culture itself. Accordingly the educational philosopher not only needs every encouragement but the active cooperation of all the disciplines, philosophic and scientific, that bear upon his task.

WHAT IS PHILOSOPHY
OF EDUCATION?

ALBERT J. TAYLOR

In a sense, the easiest route to answering the question, "What is philosophy of education?", is to exercise our freedom of stipulation. A survey of the books on philosophy of education would probably indicate that this is the most popular approach. Yet, lest we choose this alternative too hastily, we should pause to consider that by dismissing it thus hastily, our choice may leave us with an uneasy feeling that we have implied by our abstract or utopian definition that philosophy of education, however we define it, is something that is unrelated to the way people behave, i.e., unrelated to what we do when we philosophize. This seems implied when we consider the number of books whose authors begin by stipulating a definition and then proceed to philosophize by taking the reader on a grand tour of the various philosophical positions regardless of what their definition has been. They seem to say, "That is what philosophy is, but this is what we are going to do."

This is not to say that we ought to deprive them of their freedom of stipulation, but only to suggest that once having stipulated what philosophy of education is, they could more soundly justify their definition by acting on their stipulation when they begin to philosophize in education. Of course, this would not solve the manifold problems involved in determining by stipulation what philosophy of education is.

Another approach has been that of stipulating what philosophy of education *ought* to be, but this creates even more problems than a stipulation of what it is. Less provocative but equally popular, and beguilingly nostalgic, is a definition of what philosophy *was*. Concerning this approach, it is interesting to note that by some strange chemistry, those who use this also inevitably define education in classical or traditional terms.

All of this is a way of saying that the question is still an open one, and seems likely to remain so. This paper can only suggest another basis for approaching the question, but it is with no illusion that the author will thereby have closed the question.

In attempting to answer the question, we will try to derive a definition that

---

FROM *Educational Theory*, 13 (April, 1963): 95–104*ff.* (Reprinted by permission of the publisher and the author.)

designates, rather than denotes. This is based on the assumption, that if we can arrive at the characteristics which designate philosophy of education, we will then know the conditions of applicability. This would seem to be a more useful approach then to define what philosophy of education is by indiscriminately listing all the various and varied activities that have come under this heading. Therefore, our attempt to indicate what philosophy of education is will involve refining as well as defining.

As our inquiry proceeds, we shall attempt to distinguish between those characteristics of philosophy of education that are defining, and those that are merely accompanying. In other words, we are going to look at what philosophers say and do in relation to philosophy of education; from this, we hope to be able to distinguish between those characteristics of philosophy that are invariably present when they are philosophizing, and those that have been only parts of particular instances of philozophizing.

An examination of opinions concerning philosophy of education and what it is would reveal a range from regarding it as a genuine field of inquiry, through considering it an aspect of a general discipline of philosophy which is the supreme and absolute science, to dismissing it as useless ivory tower speculation.

More specific attitudes toward what we do when we philosophize would indicate wide variation, from requiring a full complement of building a metaphysics and deducing an epistemology and value theory before we would bestow the title of philosophy on the activity, to regarding philosophy of education as an analysis of the language we use in speaking of certain problems of education. If variety be the spice of life, one would surely find this multitudinous variation too highly seasoned for most tastes. We shall hope that some reasoned consideration will make it more palatable.

Let us begin our inquiry by considering briefly what philosophy has been. To the Greeks who first articulated systems of philosophy, it was science. Not science in any such empirical and contingent sense as we see science today, but science according to the Greek formula, i.e., that which we *know* as opposed to that which we merely believe. As such, it was only reasonable that it should concern itself with knowing everything, even including what knowledge itself was. It was a science which promised much. It promised to explain the universe, to answer such questions as what reality is; what the universe is made of and why it is here; what man is in it, and to it, and what he is to God; it would even answer what God is, what the world is to God, and in fact, what the world is. It would say what beings are and what they mean; what the very nature of human nature is. It promised to tell what we could know and how we would know it, i.e., what knowledge is and how men could come by it. It promised to answer questions about what was good and what was evil. It would tell us what beauty is. In short, it was the job of philosophy to deal with everything. And philosophy promised to do this, not contingently, but certainly.

Philosophers did in fact inquire into everything possible for them. Perhaps we should say that they *considered* everything, since we would have to qualify our use of the term "inquire" to describe some of their activities.

But philosophy did even more than this. Sometimes incidently, and sometimes intentionally, philosophers held a mirror up to the society in which the particular philosopher was living. It commented on the way men and societies lived, and subjected these ways to analysis. In this way, philosophy showed signs of being a method, or process, as well as a body of knowledge. And examples would range from Socrates, who died for his criticalness, through Kant, who had priests name their dogs Immanuel Kant in return for his "defense" of religion, to today's philosophers.

But between the time of Socrates and the time of Kant, a great deal had happened to philosophy. Some of its certain knowledge had proved, and was proving, to be contingent indeed. In fact, in some areas, a particular province in the realm of philosophy was being taken over by specialists who did not call themselves philosophers. These specialists were, in fact, ignoring philosophy's claim to supremacy, were deserting philosophy and splitting knowledge into separate and highly specialized fields. What is more, they were using a new method that did not depend on the traditional tools of philosophy, introspection, intuition, revelation, or deduction from self-evident first principles.

Philosophy surrendered much; but it could afford to surrender because these specialists, while invading certain provinces, showed signs of repulsion for the areas of "ultimate significance." They were interested mainly in the "whats" and "hows", and only after a fashion in the "whys". They dealt chiefly with empirical matters, the observable rather than the ultimate, or the spiritual, or the "why behind the why." So philosophy surrendered some provinces, albeit with much reluctance and much rationalizing.

But, unwittingly, traditional philosophy was surrendering much more than it had intended. Whereas it had promised to answer questions with certainty, and had claimed to have a special method of knowing which enabled philosophers to do this (usually one or a combination of the four methods mentioned above), its answers were as various and varied as the philosophers themselves. And in respect to method, the new sciences were demonstrating their superiority to the point that philosophers were being forced to give ground. Instead of giving support to the tenets of the ancient and medieval philosophers, the new sciences were replacing those tenets with testable and tested laws. In giving up particular items of belief, which they had regarded as knowledge, the traditional philosophers were recognizing that the newer sciences had developed a method for creating knowledge. Without exception, when the new, empirical sciences clashed with traditional philosophy, it was philosophy that gave ground. While still trying to hold onto the claim of having special ways of knowing, the traditional philosophers, with every surrender, were admitting that their special methods had not created knowledge, and that knowledge had to be publicly testable, had to predict accurately, and had to fit with everything else we know, if it were to remain as knowledge.

... the traditional philosophers promised much more than they were able to deliver and ... their claims to interpret the universe on a grand scale must be rejected for just the same reason that the claims of alchemists, astrologers, or magicians are now rejected.[1]

[1] D. J. O'Connor, *The Philosophy of Education* (London: Routledge and Kegan Paul, 1961), p. 17.

What have we hinted at here? We have suggested that even the traditional philosophers themselves were beginning to grant that certain characteristics of philosophy that had seemed defining were perhaps only accompanying characteristics after all. At any rate, even after implicitly, if not specifically, admitting that a special way of knowing was not a defining characteristic of philosophy, they continued to philosophize.

To continue our attempt to distinguish between defining and accompanying characteristics in order to decide what philosophy of education is, let us consider some views from among the variations we suggested earlier. A brief survey would indicate that there is still much support for including everything that philosophy has ever been in our list of defining characteristics. At any rate, there are many who say that philosophy of education ought to include everything that philosophy has been. For example, we find John Wendon, of Wabash College, expressing a belief that philosophy is:

> ... the love of that knowledge which deals with ultimate questions of reality or of the principles of things. In respect to education, philosophy—if it means anything—should therefore be concerned with the ultimate principles of education, which may well be a far cry from practical policies and ethical precepts.[2]

Although he does not specify that he is referring to metaphysics, this is the sort of language traditional philosophers have used when referring to metaphysics. He also suggests epistemology[3] as a choice, and grants that education is a realm of choice.

Harry S. Broudy seems to hint vaguely at this position, and more, by listing "logic, epistemology, metaphysics, aesthetics, ethics, and value theory in general," as the proper content for philosophy of education.[4]

In an article following Broudy's in the *Journal of Philosophy*, Kingsley Price, in discussing "Is a Philosophy of Education Necessary?", indicates that his requirements for a philosophy of education would include "an analytical treatment of education together with an attempt to relate it in a certain way to metaphysics, ethics, and epistemology."[5]

In another article, in *Educational Theory*, Professor Price states that:

> When we ask the question, "What is a philosophy of education," we are asking either one or all of three different questions; ... The first of these questions is, "What is an analysis of education"; the second, "What is a metaphysics of education"; the third, "What is an ethics of education."[6]

He dismisses aesthetics, epistemology, and logic, since he cannot imagine what these questions would come to. This view would seem to be supported by J. G.

[2] John Wendon, "On Philosophy of Education," *Educational Theory*, Vol. V, p. 24.
[3] *Ibid.*
[4] Harry S. Broudy, "How Philosophical Can Philosophy of Education Be?" *Journal of Philosophy*, Vol. LII, No. 22, p. 614.
[5] Kingsley Price, "Is A Philosophy of Education Necessary?" *Journal of Philosophy*, Vol. LII, No. 22, pp. 625–626.
[6] Kingsley Price, "What is a Philosophy of Education?" *Educational Theory*, Vol. VI, No. 2, p. 89.

Brennan of Columbia, who, in his book, *The Meaning of Philosophy*, takes philosophy to mean analysis, metaphysics, and valuation.[7]

To see a totally different approach to our question, we might note the position taken by C. D. Hardie, who discusses "The Philosophy of Education in a New Key," in *Educational Theory*.[8] Professor Hardie believes that philosophy's task has been so altered by the modern sciences that its function now is to develop methods which lead to the clarification of different kinds of knowledge; i.e., whether knowledge is the knowledge of common sense, or mathematics, or science; and that philosophy has no direct message for or bearing on education. He sees philosophy's method as linguistic analysis, by which we determine whether problems are technical problems for a particular science, or simply verbal problems, or merely phoney questions. Our philosophy of education then would be "the philosophy of curriculum" consisting of philosophy of language (the most important phase), philosophy of mathematics, philosophy of science, and philosophy of history.

The widest spectrum of views on philosophy of education that one could encounter in a brief time is that presented by the Spring 1956 issue of the *Harvard Educational Review*. The contributors dealt with the question: "What should be the aims and content of a philosophy of education?" With contributors such as George Axtelle, Theodore Brameld, James K. Feibleman, Charles Frankel, Sydney Hook, I. L. Kandel, Arthur Pap, Robert Ulich, and John Wild, among others, we are bound to get a sampling of divergent views. This follows that pattern we have described earlier, from requiring a full tour of traditional philosophic patterns to limiting the field to linguistic analysis.

Perhaps, however, our use of "spectrum" and "range" is misleading, because the points of view seem more discrete than continuous. In other words, as we look closely at the positions which the various philosophers occupy, it seems that they form two major clusters. (It is hoped that statisticians will forgive the borrowing of terms.) We might identify the two clusters as traditional and modern, but this does not really convey much about them. However, it does seem that there is a thread running through them that ties the members of each of the two groups together. The one group tends to present philosophy as a "discipline", in contrast to the other group's identifying philosophy as a method. The former group does not deny that philosophy involves a process. The distinction they seem to make is that a specific body of knowledge is a defining characteristic of philosophy of education, as is the "method" of philosophy which they are willing to grant is some kind of critical analysis. It is this point that seems to require consideration next.

Since all the characteristics of philosophy of education that anyone has assigned seem to have been included in Broudy's definition, we might profitably use this as a point of departure for further determining which characteristics are defining and which are merely accompanying.

[7] See J. G. Brennan, *The Meaning of Philosophy* (New York: Harper and Brothers, 1953), pp. 1–9.
[8] C. D. Hardie, "The Philosophy of Education in a New Key," *Educational Theory*, Vol. X, No. 4, pp. 255–261.

If we examine the "cluster" represented by Broudy's position, we will find that this would require four main areas of consideration. To be philosophical, philosophy of education would be required to have a metaphysics, an epistemology, a value system, and it would have to be critically analytical. Let us examine each of these and determine whether or not all are defining characteristics.

How necessary is a metaphysics to philosophy of education? Whether we are going to see metaphysics as beliefs about reality in the popular sense of the word reality, or as being concerned with "ultimate reality" (i.e., beyond that which is empirically observable and testable), it is not unreasonable to require that metaphysics have some import for education, if it is to be part of philosophy of education.

There are two bases, however, for questioning whether or not a metaphysics can meet this requirement. If we see metaphysics as a system which explains the universe, i.e., the "real" universe in the popular sense of the word, then we must question in what way it does this. No one any longer identifies metaphysics with science in this sense. Therefore, we have the problem of the relationship between the two in the matter of explaining the universe.

If we are going to maintain this view of metaphysics, then we must deny science and rely on metaphysics to explain the universe. The only alternative to this, other than denying metaphysics and relying on science, is to assign to philosophy whatever temporary residue may be left after the sciences have indicated their present but expanding boundaries. But, to do this is to imply that philosophy is at best a stop-gap until science takes over, and that the field of philosophy will be a rapidly and constantly diminishing one, and that where the sciences choose to explain, we will accept the knowledge that science establishes. Where science and philosophy conflict, we will then rely on science to explain the universe. I would suggest that this comes close to describing the role of traditional philosophy.

Although there are some philosophers, Maritain[9] for example, who claim that philosophy, and metaphysics in particular, is the supreme science, their claim is purely verbal. They do not act on it. With the surrender of the belief that philosophy had some special way of knowing has gone any valid claim that we rely on metaphysics to explain the universe. Rationalize it as we will, it is science that gives us knowledge of the universe. In education, when we want to teach about the universe, we call on the sciences.

If, on the other hand, we refuse to surrender, and maintain that metaphysics deals with "ultimate" truths, then we may properly ask what significance this has for education. Let us grant that, as our metaphysics tells us, there is a god, and man has an immortal soul. What does this say about what we ought to do in education? As Hume pointed out concerning "is" and "ought" statements, there simply is no connection. We cannot move logically from statements which say "is" or "is not" to statements which say "you ought." The only way we can move from statements of fact to statements of "ought" is to make an "Irrational Leap." But since there is no "ought" implied in statements of fact, there is nothing to tell me in which direction I "ought" to leap, or even if I ought to leap at all.

[9] See Jacques Maritain, *An Introduction to Philosophy* (New York: Sheed and Ward, 1959), chapter V.

Since Hume has already clarified this point, there is no need to labor it further. The point this makes clear is that since a metaphysics either does not make good its promise to give us knowledge of the universe, nor, when it deals in "ultimates" does it prescribe anything for education, it is obviously irrelevant and is therefore not a defining characteristic of philosophy of education.

Before leaving this point, let us make clear that we are not talking about what people say; our concern is with the way they act. The objection may be raised that others are not so willing to dismiss metaphysics. I would not deny that there are those who display a certain sentimental attachment to metaphysics in their writing. But when they are acting, they rely on the modern sciences for knowledge about reality, and it has been obvious that, in spite of all the rationalizing that has been done during the past couple of centuries, when the knowledge established by the sciences comes into conflict with the knowledge that had been established by metaphysics, it is the metaphysician who has surrendered. Even Maritain, for all his insistence that metaphysics is the supreme science, and that when the two come into conflict, the science is false, still leaves himself an out by saying, in effect, "Well, philosophers can be wrong, even though philosophy is infallible."[10]

A second characteristic, generally listed as a defining characteristic of philosophy of education, is epistemology. Traditionally, this has been a vital part of philosophy, and it might seem that beliefs about knowledge should have much to say to education. However, just as the so-called "natural philosophy" became the various fields of modern science, so men's attempts to synthesize general statements about knowledge have gradually drifted from the traditional philosophic fold to become a new science, psychology. Although there are some traditional philosophers who have claimed that it is possible to deduce a system that is concerned with knowing and knowledge from a system of metaphysics, they do not act on this. When new findings or new theories in psychology come into conflict with these beliefs, the beliefs are altered even though they, and the metaphysics from which they have been derived, are supposed to be certain and not contingent knowledge. The beliefs are altered, not on the basis of logical deduction from metaphysics, but to fit the new findings in psychology. Again we could look to Maritain, who makes many recommendations for educational practices that take into account our new knowledge in the science of psychology.

Sydney Hook points out another significant factor in an article in the *Harvard Educational Review*.[11] He notes that men as far apart in metaphysics and epistemology as Dewey, Bertrand Russell, and Felix Adler will agree on accepting the findings of psychology about the learning process. On the other hand, we have other philosophers who profess support of the same metaphysics and epistemology and yet propose distinctly different methods in education. As Hook points out:

> No one ever derived a single item of new knowledge about learning either from epistemology or epistemology of education. What we know about reliable procedures by which

[10] Maritain, p. 84.

[11] Sidney Hook, "The Scope of Philosophy of Education," *Harvard Educational Review*, Vol. XXVI, No. 2, p. 147.

learning may be furthered, we know through scientific or empirical psychology without benefit of epistemology or metaphysics.[12]

We will grant that metaphysics and epistemology have been included in certain philosophies of education. However, it seems obvious that the role they once played has been taken over by the several fields of science, and that, where these systems are included, it is merely as an accompanying and not a defining part of the philosophies. Since both areas are irrelevant to education, we could not properly call them vital to philosophizing in education. A few philosophers have attempted to support their desire for an epistemology by including logic as a part of epistemology and claiming that logic is required for critical analysis. No one would dispute this latter claim, but even their assertion in defense of epistemology indicates that it would be more fitting to see logic as a part of this tool of philosophy than as a part of a system of beliefs about knowledge. Therefore, even this attempt fails to salvage epistemology.

Occasionally, a philosopher will claim to have found a logical connection between metaphysics or epistemology and educational practices, but analysis invariably reveals either that his metaphysical or epistemological premise is a disguised value judgment, or that the connection is a psychological rather than a logical one.

The area of values is likewise an area with which philosophy has traditionally dealt. As with metaphysics and epistemology, traditional philosophers promised much. They promised to give us a set of universal "goods." However, since each system claimed to be complete, and since the universal goods were supposed to be implied in the metaphysics of the system, every new metaphysical system had its own system of values, complete and universal and thereby excluding all other systems. There were, however, the embarrassing situations of (1) having competing value systems deduced from the same metaphysical system, and (2) having two competing metaphysical systems deduce similar value systems. For example, we have the Christian philosophers looking to pagans as the fountain head of Christian wisdom.

On the other hand, we have in more recent times had philosophers reject the absolute position and claim that values are relative. What are they relative to? They are relative to each other and to the whole context in which they occur. This has some significant implications because it gives added strength to the argument against dictated values. We cannot deduce values from a metaphysics not only because they are not implied in the metaphysics, but also because, if they are related to the context in which they occur, this in itself makes them contingent and not necessary; i.e., they are related to particular circumstances and not to universals. Obviously, then, values can come into conflict, and what then? This would seem to throw the door open to human judgment, and the judgments themselves would have to be in terms of, or subject to, the context and other values, rather than in terms of or subject to a metaphysics.

Unfortunately, we cannot look to science alone to solve all the problems involved in this area. We can resolve to use the scientific method, or to use reflective intelligence, but these, in turn, imply a value system. We are faced with such questions

[12] *Ibid.*, p. 148.

as: What ends do we hold to be valuable? How can we effectively realize these ends? What do the ends imply for practices?, etc. In other words, we are faced with problems of value judgments that the methods of science alone cannot solve or settle. This in itself poses another question: What sort of methods will solve such problems? And still another: Assuming that we are going to rely on human reason, and no one seriously disputes this, how will we know that we have arrived at an appropriate answer?

It would appear, not only that this area is a proper one for philosophy to operate in, but that in this area, philosophy can be synthetic, in a sense. This is not to say that philosophy of education is going to develop or produce new knowledge; that is the role of sciences. But it can take knowledge into account, and relate it to our problems; and it can suggest possible alternatives. It can examine the relationship between ends and means, in addition to examining these, and can evaluate consequences.

All we have said concerning this area seems to indicate that this is a defining rather than an accompanying characteristic of philosophy. There are quarrels about the way we ought to proceed in the area of values, but there seems to be no way we can remove it from the realm of philosophy. To choose to do so would involve us in values. We cannot solve all the problems involving values merely by collecting empirical or observable data nor by mathematical deduction. In fact, a choice of either of these methods would itself be an act of valuing. If these methods are inappropriate, or at least not entirely adequate, then what method can we turn to? This naturally leads us to our next characteristic. If valuing is to be something more than idle speculation, and this is another choice to be made, then perhaps we should look for a proper method, just as the sciences have their methods and mathematics has its method. If we can agree that it requires a method, perhaps that method is critical analysis.

When we speak of critical analysis, we are referring to linguistic analysis. We are not limiting ourselves to the claims of the extreme logical positivists that statements of empirical fact which can be confirmed by sensory observations, and statements of mathematics and logic that can be checked by calculation, are the only kinds of statements that can have cognitive meaning, and that therefore all other statements are meaningless. We are referring to the linguistic analysis which merely says, language has many uses; let's examine the way this language is used so that we know how to treat this proposition.

As we mentioned earlier, logic is an integral part of this process. Without getting involved in the argument of whether logical statements are always true statements or whether we can gain knowledge from logic, we would have to admit to at least a pragmatic justification of the principles of logic and recognize their usefulness in discourse and argumentation. In spite of questions being raised, no one truly doubts these, and we all use them.

The use of such a tool, or method, in philosophy has been an invaluable, in fact an indispensable, part of philosophy. It has great significance for education. Certainly, philosophy would have a significant role to play if it did no more than subject slogans and rules of thumb to critical analysis. Analysis has been the single area in which philosophy, including traditional philosophy, has made its greatest contribution. Regardless of how meaningless the metaphysics and epistemologies of various philosophies have been, the critical function has consistently performed a significant service. And since every attempt to philosophize has been made within a particular context, it has involved, implicitly if not overtly, an analysis of that context, we must admit analysis as a defining characteristic of philosophy of education.

On the basis then of defining philosophy of education by examining its characteristics in terms of whether they are accompanying or defining, we might support the following conclusions: Although metaphysics and epistemology have been parts of philosophy, the sciences have rendered them irrelevant. We could justifiably grant no more than that they have accompanied particular instances of philosophizing. Philosophy of education, then, would not be a body of knowledge, but a process. The process appears to have two aspects, or phases; analysis and synthesis.

The critical analysts have built a convincing case in this regard, at least up to a point. We have indicated that values are a defining part of philosophy of education, and there is a strong case for saying that the only method we have for dealing with values is the method of critical analysis. When questions concerning matters of fact arise, we can turn to the sciences to answer these, but there are apparent difficulties in applying the methods of science to values. Yet, a problem arises when we say that this is all there is to philosophy of education. In granting that linguistic analysis is one of the elements of philosophy of education, we are not saying that it *is* philosophy of education.

Let us grant that analysis is a vital process, and that our words and propositions need to be examined in terms of clarifying what they mean. Let us even agree that by the use of critical (linguistic) analysis, we may come to see that some apparent problems are really only verbal ones, and that they can be resolved by a critical analysis that leads to clarity. We could grant that this is a defining characteristic of philosophy and no one could seriously deny it. But, still, this is not all there is to philosophy of education.

At this point of granting all this, we have reached a stage where we will rely on the sciences to give us knowledge of the universe. We can rely on the psychologists to tell us how learning takes place. We have also, by critical analysis, clarified our statements of values. Where do we go from here?

Our fact statements can say, "If A, then B," but there is not just one such statement. We cannot possibly know all the knowledge that men have accumulated, and therefore, the various items of knowledge are competing for our attention. When we choose "If A, then B," as the fact we shall concern ourselves with, then we have eliminated "If B, then C," "If D, then E," etc., simply because we cannot know them all. How then are we to choose? An item of knowledge does not choose itself to become known to us. It is we who are selective, and facts of knowledge tell us nothing about which facts of knowledge we are going to select.

Perhaps this is a matter that involves value, then. But, here we find a similar situation in that values are also in competition. There is no absolute hierarchy of values to tell us that in every situation A is to be more valued than B, which is more valued than C, etc. What is highly valued in this situation may not even be relevant to that one, but values do not tell us this themselves. Even after they have been thoroughly analyzed, and our proposition concerning a particular value is clear, it does not choose itself. We can be relatively certain as to what it is that we value, but this still does not say, "Choose this value," because values have a way of changing in value, and coming into conflict. We can vow to value honestly, and be clear on what this means, but the choice never seems to be between honesty and nothing. It is frequently between honesty and something else that is valued.

All of this is merely a way of saying that philosophy of education is more than critical analysis. As we said earlier, it is a process with two aspects: (1) clarifying the problems of education; (analysis); (2) presenting possible alternatives, (synthesis). This activity will operate chiefly in the area of values, but it must also take knowledge into account. Although it would undoubtedly require another paper to explore this area, I would suggest that this presentation of possible alternatives would be not only in terms of values, but would involve a consideration of possible consequences, i.e., that we cannot possibly assess value choices adequately without such consideration. I would also suggest, without going into detail, that this process of suggesting or presenting possible alternatives is the area in which we would introduce the scientific method into philosophy of education. But that topic, too, would require another paper, if we were to explore it adequately. We will be content with the hope that herein we have adequately indicated what philosophy of education is.

CAN EDUCATIONAL THEORY GUIDE PRACTICE?

D. B. GOWIN

The honorable Robert Boyle, in 1680, complained of "theories which either like peacocks feathers make a great show, but are neither solid nor useful; or else like apes, if they have some appearance of being rational, are blemish'd with some absurdity or other." [1] The contemporary scene in the science of behavior finds Professor B. F. Skinner asserting that the science of behavior needs no theories, that

FROM *Educational Theory*, 12 (January, 1963): 6–12. (Reprinted by permission of the publisher and the author.)

[1] As quoted by Agnes Arber in *The Mind and the Eye*, Cambridge University Press, 1954, p. 28.

theories of learning, for example, are not necessary.[2] That Skinner himself actually uses a theory in his work, as Michael Scriven[3] declares, is not for us to examine here. It is enough to note that there is a problem concerning the nature of theory, the functions of theory, and, in general, what we mean by theory. So long as there is a general confusion about the meaning of the term, theory, there will be confusion about theories as a guide to educational practice.

How shall we conceive of theory? In general, theory seems to be defined as some set of abstract propositions logically-related to each other through assumptions, postulates, axioms, definitions, and hypotheses; and these are related by operations and/or observations in the empirical realm to some set of data, facts, events, things, processes, entities. The two main dimensions of theory seem to be the logical dimension and the empirical dimension.

Let me cite a few definitions of theory. Professor Herbert Feigl writes:

Theory is a set of assumptions from which can be derived by purely logico-mathematical procedures, a larger set of empirical laws. The theory thereby furnishes an explanation of these empirical laws and unifies the originally relatively heterogeneous areas of subject matter characterized by these empirical laws.[4]

This is the definition accepted by Professor Andrew W. Halpin in his study of theory in educational administration.[5] Also accepting Feigl's definition is Professor Daniel E. Griffiths in his work on administrative theory.[6] Both of these theorists in education think that Feigl's definition has relevance for educational work. The logical and empirical dimensions of the definition of theory are clearly evident in Feigl's definition.

Professor D. J. O'Connor[7] defines theory in the following four ways:

1. sets of verified hypotheses, logically connected, e.g., scientific theories

2. an organized and unified conceptual framework, e.g., a theory of numbers, a theory of games

3. a body of related problems, e.g., a theory of knowledge, theory of value

4. a set of prescriptions or rules used to govern some behavior, e.g., a theory of plumbing or violin playing, or teaching

Still other uses of the term theory are to be found. Theory is sometimes defined, etymologically, as "spectacle, a viewing." Professors Combs and Snygg use it in this sense. They write, "... a theory ... is nothing more than an organization of data, or a way of looking at data, to make them meaningful."[8]

---

[2] B. F. Skinner, "Are Theories of Learning Necessary?", *Psychological Review*, Vol. 57, 1950, pp. 193–216.

[3] Michael Scriven, "A Study of Radical Behaviorism," *Minnesota Studies in The Philosophy of Science*, Vol. I, University of Minnesota Press, 1956, pp. 88–130.

[4] Herbert Feigl, "Principles and Problems of Theory Construction in Psychology," in W. Dennis (ed.), *Current Trends of Psychological Theory*, pp. 174–213, Pittsburgh: University of Pittsburgh Press, 1951.

[5] Andrew W. Halpin, *Administrative Theory in Education*, Midwest Administration Center, University of Chicago, 1958, p. 7.

[6] Daniel E. Griffiths, *Administrative Theory*, Appleton-Century-Crofts, Inc., New York, 1959.

[7] D. J. O'Connor, *An Introduction to Philosophy of Education*, Philosophical Library, New York, 1957, p. 72 and *passim*.

[8] Arthur W. Combs and Donald Snygg, *Individual Behavior*, Harper and Brothers, Inc., New York, 1959, p. 7, and *passim*.

For Plato theory is a contemplated truth. According to Harold Rugg, theory is a thought model of reality. Aristotle opposes theoretical knowledge to practical knowledge. And the man in the street is likely to think of theory as idle armchair speculation divorced from evidence about the real world, or—as one person said to me when I asked him about the meaning of the word "theory"—"Well, when you don't know what you are talking about, you use a theory." Theory here is being used in the sense of a guess; in the absence of knowledge one relies on theory. Notice that this definition is not Aristotle's contrast of theoretical to practical knowledge; this meaning is theory as the absence of knowledge.

Let us consider two other definitions of theory. Professor Max Black, in the *Dictionary of Philosophy*, gives the following definition of theory:

(1) Hypothesis. More loosely: supposition, whatever is problematic, verifiable but not verified.

(2) (As opposed to practice): systematically organized knowledge of relatively high generality (See 'the theory of light')

(3) (As opposed to laws and observations): explanation. The deduction of the axioms and theorems of one system from assertions (not necessarily verified) from another system and of a relatively less problematic and more intelligible nature.[9]

Another definition of theory comes from Professor Lawrence G. Thomas in a paper entitled "Building a Theory of Teacher Education."[10] Thomas lists the parts of an experimental theory as: an agreed upon frame of reference for inquiry, operational definitions of key terms, the use of control conditions, the requirement that verification of hypotheses be attempted under conditions where falsification is possible, and the logical interdependence of postulates, assumptions and hypotheses. Thomas asserts two major requirements of theory: that it be scientific and that it be logical.

These writers differ somewhat in the accent they place upon the logical or the empirical. Feigl and Black seem to stress the logical (deduction and explanation), Combs and Snygg and Thomas seem to stress the empirical and the experimental. The exact relation between the logical and the empirical is a perennial issue among philosophers of science.

Many writers on the concept of theory ascribe to it three chief functions: description, explanation, and prediction.[11] These functions of theory seem to refer to the phenomena which the theorist is seeking to understand. That is, theory describes facts, outcomes, and explains (gives an account of) phenomena. Theory here is stated as it functions in relation to the things of nature (or the nature of things).

But turn theory around and point it toward the person using the theory. A different set of functions seems to be prominent when we look at the theorist at

[9] Max Black, *Dictionary of Philosophy*, Philosophical Library, New York, 1942, p. 317. "Note: Since criteria of what is 'intelligible' and 'problematic' are subjective and liable to fluctuation, any definition of the term is bound to be provisional. It might be advisable to distinguish between *laws* (general statements in a system), *principles* (axioms), and *theories* (methods for deriving the axioms by means of appropriate definitions employing terms from other systems). M. B."

[10] Lawrence G. Thomas, "Building a Theory of Teacher Education," *Educational Forum*, Vol. 8, 1943, pp. 43–54.

[11] O'Connor, *op. cit.*, p. 81.

work in research. Here the theory helps the researcher to *analyze* data, to make a short-hard summarization or *synopsis* of data and relations, and to *suggest* new things to try out.[12] Theory functions in analysis, in synopsis, in power of suggestion or speculation. Theory functions as something to think with, to help in one's work.

In this second context theory is appraised in terms of the kind and quality of research it helps to generate. As Professors Hall and Lindzey say ". . . all matters of formal adequacy pale alongside the question of what empirical research is generated by the theory."[13] Some theories, like Wheeler's organismic theory, are dropped from consideration when they are not revised in the light of empirical research relevant to them.[14] Other theories, like Lewin's field theory, despite trenchant criticisms of its formal adequacy,[15] continue to influence the research worker; field theory has borne fruit in the empirical realm despite its shortcomings in the logical realm.[16] Therefore, in looking at the behavior of scientists, we might answer our question in this way: it is a job of scientific theory to guide the practice of empirical research.

Now for the leap to educational theory. In a similar manner, it is the job of educational theory to guide educational practice. Indeed, what other prime function could an *educational* theory have but to guide educational practice? That is what the theory is for. Yes, you might say, but do we have any educational theories?[17] If we discount the criterion of formal adequacy of the theory, then a list of the theories we are most familiar with would qualify. For example we can think of Rousseau's theory of natural development, Dewey's theory about the child and the curriculum (to mention only one), Kilpatrick's theory of the project method, and the theories of life adjustment, of human relations in administration, of group dynamics in counseling, and so forth. All these theories have generated important educational practices.

But it is easy to sense impatience with this answer. You might say that you mean by theory something else. A theory should have formal adequacy to be a theory; it must have logical rigor. Moreover, theories should not carry such a heavy load of prescription, of value-laden propositions. Theories should be value-neutral. A

---

[12] Looking at theory in terms of its functions in guiding the researcher might enable us to expand the definition of theory to include such heuristic devices as models, metaphors, analogies. We might call these "theoroids" since they are not theories in the usual meaning of the term. We might even include the skeptical Skinner's Law of Serendipity.

[13] Calvin S. Hall and Gardner Lindzey, *Theories of Personality*, John Wiley & Sons, Inc., New York, 1957, p. 20.

[14] Ernest R. Hilgard, *Theories of Learning*, Appleton-Century-Crofts, New York, Second Edition, 1956, p. v and p. 225.

[15] Kenneth Estes, in A. T. Poffenberger, editor, *Modern Learning Theory*, Appleton-Century-Crofts, Inc., 1954, p. 335 and *passim*.

[16] D. B. Gowin, "Comments on Cognitive Field Theory of Learning," *Proceedings of The Philosophy of Education Society*, 18th Annual Meeting, 1962, pp. 189–194.

[17] Professor O'Connor claims that education does have a "body of established hypotheses that have been confirmed to a reliable degree. They enable us to predict the outcome of their application and to explain the processes that we are trying to control. They are, to that extent, genuine theories in the standard sense of the word." The theories he cites include "present day knowledge of perception, learning, motivation, the nature of 'intelligence' and its distribution and development, the causes of educational backwardness, and many other matters of this kind." O'Connor, *op. cit.*, p. 109.

theory cannot tell you what you ought to do. Rather, a theory is like a map.[18] And maps—as distinguished from itineraries—do not tell you where you ought to travel. The reply, of course, is well then, it is not an educational theory, for we mean by educational theories that they generate and guide practice.

How then shall we conceive of "guiding practice?" A handbook of plumbing is a guide to action. A set of directions in a do-it-yourself kit is a guide to action. A written monograph on a particular surgical operation is a guide to action. A musical score is a guide to action. The sign "In case of fire, break glass, reach inside, open door, exit on fire escape at rear" is a guide to action. These guides contain conditional "oughts." They seem to proclaim: if you want such-and-such a result, then act in the indicated fashion. If you want to escape a fire, then you ought to break the glass.

A brief examination of the status of theory in educational administration is a case in point. Does theory guide the administrator? If so, in what sense? Professor Getzels likens his social process theory of administration to a map. Paraphrasing the Kantian statement, he writes "theories without practices like maps without routes may be empty, but practices without theories like routes without maps are blind."[19] Getzels argues that theory does guide practice in the sense that theorizing or "map-making" is inevitable in *all* human affairs. "The question of whether we should use theory in our administrative behavior" writes Getzels, "is in a sense as meaningless as the question of whether we should use motivation in our behavior. Our actions are inevitably founded in our motives and steered toward goals by the relevant explicit or implicit theories that we hold."[20] Getzels argues that we should make implicit theories explicit, and he, for one, makes his theory clearly explicit.[21] We may doubt, along with McClellan,[22] whether a set of propositions as such can ever be implicit; clearly it is difficult to see how a set of verified hypotheses could ever be implicit in one's behavior.

But does Getzels' theory tell an administrator what he *ought* to do in practice? The theory is a set of abstract, ordered relations connected at some point to observable processes. Assume (notice that this is a big assumption) that the requisite scientific work has been done so that the logical ordering developed in the theory is well-connected empirically to the observable processes. These observable processes, or data, constitute the existential "is-ness," the empirical referents. The directions for the use of the theory, then, constitute the relevant "conditional oughts." If the map states "for one mile read one inch," then you ought to use this conversion rule if you want to get to your destination. If the theory states

[18] Stephen Toulmin, *Philosophy of Science*, Chapter IV, "Theories and Maps," Hutchinson University Library, London, 1953, pp. 105–39.
[19] Jacob W. Getzels, "Theory and Practice in Educational Administration: An Old Question Revisited," in Roald F. Campbell and James M. Lipham, *Administrative Theory as a Guide to Action*, Midwest Administration Center, University of Chicago, 1960, p. 42.
[20] *Idem.*
[21] Arthur P. Coladarci and Jacob W. Getzels, *The Use of Theory in Educational Administration*, Stanford University Press, 1955.
[22] James E. McClellan, "Theory in Administration," *School Review*, Vol. 68, No. 2, Summer 1960, p. 210.

that behavior is a function of role and personality $(B = f[R \times P])$, then you ought to use this concept in observing and controlling the behavior of those for whom you as an administrator are responsible; you cannot use Lewin's formulation that behavior is a function of person and environment $(B = f[P \times E])$.

One school superintendent reported that all decisions he made were the result of following Getzels' theory; he constantly referred to the map before charting his course. His comment gives us a clue. The theory turns out to be a guide to thought; it is a screen, a way to think about fundamental problems, a way to reach a decision. But, when it comes time to *act*, the theory is put aside as the action takes place. It is not a guide to action in the same sense that a musical score is a guide to the action of a performing musician. It is a guide to the action of thinking, as it were, but not a guide to direct acting.

It is very possible that education needs to train a new kind of specialist—the planner or developer. This person would be able to understand theories (but not required to create them), and to understand practice well enough to draw up plans for the practitioner. This planner would not necessarily be able to put the plans into practice; he might not have the requisite skill of the artful teacher or administrator. Like the theorist, he would work chiefly with verbal symbols. Unlike the theorist, he would be able to relate his understandings to the practical school situation. Unlike the teacher, he would not necessarily be able to make the plans work in actual practice.

A proposal for a specialist of this kind has recently been made. It comes out of the University of Chicago studies in administrative theory.[23] Professor Roald Campbell calls for a three-way division of labor: the scientist, the developer, and the practitioner. The developer, for Campbell, is the professor of educational administration who develops the theories of the social scientists on the one hand and who on the other hand works with the practicing administrator in showing how the theory can be used in guiding practice. The developer must know the different languages of the two kinds of work—research and practice—and must understand the process of both. It is one thing to build a theory and to use it in the practice of research; it is another thing to use theory to guide educational practice. The conception of "practice theory" put forth by Ernest Greenwood might serve Campbell's developer. Greenwood writes:

. . . scientific theory is descriptive; practice theory is prescriptive. Scientific theory consists of laws describing and explaining nature; practice theory consists of principles prescribing ways of controlling nature. The proposition that every organized group eventually develops a subculture of its own is a scientific law. The proposition that every therapeutic plan must consider the subculture of the client is a principle of practice.[24]

---

[23] Campbell and Lipham, *op. cit.*, p. 171 and *passim*. Note: Henry Brickell's report, *Organizing New York State for Educational Change*, contains a similar recommendation to the effect that three kinds of work are involved in instructional innovation: *design* in enriched circumstances (for the theorist primarily), *evaluation* through field testing (for the measurement specialist primarily) and *dissemination* through demonstration and re-education (for the practitioner primarily).

[24] Ernst Greenwood, "The Practice of Science and the Science of Practice" as quoted in Warren G. Bennis, Kenneth D. Benne, Robert Chin, *The Planning of Change*, Holt, Rinehart and Winston, New York, 1961, p. 78.

Greenwood's article is an interesting one, but set more in a social work context than an educational context. I agree with his final remarks concerning what we must do if we believe in the value of a science-practice collaboration.

We cannot rely on isolated applied-oriented scientists and theory-oriented practitioners to collaborate on a voluntary, individual, and informal basis. . . . We must experiment with new forms of social organization and new social roles.[25]

If we do develop a new social role for the Developer, or the Practice Theorist, some detailed philosophizing will have to be done to delineate the pattern of logic and language useful to this person, for much of his task will be a translation problem. And while he may not be qualified to do research as a scientist, he will have to be able to criticize research work—to analyze assumptions, to identify and judge the typical types of definitions made in research, to read statistical tables with understanding, to follow and judge the inferences made in moving from findings to conclusions. His role, in short, will have some of the characteristics of the philosopher of science.

Let us examine briefly the remarks of Professor W. W. Charters, Jr.,[26] in commenting on the usefulness of Getzels' theory in guiding administrative practice.

Charters asserts that it is the concepts, and not the findings, of social science theory which will be of greatest help to the administrator in guiding practice. It is the logical aspect, not the empirical, that an administrator may find useful. The reason he gives is that findings are always only probable, never certain, and social science findings always are small and limited in comparison to the range of reality the school administrator must deal with. But the concepts, the ideas, may be used as each administrator tries to make sense of them with reference to his own local situation and his own personality and need. Without what Northrop calls the "for-me-ness of theory"[27] or the decision of principle in Hare's terms,[28] the concepts will never be used to guide practice.

Part of the reason for Charters' conclusion may be that Getzels' theory is long on concepts and short on empirical data. Getzels seems to accept the definition of theory as a unified conceptual framework rather than the definition of theory as a set of logically-connected and verified hypotheses. Educational theories, to date, still lack the power of theories in the physical sciences.

Professor Halpin, who formerly took a hard science line, and who accepted Feigl's definition of theory, and who did much personally to promote the notion of administrative theory in education, sums up: ". . . there does not exist today, either in education or industry, a single well-developed theory of administration that is worth getting excited about."[29] This condition may not be entirely the theorist-scientist's fault. The fault (or difficulty) may lie in the nature of the beast

[25] Greenwood, *op. cit.*, p. 82.
[26] Campbell and Lipham, *op. cit.*, p. 175, *passim*.
[27] F. S. C. Northrop, "Ethical Relativism in the Light of Recent Legal Science," reprinted in S. Hook, *American Philosophers At Work*, Criterion Books, Inc., New York, 1956, p. 452.
[28] R. M. Hare, "Decisions of Principle," *The Language of Morals*, Oxford Press, 1952, pp. 56–78.
[29] Campbell and Lipham, *op. cit.*, p. 5.

we have to contend with. Halpin gives us a clue by citing the psychoanalyst Erik Erikson, to wit:

Erikson admits that we can learn about the nature of things as we find out what one can do *with* them. But people are not things; '. . . the true nature of man reveals itself only in the attempt to do something *for* him.' But the moment you do things for other human beings, you must assume moral responsibility for what you do. And this is the very responsibility which the analytical scientist has refused to accept, has declared as none of his concern.[30]

In a way Halpin provides us with a good reason. It may be the reason why educational theory will have to be formulated in an essentially-different pattern of formal adequacy than scientific theory. The background theory of science is well known to scientists—to gather facts, perform experiments, make observations, explore nature, discover things. Hence, they know how to use a theory in practicing their work. The goals of educational practice may be as well known in our common background theory: form character, cultivate intelligence, promote knowledge, generate wisdom and the good life. But these referents for the background theory always involve human beings. To put it simply, science deals with things, and when it deals with people it treats them as things. But education deals with people, and when it works with them it can never forget or deny that they are human beings. Hence, educational theory will always carry a component of moral responsibility. While the scientist has moral responsibility in his discipline, the referent for the moral responsibility is to other scientists and not to the things with which he deals. I submit the following argument in capsule:

1. An educative act involves an educator trying to do something *to*, *with* and *for* another person.
2. An educative act involves a moral responsibility on the part of the educator.
3. An educational theory must make reference to an educative act.
4. An educational theory, in accounting for educative acts, must make reference to the person-to-person relation.
5. An educational theory will differ from scientific theories in that, although they both guide practice, the referent for the guidance is a person-being-educated in one theory, and a thing-being-studied or manipulated in the other theory.

Therefore: any educational theory will necessarily differ from any scientific theory; it is impossible for a scientific theory (as a set of propositions in the logical realm) to guide educational practice; if we wish to get our educational practice under intelligent control, then we must specify in our educational theories the nature of the moral responsibility so entailed by the nature of educational theory itself.

[30] Idem., p. 7–8.

THE EDUCATIONAL
PHILOSOPHER AS
"LIAISON OFFICER"

THEODORE BRAMELD

The stereotype of the philosopher, including the educational philosopher, is one of the reasons why he is utilized less effectively in professional as well as lay activities than he ought to be.

We are all aware of typical features of the stereotype: an aloof, somewhat absent-minded creature absorbed in abstractions and obsessed by ivory-tower speculations that have little if anything to do with the really vital affairs of "every-day life" and even less with "common sense."

It must be granted that, like other stereotypes, this one is not altogether false. Philosophers do frequently seem remote, and the standard college courses offered in their field may on occasion reinforce that reputation. In the United States, the recent preoccupation of many professional philosophers with symbolic logic and other erudite competencies removed from the great moral and political struggles of our time has scarcely served to weaken the stereotype.

And yet, as anyone knows who has studied the history of philosophy, some of the greatest thinkers from Plato onward have also been men of action—men profoundly immersed in the fighting issues of life. Even in our own day one thinks of Bertrand Russell, John Dewey, Benedetto Croce, Thomas G. Masaryk, and Albert Schweitzer.

While the philosopher of education can hardly hope to approximate these world figures, nevertheless, precisely because he has chosen to apply fundamental theory to the eminently practical field of education, one would expect him to be eager to bring his training and experience to bear in as many concrete ways as possible. That he has not always done so is probably his own fault as well as that of his associates: his own, because he, too, sometimes escapes into "theory for the sake of theory"; his associates', because sometimes they show little interest in discovering what the educational philosopher might offer to the enrichment of other fields within the scope of teacher education.

FROM *Journal of Education* (Boston University), 141 (October, 1958): 25–28. (Reprinted by permission.)

Perhaps it would be helpful to consider a few of the ways in which such enrichment might occur. Of a number that might be selected, let us consider four: (1) the philosopher of education as resource person in other areas of specialization: (2) the philosopher of education as interdisciplinarian; (3) the philosopher of education as co-researcher; and (4) the philosopher of education as policy shaper.

(1) No subject matter in teacher education, or for that matter in anything else, is devoid of its own philosophic aspects. We are thinking here primarily of one important feature of philosophy—its critical concern with the nature of assumptions presuppositions, and premises. For no educational authority in any subject matter is able to proceed without these starting-points even when, as is often the case, they are not consciously inspected by that authority.

To suggest, then, that the philosopher of education serve as a "resource person" in other fields than his own—in curriculum, administration, learning, measurement, or any one of a dozen others—is first of all to suggest that he be utilized to sensitize students and instructors to what Harold Laski aptly called their "inarticulate major premises." The value of this contribution should be obvious: it helps to create awareness that the strength of, say, an explicit curriculum superstructure is only as great as its implicit foundations—foundations which, if one takes the trouble to examine them, may prove to be flimsy indeed.

To put the point in another way, the potential contributions of the educational philosopher as resource person are epitomized in his obligation *not* to take for granted what other people often do take for granted. We are not saying that he functions merely as a skeptic; he may thus function, certainly, but he may also wish to examine educational starting-points not to demolish but to strengthen them by greater discernment of their meaning. Nor are we saying that the resource role is limited solely to critical analysis of these starting-points: there are other contributions, too, which will often emerge in the process of making the first—contributions perhaps better described in terms of the three remaining liaison roles.

(2) In speaking of the philosopher of education as "interdisciplinarian," the implication is that he is, or surely ought to be, concerned not only with the relations of all educational fields to one another but, in turn, with the relations of these to the still wider spheres of art, science, religion, politics—in short, to the world. Here his service could be the invaluable one of providing perspective—of helping his associates more clearly to perceive the significance of their particular specializations to other specializations and to the still wider contexts of culture and nature.

To deny the need of this service today would be foolhardy. At least as much as any institution, education has suffered because it has not maintained adequate perspective. It has not viewed itself from a distance, as it were, so that when a crisis occurs . . . it is unprepared to do much more than go on the defensive with loud and unintelligible noises.

More concretely, the educational philosopher should be called upon to join forces with experts in a variety of fields besides his own—and to work cooperatively in the study of problems that, by their nature, cannot be solved by any one of these experts. The interdisciplinary approach to, say, problems of personality is today becoming more and more recognized as essential—a fact exemplified by the increasingly popular term "behavioral sciences" to encompass all the disciplines from psychology and psychiatry to economics and anthropology that deal with human experience. In education, the crucial importance of the behavioral sciences goes without saying, though interdisciplinary approaches in teacher-training programs are still more the exception than the rule. Even fewer, however, are those programs that include the educational philosopher in cross-departmental courses, should any exist. Yet he, more than anyone else, should be equipped by his training to throw light upon relational dimensions of the problems under consideration, to press for warranted integrations, and to keep the entire effort in cultural as well as educational perspective.

(3) "Co-researcher"—the third of the four liaison roles—overlaps with the second. For when the philosopher participates in fundamental educational research with his associates he again performs an interdisciplinary function. Here, however we are thinking less of courses of study than of field and laboratory investigation and experiments.

In education, as much as any profession, research is constantly carried on that involves, for example, attitudes and beliefs about a vast range of germane issues—from sexual morality, at one extreme, to international relations, at another. The philosopher's contribution is, of course, to make sure that the most significant attitudes and beliefs are focused upon—a task also related to his special concern with assumptions and other starting-points. Thus, as such a co-researcher he could share more often in the formulation of questionnaires and other instruments of investigation. He could, were he invited to do so, participate directly in field work in order to offer guidance and to learn first-hand. Similarly, in the case of doctoral and other studies confined chiefly to library resources, he could demonstrate his usefulness by counseling candidates in methods of research practised by philosophers themselves—research in the history of concepts, in evaluation, and many other areas.

Teacher-training institutions need to carry on many more community-and-school experiments to test out fresh ideas—pilot projects that could, if successful, develop into accepted practices. In these endeavors, the educational philosopher should be an ally: thus he should help to formulate hypotheses in the most fruitful ways possible and to suggest avenues of exploration that might not occur to colleagues with other kinds of background.

(4) The role of "policy shaper" has also been anticipated. For, to help in shaping policies for professional education is to perform all three previous roles as well. It is, first, to serve as a resource person especially aware of the assumptions and premises that govern, for example, the requirements for a degree. It is, second, to encourage awareness of the interrelations of departments, courses, and contents, and hence to press for less "atomism," more "organism," in the total program. And it is, third, to stimulate kinds of student and faculty research that may be less pedestrian, less piecemeal, more audacious, and more comprehensive in its preoccupation with educational problems on the cutting-edges of society and school.

More than all this, however, the educational philosopher should be involved at every stage in the effort to formulate and translate into practice new designs for education itself. Thus, in addition to his roles as critic of premises and as synthesizer of disparate parts, he is rightly interested in norms—which is to say, with what ought to be but is not yet. In this responsibility we are, of course, calling attention to what some of his peers think is the only legitimate interest of the educational philosopher—namely, the realm of values. This view is as naive as it is constricting. But certainly one of his interests—a major one, too—is to analyze and validate as far as possible the purposes of education and hence the values which constitute the substance of all purposes.

In teacher education itself, these purposes are being subjected to renewed scrutiny, and the question of whether the principles that have governed its programs are defensible is now of uncomfortable urgency. The philosopher of education should be directly involved in every attempt to clarify and crystallize educational policies commensurate with the revolutionary age in which we live. He should eagerly serve on key committees devoted in any way to this paramount objective. And he should bring to bear upon their deliberations the best available knowledge from the branch of philosophy most concerned with values—the field of axiology.

To suggest that the educational philosopher serve by these means as "liaison officer" is simply a way of saying that he desires to make philosophy count. It is not to suggest the slightest lessening of tough, thorough study of the field itself. Nor is it to suggest any radical departure from what the philosopher has always tried to do when he has been an influential force. His role as resource critic of assumptions has a tradition behind it of more than two millennia—that of the Socratic "gadfly." His roles as interdisciplinarian and co-researcher are, in last analysis, those of the maker of *weltanschauungen*—of steady and harmonious views of the world. Lastly, his role as policy shaper is that of creative visionary—of suggester and projector toward better ways of performing necessary educational tasks.

All of these roles, however, require for their performance a new rapprochement from two sides—from that of the educational philosopher, and from that of colleagues who can no more afford to isolate him from the mainstream of their endeavors than he can afford to isolate himself.

PART IV
EDUCATIONAL PHILOSOPHY AND THE TEACHER

Can the study of philosophy help the teacher and, if so, how? The question is fraught with ambiguity, but it deserves some frank answers. What is wanted is a defense for the claim that philosophical ideas can assist the educational practitioner confronting the workaday realities of a classroom. Criticisms are leveled often at philosophy because it does not seem to have a convincing relevance to the exigencies of daily life, much less the immediate, pressing concerns of educational practice. The idea that the solution of pedagogical problems depends in some measure on one's views of reality or the nature of knowledge and value is dismissed as an intellectualist superstition. Many will argue that an appeal to ordinary facts and purposes will usually be sufficient for dealing with schoolroom problems, and when they are not it is highly unlikely that philosophical considerations will provide much assistance.

The skeptic sees little relationship between obtruse speculations or technical philosophical analysis and the down-to-earth practicalities of everyday life. As one teacher of a course in philosophy of education once wryly remarked,

Teachers-in-training feel that, once they have passed our examinations, they will never have occasion to use (in the classroom) anything of what we have made them put into their term-papers and finals, if not into their heads. Systematic thinking they find hard to follow. Abstract reasoning leaves them untouched. An inspiring address on the beauty and spiritual significance of teaching as a life-work, they applaud—is it not a recognized morale-builder? Indeed, will they not expect something of the sort to be featured on their convention programs? But, among themselves, they are convinced that anything savoring of "general issues" is of no practical use in their day-to-day work. "Philosophy cuts no ice and bakes no bread." [1]

Thus, it is argued that philosophical theories and concepts are of such a general character that it is well nigh impossible to deduce straightforward and specific practical consequences from them which can be put into practice.[2]

This latter claim must be conceded unequivocably. Precise rules and particular injunctions do not seem to follow in a strictly deductive pattern from some *a priori* philosophical generalization. It seems precarious to think, for example, that there is some isomorphic correlation between a given philosophical position and a system of imperatives for action that constitutes an educational policy requiring only that it be implemented. There are *general* conclusions that can be drawn by implication from a philosophical position perhaps, but nothing approximating the degree of specificity usually called for in the conduct of a classroom. In other words, no strictly deductive model seems adequate for understanding how philosophical theories can be "applied" or "put into practice" in the ordinary sense of these expressions. Despite the fact that we sometimes talk of putting our philosophy into action, philosophy does not function directly this way.

Yet if there is no such thing as a "philosophical technology" roughly analogous to scientific technology, if the diffuse and mutually entangling inquiries of philosophy bear at best a tenuous relation to particular practices, then how can philosophy bring any benefits to the teacher in his or her work?

One might argue that an important question has been begged by assuming that philosophical thinking is something that is being done in a separate compartment, in which case the practical benefits of such reflections will be minimal. If, however, thoughtful reflection upon philosophical themes relevant to education has become thoroughly assimilated, made an integral part of the person's total reorientation, then there is some reason for affirming that philosophy can "bake bread" insofar as that person's perspective and personal commitment are concerned. This may not mean that philosophically the teacher-to-be will acquire any blueprints for action. It is not suggested that philosophical thought will yield up a set of imperatives to guide pedagogical practice. Yet there is still some basis for claiming that sustained consideration of educational ideas in the light of their fuller philosophical dimensions can be beneficial.

Moreover, asking for rules or recipes from philosophy for teachers may not simply involve a misconception of philosophy but also a wrong-headed

---

[1] Rupert C. Lodge, "The Essence of Philosophy of Education," *Educational Theory*, 3 (October, 1953) 353. (Quoted with the permission of the publisher.)

[2] See Louis Arnaud Reid, "Philosophy And The Theory And Practice of Education," in *Philosophical Analysis and Education*, Reginald D. Archambault (ed.). New York: Humanities Press, 1965, pp. 28*ff*. The following exposition borrows freely from Reid's arguments.

notion of what it means to teach. One venerable and popular stereotype of the teacher is that of a technician who acquires certain techniques and then comes to the classroom situation to apply them. Quite obviously one wants practical formulae to put into operation. The teacher needs prescribed modes of procedure firmly grounded in the best findings of the relevant scientific disciplines. In this sense, the need for an improved "science" of education is almost self-evident unless we assume that teachers today have attained some educational utopia admitting of no further improvements in conception or technique. But there is another side to teaching—the "art" of teaching which transcends simple rule-governed behavior. Good teaching is not identical with applying rules inflexibly without proper regard for the particular idio-syncrasies of a given situation. Here the analogy of the artist is more apposite: his tools and techniques in the practice of his art are employed all the time. But they are subsidiary to the central artistic purpose of creating something; although used all the time, his techniques have become "second nature" to the artist. They have been assimilated so thoroughly that he is free to be creative. These observations apply with equal force in the case of the teacher.

The outcome of this is that if teaching is not identical with the application of techniques, it is meaningful to assert that philosophy can be beneficial to the teacher although a poor source for instructional tools and methodologies. The potential contribution of philosophy for teachers ought not to be sought in terms of answers so much as in terms of questions. As Bertrand Russell once remarked, "Philosophy is to be studied, not for the sake of any definite answers to its questions . . . but rather for the sake of the questions them-selves; because these questions enlarge our conception of what is possible, enrich our intellectual imagination and diminish the dogmatic assurance which closes the mind." Even if this is too one-sided, even if we need not give up the hope for tentative answers, no mean significance inheres in exposure to ideas where the effects are a sense of life's depths and continuing complexities and an impatience with panaceas or ready-made answers in a difficult enterprise where few final answers seem adequate.

It is easier to make claims for philosophical reflection than it is to substantiate such claims. Still, there seems to be no way of either affirming or denying such claims generally in a scientifically accepted way. An assessment of the claimed benefits of philosophy of education cannot be scientific because any generalizations would have to be based on a number of studies, each in-volving value-laden variables that are not susceptible of investigation by strictly scientific procedures. If any salutory benefits are integral with the teacher as a whole person, a judgment of benefit would be inseparable from the total personality of that individual teacher and his influence upon his students. It appears impossible to envision any procedure that can evaluate such a globalistic effect as opposed to the observable data with which scientific investigations ordinarily deal. The "case study" method of rendering a judgment seems most nearly applicable, but even here the criteria for any judgment are multiple and nonobjective. Even were a satisfactory conclusion reached with respect to one single teacher, such as that teacher taught "better" for having studied philosophy of education, generalizations applying to a number of individuals become so vague as to be meaningless.

Nonetheless there can be rational judgments as to the benefits of the study of educational philosophy. They involve the introspective comments of experienced teachers who assess their own teaching and relate it to their philosophical development. Conceivably, comparative studies of teachers who had not studied philosophy or adopted a philosophical posture as opposed to those who had might shed further light on the question of the benefits to be derived from philosophy. The irony here is that the criteria for evaluating the results of any such studies might themselves necessitate philosophical reflection. Questions such as what is meant by "improved" teaching and the like contain concepts requiring philosophical clarification and analysis.

Typically, the curriculum of a professional teacher preparation program is overcrowded with course requirements. Ought room to be made for a separate course in philosophy of education for teachers? Or perhaps philosophical considerations should be raised within the contexts of all the various courses in curriculum, instruction, and soon. The possibility suggests itself that students in a separate course in educational philosophy will be more likely to compartmentalize their thinking. They may fail to draw the connections between philosophical points under consideration and the substance of other courses taken. The relevance of ideas discussed in one particular class in philosophy of education to the problematic situations encountered in initial teaching experiences, for example, may go unnoticed, whereas if philosophically grounded themes are part and parcel of the total preparatory curriculum, maybe the objectives of the philosophical study of education can be better realized.

The difficulty is, as in most such instances, if something is everybody's responsibility, it turns out to be no one's. Most teachers of education courses themselves lack the training and ability to frame their special competencies in a subject area within a larger philosophical context. Thus, despite its special hazards, the conventional arrangement has provided for a separate course in philosophy of education.

What should such a course be in terms of scope and content? With what substantive issues should it be concerned? What instructional strategies seem most promising? What should students "get out of" a philosophy of education course? The authors of this section address themselves to questions such as these. In a sense, the discussions are an extension of the ideas raised in the previous section. Arguments concerning the function and nature of philosophy, the content of a philosophy of education, the role of the educational philosopher all continue. The difference is primarily one of emphasis. In diverse ways, each of the following papers is involved with the broad question of the relation of philosophy and the teacher and, directly or by implication, with the question of what a course in philosophy of education ought to attempt to do.

Hall-Quest begins with an historical look at the relation between philosophy and the study of education. The value of philosophical inquiry, he notes, has frequently been misunderstood, partly because of a perennial American aversion to "theory" in favor of the immediately "practical," and partly because courses in the philosophy of education have lacked a coherent focus. Rather than a *mélange* of theoretical studies culled from disparate social disciplines, a more meaningful focus for educational philosophy, he argues, is "The nature of subject matter as distinguished from its organization as subjects or as curricula." Hall-Quest illustrates his thesis with an enumeration of substantive issues with which courses in educational philosophy might be profitably concerned. Finally, the potential of educational philosophy as a cohesive force in programs of teacher preparation is explored. Although written over three decades ago, many of Hall-Quest's fundamental themes can be discussed with profit in the changing educational world of today.

Paul Woodring echoes the thesis that educators tend to be philosophically illiterate. Although the factors responsible for such illiteracy are diffuse and difficult to trace historically, today more than ever teachers require the sophistication which only a philosophical consideration of contemporary educational problems can provide. Although philosophy may have no direct message or specific proposals to hand over to teachers, it has a profound bearing, C. D. Hardie suggests, on the clarification of puzzles and problems in curriculum construction. Hence, prospective teachers ought to be exposed to the study of what Hardie terms "the philosophy of the curriculum." Such an exposure might not produce a new revolution in educational theory and practice, but it might assist in developing changed habits of thinking on the part of teachers in classrooms.

A strategy for fostering such improved thinking habits is proposed by Castell. Rather than looking to the implications of philosophical positions for education, it is argued, courses in educational philosophy should be the occasions for examining educational matters in such a way that one is brought to philosophize about them. Clyde Curran posits much the same argument, while rejecting the notion that philosophy is "the obscure study of difficult writings." The encounter between teacher and student or the dynamics of the learning process, for example—these are rich sources for philosophical analysis. Similarly, Brickman pleads for a philosophy of education that concerns itself with an analysis of the fundamental issues of contemporary education. In particular, the underlying objectives of American education need to be brought in for philosophical inspection; in an age demanding priorities among what should be taught, teachers must formulate a coherent and comprehensive philosophy that will actually direct classroom instruction.

Arthur Pap, on the other hand, takes a more restricted view of the function of philosophy. Reflective of the critical, analytic temper of modern philosophy, he holds that we look in vain to philosophy for far-ranging objectives and broad directives. If there is to be an integration or center of focus in education, the contribution of philosophical analysis is very different than that envisioned by Brickman. Louise Antz, William Frankena, and Max Black, in sharp contrast, offer a wider, more "traditional" conception of the role of philosophy and accordingly a different perspective on its significance within the context of teacher preparation.

A familiar theme in apologetics for the philosopher is the invaluable contribution that he can make as a Socratic gadfly. The philosopher, as Demos sees it, offers an intellectual astringent, which—to mix a metaphor—constitutes a "semantic purgation" of the clichés and poorly understood slogans that abound in educational talk.[3] The philosophical gadfly performs a critical function in requiring educators to clarify and refine those basal concepts that underlie educational theory. Although the philosopher may not presume to legislate for the teacher, he can raise the kinds of questions that professional educators might otherwise ignore. By implication, courses in philosophy of education ought to perform an analogous function for prospective as well as practicing teachers.

As seen in earlier sections of this work, there is little unanimity of opinion on specifically what types of questions are especially appropriate for philosophy of education or on the methods to be utilized in providing answers. James Gutmann draws attention to the fact that since the range of professional concerns among teachers is so diverse, a tremendous problem arises in constructing a course in philosophy of education that can encompass such diversity. Nonetheless, a divorce between teaching and scholarship—including philosophical scholarship—is untenable. Thus, Peter Bertocci submits some guidelines for uniting "philosophy" and "education" in a common set of concerns. The very comprehensiveness of the task of philoso-

---

[3] The phrase is Professor Broudy's. Cf. pp. 114-121; and Demos, p. 285.

phy of education poses formidable hazards, among them the one noted by Gutmann—that is, the planning of a course to encompass the range of issues in education that need to be treated philosophically. As Robert Ulich illustrates, however, the educational practitioner and the speculative philosopher need to be bound into a "covenant of mutual responsibility." This is the difficult challenge that courses in philosophy of education must confront. Hetenyi offers a thoughtful review of most of the issues considered previously and outlines some of the possibilities for a course in philosophy of education in an undergraduate program of teacher preparation. His summary observations seem to suggest that a meaningful link can indeed be forged between the educationist and the academician via courses in educational philosophy, to the ultimate benefit of both.

Philosophers of education may easily fall prey to the delusion that they enjoy a monopoly of wisdom in matters educational. In conclusion, Chambliss and Phillips pose a reminder that efforts to improve educational practice and to engender more informed discussions in education requires more than a proliferation of courses in philosophy of education. What is needed is a creative attempt to involve the larger public in dialogue about education. The contributions of philosophy for teachers have been discussed at some length. Beyond this concern lies a larger task: locating means for bringing philosophy out into the marketplace where, ultimately, the decisions are made that shape the success or failure of education in a democratic society.

DESIGN FOR PHILOSOPHY
OF EDUCATION

ALFRED L. HALL-QUEST

Among the questions that need discussion in this critical hour of American education one of the most significant is the rôle of philosophy in the education of teachers.
The trend of the times seems strongly unfavorable to the development of a field
which, historically, is profoundly concerned with problems of education. The
question involves not so much the status of philosophy among other courses
deemed necessary for the education of administrators and teachers as the functional
value of philosophy in the practice of education. A similar question is now being
asked regarding the value of courses on the theory of jurisprudence in law school
programs. At a time when the promotion of new forms of government is based
upon a serious study of philosophy by the proponents of what is loosely called
radical movements, and, at a time, when popular interest in discussions broadly
philosophical is increasing, there would seem to be need of examining the value of
philosophy for the members of a calling which has derived many of its concepts
and values from this source. Stated differently the trend of the times in professional
education seems to be rushing away from theory toward the immediately practical.
If philosophy can not justify itself as necessary for the practice of Education it will
become as outmoded as the dialectics of the schoolmen.

The association between philosophy and the study of Education has had in the
United States a development of far-reaching significance in the organization of
programs of teacher education. It is well known that the study of Education on the
university level gathered momentum little more than a generation ago. Education,
to be sure, is frequently referred to in the history of philosophy and history in
general, but as a distinct discipline with its own concepts and literature. Education
is much younger than teaching itself. Pedagogy as studied in the normal schools
had important connections with philosophy, as can be seen in an examination of
Froebelian, Pestalozzian and Rousseaulian theories. Plato and Aristotle have much
to say on education; but not until educational theory flowered under the influence
of the Renaissance did the fruitage of Education as a discipline begin to form.

Between scholasticism and the modern study of Education there is an especially

FROM *Educational Forum*, 1 (November, 1936): 116–126. Copyright by Kappa Delta Pi, an Honor Society
in Education. (Reprinted by permission.)

close bond. The schoolmasters of the Middle Ages were monks intent upon the defense of church dogma and to this end employed Aristotlean principles of definition and classification, one result being the establishment of the great universities of Europe as centers for the study of philosophy, then confined to logic and dialectics. Thus came rationalism with its emphasis on deductive reasoning based upon assumptions or faith. The modern university of America is largely patterned after its European models, and today with all of its expansion in its liberal studies is largely rationalistic. The philosophy of idealism, for example, is the dominant academic philosophy in America.[1]

In time the study of philosophy, originally synonymous with higher learning, became one of several departments within the university or college, retaining, however, its historical prestige. In view of the fact that the study of philosophy on the undergraduate level was little more than an historical survey of major systems of thought, it was logical to take this material and organize it around the central interest of education. Thus the original courses in Education on the higher level were chiefly within the field of the history of education, and were listed under philosophy. Education was a branch of philosophy.

The scientific movement in Europe evolved research laboratories, among them physics, and here another emergence began, destined to have far-flung influence on the study of Education. Weber and Wundt were heirs of the new laboratory and through them three Americans acquired a point of view which quickly affected educational practice: namely, Titchener, Cattell, and Thorndike. Psychology, however, had long been another branch of philosophy, a very natural branch since philosophy was concerned with the meaning of mind. Early psychology was an introspective study of mind, rationalistic and analytical, without any pretense of being scientific. Weber through his studies in physiology and Wundt through more highly developed technique of research provided a new medium for the study of mind as measurable behavior. Education as concerned with learning, a distinct type of mental behavior, was divorced from philosophy and wedded to psychology. The results are well known. Beginning now as a branch of general psychology, rather than continuing as a division of philosophy, education evolved a further forking within psychology itself, and thus educational psychology came forth as an independent field of study and research, with philosophy far in the dim background and general psychology as a frequent substitute or prerequisite.

A few years ago another radiation from philosophy shifted the emphasis from educational psychology to sociology, more specifically educational sociology; and in some institutions this field is now considered as more important than educational psychology. Our present interest, however, lies in the fate of philosophy and its relations to Education.

It is, of course, incorrect to state that philosophy has been wholly abandoned. To some degree all institutions for the education of teachers offer courses in the

[1] Indicative of the changing philosophical scene in America, this statement might well be challenged today by those who see the philosophy of existentialism and the newer analytic movements as dominant. (Editor's note.)

philosophy of education. Usually in teachers colleges philosophy and history of education share a semester's or year's work. In addition to this compact course there are opportunities to study the principles of education, the principles of teaching, educational values, all of which derive not a little of their content from general philosophy. Universities, as a rule, include courses in the philosophy of education together with courses in curriculum making, the latter being related to earlier considerations of educational values and to courses in educational objectives, both of them organized selections of philosophical themes. Here two tendencies have begun to merge, the study of educational sociology and the study of philosophy as a distinct field of social theory. Much of current educational philosophy, therefore, is philosophical sociology or social philosophy. In a measure courses on character education reflect ethical theories and again the connection with general philosophy is obvious.

The philosophy of education, however, is typically quite different from historical philosophy. The latter embraces logic, aesthetics, ethics, politics and metaphysics, and is a synthetic expression of age-old human interest in the unknown or that only partially and inexactly known. Its broad original meaning was love of wisdom, and wisdom involved a knowledge of the general principles or laws through which anything might be explained. To the ancient Greek, before Aristotle, philosophy was synonymous with culture. Aristotle gave it two meanings: speculative knowledge and the study of metaphysics. Much of philosophy throughout its development has been deductive or rationalistic, but Bacon shifted the emphasis to the inductive, and from this came the scientific method and philosophy of positivism. Descartes was the great humanizer of philosophy through his insistence on the observation of nature and human life. However classified or defined general philosophy has been concerned with certain major questions: what is substance, what is knowledge, what is value? All of these questions have educational significance, but in educational philosophy they are only indirectly stated and answered at the present time.

In American education two systems of thought have been dominant—the idealistic, represented by Josiah Royce, and the pragmatic, sponsored by William James and John Dewey. The many shades of differences within both of these systems can not be considered in this discussion. Suffice that their respective corresponding courses in programs of teacher education are general and concerned chiefly with the problem of values. After a rather desultory investigation over several years I have failed to find any course in educational philosophy which includes *specific philosophies of subject matter*. All courses in the philosophy of education consider the meaning and significance of the principles underlying learning. ... I find that the usual themes have been: adaptation-adjustment and specialization of functions, the significance of the nervous system for education, the theory of recapitulation, the culture epoch theory, instincts, nature and nurture, inheritance, correlations between mind and body, work and fatigue, memory and association, imagination, apperception, thinking, interest, will, discipline, curriculum construction, orientation, logical and psychological organization of subject matter, the project method, democratic movements in education, culture and education, the scientific method, mental tests, experience, the nature of society, socialization, the nature of the individual, activity, the good life, the meaning of democracy, progress, the state, the problem of method, moral education, the child, the meaning of education, the function of the school and of the teacher, the meaning of science, freedom, personality, the nature of knowledge, etc. Here over a twenty-five year period is a strange *melange* of physiology, neurology, psychology, political science, mental hygiene, economics, sociology, social psychology, peda-gogy, science and ethics—all of it classified as philosophy of education and all of it taught in the schools of Education in American colleges and universities. In none of the books that I have examined appear discussions of the philosophy of mathematics, of science (save as scientific method of thinking), of history, of art, of music, of language, etc. There are valuable discussions of the sociology and psychology of these and other subject matter fields with emphases on the social value of such knowledge, and the psychological principles that seemingly control the process of teaching and learning in these fields. The historical, philosophically critical view of great meanings in these fields seems to be avoided.

Students in schools of Education have often asked: what is the value of such content for actual classroom purposes? Obviously much of the research in curriculum construction has professional and practical value in establishing attitudes, aiding child study, facilitating diagnostic teaching, enriching subject matter content and so on. In the present discussion there is no intention to wax cynical toward the vast amount of work done by conscientious investigators seeking for deeper understanding of the purpose, content, method, and problems of education. That some of it is worthless will be readily admitted by any critical reviewer; that much of it has far more value than the typical teacher realizes is equally true. Over a period of a quarter of a century important gains have been made and in many respects schools today are better than at the beginning of this period. My present interest lies in the contemplation of *a wholly different type of philosophy of education in which the emphasis rests upon the nature of subject matter as distinguished from its organization as subjects or as curricula.* Here is an approach to teaching efficiency and teacher leadership that may bridge the long existing gap between theories of education or of teaching on the one hand, and penetrating insight into the meaning of subject matter as a basis for artistic and inspiring exposition and appreciation, on the other hand. I have chosen two fields as illustrative of the meaning of educational philosophy about which I have long been thinking.

LITERATURE

The term "literature" has a two-fold meaning: artistic creative writing, and a collection of writings about or on a particular subject field. Thus the story, novel, drama, poetry and essay belong to literature as one of the arts, and the collective writings about or on the nature of matter would be philosophical or scientific literature. I am here confining the discussion to the first meaning of literature, as one of the arts. The question, therefore, is: what is the meaning of the philosophy of literature and how may an understanding of this philosophy aid the teacher of literature?

Philo M. Buck in *The Great Age*, recently published by the Macmillan Co., states that the problem of all great literature is to answer the question: "How to discover an adjustment in this new and expanding universe; how to live in it rightly and comfortably and justly; how to bring it into conformity with man's deepest desires; or, what seems much harder, how to bring one's deepest desires into conformity with it?" Here is a view of literature that is clearly philosophical. Literature is great to the degree that it reveals profound insight into universal problems of living. But it is exactly with these problems that philosophy is ultimately concerned. History clearly shows that these problems are timeless; they transcend all the artificial divisions of human endeavor into historical periods. They are the quests of man from the dawn of history down to the present hour, and to only a slight degree are they affected by national identities. Consequently the philosophical approach to the study of literature results in the discovery of vast world-inclusive literary movements. Just as philosophy critically examines ideas or concepts which are universally of value (for no system of philosophy can be exclusively or even chiefly national) so literature reflects human nature and experience. But human nature and experience have national or periodic significance only within narrow range. Man is essentially more cosmopolitan than national. Great literature, like philosophy, belongs not to a particular people, but to all.

Accept this broad interpretation of literature and immediately it appears as vastly more than a series of individual creations of the imagination. In High School literature should be, as it is, international in scope. So viewed, through the wide lens of mankind as a restless multitude seeking satisfactions, literature can be seen to express various levels or areas of racial thinking on or in each of which certain conceptions of the universe as a whole are given treatment in a variety of forms— myth, drama, history, poetry, novels, essays, etc.

On the first level, let us say, appear myths, fables, naïve narration and description as in the Bible, Homer, The Egyptian Book of the Dead, The Code of Hammurabi, the Ramayana, the Koran. In these writings we see a world sweep of elementary questioning and answering or wonderment in which imagination roams through longitudinal and latitudinal corridors dim-lit, mysterious, awesome with only an occasional beam of sunlight to mark the way. On another level we discover that Aristotle, Descartes, Newton, Spencer, Havelock Ellis, Dreiser, Galsworthy, Thomas Wolfe, are closely kin. On another we observe Aristophanes, James Joyce, Eugene O'Neill and Freud as literary companions. On each level there are the same fundamental questions, the same uncertain answers, the same fog-bound problems, all related to the meaning of life, the meaning of experience, the labyrinthian course of thinking, the scope of human freedom, the setting process of discipline. But all of them are likewise the problems and themes of Education.

For the teacher of literature, therefore, a philosophy of education needs to draw material not merely from philosophy itself but from the handmaidens of philosophy

—the literary arts. Literature is not a fund dissociated from other areas of human endeavor—it depends upon experience; it interprets life. All great literature has deep-running connections. Hamlet, Jean Valjean, Don Quixote, Ulysses and King Arthur are tragic characters, disillusioned, betrayed, bewildered in the presence of injustice and brutal reality. But notice that between Ulysses and Valjean stretch a thousand years. Notice that here are fictive characters beset by the problems that education would seek to answer. Here are examples of personality, of character. They are victims of environment. Upon them social pressures have laid their weight. In a word, they are vital and with such as they education must deal in all climes and times. Their place in literature courses is assured not merely because they belong to a significant cultural heritage, but because they represent educational forces, ideas, problems. Educational content must be related to understanding, imagination, thinking, the recognition of problems, the judgment of values, etc. Attitudes are not less important than skills; valuated interpretation is not less important than information.

A more detailed reference may make my meaning clearer. The Arthurian legends are one of the most popular units in the Junior High School course in literature. They are stories of adventure, tales of heroism. But they have wider significance, as descriptions of the age of Chivalry. The knightly brotherhood corresponded to the monastic brotherhood and both during the Middle Ages had become guardians of church doctrine. Knighthood involved loyalty to the church, to the lord of the manor, and to the lady of the manor. Its ideal was gentlemanly conduct. In the Arthurian tales, however, as told by Sir Thomas Malory, Tennyson and Lowell, knightly conduct is far from the ideal of gentleman developed later. In these tales evil conquers the good, and knighthood at King Arthur's court dissolves because the knights are unfaithful to their vows! But surely this is not the educational value of these tales. The value lies, I believe, in their being part of a continental movement, dominated by the church and directed toward preserving not only religious dogma but a method of reasoning whereby the doctrines of religion were formulated and departures therefrom detected. In the midst of such a scholastic regime human conduct might well appear far more evil than it probably was. The rational ideal, therefore, must be viewed critically. The life of reason during the Middle Ages was quite different from the ideal of reason in ancient times. The Arthurian tales, therefore, have a place in the history of education and in the evolution of educational theory, both of them sources for a study of educational philosophy. The educational ideal of the gentleman, as expounded by Montaigne, for example, must be viewed in the long gallery of personality portraits drawn against the background of national ideals: as in Sparta, the soldier; in Athens, the philosopher or sophisticated politician; in Rome, the orator, and so forth. An appreciational interpretation of the Arthurian Tales would involve a study of Feudalism, Chivalry, the Crusades, Don Quixote, as well as the Aristotelian system of definitions and classification, and the aim of living.

Teachers of literature need to understand the relation between their field and the broad concepts of education examined in the philosophy of education. The philosophies inherent in the writings of Shakespeare, Rousseau, Shelley, Hardy, Tolstoi, Dostoevsky, Scott, Ibsen, Whitman need to be connected with the whole background of educational philosophy if the school and the curriculum are to be conscious applications of educational principles. The department of literature in the high school bears a relation to the curriculum as a whole similar to that of the department of philosophy to the college curriculum. The fact that this relation all too often has not been functional is due in large measure, I believe, to the long existing gap between courses in the philosophy of education and the subject matter fields of public education.

SOCIAL STUDIES

This need is no less urgent in the education of teachers of the social studies. The major themes here direct attention to the meaning of society, experience, socialization, the nature of the individual, democracy, social control, the social process, the state, the social inheritance etc. But again these considerations are broad and usually remote from the interpretations of historical movements and historical characters as educational content.

What, for example, is the educational value, beyond the merely informational, of colonization in America in the seventeenth century? Why is it important that the young learner be guided toward an understanding and appreciation of this period? In courses on American history the instructor will doubtless consider this period against a broad background of social meanings. Spanish exploration was largely influenced by the encroachment of Mohammedanism on European soil, notably in Spain, but more than this the great European powers at the time—Spain, France, Holland and England—were beginning to hear the rumblings of a new disturbance, the assembling of the middle class only recently born after the travail that followed the dissolution of feudalism. Men were now aware of a new place in the scheme of things. The huge baronial estates were disintegrating. Unemployment prevailed over Europe. Governments faced bankruptcy because income from baronial tributes had ceased to flow. In France, for example, a central government was little more than an hegemony as in the case of Sparta, Athens and Thebes at different periods of Greek history. The European countries named needed trade expansion, new sources of raw materials. The explorations of the fifteenth and sixteenth centuries sought convenient trade routes. One result of such explorations was the discovery of new lands, among them the lands later to be known as North America and South America. A frantic race began to establish squatter's rights. Holland had found promising lands south eastward. Spain, France, and England concentrated on the west. In England reports presented by Raleigh, for example, stirred popular imagination. Land companies were formed, stocks were sold, passage for the adventurous unemployed was assured in return for indentured service. Creaking ships sailed west and in time dropped anchor near the shore known as Virginia. Others found harbor farther north along shores now known as Canada, Maine, New Hampshire, Massachusetts and Connecticut. Holland belatedly joined the race and settled New Amsterdam but England changed that to New York. The son of an English religious zealot eventually received a grant from the crown and thus Pennsylvania was added to the English colonies. Further details need not be recited. Suffice that colonization was a vast economic movement following the breakdown of feudalism, a movement sponsored by governments with depleted treasuries, and supported by thousands of men and women seeking economic security. More than this it was the beginning of the westward flow of migration which would soon spread into the American midwest and two centuries later reach the far west, and thus write the rough notes from which a James Truslow Adams could create *The Epic of America*. Obviously colonization is a projection of the utilitarian and naturalistic philosophies.

Here is a broad canvas to which must be added the great treks of ancient times. It is a canvas that tells the story of man's daring search for the bare means of subsistence, the story that explains the revolution of life, ever westward, driven by the same forces that hurl the atoms along unpredictable paths, the same energy that spins the nebulae into worlds. Can we not see in the epic migrations of man manifestations of cosmic activity, and in this the meaning of life as ceaseless activity with rest periods that we call today civilization or products of progress only momentary. And what is death but a pause in the rhythmic whirl, eternal and infinite?

How shall the teacher of social studies guide the pupils toward an understanding of the present unrest throughout the world? The leaders of the current protestants are young people. Do they understand the ideas and the ideals they champion? What lies back of socialism, communism, fascism, democracy, share-the-wealth-ism? Is there anything in nature that promises an equal distribution of minimal essentials? Is life a free gift? Does the world owe man a living? a share in the fruits of others' labors? Is profit wrong, anti-social? Can there be economic justice by definition in the midst of biological inequalities observable among all life forms? Does intelligent adjustment mean stabilized existence? If I have correctly understood my readings in ethnology it is only among extremely primitive peoples that tribal ownership of all things, including children, prevails. As group man rises individuality and personality gain value. Individual capacity results in differentials of sharing. The bride has value in terms of dowry; she can be bought for so many heads of cattle or other evidences of wealth. Private profit and ownership are therefore not anti-tribal; they have been earned or won by effort of prowess. The biological factor, including the mental, works selectively. Even in the ancient descriptions of the celestial world there are ranks among the spirits, and this hierarchy became the pattern of the ecclesiastical even in primitive Christianity, both of them being, of course, human interpretations of the composition of an ideal existence. Why did Marx and Engels evolve their economic theory? Whence the source of Hegel's state? What lies back of the theory of the social contract?

Here are profound philosophical questions that teachers of social studies should wrestle with. Here are trails that lead far back into social biology as well as social psychology. It is of such stuff that a vital philosophy of education is made.

Back of the social studies are inspiring, breathtaking meanings of life as the awesome evidence of an ever-gripping mystery. Bringing the teacher of social studies face to face with this fundamental meaning of the record he has the privilege of interpreting surely is one of the obligations of a course in the philosophy of education.

But many may object by asking: Do not or should not courses in subject matter for teachers take care of this need? The answer is that courses in biology, sociology, economics, physiology and even physics, to mention only a few, treat of materials included in the typical philosophy of education. As Dewey has clearly shown in his little volume on *The Sources of a Science of Education*, Education is a borrowing or applied science. It has evolved little, if anything, that is distinctly its own, save reorganization and interpretation of the materials it has borrowed and applied to preferred meanings of education. Strangely enough it has not borrowed from literary or art criticism! It has not borrowed from the philosophy of science or of mathematics or of history! In other words, it has not focused attention on the philosophy of subject matter but upon the philosophy of organization of subject matter and the objectives that such organization is designed to reach.

The problem of educational values involves not only subjects or courses as administrative units but the detailed content of these units, as well. Synthesis rests upon analysis. The widespread controversy about subjects versus activities may be viewed as chiefly a contention over the relative merits of the past and the present, subjects being viewed as systems of accumulated knowledge and activities a knowledge in the making through vital, immediate, and direct experiencing. The contention, however, is more verbal than fundamental. Such subjects as aviation and broadcasting are distinctly in the present. In both, especially the former, there is a body of knowledge that must be thoroughly understood through painstaking, progressive experiencing. Doubtless each item in a course on aviation has educational value in the sense that licensed flying depends upon proved understanding of what it means to pilot a plane. Among the essentials are certain items in physics and mathematics, both of them organized knowledge. In other words the principles of flying are of paramount importance.

A philosophy of education needs to be concerned with not only the purpose and meaning of education but with the content of educational practice. How are the principles of school administration, for example, related to this purpose and this meaning? How is cost accounting related thereby? What is the educational significance of any of the content in programs of teacher education as related to the purpose and meaning of education? Similar questions need to be studied on the public school level. Philosophy of content is no less vital than philosophy of purpose, process, organization.

In as much as Education has borrowed from numerous fields of knowledge deemed significant for an understanding of the meaning and value of the educative process it may be asked, why has there not been borrowing from the philosophy of history, of science, of mathematics, of art, of music, of literary criticism, of language; in a word, from the literature on the meanings underlying the content of education?

The relations of these meanings to the purpose and meaning of education need to be examined by the educational philosopher and discussed by all prospective teachers and administrators. The department of educational philosophy, as here viewed, is the central and synthesizing agency in any program of the education of teachers.

The philosophy of education that is envisaged by this discussion may be achieved by one or all of several kinds of organization.

1. The revision of present courses whereby much of the present content will be deleted and a wholly new content substituted in its place. This new content will consist of such emphases as I have tried to illustrate.

2. A wholly new course, entitled "The Philosophy of Subject Matter" might be organized within an expanded department of educational philosophy. This new course would be a fusion of the meanings that underlie the subject matter of public education.

3. The department of the philosophy of education might become the core of the school of Education and in and through it all other departments might be philosophically interpreted to the end that the student may see the many interpretations of what he doubtless now views as a loose aggregate of courses in Education that lack cohesive unity in a program of teacher preparation. Such a fusion would include all courses in educational method and student teaching.

4. Between the school or college of education and other departments of the college or university a cooperative arrangement might be evolved whereby these other departments would offer in their respective fields interpretations of professional value for teachers, such interpretations to be derived through a reviewing board composed of representatives of the various interests concerned.

5. A wholly new course in the philosophy of education might be taught by a number of professors from various fields, the course continuing through the year and each instructor responsible for a four or six weeks' unit, the course as a whole to be directed by the professor of the philosophy of education.

6. A series of lectures by subject matter specialists might be planned, each lecturer to conform to the design of the series as philosophical in the sense used in this discussion, and each lecture based on a mimeographed or printed syllabus with bibliography; credit value to be allowed on the basis of intensive study of the philosophy of subject matter in the student's subject matter specialty.

Local conditions will determine the most workable arrangement of the type of course adequate for the purpose in view. First all of there needs to be not only awareness of the problem but professional interest in thinking toward its solution. Much is being said these days about integration. If this term is to mean more than an additional slogan or shibboleth and signify a vital control of the educative process efforts in constructing public school curricula must begin, I believe, with plans to integrate the curricula within the institutions responsible for the education of teachers. Important as are curricular patterns of even greater importance are the bases upon which the content of the curriculum is interpreted to the pupil. Subject matter is not important in itself. Its significance and value lies in its being the results of human striving, thinking, growing. It is both the result of energetic behavior and the instrument for further and perhaps more intelligent effort to live through adequate readjustment. But back of subject matter are huge questions and trembling answers concerned with the meaning of the universe, the meaning of man, the meaning of life. These questions and answers need consideration in every subject matter field. It is the privilege of the philosophy of education to review them.

THE VALUE OF
PHILOSOPHY FOR TEACHERS

CLYDE E. CURRAN

Few studies for the professional training of teachers receive more emphasis than philosophy of education. Most directors of teacher training consider a comprehensive philosophy vital to good teaching. Thousands of courses in principles, theory, and philosophy of education offered by colleges and universities testify to the importance placed upon philosophic training for educators. Yet few teachers have well-rounded philosophies of education.

When a group of teachers discuss their "philosophy," what do they say? Do they refer to first principles, human and cosmic foundations, theories regarding the learning process, the nature of society, the role of the school in relation to society, or problems in ethics and esthetics as they relate to education? No. Most educators do not treat these fundamental matters. When discussing their "philosophy," teachers usually refer to miscellaneous practices performed in classrooms regardless of inconsistencies, ineptness, or excellence. They manifest a great deal of impatience towards anything theoretical. Crowded by the demands of the day with schedules to meet, large classes to organize, budgets to arrange, and examinations to grade, teachers consider theory a waste of time. Their interest centers upon effective ways of teaching spelling, writing, chemistry, or mathematics. The suggestion that a theoretic analysis of practice facilitates teaching usually draws a reply like this:

"How in the world can studying the nature of man and society help me teach reading in the fifth grade? Teachers want to do a better job, but how can reading and talking about theory that teachers don't understand, and about which philosophers themselves are confused, help when I stand in front of a class of from forty to fifty youngsters?"

FROM *Educational Theory*, 3 (January, 1953): 81–83. (Reprinted by permission of the publisher and the author.)

The foregoing challenge raises an important question: Of what value is a philosophy of education to teachers?

There is a reason why teachers have found much of the required work in philosophy of education of little value. Traditionally philosophers of the western world have dwelt in the realm of abstraction. The eyes of great visionary thinkers like Plato, Kant, and Hegel have turned from the flesh and blood realities of people struggling to the pristine quietude of metaphysics. Their writings, containing unexplained mysteries and couched in formidable, often obscure, language, perplex more frequently than they enlighten. No wonder teachers become appalled when told such philosophy will improve their classroom practice.

To dismiss philosophy with a shrug and the ejaculation, "I have tried it but it didn't help me a bit," overlooks what penetrating thinking can do. Although educators may find classical philosophic writing unfathomable, they teach under conditions that call for philosophizing. People trying to live together harmoniously present dilemmas that require the deepest reflection. If instead of finding sanctuary within ivory towers, thinkers (teachers belong to this group) ply their tools in the mire of human relations, philosophy can move from the twilight of idle speculation to the world of practical affairs. Rather than living the shadowy life of a saintly recluse, the philosopher can become a man of action, seeking the causes and furthering the alleviation of human conflict. Philosophy looked upon in this light has value for teachers.

When developed as a thoughtful, consistent description and analysis undertaken to build an ever-increasing harmony among people, philosophy has meaning for educators. From this view the process of philosophizing and the educative process are the same. Teacher-philosophers project their work against a background of human struggle where they seek to understand why people behave as they do, how human nature develops, and through this insight facilitate understanding among men. Classrooms, instead of dreary cells where hollow voices drone out lessons in spelling, arithmetic, or reading, become laboratories in human relations. Success in teaching is then marked by the effect the school has in developing character and not only by the quantity of reading, spelling, or arithmetic learned.

Teachers who plead, "Show us how confused philosophic theory can help us teach arithmetic, spelling, or reading," assume that all philosophy is abstract, controversial, and of no use whatever in educational practice. Associating philosophy with the never-never land of dreamers, they overlook the place of philosophic thinking in relation to human problems. Furthermore, they assume that the purposes of education revolve around teaching subjects. Students certainly need to know subjects, but for what? What does it avail men if they master the intricacies of science, relish the great classics of art, music, and literature, span the earth with steel and cement, yet know not how to live in harmony?

What do teachers as philosophers do? They seek to understand what accounts for human conflict. They study the sciences, especially anthropology, psychology, sociology, economics, and government to discover reliable data about men and societies. They turn to the humanities, the history of civilization, for further evidence. Teachers need to know facts. But facts are not enough. They must also hold a glowing ideal before their eyes. What better ideal can teachers find than the Christian ethic of men living as brothers? This serves as a goal, the vision of men fulfilling their capacities by developing human understanding. Teacher-philosophers do not perform these tasks in the serenity of armchairs, but engage in inquiry, muster evidence, keep ideals before them for direction during periods of conflict. They work in the world of practical affairs, marriage and parenthood, business and vocations, and community relations both local and international, to determine areas of confusion, to participate with all concerned in building policies and practices that will further understanding among people.

Their special province is the classroom. Here teachers endeavor through mature judgment to so guide pupils that they develop strong characters. What kind of characters? Young people with habits and dispositions of curiosity typify characteristics philosopher-teachers seek—boys and girls so charged with enthusiastic imaginations that a lifetime is too short for satiation; youths growing in their ability to think reflectively, to reap the rich harvest of love in marriage and parenthood, to achieve satisfaction in their work, to create and consume beauty, and most of all to communicate, not in the narrow sense of reading and writing, but of using all skills to strengthen bonds of human understanding.

Educators may ask, "Isn't this expecting too much of teachers?" We require doctors to have thorough scientific training that takes years of intensive study. They must devote their lives to their work. Only men with outstanding personal qualities succeed in medicine. The maintenance of public health and care of the sick demand the best. In turn, practitioners of medicine have reached a high place in our society. Should we expect anything less from practitioners of education, who virtually hold the destiny of civilization in their hands?

Teachers might complain that the above description of philosophy in education does not give answers to questions about specific problems and practices. No, it doesn't. It is not supposed to, any more than a hammer or saw is supposed to build a house. People, not tools, build houses. Philosophy, the process of using reflection to eliminate human conflict, is a tool. When used properly, it can build mansions or it can lie idly by while men live in shacks and caves. No, philosophy does not give the answers. Neither does science, history, literature, or whatever you wish to name, for that matter. People must work out the answers. They must bring their ideals into reality by determining obstacles and jointly working for agreement. Perhaps the most serious block is conflict of ideals. People of divergent cultures need to work out harmony. We have the tool—the process of reflection applied to human affairs—philosophy. Teachers are among the most important workers in this building of the mansion of humanity. We have had the plans for a long time—ever since Jesus taught the ideal of brotherly love.

Traditional thinkers made the gigantic error of considering philosophy a castle ready-made—one in which men could dwell by exercising lofty thinking removed from the world of practice. They knew they had the supreme answers to all existence. Once entrenched in their convictions, they proceeded to mount the marble steps leading into the clouds, shouting loudly, "Follow us. Ahead lies the Promised Land." From this high perch they could no longer see the populace tearing at one another's entrails.

If we lived in a perfect world, one free from conflict, if decisions were never necessary because each life abounded in the highest satisfactions, if we knew the best possible way of teaching the absolute truth, then philosophy of any kind would be unnecessary. People living in such a Utopia would need only to conserve and consume the bounties of eternal beauty. Our world is not this kind of place. The panorama of history (both present and past) presents confused scenes of noble achievement contrasted with human degradation, enlightenment with ignorance, love with hate, and benevolence with bestiality. The fact that history yields no clear-cut idea of a fixed good complicates the picture even more. What some cultures revere as good, others despise as ignoble.

There are no well-paved highways leading through the jungle of human misunderstanding. Despite great cultural advances, this jungle threatens to engulf us. Because of human conflict, modern civilization stands on the brink of disaster. Either we learn to live together harmoniously or face destruction. We must penetrate the vast puzzle of human relations. Teacher-philosophers must lead the way.

THE DECLINE OF EDUCATIONAL PHILOSOPHY

PAUL WOODRING

It is my thesis that educational philosophy in America has fallen upon evil days. The difficulty is not so much that we have accepted false philosophies, or even that we have no philosophy at all, though that is true of far too many educators, but that we have ceased to give proper attention to philosophical problems.

Because we have neglected these problems we make decisions about the curriculum on an *ad hoc* basis without proper attention to the basic problem of the aims, purposes, and meaning of education. Because we have no clear intellectual basis for rejecting their demands, we give in all too easily to noisy minorities within each community who demand additions to the school's responsibilities without first asking whether these are consistent with the important educational aims. Because we have not given sufficient attention to philosophical problems, we are afraid to

FROM *Phi Delta Kappan*, 40 (October, 1958): 6–10. (Reprinted by permission.)

attempt to discriminate between the profound and the trivial or even to see that we must.

It is true that the public schools in a free nation must be responsive to the will of the people in the long run, but because many of our teachers and school administrators are innocent of philosophy they have confused this to mean that they must satisfy each demanding citizen in the community. If a few noisy citizens demand a marching band, they get a marching band with a bevy of drum majorettes thrown in. If a few parents complain about high standards, we lower the standards for all the children. We have become afraid to say no. But this is not a proper application of the principle of basing our free institutions upon the public will. The public will is not to be determined by the whims of the few but rather, as Walter Lippmann has put it, "the public interest may be presumed to be what men would choose if they saw clearly, thought rationally, acted disinterestedly and benevolently." Educational leadership requires the ability to assist the public to see educational problems in perspective and to think clearly about them, so that their decisions may be disinterested and benevolent. This will be possible only if the leader himself has a clear understanding of the philosophical issues underlying educational decisions.

In saying that we ought to be more sophisticated about educational problems, I do not at all mean to say that we must agree. In our pluralistic culture, full agreement on philosophical issues is neither possible nor necessary. But tolerance of diversity does not mean that any individual who aspires to leadership can be excused from the responsibility for having some firm convictions of his own, based upon evidence, clear thinking, and value judgments.

I have before me the answers to a questionnaire in which each of a group of teachers, all of whom hold master's degrees, was asked to state in his own words his philosophy of education. The answers of more than half are truly appalling. "We learn by doing," said one. "Education is life," said another. "We learn what we live," said a third, while a fourth opined that "education is growth." None seemed to be able to explain what he meant by these venerable cliches and none seemed to understand that a cliche, however ancient, is not a philosophy. I assume that if one of these teachers is later asked by a citizen whether driver education is consistent with his educational philosophy, he will reply, "Education is life," and leave the questioner with his mouth hanging open. I wonder what he will reply if asked his views on racial segregation.

I hope I am making it clear that my criticism of these teachers is not that their philosophy was faulty, but that they gave no real evidence of having any philosophy. Happily, a much smaller number of those questioned were able to state their philosophy with varying degrees of clarity.

No one of us has the right to say what is the "proper" educational philosophy for American teachers; all we have a right to do is express our own views for their acceptance or rejection, using the most forceful arguments at our command. But while we cannot say what is the best philosophy, we can certainly say that some points of view are not philosophical at all. A refusal to make decisions or to organize our ideas in such a way as to reveal internal inconsistencies is not a philosophy. Philosophy, says Philip Phenix, "involves the organization, interpretation, clarification, and criticism of what is already within the realm of the known and the experienced."[1] If an individual fails to organize, interpret, clarify, and criticize his own ideas, he is not dealing with problems philosophically. Bertrand Russell prefers to place the emphasis on the last step. "Philosophy," he says, "is the criticism of criticism." But this is an incomplete statement, for philosophy must surely include the organization and interpretation of a set of consistent ideas.

How much of our failure in educational philosophy can reasonably be attributed to the impact of progressive education? Many people have assumed that progressivism was a philosophy and some of the critics who have accepted this assumption have attributed all the ills of our schools to this philosophy. This, I think, is mistaken on two counts. First, because the great majority of American teachers have never accepted more than randomly selected portions of progressive education and second, because it was not, properly speaking, a philosophy at all.

"The fact that the progressive movement has never come across with an adequate philosophy of education warrants the presumption that it does not have any,"[2] said Boyd Bode. I should prefer to accept Carter Good's definition of progressive education as a reform movement, with the added comment that reform movements, however necessary and useful, are usually much more clear in what they oppose than in what they stand for. Dewey saw the danger in this. In 1938 he wrote, "Those who are looking ahead to a new movement in education should think in terms of Education itself rather than in terms of some 'ism about education, even such an 'ism as progressivism. For in spite of itself, any movement that thinks and acts in terms of an 'ism becomes so involved in reaction against other 'isms that it is unwittingly controlled by them. For it then forms its principles by reaction against them instead of by a comprehensive, constructive survey of actual needs, problems and possibilities."[3]

As a reform movement, progressive education was successful in clearing away much of the educational debris that had accumulated over the centuries. It was successful in focusing the attention of the educators upon the child as a responding organism. But as a philosophy it was far from complete, for it failed to establish a clear and consistent sense of direction, and this lack has led to aimless wandering in search of a goal. Some progressives have talked as though growth were the goal of education, but growth itself is by no means a satisfactory goal. A cancer grows. The very use of the term "growth," when used to describe a complex process involving both maturation and learning, has led to educational confusion. A philosophy of education must include within itself a clear order of priorities, however these may have been arrived at.

The decline of interest in educational philosophy surely cannot be attributed directly to John Dewey, for no one had a greater interest in philosophical problems

[1] Philip Phenix, *Philosophy of Education*, New York: Holt, 1958, p. 4.
[2] Boyd Bode, *Progressive Education at the Crossroads*. New York: Newson, 1938, p. 85.
[3] John Dewey, *Experience and Education*. New York: Macmillan, 1939, p. vii.

than he. But indirectly, through his interpreters and misinterpreters, he may unwittingly have contributed to the decline. Dewey was far too tolerant of those who distorted his most important ideas.

Educators are fond of pointing out that the critics of modern trends in education are prone to use Dewey as a scapegoat without having read or understood him. All too often this has been true, but it ought to be mentioned in passing that a great many teachers and school administrators haven't read Dewey either, and many who think they understand him have gotten their impressions through secondary sources such as textbooks or selected readings where his views have been so highly selected as to distort their true meaning. No one who really understands Dewey would be in favor of soft education or afraid to say which kinds of education are "soft." No one who has read him carefully can believe that all experiences are equally educative or that it is unnecessary to set up a list of priorities in education. No one who understands him would question that every professor of educational philosophy must have a wide acquaintance with philosophies other than his own. It was Dewey himself who pointed out that, while experience is educative, not all experience is equally educative. An understanding of this principle requires that the educator make decisions regarding which experiences, which subjects, and which activities are *most* educative.

WHY CAN'T WE DEAL WITH THE CRITICS?

Our failure to grapple with the philosophical problems has made us much less effective than we ought to be in dealing with the critics of the public schools, for much of recent criticism is philosophical in its import. In answering the criticisms of Bestor, Hutchins, Adler, and Mortimer Smith it is futile to content ourselves with pointing out the over-generalizations, the exaggerations, and the occasional misstatements of fact, for the intelligent reading public regards these as but minor details, even as legitimate literary devices. The important issues are philosophical, and so long as the literate public believes that the critics have a firmer philosophical base than that of the educators they will continue to lend their support to the critics.

If you wish to reply to Mortimer Adler, it will do no good to point out that Adler ignores the measurable facts of individual differences in learning capacity—though it is true that he does. It will do no good because Adler holds to a philosophical position that is prone to reject empirical evidence or at least to subordinate it to rational thought. If you wish to reply to Adler you must do it by a direct attack upon his view of the ultimate nature of man, which he holds to be everywhere and at all times the same. If you wish to undertake such a task you would be wise to make sure that your own logic is impeccable, for Adler is skilled in forensics.

If you wish to take on Bestor, a somewhat simpler but still not an easy task, you will find it futile to point out the sweeping generalizations in some of his earlier publications, for it is not these that have won him a wide following. Nor will it do much good to point out that he is biased against educators or, as he prefers to call them, "educationists," because too many of your readers share his bias. Bestor's popularity grows, in large part, from his concept that the proper role of the schools is intellectual development and that all other aims must be held in due subordination to this fundamental purpose. He holds, too, that the most effective way to develop intellectual excellence is through the academic disciplines taught as separate subjects. Of these two issues the first is clearly philosophical and the second has important philosophical overtones.

A great many intellectuals, in and out of universities, share Bestor's views on both these issues. Any educator hoping to make a successful counter-attack must come squarely to grips with them. Merely demonstrating that other goals—social, recreational, or vocational—are desirable *social* aims will not weaken the position of Bestor and other critics of recent educational trends; any effective reply must include convincing evidence that these are the proper aims of the public school and that no other agency can achieve them as well. And any effective attack on the position that intellectual development is best achieved through the separate academic disciplines must include evidence that it is best achieved in some other way with the teachers available or likely soon to become available.

The literate public is not greatly interested in the conflicts between professional educators and academic groups within the universities, but it is very much interested in the question of what is the primary purpose of institutionalized education and the question of how this purpose may best be accomplished. At the present moment in history it is prone to agree with the critics that the schools have tried to do too much, have accepted too many of the responsibilities best retained by the home, and that as a result they have neglected their fundamental responsibility.

LET'S ASK THE RIGHT QUESTIONS

Educators and their critics alike have been too much concerned with the question of whether the schools of fifty years ago achieved their academic aims better than do the schools of today. Critics are fond of trying to prove that the schools of grandfather's day had admirable aims and achieved them. The evidence does not support them, but neither does it support the view of many educators that the older schools were iniquitous institutions fit only for scorn and ridicule. Let us learn what we can from the past while resolutely facing the future. The real and important question is not whether the schools of 1900 were better or worse than those of today but whether the schools of [today] are as good as they might be, ought to be, and can become. Children entering the first grade this fall will not yet be fifty when the year 2000 rolls around; the question is whether we are adequately preparing them for the age in which they will live.

EVERY TEACHER A PHILOSOPHER

To fill the philosophical vacuum in the schools will require that every teacher and every administrator take a more sophisticated view of the fundamental problems of education. Each teacher should have a clear idea of what he is trying to accomplish and of how his aims are related to the basic problems of reality, of truth, and of value. The secondary teacher should understand how his subject fits into the scheme of things and should understand its limitations and its relation to other subjects and other activities. Any teacher should have a clear view of the role of the school in its relation to other social institutions in order not to preempt the responsibilities of the home and the community. The administrator, even more than the teacher, should be able to interpret the role of the school to the community and to work with community leaders in re-defining that role. If he is to do this effectively he must be at least as well oriented philosophically as the most intelligent adults in the community, for his job is not that of "selling" a program but that of participating in intellectual discourse at the highest levels.

How can we achieve the necessary philosophical sophistication on the part of teachers and administrators? In commenting earlier on the replies of teachers to a questionnaire regarding their own philosophies of education, I observed that a small group of teachers did give evidence of clear views while the larger group did not. When we have analyzed the difference between the backgrounds of these two groups we may have an important clue.

I suspect that we shall find that those teachers who have a sophisticated understanding of philosophical problems got it from a wide variety of sources, some in a course called educational philosophy, others in courses in history of education, some as a part of their liberal education, and others through random reading and discussion outside of class.

If a college has on its staff a professor with the proper interests, scholarship, and enthusiasm for the subject, it seems to me to be best that the philosophical problems of education be explored in a separate course. Whether this course should come at the undergraduate or the graduate level has been a subject for debate and we have little clear evidence as to which is more effective. But if the major course is postponed until the fifth year—which means that for many students it will not come until after a period of teaching—it seems essential that the student be at least introduced to philosophical problems in his first professional course. At the point where he moves from liberal into professional education he should begin to ask what education is all about. His views about the nature of reality, truth, and the good life should be challenged. The questions will not be answered at this point— they will never be fully answered—but he should become aware of the problems, of the fact that people differ and have a right to differ.

If the liberal portion of his education has been truly liberal, these questions will, of course, have been asked earlier, in courses in literature, social studies, science, and general philosophy. The problem now is to relate them to the problems of education.

HAS PHILOSOPHY BEEN BADLY TAUGHT?

On questionnaires in which graduates have been asked to rate the value of their professional courses, educational philosophy often falls low on the list. I think it would be hasty indeed to conclude from this that philosophy is unimportant to the teacher. The more probable explanation is that teachers think it is unimportant because they have no real depth of understanding and it is difficult to see the importance of anything one does not understand. If teachers react unfavorably to their courses in educational philosophy, it is probable that it has been badly taught, often by individuals without the proper preparation and interests.

A philosophy of education should be related to actual experience with children in a learning situation, but it will not stem directly from such experience. A teacher may spend forty years with children and yet never achieve anything even remotely resembling a philosophy. The development of a truly philosophic point of view requires intellectual activity: reading, thinking, discussion, and critical evaluation—activities most likely to be found in a college classroom in the company of one's intellectual peers.

The graduate schools of education have a clear responsibility for making sure that each candidate for a doctoral degree in education has a firm grasp of philosophical issues. The fact that the student plans to be a school administrator or guidance specialist in no way reduces this responsibility. The administrator who cannot deal effectively with problems of goals and values is at best a manager rather than a true educational leader, and the guidance specialist who has no clear idea of the overall aims of education runs a serious risk of guiding in the wrong direction. But graduate schools should give particular attention to the preparation of those who are to teach courses in the foundations of education in our colleges and universities. If these individuals are philosophically naive, the whole program of teacher education will become a shambles.

The long-range solution to our problems will require that teachers on all levels, including the academic scholars in our universities, take a more knowledgeable and sophisticated view of the philosophic issues in education. Classicists, scientists, and historians, particularly those who plan to devote a large part of their time to college teaching, need the same broad orientation in fundamental educational issues as do the elementary and secondary teachers, and eventually this orientation will become a part of the preparation of college teachers. When this occurs, the tensions between professional educators and scholars in other fields will be greatly lessened, but this happy day seems a long way off because of the sad state of confusion in educational philosophy. First, we must put our own house in order.

THE PHILOSOPHY OF EDUCATION IN A NEW KEY

C. D. HARDIE

Many of those who work in the field of education like to feel that they are helping to change the world. Indeed one of the reasons often given by students who are going to teach for their choice of profession is that they want to influence other people's lives, and in that way produce better individuals and hence a better world. This power of education is certainly very real and is not likely to be forgotten or ignored. But the converse relationship is sometimes ignored. By this I mean that some people who are interested in education do not realise the extent to which changes in the world and in our knowledge of it produce changes in education.

In the days of ancient Greece ideas about education were determined largely by (a) the position of mathematics in the scheme of knowledge, and (b) the facts associated with a slave-owning society. In the Middle Ages ideas about education were very different, because for mathematics and a slave-owning society were substituted theology and a feudal society. These have now been replaced by science and democracy. Several of the problems which puzzle people today are due to the fact that they are confused in their minds, and have not explicitly recognized the change that must result in education from the changes which have taken place in the way in which we think about the world.

In this paper I want to consider one aspect of this change, namely, the effect which it should have on the philosophy of education. Most people are probably willing to admit that the increased and increasing importance of science should be reflected in a changed curriculum, but not so many realize the change that should take place in education from the fact that a clearer understanding of science has resulted in a clearer understanding of the nature of knowledge itself. Scientific knowledge has come to dominate our way of life, not just because of its practical and theoretical successes but because it is in fact coextensive with the entire field of knowledge.

The relevance of this to the philosophy of education has not yet been properly appreciated. Much teaching and writing in the philosophy of education still assumes a view of philosophy that can no longer be justified. As this view is perhaps most ably expressed in a passage in Russell's *History of Western Philosophy* I make

FROM *Educational Theory*, 10 (October, 1960): 255–261. (Reprinted by permission of the publisher and the author.)

no apology for quoting it in full. "Philosophy, as I shall understand the word, is something intermediate between theology and science. Like theology, it consists of speculations on matters as to which definite knowledge has, so far, been unascertainable; but, like science, it appeals to human reason rather than to authority, whether that of tradition or that of revelation. All *definite* knowledge—so I should contend —belongs to science; all *dogma* as to what surpasses definite knowledge belongs to theology. But between theology and science there is a No Man's Land, exposed to attack from both sides; this No Man's Land is philosophy. Almost all the questions of most interest to speculative minds are such as science cannot answer, and the confident answers of theologians no longer seem so convincing as they did in former centuries. Is the world divided into mind and matter, and if so, what is mind and what is matter? Is mind subject to matter or is it possessed of independent powers? Has the universe any unity or purpose? Is it evolving towards some goal? Are there really laws of nature, or do we believe in them only because of our innate love of order? Is man what he seems to the astronomer, a tiny lump of impure carbon and water impotently crawling on a small and unimportant planet? Or is he what he appears to Hamlet? Is he perhaps both at once? Is there a way of living that is noble and another that is base, or are all ways of living merely futile? If there is a way of living that is noble in what does it consist, and how shall we achieve it? Must the good be eternal in order to deserve to be valued, or is it worth seeking even if the universe is inexorably moving towards death? Is there such a thing as wisdom or is what seems such merely the ultimate refinement of folly? To such questions no answer can be found in the laboratory. Theologians have professed to give answers, all too definite, but their very definiteness causes modern minds to view them with suspicion. The studying of these questions, if not the answering of them, is the business of philosophy." [1]

Such a view of philosophy led to the principal traditional subdivisions of the subject. (1) Metaphysics, which was supposed to deal with what is ultimately real in the universe—the reality of mind and matter, the existence of God, the nature of Space and Time, and so on. (2) Moral philosophy, or ethics, which was supposed to deal with the nature of moral concepts and with the grounds that exist for justifying moral judgments. (3) Logic and epistemology, which were supposed to deal with reasoning and the nature of knowledge. The answers which philosophers have given to problems in those traditional subdivisions have been about as numerous as the philosophers, but certain broad types of answer could be distinguished, the most important of which were called Idealism, Realism, and Pragmatism.

This division of philosophy explains why it is that in many books on the philosophy of education it is possible to distinguish quite clearly three different kinds of statement. First of all there are metaphysical statements. "Froebel's God is an active source of continual creation in both nature and mind." [2] "The Herbartian soul is real, unchangeable, independent and without faculties; the contact of this

---

[1] Bertrand Russell, *History of Western Philosophy* (Allen and Unwin, 1946), pp. 10–11.
[2] S. J. Curtis and M. E. A. Boultwood, *A Short History of Educational Ideas* (University Tutorial Press, 1953), p. 363.

soul with the reality of the body brings about the thought and motivation of the live man." [3] Then there are judgments of value, which, implicitly or explicitly are part of any statement about the aims of education. "Pestalozzi saw education as a means of social reform." [4] "Perhaps, unconsciously, he (Comenius) held fast to many of the tenets of Plato and Aristotle and sought to inculcate in all children the habits of thought, behaviour, and activity which would later ensure the fulfillment of the duties and responsibilities of citizenship and Christianity." [5] Finally, there are statements about the nature of knowledge. "A knowledge of the external world is arrived at through the activities of the sense organs." [6] "The beliefs, thoughts, efforts which may constitute a person's enquiry have no truth or falsity, they are either satisfactory or unsatisfactory." [7] It is evident that these statements, all taken from one book on the philosophy of education, are typical philosophical statements in Russell's sense.

With the teaching of Wittgenstein, however, this view of philosophy has had to be abandoned, and the reason for this is of great importance for students of education. For many people spend a great deal of their time speculating about traditional philosophical questions, or, at least, about questions which fall in the metaphysical and ethical subdivisions of philosophy; and if they are being misled in doing so, then it should be one of the tasks of education to cure them of this confusing and wasteful habit. The reason for the abandonment is that before any problem is solved we must at least know what kind of evidence would have a bearing on it. If, as is the case in most of the problems of traditional philosophy, we have no idea what the relevant evidence would even be like, then we must admit that such problems are not meaningful ones. This criterion for the meaningfulness of any question or problem, adopted by practising scientists, must now be accepted for the whole of knowledge.

Philosophy, therefore, is not a subject which provides knowledge about the universe—either about the physical environment of man or about man himself. If it is sensible to inquire whether the world is divided into mind and matter, and if so, what is mind and what is matter, then it is quite certain that the answers will not be found in any book on philosophy. It is certain not because philosophers have so far been unsuccessful in such inquiries, but because philosophy cannot by its very nature make pronouncements about the nature of the world—that is the function of the sciences or of common sense. It follows that it will not be possible to deduce a philosophy of education from a general system of philosophy which claims to have inside knowledge about the nature and destiny of man, or about the nature of ultimate reality, for the claims of any such system must be spurious.

The task of philosophy is much more modest, but at the same time much more useful. It is to develop methods which lead to the clarification of different kinds of knowledge, whether it is the knowledge of common sense, or of mathematics, or of the sciences; and in the last thirty years or so considerable progress has been

[3] Op. cit., p. 345.
[4] Op. cit., p. 325.
[5] Op. cit., p. 183.
[6] Op. cit., p. 221.
[7] Op. cit., p. 456.

made, so that as a result of the labours of recent philosophers we understand very much more clearly the nature of the knowledge attained in these different spheres.

Philosophy has thus no direct message for education. Traditional accounts of the philosophy of education often start with the kind of question posed by Russell and then proceed to discuss the various answers, such as realist, idealist or pragmatist, that have been given by philosophers. The answers to various practical educational questions, for example, the construction of curricula, are then made to depend on the type of philosophy which has been approved by the author. Even if the philosophical questions were genuine, it would be difficult to take this seriously. I think most people who have had experience of teaching such a course would admit that students find it somewhat strange that they are not expected to give an answer to a straight-forward teaching problem until they have made up their minds on speculative philosophical issues that are quite remote from the practical affairs of every-day life and of the school-room. But the situation is even more fantastic when we realize that many philosophers have at last admitted that such issues are not in fact genuine intellectual problems at all.

But although philosophy has now no direct bearing on education, it is probably much more important than before because of its indirect bearing. Whatever subject one is studying and proposing to teach it is true, I think, that there are problems or puzzles, not so much in the subject as about the subject, which have to be tackled by the methods developed in recent philosophy. The analyses of these problems may show either that they are technical problems in the subject or that they are technical problems in a related subject, or that they are linguistic or verbal puzzles, or even perhaps that they are bogus questions.

The philosophy of education which students ought now to study is therefore something which might properly be called "the philosophy of the curriculum." For this purpose four basic courses should be given (or an integrated course covering the same ground)—the philosophy of language, the philosophy of mathematics, the philosophy of science, and the philosophy of history. In all of these there are problems that can profitably be clarified by modern philosophical methods, and even the results that have already been obtained could lead to far-reaching improvements in education. Let us consider each field briefly.

THE PHILOSOPHY OF LANGUAGE

This is perhaps the most important of the four, for the results obtained in this are to some extent presupposed throughout the other fields. Any selection of topics must be rather arbitrary, but I think it would be generally admitted that the following are of importance to students of education.

(a) The problem of meaning. (b) The similarities and differences between sentences expressing factual propositions and those expressing evaluative (including ethical) propositions. (c) The tautologous nature of logical truth.

The discussion of the problem of meaning throws a great deal of light on the conditions necessary for anyone to acquire a knowledge of language and on the conditions which render communication possible. As so much bad teaching is in fact just failure of communication, the importance of this topic can hardly be overemphasized. Under (b) the distinction between the kind of meaning possessed by factual propositions and that possessed by evaluative propositions is fundamental in any talk about the aims of education. It must also be fully appreciated if the student is to have any understanding at all of what has been traditionally called moral education. In the past this has all too often been a tragic failure, but that is hardly surprising, when one reflects on the enormous confusion surrounding the subject. Some study of the philosophy of language would help not only in making clear the differences between factual and evaluative propositions, but would also expose the "category mistakes" of the traditional mind–body doctrine, on which much of the moral education (improvement of the soul by means of physical punishment) conducted in schools in the past has been based. The clarification of the concept of logical truth in topic (c), which has been achieved by the demonstration of its tautologous nature, removes a frequent source of support for essentialism and kindred doctrines. Necessarily true propositions acquire their necessity from the language in which they are expressed.

THE PHILOSOPHY OF MATHEMATICS

It is probably desirable that this should be covered in two parts; one part suitable for the general elementary school teacher, and the other part suitable for specialist teachers of mathematics. The first part would deal with the foundations of Arithmetic, and include the derivation of the positive and negative integers, the fractions, irrational and complex numbers from the natural numbers. It could then go on to consider the problems of measurement—the device by which numbers are attached to objects in virtue of certain properties. In this way students could understand what logical justification there is for educational measurement, and would have some defence against both the hostile critic and the excesses of the psychometrists. The second part of the course would cover more specialist topics, such as axiomatic systems, theory of proof, and problems of consistency and completeness. It is surprising how often quite good mathematicians are ignorant of such topics, and a teacher's explanation of the "laws of algebra" to a twelve-year-old class is generally improved out of recognition if he himself has understood the axiomatic treatment of different algebras. Moreover, once a student has been taken through the moves in the kind of argument that is raised between the Intuitionists and those who support a classical view of mathematics, he has had an excellent training in smelling out bogus philosophical questions.

THE PHILOSOPHY OF SCIENCE

There are two big problems in this field which are of importance to the student of education. There is first of all the problem of the relation between scientific knowledge and our commonsense experience. I think it was in the 1920's that the late Sir Arthur Eddington published a delightful story about the man in the street and a distinguished physicist who were both on the threshold about to enter a room. The man in the street, of course, stepped forward and entered. But the physicist had to face up to several difficult problems. He had to remember that he had to put his foot on a plank of wood travelling at some twenty miles per second round the sun, and that he had to do this while he was hanging head outward into space. Moreover, what was for the man in the street a solid unyielding plank was for the physicist mostly emptiness; and to add to his difficulties, the atmosphere was pushing against him with a force of fourteen pounds on every square inch of his body. After several long calculations, however, the physicist concluded that the feat could be accomplished, and he proceeded to emulate the man in the street. In other words there appear to be two worlds—the world of the man in the street (or commonsense), and the world of science. But how are these two worlds related? The obvious answer that we start from knowledge of common sense and gradually build up or deduce the knowledge of science leaves us in a difficult logical position, committing us to the conclusion that the commonsense view of the world is false. (If p implies q, and q implies not -p, then p must be false.) Now some skill in handling this kind of question should be acquired by teachers. For a teacher is, first and foremost, an interpreter of knowledge, and he must not only have some understanding of science, but he should be able to explain the part which scientific knowledge plays in human affairs and the relation it has to our ordinary everyday experience. Otherwise science tends to become a kind of magic, pursued by members of a secret cult, who are appealed to when the man in the street is confronted by technical difficulties, but whose magic has otherwise little to do with ordinary ways of living and thinking.

The second big problem that should be considered by the student is what is often called scientific or statistical inference, or perhaps even the problem of induction. This is a large and difficult topic; nevertheless the essentials of the problem can be explained quite simply, and apart from the importance which the problem has in the understanding and interpreting of scientific knowledge it is of considerable domestic value in the treatment of statistical data which arise out of educational practice. Indeed the customary course on statistics for students of education is highly unsatisfactory. It gives them some skill in making routine calculations and drawing inferences according to text-book rules, but it gives them little understanding of the justification of such inferences—a problem which is the correlative of topic (c) in the course on the philosophy of language.

THE PHILOSOPHY OF HISTORY

Anyone who is preparing to teach History is at some time concerned with such questions as "How do I know that so-and-so happened?" "What does it mean to say that so-and-so happened?" "How is the happening of so-and-so in the past related to the present?" etc. These questions are obviously closely connected with the problems of meaning and verification that are considered in the course on the philosophy of language. But in addition to these puzzles about the past, there are those associated with the philosophy of any social science. It is idle to deny that the social sciences have not attained the prestige, or even the respectability, of the natural sciences. Now the teacher of any of the social sciences (and History is the most important of those that are generally and seriously taught in schools) ought to be able to justify his subject as a respectable branch of human knowledge, and he will be able to do this only if he understands the methodology of the social sciences sufficiently to answer the sallies and quips of his colleagues in the older sciences.

In each of these four spheres, the philosophy of language, the philosophy of mathematics, the philosophy of science, and the philosophy of history, revolutionary changes have taken place in the last few decades, and I believe that if a knowledge of these changes were disseminated by University Departments of Education several important advantages would be secured. The most important is that students would gain much more understanding of the different subject-matter fields than they have at present. This obviously must make them better teachers, or interpreters of knowledge, but it also makes them better specialists. In the second place, the kind of adolescent interest which many students show in philosophical problems of the traditional kind can be safely channelled into these four courses. By being shown how to tackle such problems in the field of their own subject-matter, they can be taught quickly to realize the hollowness of traditional philosophical claims. They will see that it is misleading to say that education must have a sound philosophical foundation, that rather the reverse is true. For with sound education people should be able to think themselves out of any philosophical tangles in which they may occasionally be trapped. Finally the study of Education acquires an intellectual difficulty that it has often lacked in the past. For in each of these four courses there is ample scope for the most intricate argumentation, the most subtle distinctions, the deepest insights.

It would be extravagant to claim that these advantages would lead to a revolution in education corresponding to the recent revolution in philosophy. But they would lead to revolution in the thinking habits of teachers, and it is only in that way that a worthwhile revolution in education can be achieved.

EDUCATION AS A
GOAD TO PHILOSOPHY

ALBUREY CASTELL

I wish to preface my remarks with an expression of appreciation. For some years now it has been my privilege to teach a course in the philosophy of education. It is a course which I thoroughly enjoy. It provides access to topics and materials which

FROM the University of Washington *College of Education Record*, 28 (November, 1961): 1–9. (Reprinted by permission.)

are perennially interesting and rewarding. While the class is in session, everything
is fine. But in the corridors and offices, the going can get bleak. You face a dilemma.
If a colleague is in philosophy he will not be greatly interested in education; and if
he is in education, he will not be greatly interested in philosophy. As a result, the
conversational pickings are slim. And then I learned of the existence of this group
whose members meet periodically for the purpose of actually talking shop about
philosophy of education. This is fine. If I am not mistaken, a great deal of "shop"
needs to be talked by those who are professionally interested in the teaching of
philosophy of education.

I began teaching our course some seven or eight years ago. I remember that,
from the start, two things bothered me. One was the way in which many textbooks
in the field were organized—how they conceived of the subject matter of the course,
what topics and materials they proposed to have the course deal with. The other
was the extent to which, among education people, psychology had outdistanced
philosophy in the interest it commanded and the influence it exerted. You could
put it this way: one is not considered ready for the pedagogical firing line until he
knows his way around in, or, at least, has been exposed to, general psychology and
educational psychology; whereas people do not think that way about philosophy or
philosophy of education. I have come to suspect that these two matters—the scheme
according to which the textbooks present their material, and the greater prestige
enjoyed by psychology among educators—are not unconnected. There is an air of
unreality about many textbooks in philosophy of education. They do not address
themselves directly to what they purport to talk about. That is to say, they do not
philosophize about education. Whereas, it seems to me, the psychologists do
"wade in," do set themselves to psychologize about education. For example, the
self as the object of pedagogical concern ought to be a big theme for philosophy of
education. It is not. Whereas the psychologists have plenty to say on it.

The sort of text-book in philosophy of education I have in mind is, I imagine,
familiar to all of you. It gives a general account of certain philosophical "isms"—
e.g., idealism, pragmatism, realism, and one or two others, and then explains
what such "isms" have to say about education. Thus one comes by the
expressions, "Idealism as a philosophy of education," or "The Idealist Philosophy
of Education," or "The Implications of Idealism for Education." And
similarly with pragmatism, realism, and other "isms" fetched from general
philosophy.

I make bold to suggest that this way of conceiving the task of philosophy of
education is unsatisfactory. The results are artificial and loosely put together. I
have seen defences of this conception of the philosophy of education attempted
now on one ground, now on another. I do not find the defences convincing. If
you know what it is to philosophize, then the central "arranging" question is: In
what ways is education a goad to philosophy? At what points will participation
in educational activity goad you into philosophizing? What problems, philosophical in character, are you faced with as a consequence of direct experience of
educational activities? If the goading does not come from the fact that the activity

is education, then it is not clear to me that there *is* such a thing as "philosophy of " education.

If you go among "philosophies of," you will find philosophy of science, philosophy of art, philosophy of language, doing a thriving business. Now, in these and other lively "philosophies of," one does not proceed by setting forth such "isms" as idealism, pragmatism, realism, etc., and then spelling out their implications for science or art or language or whatever it is. Why has philosophy of education got trapped in this dead-end procedure? To ask, e.g., "What does idealism say about education?", is not to ask a philosophical question about education. At most, it is to ask a question, and a relatively unimportant one, about idealism. These "isms" did not arise in response to questions about education; and it is not clear to me that they throw any important light on education.

If you ask "What topics and materials should philosophy of education deal with?" I do not have an answer ready. I have some hints and suggestions; but beyond that only a firm conviction that philosophy of education will die on the vine unless it gets away from the procedure I have described. Philosophy of education should not be thought of as a sort of "Philosophy I" to be taken by persons in education. The task of Philosophy of Education is not to make known what "philosophies" say about "education." That is to get the cart before the horse. The task is to introduce people to education with reference to those matters in education which will goad you into philosophizing. Philosophy of education should not be conceived of as an "introduction to philosophy" presented so as to interest teachers, but as an introduction to education with reference to aspects that goad a person into philosophizing.

Where then, might a course in philosophy of education begin? I have a suggestion to make. If you consider such enterprises as logic, or ethics, or aesthetics, you will notice that, in each case, there is some activity, some mode of behavior, that gives rise to these and similar disciplines. If people did not perform the activities in question, there would be nothing for these philosophical disciplines to ask questions or propose theses about. (1) Thus people perform an activity called "inferring" or "reasoning"; take something as given and proceed to infer or reason from it. If there were not this activity of inferring, if no one ever inferred anything from anything, there would be nothing for logic to ask questions and propose theses about. Hence you have Prof. Bosanquet saying of his small book on logic: if it teaches you what an inference is, that is something. (2) Again: people perform an activity called deciding between right and wrong, doing something because it is right, refraining because it is wrong. If there were not this activity, if no one ever distinguished between right and wrong, never at any time did something because it was right or refrained because it was wrong, there would be nothing for ethics to ask questions and propose theses about. Hence you could say of a small book on ethics: if it teaches you what a moral judgment is, that is something. (3) Once more: people perform an activity called producing a work of art. If there were not this activity, if no one ever produced a work of art, there would be nothing for aesthetics to ask questions and propose theses about. Hence, you could say of a small book on aesthetics: if it teaches you what a work of art is, that is something.

Now, I think there is an activity, related to philosophy of education as these other activities are related to logic and ethics and aesthetics. I mean learning. If there were not this activity, if no one ever learned anything, there would be nothing for philosophy of education to ask questions and propose theses about. Hence you could say of a small book on philosophy of education: if it teaches you what learning is, that is something.

The question "What is learning?" is easier to ask than to answer. In this respect, however, it does not differ from the question "What is inference?" or "What is moral judgment?" or "What is art?" Part of the difficulty arises out of the fact that we use the term "learn" in different senses. Where this is so, we must indicate which sense we intend.

There is a certain sense of "learn" which, I think, runs through the following illustrations. For example, we say "You didn't learn that; someone told you." Here learning is distinguished from being told. Again, we say "You didn't learn that, because it isn't so." Here learning is distinguished from acquiring a false belief. Again, we say "You didn't learn that; you already knew it." Here learning is distinguished from knowing. Again, we say "You didn't learn that; you inferred it from something you did learn." Here learning is distinguished from inferring. Again we say "You didn't learn that; you were conditioned into it." Here learning is distinguished from being conditioned. Again, we say "You didn't learn that; I did." Here learning is distinguished from something else, possibly cribbing, by distinguishing the learner from someone else. Again, we say "You didn't learn that; you merely came to believe it." Here learning is distinguished from merely coming to believe. Again, we say "The machine didn't learn that; it was designed to do it." Here learning is distinguished from something a machine does because it was designed to do it.

I suggested a moment ago that there is one important sense of "learn," or "learning," which runs through these examples. If I am not mistaken it is the sense of "getting to know," either "getting to know that" or "getting to know how to." In this sense learning presupposes ignorance. If everyone knew everything there is to know, then no one could learn anything. Less sweepingly: If you are not ignorant of X, you cannot learn X, you cannot "get to know X." In this sense learning equals the liquidation of ignorance. I think it is fair to say that whatever else "learning" may mean, it means *that*. Suppose an astronomer is ignorant about the behavior of the solar system. Here is something he does not know. Suppose he goes through the steps necessary to liquidate his ignorance. He illustrates what I mean by "getting to know," or "learning." [1] Now, what questions can we ask, and what theses can we propose about learning so understood?

So understood learning is a mode of behavior. Considered as a mode of behavior it differs radically from, say, the behavior of the solar system about which the

[1] This notion of the liquidation of ignorance is set forth in a brief paper, in *The Spectator* for 1957. *The Spectator* is the bulletin of the National University Extension Association.

astronomer was ignorant; and from say, the behavior of his brain and nervous system while he was engaged in liquidating his ignorance. You can say of the behavior of the astronomer that it is (a) fallible (b) purposive (c) critical (d) experimental (e) corrigible (f) reasoned, or reasoned out (g) judgmental, hence verifiable or falsifiable (h) response to a challenge (i) and that it has presuppositions.

You not only can say these and many similar things about the behavior of the astronomer—you must say them. If you denied any of these characterizing marks, you would distort your account of his behavior. On the other hand you cannot say any of these things about the behavior of the solar system or about the behavior of his brain and nervous system. If you were to talk about the behavior of either of those "systems" as you *must* talk about his behavior, you would "personify" those systems, and hence speak in metaphor. If, on the other hand, you were to talk about his behavior as though it were no different from the behavior of those systems, you would "thingify" his behavior, and hence speak in metaphor. We have then, two modes of behavior: the one illustrated by the astronomer when he is astronomizing; the other illustrated by the solar system and by his brain and nervous system. This is a dualism. I suggest that we call the one mode of behavior "activity," and the other, "process." The behavior of the astronomer in getting to know, in learning, is an instance of activity. The behavior of the solar system or of his brain and nervous system, is an instance of process. The statement I am trying to get into a position to make is this: learning is an activity, not a process.

I have been drawing attention to the distinction between process and activity, and to the fact that learning is an activity; i.e. not a process. At this point I propose a question which is both serious and far-reaching not only for philosophy but also for philosophy of education. If you admit the distinction between process and activity, do you go a step further and admit that activity implies an agent whose activity the activity *is*; an agent who performs the activity? Some persons will answer "no" to this question. They will say: "Activity may differ, as you say, from process; but activity does not imply an agent. We will grant you a dualism of process and activity; but not a dualism of activity and agent." There is much to be said *to* such persons; and given the time and place, it has to be said; because refusal on this point amounts to defeat, and should not be conceded without a dialectical struggle. Since I am not free to commit any of you on this crucial point, I shall simply speak for myself and say, "Yes; activity does imply an agent." In the case of learning, this gives you the metaphysically important thesis: "learning implies a learner." Hence for me two dualisms: process and activity; and, activity and agent. Tradition has different words one may use in speaking of agents; e.g. the pronouns I, you, he, she, and the like; and the nouns person, ego, self, and so forth. I suggest the word "self," meaning the agent whose activity you are interested in.[2] I want, then, to say that teachers have a professional stake in the reality of selves, particularly in the ignorance with which selves are born into this world; more particularly in the activity (learning) by which this ignorance is liquidated; and more

[2] The dualism of process and activity is argued for in the *Philosophical Review* for 1951; the dualism of activity and agent, in the *Faculty Forum* for 1960.

particularly still in what I call the "pedagogical encounter" in which the teacher seeks to initiate and sustain those activities on the part of the pupil which, carried through, liquidate his ignorance. Briefly: a teacher is interested in selves because they are ignorant and because through the learning activity on their part their ignorance can be liquidated. Here is the basic situation to which philosophy of education addresses itself. What questions can be asked; what theses proposed?

(1) For example, we have institutionalized our attack on ignorance. We have schools. One striking fact about our schools is the source from which they draw their financial support. It may be government wealth, or private wealth, or church wealth. Our schools are hence public or private or parochial. What is the significance of this three-way division of labor? Ignorance is ignorance, you might think. Why, then, do three distinct institutions generate their own schools? It is not the primary business of governments or private property or churches to liquidate ignorance. What stake have they in arranging for it to be done? Is there any truth in Spinoza's remark here: "Academies founded at public expense are instituted not so much to cultivate man's natural abilities as to restrain them"? If so, would it hold also for private or parochial "academies"?

(2) Academic freedom is a relevant question. A self is ignorant. You propose to liquidate this ignorance. An authority intervenes: the ignorance of that self on that matter is to be preserved. This is the basic issue in academic freedom; freedom in the academy, the place to which people take their ignorance to have it liquidated; freedom on the part of the pedagogue to have at ignorance whenever it confronts him. To deny academic freedom is comparable to denying medical freedom. If there is disease, and a way of liquidating it, the doctor demands a chance to have at it. If there is ignorance, and a way of liquidating it, the teacher demands a chance to have at it. Is there a "right" to have one's ignorance liquidated? Is there a duty correlative with this right?

(3) There is a related issue for which we lack an accepted name. You cannot call it academic freedom, because, by convention, that phrase refers to the right to learn. What I have in mind is the right to refrain from learning something. Suppose there is something you don't know and don't care to know, or don't want to learn at the expense of having to leave something else unlearned. Suppose you are given no choice in the matter. This is not the school or the state protecting your academic freedom, your right to learn. It is being told that you must learn something which, left to yourself, you would leave unlearned. This issue is by no means unreal or infrequent. In my experience it is more intrusive than the question of academic freedom. And, as state education becomes bigger, as alternatives to state education become more difficult, as state education becomes tied in with federal regulation and support, this question could become increasingly urgent. What principles and presuppositions are operative in arriving at rationally enforcible decisions here?

(4) Religion in education is a relevant question. There is an ambiguity here. The phrase may suggest that there is religious ignorance, that we can diagnose it, and that we possess the knowledge to liquidate it. I doubt this. I think we confuse

knowledge here with faith. You can do wonders with faith, from saving souls to moving mountains; but there is one thing you cannot do. You cannot liquidate ignorance with it. For that you must use knowledge. However, the phrase may suggest ignorance *about* a religion or *about* religions. A person may say "I am ignorant about Mohammedanism." If we know about Mohammedanism we can help him. But a person informed *about* a religion, or about all religions, is not *ipso facto* a religious person. He is an informed person. He may still be, in the first sense, religiously ignorant. As a tribe I do not think we can help him. A primary demand, in our profession, is not to pretend that we are in a position to initiate the learning activity when we are not.

(5) Punishment in education is a relevant question. As much as any, it helps to bring out the essential ingredients in what I have called the pedagogical encounter. A teacher who can give a philosophically adequate account of the nature of punishment in education will have come a long way in philosophy of education. For example, what precisely is punishment? When is it justified? What do you presuppose about a self when you punish it? What account are you entitled to give about punishment if you reject the dualism of process and activity? Or the further dualism of activity and agent? What account are you entitled to give if you reject the metaphysical notion of personal identity or the equally metaphysical notion of free will? I would not suggest that a grade of "F" is a mode of punishment; but under assignable circumstances, it might be. And there is enough similarity between punishing and failing to give rise to this question: When a student does not pass why don't we give the grade of "F" to the teacher? If the pedagogical encounter is what I think it is, it might well be that we need two "F"-grades; one carrying the subscript $p(F_p)$ for pupil and one carrying the subscript $t(F_t)$ for teacher. The question "What do we presuppose about the student when we fail him?" is obvious. But the question "What do we presuppose about the teacher when we do not fail him?" is there for the asking.

(6) The sciences vs. the humanities in education is a relevant question. Indeed, next to the question of punishment in education, there are few questions better calculated to goad a person into philosophizing about education. You can meet this question in the pair of papers which T. H. Huxley and Matthew Arnold wrote for Victorian England, or in Sir Charles Snow's lecture "The Two Cultures." It is this: If the pedagogical encounter liquidates ignorance, how do the humanities function in that encounter? In the case of the sciences, the answer is easy: they are knowledge, and knowledge is what you use when you liquidate ignorance. No problem there. But can the same be said for the humanities? Are they knowledge, too? Is there humanistic ignorance, requiring for its liquidation the use of humanistic knowledge? What do you learn *about*, in getting to know a play by Shakespeare or a quartette by Beethoven or a still-life by Cezanne? To be sure there is knowledge *about* the humanities, just as there is knowledge *about* religions, but knowledge *about* the humanities is not *ipso facto* the same as humanistic knowledge. A person can be informed about the humanities and yet not be humanized. My point is, there is a philosophical problem here, and it is germane to education.

(7) The relation of value (or values) to education is a relevant question. It is frequently put this way: "Can you teach values? Can values be taught?" Something very close to this question was raised by Socrates in his conversations with the sophists: "Can virtue be taught?" The question "Can you teach values?" seems to be a way of asking "Can you teach a person to value?"; e.g. "Can you teach this boy to value this tool?" Or, "Can you teach this boy to value some things as means and some things as ends?" Is the distinction between instrumental value and intrinsic value one which poses a problem for education? I word it that way because it is not clear to me that one "teaches values." One teaches X to value Y; or one teaches that Y has the value Z. Regardless of how the basic question is worded, you have here a difficult and important question for philosophy of education. If teaching equals initiating the learning activity, the activity called getting to know, then to teach X to value Y is to get X to learn something about Y which, when known is seen to be a reason for valuing Y.

(8) Learning theory is a relevant question. Indeed it is the *pièce de résistance* among the questions relevant to philosophy of education. Here the psychologists have moved in and taken over; so much so, that you gather that questions about learning *are* psychological questions, because as they say, learning is itself a "psychological process." Here, so far as I can see, much remains to be done. I know of only a few books of learning-activity written by persons in philosophy. The difficulty here is one of dispelling what amounts almost to academic complacency. Philosophy people must somehow come to see that learning does raise philosophical questions, and that a theory of learning is not the same as a theory of knowledge. Epistemology is not just another word for learning-theory. However, philosophy people do not have a monopoly of academic complacency in this matter of learning-theory. Psychology people must somehow come to see that learning is not what is called a "psychological process." Why is it "psychological"? Because it goes on in or is performed by psyches? Why is it a "process"? Because it goes on over a stretch of time? If I could get a philosophy person and a psychology person to talk out this question of the status of learning-theory, I would contribute some questions for them to warm up on, some setting-up exercises. My hope would be that one or other of these questions would dispel the two sorts of complacency I mentioned above. For example:

(a) Suggest an experiment to decide whether a piece of behavior is process or activity.

(b) Mention a process which is "not even psychological." Another which is "merely psychological." Can you mention one which is "more than psychological?"

(c) Make a tape recording of a person reasoning aloud. Play the tape back. Does it do any reasoning? Did it do any learning?

(d) A log bumps into a rock in the middle of a stream. It bumps again and again, until it swings clear and drifts down stream. Is this trial-and-error learning?

(e) Can a person learn that $2+2=5$?

(f) If education is conditioning, then, when a student fails a course, who should receive the grade of "F"?

(g) Is ignorance a presupposition of learning?

(h) Philosophers speak of laws of thought. Psychologists speak of laws of learning. Which of these are operative in the activity of learning?

(i) Would either of the following, if true, be an example of a law of learning? If not, why not?

(1) As insight into rationale deepens, learning proceeds more rapidly.

(2) As insight into rationale deepens, errors become less frequent.

(j) If you cannot diagnose purpose, can you diagnose failure? If you cannot diagnose failure, can you diagnose error? If you cannot diagnose error, can you propose criticism?

(k) It is said that physical or chemical or physiological processes are "value-free." Does the same apply to psychological processes? For example, learning?

(l) Is there a difference between exploring human nature with a view to (1) controlling it? (2) educating it?

(m) "Learning is modification of behavior." Why not: "Modification of behavior is evidence of learning?"

I would invite you to consider item (h) in my list of questions. This question is built around the distinction between laws of thought and laws of learning. It wants to know not only what the relation is, but also what the distinction is between these two sorts of "laws;" and what each has to tell us about learning, the activity called "getting to know." As traditionally understood laws of thought are prescriptive, whereas laws of learning are descriptive. Laws of thought thus state conditions which you must observe, adhere to, if your activity is to be a learning, a getting to know. That is to say, laws of thought are prescriptive for the learning activity. Laws of learning describe something in which laws of thought are already operative; that is, laws of learning presuppose laws of thought. That is, you have a case here in which the presuppositions of educational psychology are supplied by philosophy.

By way of conclusion let me summarize. Philosophy of education is not doing itself any good by setting forth certain philosophical "isms" and then spelling out the implications of these "isms" for education. What might it do instead? My suggestion has been that it turn the spotlight on the learning activity and on the pedagogical encounter. These define the pedagogue's world. Then let it raise questions which come out of this world and refer back to this world. And let these questions be philosophical, let them be the sort which goad a person into philosophizing. If its questions come out of the heart of the teacher's world, and if they incite to philosophy, then philosophy of education belongs properly enough in that world.

THE MEANING OF
"PHILOSOPHY OF"
EDUCATION

BENJAMIN BRICKMAN

It has been fashionable for some time now to employ the expression *philosophy of* and to link it with a variety of intellectual fields. A glance through a university catalogue will show courses in the philosophy of history, government, law, religion, mathematics, science, art, language, and education. The common denominator running through these courses will generally consist of a thorough investigation and a critical analysis of the fundamental character of the field, including the ideas of past and present-day thinkers. Thus, the *philosophy of* history (referring not to the written record of human events, but to the events themselves), will deal with such views as the great man theory (men make history), the economic interpretation of history (all social institutions are determined by economic factors), the inexorable force toward social amelioration, and the civilization theories (e.g., Oswald Spengler's). Similarly, an investigation and analysis of the institution of government will include such views as Hobbes' theory of absolute government and Locke's theory of constitutional government.

How did the expression *philosophy of* come to be used for this kind of inquiry into the nature of a field? One can conjecture two explanations. First, the term *philosophy* itself consists of an inquiry into the fundamental nature of the universe, reality, knowledge, and human conduct. It is thus a simple matter to use the modified expression for an inquiry into the fundamental nature of any field. Second, the nineteenth century witnessed the rapid growth of disparate intellectual disciplines. Since it was important to inquire into the fundamental nature of each of these disciplines, why not employ the term *philosophy of* to connote such inquiry?

A further linguistic clarification is in order for the use of the singular and plural of our basic term. We can speak, for example, of Carlyle's philosophy of history or of Spengler's philosophy of history. A course textbook expounding their theories, as well as other theories, may be called either *Philosophies of History* or *Philosophy of History* (in the generic sense). Practice seems to favor the latter usage.

FROM *Journal of General Education* (October, 1963) 212–220. (Reprinted by permission of The Pennsylvania State University Press and the author.)

Concerning a *philosophy of* education, what would a thorough investigation and critical analysis have to include? Let us first make clear the meaning of the term education. For our present purpose the broadest possible definition is necessary: a deliberate effort to insure the acquisition of certain preferred cultural elements by youth. This inclusive definition can embrace many widely divergent practices: from the ancient Roman father's responsibility to the Spartan community enterprise, from a tribe of cannibals' concern for the continuity of cannibalism to a civilized society's interest in the continuity of its ideals, from the schooling controlled by a religious society to one controlled by a materialistic one, from the educational practice of a democratic society to that of a totalitarian society.

The crucial term in the definition of education is *preferred*. Preference involves selection, and implies a basis for selection, and it is around these ideas that philosophy of education is developed. About half of an Athenian boy's schooling was physical education, with the objective of developing physical power and bodily grace— the former mostly for military skill, and both for athletic prowess. International relations necessitated military preparedness, and worship of bodily grace gave impetus to gymnastics. So highly valued was athletic skill among the Athenians that it constituted one of the main features of religious festivals, at which the victors were crowned with wreaths and immortalized in odes. (How sacrilegious would we today regard, say, a baseball game to celebrate a religious observance!) Conspicuous by its absence was what we would call industrial education. Since formal schooling was limited to the privileged class, most of whose wealth was produced by slave labor, there was little need for practical education—indeed, it was regarded as beneath the dignity of the aristocracy. Contrast the Athenian preference first, with the Roman father, who regarded it as a major duty to train his son in the skill of agriculture, and with the early Christians, who held bodily grace and excellence in low esteem, of no importance to the spiritual life.

EDUCATION AND CHANGE

Examples can be multiplied to show that education is an enterprise organically linked with the major social and cultural values of the group in question. However, the instances cited were, so to speak, moments in history, without reference to change. But what about change? Suppose incipient modifications in social and intellectual values appear on the horizon, should education keep pace with them, ignore them, adopt a "wait and see" attitude, evaluate them critically with a view to either stimulating them or opposing them? May education take it upon itself to suggest modifications of values in the society in which it is operating? To put the question differently, granted an organic link between education and society, what should be the nature of the link? Is education to be part of a lock-step mechanism, or should it be allowed some "free-wheeling"?

AREAS OF CONCERN

Unfortunately, these questions can have only theoretical significance in a totalitarian society, where schooling is under the iron grip of political power, often with the endorsement of schoolmen in agreement with that power. Still, one can conceive of the possibility of a secret educational initiative allied with an "underground" striving to spread ideas of freedom. While their chance of success would be very slight, these efforts would represent a purpose of education sharply critical of the social milieu in which it found itself. In a democratic society, where one usually finds an open market of ideas, a ferment of social change, and an interplay of diverse sets of values, education can pursue a variety of directions. Indeed, it can be a chaotic mass of diverse points of view, or a combination of outmoded and new values—a sort of house divided against itself—or a composite of fairly consistent values. While this last type has the virtue of harmony, the big questions still remain: with what aspects of the social and cultural values should education concern itself, and what should be its position respecting each of these aspects? Taking America today as an example, the major areas of concern seem to be:

1. The nature of democracy in America.
2. Cultural heritage.
3. Spiritual values.
4. Nonformal "educational" influences.
5. National interests and world understanding.

An analysis of the role of education with respect to each of these areas constitutes the substance of the *philosophy of* American education. This article offers only an outline treatment.

It is in order to comment on the practice of some writers of regarding *philosophy of* education as though it meant *philosophy and* education: for each of the major schools of philosophy—idealism, realism, pragmatism, and so on—a comprehensive world view is described; each school is presented, following Josiah Royce, as an attempt to get a reasoned conception of the universe and man's place in it. On the basis of the metaphysics, epistemology, and ethics characteristic of each school, these writers develop a view on education deriving from, or consistent with, it.

No one will dispute the intellectual strength of the time-honored schools of philosophy. But to regard *philosophy of* education as *philosophy and* education seems to me unsound. First of all, the expression *philosophy of*, when used for other fields, such as history and government, means nothing more than an analysis of the fundamental character of the field in question. Perhaps a better expression should have been used, such as "theory of" of "theories of." Secondly, one sometimes suspects that writers on philosophy of education are awed by the majesty of the word *philosophy*, or feel that greater respect will be gained for education if it is developed as a derivative of philosophy. They thus make philosophy the *sole* source of educational values. (Conceivably they would have done the same thing were the subject called *Theory of*, and not *Philosophy of Education*.)

The result is a severely limited, and, at times, even distorted view of education. For example, how, "logically," can one determine from realism, naturalism, pragmatism, etc., what position education, as a social enterprise in democratic and totalitarian states, would be justified in taking with respect to a movement to replace the existing social system with some other system? Any attempt to show the link would be based on a labored, if not tortured, logic. Similarly, by what "logic" can one derive from each of the several schools of philosophy an answer to the question of whether educational emphasis should be on the humanities or on science? These educational questions, as well as many others, are linked with the traditions and aspirations of a particular nation, as well as with its needs and problems of the day. To be sure, the answers will sometimes also be consistent with a certain aspect of philosophy. In other words, the sources of educational values may include certain philosophical systems. But it is one thing to locate the sources of educational values in the cultural traditions and the social values of a particular society, as well as in certain philosophical positions. It is quite another thing to formulate theories of education *exclusively* as derivatives of schools of philosophy.

BASIC PREFERENCES

In brief, then, the *philosophy of* education, meaning simply, *theory of* education, concerns itself with an analysis of the fundamental nature of education. Since its fundamental nature includes basic preferences deriving from certain values, *philosophy of* education will deal with these preferences and their sources.

1. *The nature of democracy in America:*—While there is general agreement on the fundamental meaning of democracy, namely, a social theory emphasizing the dignity and worth of the individual, the specific ways of fulfilling democracy vary from country to country, and, in each country from period to period. For example, at one time in our history property ownership was a qualification for voting, at other times taxation for the support of public schools or enactment of minimum wage laws were regarded by many as infringements on personal liberty. In time, the first disappeared, and the last two were adopted as essential fulfillments of democracy. In other words, at any one moment in our history the character of democracy in operation consists of a fairly well accepted nucleus—an unquestioned, hard core already frozen into our tradition—surrounded by an area of unsettled issues that constitute a ferment of social change. Conceivably too, some new issue may even disturb an element in the nucleus. What view should education adopt respecting the ferment of social change? For example, after the "separate but equal" doctrine was enunciated by the Supreme Court in 1896, should education in the North have given it its blessing? Suppose there had been white northerners in education who disagreed with that doctrine, would they have been justified in advocating in their teaching desegregation of races? Is education just a chorus echoing the status quo, or may it be bold enough to assume the initiative for change, or may it at least be prophetic of modifications in our social arrangements?

2. *Cultural heritage:*—Every educational theory will of necessity be linked with our accumulated culture, but the values placed on different elements will result in widely divergent positions as to what counts in life. It should be borne in mind that

America (or any country) is the inheritor of the totality of human culture—all intellectual, artistic, and technological accomplishments. There is nothing inherent in the nature of democracy that inclines it *logically* towards one phase more than any other. Ours is the choice to select and to give priority to whatever we deem important. In other words, given our acceptance of the essential meaning of democracy, we are still in need of important guiding values for our individual and institutional existence. For we can be a democratic society and at the same time either accept or reject basic spiritual values, at the same time either respect or ignore things of the mind, at the same time either live deeply or superficially. As these choices converge on school practice we can ask such questions, as shall we give priority to training for practical living, characterized by such goals as vocational efficiency, duties of citizenship, and personal care, or shall we strive primarily to turn out educated people, whose education shall also include training for practical living?

3. *Spiritual values:*—The ideal of universal education in our country is implemented mostly through the tax-supported public school. Through custom and tradition, fortified in the minds of many people, correctly or incorrectly, by the principle of separation of church and state embodied in the First Amendment, religious training is excluded from the public school. The occasional manifestation of religious practice, such as Bible reading, special music, or the inclusion of the words "under God" in the Pledge of Allegiance, is so pale and meager as to be practically insignificant. One has only to look into a denominational school to note what the fusion of religion and education really involves.

For at least a decade we have been hearing a number of challenging and thought-provoking questions concerning public education: Does the principle of separation mean that our public schools are to be Godless? Is not religion a basic human experience, and should not education, therefore, concerned as it is with the whole child and not merely with his mental growth, include religious training as an integral part of his curriculum? In an age dominated by a secular science and its materialistic off-spring—technology—do we not need a spiritual influence, at least as a counterfoil? Do we not need religious values to give more meaning to life, or at least to offset the powerful attraction of materialistic gain? And finally, will not divine sanction render our moral and ethical standards unshakable at a time when they are being threatened by half the world?

These questions point to the gravity of the problem. Current meager religious practices in the schools do not begin to approach a solution. The practice of released time, and the suggestions that we include the factual study of religion or a common core of religions are only limited solutions. And yet education needs to wrestle with the problem. Shall we move in the direction of spiritualizing the curriculum of the public schools? If so, what formula can be found to harmonize the diversity in community feelings? Or is it altogether unwise to move in that direction for fear that the public school, as a creature of political authority, may, if spiritualized, lead to the union of church and state? If so, can anything else be done, short of religious infusion into our schools, to deepen the influence of education?

Can we, for instance, re-cast our concept of education so as to elevate the intellectual and artistic achievements of man? If we cannot have *Divinitas* in our public schools, can we at least get a little closer to it by devoting more attention to *Humanitas*?

4. *Nonformal educational influences:*—There is a big, powerful school outside the formal school. It includes the home (with its standards, its outlook, and its values), the vast media of mass communication, the immediate environment, religious institutions, and a variety of personal contacts. In some cases the outside "schooling" has a positive influence in support of the formal school. In other cases the outside influence tends to negate or neutralize the effect of the formal school.

In a totalitarian society, ironically enough, the task of the school is greatly facilitated by the outside "school" because all of the educational influences are tightly controlled—teaching is like rowing downstream. In a democratic society, however, the school faces the harder task of rowing upstream. At times schoolmen are understandably discouraged to see the net result far below what formal education seeks to accomplish. How should this problem be reckoned with? What viewpoint should education adopt? To ignore these outside influences would be utterly unwise. Should education seek ways of neutralizing the outside "school"? Shall we favor some sort of legal censorship? Shall we strive to unite with the leadership outside in an effort to enlarge the scope of education? Should education "bore from within" the nonformal school to raise its standards and modify its values? Does salvation lie in giving more attention to adult education, where we have only begun to scratch the surface?

5. *World understanding:*—Nineteenth-century nationalism is dying hard. One of its chief supports, colonialism, has already crumbled. The sheer need for survival is forcing a number of proud nations to move in the direction of federated blocs. The concern in the United States for the welfare of large, neglected portions of the world population, and the desire to anticipate and stem the influence of a foreign menace have resulted in radical modifications in foreign policy. Finally, the menace of this vast foreign power has brought home very forcefully the choice between coexistence and world destruction.

A COMPREHENSIVE PHILOSOPHY

In the light of these circumstances, it would seem obvious that our education needs to be refashioned with respect to the relation between the United States and the rest of the world. Still, the choice of path or policy is not yet clear. Shall education emphasize world understanding, or international cooperation, or world government? Some people in our country will not surrender their views on our superiority; others question the wisdom of limitless largesse to underdeveloped lands; still others express themselves in favor of our leadership and only partial cooperation. An interesting case in point is the quick decision to pool atomic and nuclear knowledge with friendly Western powers as a result of Sputnik I and II, when hitherto we were far from willing to share it. On these and similar basic policies, what position should education take? The choice could not only affect the chances of survival, but, if we do survive, would also affect our whole outlook toward humanity.

By way of summary, the *philosophy of* education involves an inquiry into the underlying objectives of one of society's most vital enterprises. Far from being left to a policy of catch-as-catch-can, to inactivity resulting from inertia, to manipulation by people with ulterior motives, or to professionals with half-baked ideas, the inquiry must be made by the most respected intellectual leadership. In regard to education in the United States, it would seem wise not to limit our scope to meeting the competition in satellites and ballistics. While we must insure our survival, we should also ask ourselves, *survival for what?* More than ever does our society stand in need of gifted minds to formulate a philosophy of education sufficiently comprehensive to take into account our basic traditions, immediate conditions, and the character of our continued existence.

THE ROLE OF ANALYTIC PHILOSOPHY IN COLLEGE EDUCATION

ARTHUR PAP

It is fashionable these days to lay stress on the need for "integration" in higher education. What exactly is referred to by this laudatory term is not always clear. Suppose that college majors were compelled to take specified courses in a large variety of subjects, from mathematics through biology to anthropology and music, and denied permission to specialize by electing a "major", would this constitute integrated education? Most educators, I guess, would deny it. They would say that what is needed is an awareness of the relationships between the various sciences, and further between science and other forms of the spiritual life, art, literature, music and even religion. And such awareness is not guaranteed by a lot of *special* knowledge, most of which will be forgotten by the college graduate soon after graduation anyway. But how is such a synthetic vista of man's spiritual life to be attained? Perhaps by survey courses? For example, instead of sending the student into separate courses in mathematics, physics, chemistry and biology we put him through a

FROM A. Pap, "The Role of Analytic Philosophy in College Education," *Harvard Educational Review*, 26, Spring, 1956, 114–118. Copyright © 1956 by President and Fellows of Harvard College. (Reprinted by permission.)

general science course containing a little bit of everything but spiced with philo-sophical reflections on the difference between pure mathematics and experimental science, between the phenomena of life and the inorganic subject-matter of physics and geology; perhaps even some methodology would be taught by the unfortunate teacher of such an "integrative" course. Clearly, it will be exceedingly difficult to find teachers competent to teach such courses. And if the course is taught by a staff of experts in the various sciences, including an expert in scientific methodology, then I do not see how our integrative course differs essentially from a series of courses on special subjects, except in quantity of subject-matter and (probably) thoroughness.

Now, philosophy has traditionally been contrasted with the special sciences and indeed with any sort of specialism; it was conceived as a grand synthesis capable of being performed by the profoundest intellects only. Why not enforce integrated education, then, by exalting the role of the philosophy department in the college and prescribing selected philosophy courses for all students? However, as has been well explained in two recent articles,[1] modern philosophy has undergone a silent revolution, which some have described by saying that philosophy is itself turning into a special science. If so, how can this new kind of philosophy, analytic philoso-phy, perform the function of integrating specialized knowledge? Don't we still need the traditional sort of philosophy, associated with the big names in the history of philosophy (the authors of the "great books"), in order to achieve the integrated college education which cannot dispense with the aid of those who specialize in integration? This is the question I wish to discuss.

To begin with, as has often been pointed out,[2] to contrast modern analytic philosophy with traditional Western philosophy, is actually to misrepresent it. Consider such typical problems of traditional metaphysics as the nature of truth, the nature of goodness, the problem of substance, the problem of the self, the problem of universals. It cannot be denied that the, by now proverbial, inconclusive-ness of the many discussions of these problems is to a large extent due to the fact that traditional philosophers were not entirely clear as to what the problems were. Nor should I be surprised if the more clear-headed "big names" (e.g., Hume, Berkeley, Aristotle, Leibniz, Kant) were actually grateful to the analytic philoso-phers of the 20th century for clarifying their problems, should their immortal souls have kept up with the history of philosophy. But these are all problems of analysis of fundamental concepts—in a sense of "fundamental" which is itself not easy to analyze. The early logical positivists overemphasized, as always happens in a revolution, whether political or intellectual, the differences between tradition and the new outlook. Actually, analytic philosophy consists to a large extent in an application of new precision tools, viz. the tools of formal logic and of semantic analysis of language, to old problems. That the old problems tend to be discussed

[1] I. Scheffler, "Toward an Analytic Philosophy of Education," *Harvard Educational Review* XXIV (Fall, 1954), 223–230. H. D. Aiken, "Moral Philosophy and Education," *Harvard Educational Review* XXV (Winter, 1955), 39–59.
[2] Among others by A. J. Ayer, in his manifesto-like *Language, Truth and Logic*, by myself in the preface to *Elements of Analytic Philosophy*, and by H. D. Aiken, *loc. cit.*

in what Carnap has called "the formal mode of speech" should not conceal the essential continuity with the past. For example, instead of asking whether an individual substance, like an apple or a man or a stone, is more than a bundle of universals (qualities), we ask whether subject-predicate sentences are in principle translatable into a language containing neither proper names nor predicates but only names of qualities (along with logical constants).[3] Instead of asking, in the manner of the old idealists and realists, whether a reality "outside" of human consciousness is at all knowable, we ask whether such statements as "a stone rolled down the hill at a time when there was nobody around to see or hear it" are in principle verifiable. These "semantic" formulations of the problems clarify the problems and consequently enable more fruitful discussion, but the similarity of subject-matter, if not of the formulations, in traditional and analytic philosophy is unmistakable.

The chief reason why this is not widely recognized, I believe, is that the semantic formulations of problems of analysis create the impression that the subject-matter of analytic philosophy is *language*. But surely, so the traditionalists argue, when we ask what goodness or truth or consciousness is, we are not asking how the English words "good," "true," "consciousness" are used; we have a decent command of the English language, hence we know the answers to *these* questions already! Indeed, such linguistic formulations of problems of analysis *are* misleading. When a German philosopher asks "Was ist das Wesen der Wahrheit?" he may be asking the same question which an English speaking philosopher expresses by the words "what is the nature of truth," but most certainly he is not inquiring into the use of the English word "true"; and if he were inquiring into the use of the German word "wahr", he would certainly not be asking the same question as the English speaking philosopher. For this reason, among others, I would prefer to formulate problems of analysis by speaking of *concepts*: the German and the English speaking philosopher are asking about the analysis of the same concept which happens to be expressed in German by "wahr" and in English by "true." Some analytic philosophers—some of them well known in the Harvard community—find the meaning of the word "concept" obscure, and they would not even feel enlightened if one explained that the concept of X is the *meaning* of the expression "X". But there is no contradiction in formulating problems of analysis by means of words whose clarification is itself a difficult problem of analysis, nor is this in any sense a sterile proceeding. We cannot at the start use precision tools to construct precision tools. We cannot delay asking what is the meaning of "meaning" until we know the answer.

Now, the most profitable way of "integrating" special knowledge is to analyze the concepts in terms of which it is formulated regardless of the special features of its objects. Thus any scientist, whether physicist or psychologist or economist, uses the concepts of explanation, truth, confirmation of an hypothesis, law, definition, probability, proof etc., and if the student is induced to ponder over the analysis of

[3] Cf. Russell, *An Inquiry into Meaning and Truth*, ch. 6.

such concepts, he will not have only filled his memory with a lot of special knowledge that may or may not come in handy in his later professional life, but further have gained insight into the nature of science. But this is not even the most important "integrating" function which analytic philosophy can and must perform in college education. When as a teacher of analytic philosophy I try to get students to become clear about the difference between truth and certainty, or between a priori proof and empirical verification, or between a genuine explanation and a pseudo-explanation, I only use these problems of analysis as means of teaching precise thinking and linguistic expression. The habit of precise, critical thinking in any area of life is surely a more lasting product of college education than any amount of well memorized special information. Unfortunately, a great many of the conventional courses taught in philosophy departments neither produce such habits nor do they provide anything else than some more special information: historical information about what the big names in the history of philosophy said about man and the universe. And it is a bad thing if Joe College comes out of his one and only philosophy course—history of Western philosophy, quite likely— with the ability to associate the big names with some "ism" or other, and besides the distinct impression that philosophizing consists essentially in the attempt to make sense of enigmatic writings.

I am not advocating abolition of historical courses in philosophy for college students. But I feel that the predominance of historical courses, and the frequent identification of introduction to philosophy with introduction to the history of philosophy, is due to a conception of philosophy as something that does not really progress and the best of which has been produced long ago. In this respect philosophy is, in the conservative's conception, like art, music and literature (as conceived by conservatives in the respective areas of the spiritual life), and *unlike science*. This, in my opinion, is the practically most significant contrast between the attitude of analytic philosophers and the attitude of the orthodoxy in philosophy. Analytic philosophers are regarded as highly irreverent, since they so liberally accuse their forefathers of confusions. But the more balanced of them will cheerfully admit that they see farther because they stand on giants' shoulders; only they might justly add that science progressed because scientists did not just respectfully look up to their forefathers but climbed up on them to get a better view. To deny that owing to the techniques of semantic and logical analysis developed especially since the start of this century we are now far bettter equipped to clarify fundamental concepts than Plato, Aristotle, Kant et alia, would be as foolish as advocating a return from Einstein to Newton in physics, or from American behavior theory to Aristotle's *De Anima* in psychology. And a philosophy department that minimizes the teaching of these modern techniques, accordingly, is simply trying to halt the march of history.

Many conservatives will of course reply that it is quite all right to teach techniques as long as one is aware that this is what one is doing and is not mistaking the means for the end. What is the end? "To paint a true picture of man's place in the universe, which will serve the college graduate like a chart in his intellectual and moral life outside the college campus!" Well, I cannot think of any better grist for the mill of semantic analysis than this kind of bombastic language by which the importance of "genuine" philosophy is so often emphasized. What is meant by "man's place in the universe"? Surely "place" cannot be meant in the geographical sense, for we all know that man is stationed on the earth—for the time being at any rate. Most likely the phrase has a teleological meaning: what is the *purpose* of human life? This interpretation accords with the widespread conception of "serious" philosophy—contrasted with the verbal acrobatics of analytic philosophers!—as being concerned with moral and religious questions. Now, when we use the word "purpose" in connection, not with conscious agents, but with objects and processes, we refer to purposes to the realization of which the latter are instrumental: the purpose of the axe is to cut, i.e., this is the end or function for which an axe is made; the purpose of legal punishment is deterrence of potential criminals, i.e., this is the end which those who make penal laws, if not those who execute them, have in mind, etc. But if this is the way the word "purpose" is used in the context "the purpose of human life," then the very question makes sense only relative to the theistic belief that man was created for a purpose. And then "serious" philosophy is in effect identified with theology, an identification which few secular educators will acquiesce in. Another possibility is that "purpose" is meant as a normative, not as a descriptive term, i.e., the "serious" philosopher must discuss and answer the question what people *ought* to do in this life. It is, however, just as arbitrary to identify "serious" philosophy with moral philosophy as it is to identify it with theology. Besides, to ask *in general* what people ought to do is to ask a meaningless question unless it is to ask for a general criterion of moral right and wrong. To ask the latter question is to ask, like Socrates, about the meanings of ethical terms and the closely related question how, if at all, moral judgments can be validated. One is then led into analytical ethics,[4] a respectable branch of analytic philosophy. Once again the conservative has failed to substantiate his claim that analytic philosophy is merely a technique which it may, or may not, be useful to apply to the study of "substantive" philosophical problems. For the moment one attempts to see clearly what the latter are, by dispersing the fog of pompous and metaphysical language in which they are so often formulated, they turn out to be indistinguishable from problems of analysis, or from problems the very genuineness of which is in question until subtle problems of analysis—such as whether questions which are decidable neither by logico-mathematical procedures nor by empirical inquiry are genuine questions—have been solved.

Analytic philosophy, in my view, is philosophy in the old sense of the word, and not one more special science, in being unlimited as to subject-matter. But even if a convincing case could be made for the conception of analytic philosophy as being nothing else than semantic analysis of language, and thereby limited in subject-matter to language, it would still occupy a privileged position with respect to the other special sciences: all scientific knowledge is formulated in language, and therefore the perfection of language would be of equal service to all the sciences.

4 See H. D. Aitken's article, *loc. cit.*, and A. Pap, *Elements of Philosophy*, ch. 10 and ch. 2.

Further, a solid training in semantics is equally useful whether the student chooses to become a scientist or not. As a citizen of a democracy he has the right and privilege to contribute to the election of his rulers, and if he is to do this wisely he must not be misled by oratory and slogans. The fact that analytic philosophy was equally suppressed in Nazi Germany and Stalinist Russia, and is not tolerated in most universities that are dominated by the Catholic church, shows what important function it has to fulfill in a genuinely liberal college education that defies suppression of ideas, whether the suppression come from political or ecclesiastical dictators.

SOME THOUGHTS ON PHILOSOPHY IN AND OF EDUCATION

LOUISE ANTZ

In the millennia-long drama of human thought, our lady Philosophia has appeared in many guises, many *personae*; and admirers of a particular *persona* have always been quite ready to show that here, now, is the veritable divinity, here in Wisdom, or Truth, or Synthesis, or Analysis, or Experiment, or Dialectic. The present writer, who in theology finds trinitarianism a better clue to the Godhead than unitarianism, sees the signature of Philosophia on each of these faces; but not when one of them is taken alone, the others denied, for then a sort of sickness, an anemia or corrosion, eats away the signature and something different—good and interesting in itself, very likely, but not Philosophia—is found to animate the chosen *persona*.

The metaphor will not be carried faithfully through this paper, whose business is fairly prosaic, but the claim will be at least indirectly supported, and at first through some empirically based conditional statements about the philosophy of education.

Philosophy of Education is particularly likely to lose its character as philosophy if it arbitrarily limits itself. If it becomes mainly system, with each system developing its own unique language, most people in education find something artificial

FROM L. Antz, "Some Thoughts on Philosophy in and of Education," *Harvard Educational Review*, 26, Spring, 1956, 162–171. Copyright © 1956 by President and Fellows of Harvard College. (Reprinted by permission.)

about it, doubting that reality and value are well accounted for by any closed system; but others identify themselves with one in a doctrinaire, sectarian way, and make absurd practical deductions. If Philosophy of Education becomes mainly experiment, the common sense of teachers cries for substance, content, reliable conclusions about great matters. If it becomes analysis, relegating all other "philosophy" and "truth" to the bin of "poetry," a dualism more devastating than Descartes' between matter and mind sets in, and schools, including teachers colleges, become addicted to the "proved" in knowledge and fill the curriculum with scrappy facts and dry systematic outlines; while literature, "meaningless" in respect to truth, becomes mere pleasure and practically passes out of the curriculum. Knowingly or not, many teachers colleges have had a positivistic basis, as is shown in the small place that great literature, including philosophy, has had there; and when facts take the place of literature, dullness follows, science crawls, and philosophy of course dies. If Philosophy of Education becomes mainly wisdom, it eventually changes into gnomic sayings and conventional sentiments (including so-called radical ones). If it becomes mainly dialectic, argument for argument's sake leads to sophistry and the loss of solid grounds for ethical, scientific, aesthetic, and religious values. If one Philosophy of Education is taught as being *the* truth, it too often loses the character of Philosophia by becoming a religion. While commitment in religion and commitment in philosophy have much in common, and while each has corrective principles of its own, they are different disciplines serving partly different purposes, and when they become confused they both lose. Though the serious thinker always finds certain bents in philosophy more to his own mind's taste, and spends a lifetime, perhaps, exploring and testing their meaning, nevertheless his first devotion ought to be to philosophy itself, and he ought to keep enough distance between himself and his own hypotheses and principles to recognize when his "truth" needs changing. This is more important in youth than in maturity, and in teaching philosophy to young candidates for the profession of education it is fairly criminal to indoctrinate them with the idea that one guise of philosophy is really all of philosophy, or that one particular philosophy is the only true one and that no others need be studied. Nor do we do justice if we teach that it is a matter of indifference which choice is made among philosophies, for when they are put to the test in the schoolroom it is obvious that they do not function alike. High philosophies, like high religions, all serve reasonably well, but not equally well in every respect, and there are philosophies which can be judged to be low by their sterility or destructiveness when carried into education. Pessimism, cynicism, nihilism, mechanistic materialism, extreme romanticism, and narrow or static perversions of any great affirmative philosophy are fatal, or at the least wounding, if tried as the foundation of education. In fact, a student holding strongly and persistently to any of these could hardly be recommended as a teacher. He is too likely to hate and distrust excessively, or to be foolishly sentimental. A teacher exists to serve human beings, in faith, hope, and *caritas*. Such service is possible only when the disinterested interest of science and the objective love of religion are strong in his being.

In the liberal arts college it is permissible, theoretically at least (if the professors are of these persuasions themselves, and dedicated to the truth as they see it) for a major part of the reading to be skeptical, hedonistic, cynical, romantically solipsistic, nihilistic, pessimistic, or ethically materialistic, and for the graduates to become addicted, provided they do not then decide to become teachers. A life dedicated to children and youth, as a teacher's must be, has its own special truths and values to face; and it is self-defeated from the beginning if it is permeated with any of these philosophies—philosophies which young people themselves reach often enough through their own experiences, stimulated and justified, maybe, by a phrase from Omar, Schopenhauer, Nietzsche, Mencken, or Russell. The teacher who has never been under the influence of these philosophies—dark, or offkey, or narrow, or shortsighted as they may be—nor known personally what drives youth to choose them, is hardly human or perspicacious enough to be in the profession. But these experiences are within life and not its foundation, for which conclusion pragmatic proof is plentiful.

A series of college courses in philosophy planned mainly to suit the specialties of technical philosophers or the whims of wonderful but offkey thinkers will not do for students who are going to be teachers. Further, all the great *fields* of philosophy are of importance to teachers, but with a difference. Ethics is not just for themselves as persons and citizens but for use in guiding the young in a world of confusing and conflicting standards. Logic is not just to be known but to be used from the beginning as a clarifier of real terms and issues, a tool for the exposition of ideas, a method in solving problems, and as a defense from fallacies—one's own and those of others. Logic may be applied within the profession, where the "latest" psychological or methodological or administrative theory is sometimes taught as fact before it is tested, or where contradictory doctrines are taught as truths in the same school, with no philosophic leader to point out that there is an institutional problem here or to give assistance in analyzing it. Ontology is not just interesting speculation but the more sophisticated form of a universal human interest in the ultimate nature of things, something reflected in poetry, song, ritual, and judgments of truth and worth at all levels. One's ontology makes a difference in what he sees in a human being, and in what he expects of him, and in what he thinks he owes him as his teacher.

In a college of education, there is need for philosophy in all her roles, and there should be books addressed to administration and faculty, as well as to the student candidates for the wise variety of occupations that today come under the caption *education*. My model for this discussion will be the emerging urban-located, combined graduate and under-graduate college, which serves the community and a variety of part-time students as well as its regular students. The community is served through the participation of professors, with students usually sharing as apprentice-associates, in surveys aimed at solving acknowledged problems; on both standing and temporary neighborhood committees and panels; and as experts bringing frontier ideas to business groups, churches, youth organizations, parents, health groups, and the like. The community is also served through apprentice participation of students in child-care centers, youth groups, released-time religious work, and many others—situations in which the student may gain much more than he is able to give. He is there, of course, mainly to be readied for his future. A newer service, to both the profession and the community, is the continued contact of the college with its young graduates while they are struggling through the difficult first years of teaching.

The undergraduate school has a double duty. It sees its students first as persons, young individuals growing up, with educational needs and rights of their own, and secondly, as candidates even from the freshman year for a great profession. If they do not have the physical and nervous stamina and the emotional and intellectual resources necessary to make teaching successful, they are early directed to other studies. They are inducted from the very beginning into habits of paying attention to the functions of the school in given communities, especially in interdependencies with economic, political, religious, racial, ethical, commercial, recreational, and aesthetic institutions and their human personnel.

The students receive a general education in which history is taught as history, science as science, literature as literature, but with each of these regarded in addition as something one might teach, and as something making a difference in the lives of human beings, especially of children and youth. Specialization also begins fairly early, for to become a teacher of music, for instance, in the schools of today requires a long experience with the materials, techniques, and literature of music, in addition to the knowledge about human development which science and professional practice have ascertained.

Besides class-room teachers, the college of education prepares candidates for the semi-educational arts and sciences of physiotherapy, occupational therapy, public health nursing, and recreation, and for specialties like religious education and labor education. The graduate school of the college carries all of these studies to a higher and more systematic level, and in addition prepares for college teaching in certain areas, administration of many kinds, supervisory work; also, it prepares educational specialists in psychology, religious leadership, personnel work, and civic leadership.

The role of general education in the lives of education undergraduates and graduates is the same as for any other students, but there is a difference, as was suggested above. I should like to say here that I think the term "philosophy of education" can legitimately include two things: general philosophy in all its branches so far as it connects with education, and secondly the organized system of hypotheses, methods of thinking, and applications which we call Philosophy of Education and which, like other "philosophies about", is generated by special interest in and practice of a distinguishable and perennial human enterprise. Professor Broudy, in his paper for the December 1955 meeting of the American Philosophical Association, justified with persuasive logic the claim of philosophers of education that theirs is a genuine discipline with a lively role to play both in the professional work of education and in the life of Philosophia herself. He closed his paper with a demonstration to young men and women who are thinking about Philosophy of Education as a career—men and women with a talent for philosophy and a zeal for education—that here is a vocation which will not betray their minds and hearts.[1]

For the teacher of Philosophy of Education, there are three distinct but partially inseparable offices. First, he is a philosopher; he knows his full share of general philosophy and he is an expert, to some degree a creative one, in philosophy of education. Secondly, he brings the content and uses of general philosophy and philosophy of education to at least four sets of learners if he teaches in a university and to at least one set if in an undergraduate teachers college. The four sets are: the undergraduates; the younger graduate students; the older graduate students, most of whom have had considerable and varied responsibility; and adult groups, including teachers-in-service, who ask him to lecture on philosophy or lead in community studies. Thirdly, the professor has a duty to the pupils who are his unknown philosophical grandchildren, the school-children and youth who will be taught by the men and women who study in his classes or read his books, and whose own educational experience may be hurtful or healthful because of the philosophy permeating their teachers' life.

It might be interesting to stop a moment and ask, To whom are works on Philosophy of Education addressed? Whom does the theorist hope to influence?[2] I am sure that every writer of a philosophical book about education wishes that the

---

[1] He might have added that for neophytes looking forward to membership in a professional organization, the national Philosophy of Education Society offers an unusually friendly welcome and an unusual intellectual challenge. Students majoring in Philosophy of Education may join as associate members. There are also regional branches which may be joined. The Society's membership represents all the live "isms" in Philosophy of Education and a lively, clarifying, and challenging dialectic goes on among them. There is an attitude of responsible intellectual courtesy. New creative hypotheses are being offered, especially by some of the younger members.

[2] Plato and Aristotle had in mind the citizen-leaders of the Greek community, the fathers of the state and of the family. A hundred years ago in Germany, Rosenkranz, who is said to have coined the phrase "philosophy of education," wrote for university professors and university trained schoolteachers. Herbert Spencer wrote for the educated British public, as did Matthew Arnold. In America, Emerson and Alcott wrote for lay philosophy circles and for civic leaders, parents, and teachers, and so did William Torrey Harris, in the years just before and after the Civil War. Philosophy itself as a technical study had little place in the universities until after that war, and Harris' paper, *The Journal of Speculative Philosophy*, was the first technical philosophic journal in the country. Because Harris was as interested in theory of education as in other branches of philosophy, the *Journal* reflected the dialectic among Spencerians, Froebelians, Emersonians, Hegelians, Kantians, Christians, Marxists, and others less systematically oriented. By the turn of the century, public education had become firmly settled in its present form of local and state supported and controlled systems. "External" problems, those of financial support, politics, interest group pressure, and the social status of teachers, as well as "internal" problems of aims, curriculum, discipline, functional equipment, and the training of teachers, supervisors, and administrators had become permanent on the American scene.

It had for a long time been common to hold teachers institutes, and for teachers to attend summer schools. Religious groups organized pedagogical and theological principles into philosophies of education to direct their own Sunday school and parochial school teachers. Leaders in philosophy as well as other disciplines were frequent lecturers to teachers. James' *Talks to Teachers on Life's Ideals* is a compilation of such lectures. Herman Harrell Horne says in the introduction to his *Philosophy of Education*, written in 1904, that the book is a result of lectures in the Summer Schools of Dartmouth and North Carolina, in the Harvard Summer School of Theology, and in the graduate Department of Pedagogy at Dartmouth. Dewey's *School and Society*, 1899, was a report and interpretation of the work of his experimental school in Chicago, founded as a place where "theories and ideas might be demonstrated, tested, criticized, enforced, and the evolution of new truths [take place]." It was addressed mainly to school leaders and to teachers and teachers-to-be, and most of the philosophies of education written since that time have been so addressed. Long years after he published *Democracy and Education* (1916), Dewey remarked that the technicians in general philosophy had by-passed this book because it was about education, and implied that this was a very serious mistake on their part.

general philosophers would read it, and that educated parents, business men, other professional men, and statesmen would. He may also wistfully hope that other leaders in education will read it, knowing full well that most professors of education in the teachers colleges do not bother with philosophy; they are busy with current empirical problems, with useful feeder subjects like psychology and social studies, or with special subject matters like physical education, elementary methods, or administration. Students are likewise kept largely to these matters, perhaps being advised to take a course in philosophy of education as seniors or graduates. Of course one does hear a great deal about "my philosophy of administration" or "my philosophy of the way to develop group activity," but one realizes that "philosophy" here usually means "my policy" or "my present strong opinion," localized and particular, and rarely a basic and directive set of theoretical principles.

Many professors of education like to use the word *philosophy* but object to studying it as a subject or to having their students study it. One cause of this strange situation is that in the past too many persons who were good teachers of geography or reading or some other school subject, and who had taken some additional professional courses, were invited to teach in Normal Schools; and they remained on the faculty when these schools were changed into four-year Teachers Colleges. In addition, successful superintendents and supervisors from the school systems were invited in to be professors. The smallest percentage of either of these groups had the knowledge and the techniques for teaching college students. They often taught practically the same thing in all the courses of their "load," and exhausted what they had to say in the first two months of a term. Much of this was essentially the same material that someone else taught, and so there was bred the common complaint that educational courses are boringly repetitious. Another misfortune was that the professors who were gleaned from the public school systems brought with them and taught to others the opinion that the main studies of a future teacher should be those things that he or she will teach, and that these things should be learned on the level of immediate use. This hopelessly anti-intellectual view is still rampant in colleges of education, with the result that mediocre students are attracted to them and highly able ones repelled. But I must balance this fact with another one, which is that the situation is changing with great rapidity in respect to theory, teaching, and student personnel. Some teachers colleges are outstripping liberal arts colleges in the high level of their offerings and of their student body. This should not be surprising, considering the quality and amount of interest, research, and dedicated effort which have gone into the study of education as a social and professional enterprise.

The fact that much work in teachers colleges has been under-intellectualized does not cancel out another fact, namely, that graduates of liberal arts colleges who decide to teach are often overintellectualized and overindividualized in their habits and attitudes so that they do not really want to work with and serve the young— not the real children and youth of the classroom and playground. Plato's youth who escaped from the busy cave of ordinary human life to attain knowledge and wisdom in the sunlight did not want to return to that cave, where he no longer fitted. But

Plato has him return, to adjust gradually and painfully, and then to lead his fellows to a higher quality of life. The painfulness might have been avoided if the journey in the sunlight had not been entirely apart from the people in the cave; especially, if some of the new knowledge had been about people, and if theory had been learned along with observation and participation; and if the journey had been undertaken as a mission for others as well as self. Plato has his philosopher kings live in and be a part of the community a major part of their lives, with theory coming rather late, followed by practice in minor offices. We cannot wait so long with our teachers, and the question is how to combine in the college years a maximum of liberal education and professional subject matter, with a maximum of experience with children, parents, community, society. The goal is to have the young teacher reasonably at ease and successful with his or her first classes, and equipped to grow professionally through the years. It helps to have in the tool-kit the methods and some of the content of philosophy, and to have there a fair knowledge of the philosophies of education actually prevalent, though perhaps not recognized by the administrators and fellow teachers who act on them.

One reason given for keeping philosophy out of the tool-kit is that it is too technical. But what developed subject is not, especially when there has been no previous, less formal, building up of vocabulary? Philosophy is the only general college subject which is not introduced to the young by name in ordinary social conversation or in high school. (Psychology is not taught in high school, either, but every student has heard and read about it and it is a widely elected college subject.) Another old argument is that since the philosophers are not agreed among themselves, why let them confuse the students? Well, who are thus agreed? And why should philosophers be? Are we automata, an ant colony? Some positivists may wish we were, for then surely no one would waste the mind's time with terms like *being, real self,* or *ethical truth.* But we are persons, interpreting a many-faced and partly mysterious universe.

Those who are cold or antagonistic to philosophy in all its branches have one reasonable argument, which is that too much of it is ill-written, drearily organized, verbally heavy. It is certain that the style of philosophic writing could be enlivened, and that the many ambiguous technical terms we have inherited or coined should be either aesthetically ordered and clarified in their context or else not used. If the philosopher wishes to influence a sizable public, such a public as the philosopher of education has a duty to try to reach, he ought to train himself to write with clarity, to be consistent in his usage, and, especially through contextual techniques, to help his reader catch the intention of his terms. See Brand Blanshard's *On Philosophical Style* for a real battle cry on this subject from a philosopher who believes we can achieve the goal without giving philosophy over to the positivists. *Their* doctrine that a statement means the experience that would verify it seems to Blanshard to be "at once deplorable philosophy and admirable literary advice."

Diversity in systems of philosophy of education is no more likely to disappear than is diversity of form and meaning in the arts. Although a philosopher is a logician, one who judges meanings by their coherence, by their correspondence with experience, and by their capacity to be verified, and although he checks his logic in a constant dialectic with other minds, he is also an artist, developing his own symbols with their own bearing, influenced by his own taste and perspectives, and coming to be recognized through his own mental style. To read or hear philosophy requires readiness and effort to enter the philosopher's richly complex world. But is this a reason for teachers, and their professors in teachers colleges, to avoid philosophy? It is rather a reason for nourishing the young on philosophy a good deal earlier than is customary.

We wait too long to respond to the philosophy in the young. Their minds and hearts have a real, if vague, affinity for serious things. They used to be brushed off when the facts of life which they sought were those of sex. Now they get answers everywhere, but they receive better ones about the physiology of sex than about the "I-Thou" relationship, and they still get brushed off when the sought-after facts of life are those of philosophy and religion. We have not prepared ourselves to converse with them about these things.

The young want to know about rights and responsibilities, fate and freedom, man and God. They are puzzled by differences in the ways of thinking—the artist's way, the business man's way, the religionist's way, the scientist's way, their own parents' way. They are attracted to and confused by values. What is good, when parents, teachers, ministers, comic-books, movie heroes, business men, and politicians differ about it? Who am I, what am I, what is expected of me? I do not know whether there are any high school students, for instance, who are not interested in these things or capable of being interested. Certainly the levels of response are widely different, and we have to have close association with the young to know what is troubling them and what sorts of ideas will reach home. Juvenile delinquents are often personal isolates, literally frightened at the idea of being intimate with any one, of any age; frightened at the idea of sharing their feelings and thoughts in a genuine person to person situation. The young deserve teachers who can recognize their potentialities, engage satisfyingly in personal and class-room conversation, and share books and projects with them. They deserve to have books in the ordinary philosophic branches written for them, adapted to their age and condition. This does not mean dilution, watered skim-milk, but intelligible portions, not too large, of good flavor. Only very literate persons, at home in philosophy and at home with boys and girls, could write such books. Naturally, the books would not be written with an eye to how much of a term it would take to teach them, but rather with the supposition that they would be on the library shelves of up-to-date classrooms, perhaps to be studied by the class, perhaps just to be read by individuals. Some of these books should have selections from the great philosophers, and their literary counterparts, with lively informational and interpretative running commentaries, and with enticing indications of what deeper, larger studies might come later.

In speaking with adults—even otherwise well-educated adults—about religious subjects, one notices how often they have carried into adulthood the meanings, images, and symbols they learned as children, apparently never having had in adolescence any religious studies on deeper, more adequate, more critical, and more appreciative levels. Modern church schools are experimenting with the problem. I mention it because it is of one piece with the philosophic situation: we have not as a people given adolescents enough religious and philosophic meat. We do not just baby them, we undernourish them. We have ourselves been interested in obvious and practical things, rather than concerned with theories and interpretations, and we have underestimated what the adolescent mind can manage and grow on.

But to do more justice to the younger adolescent we must first do justice to the late adolescent studying to be a teacher, and continue to enrich his professional life by keeping him in contact with the intellectual resources of the college after he graduates. When he enters upon his vocation he will have to adjust to a welter of expectations from fellow teachers, superiors, and parents. The variety of unintegrated psychologies, methodologies, standards, emotional attitudes, and goals existing in the minds and behaviors of the older personnel in the usual school would be fantastic, even funny, if it were not so wasteful, so tell-tale of hasty training and uninspiring present leadership, and so difficult for the new teacher. This semi-chaos is tell-tale also, of course, of the hasty flux in life itself, which throws problems to schools and then, before hypotheses to solve them can be tested, throws new ones which require almost complete reorientation. Both reason and human nature demand principles of order in the midst of the flux. But which principles? It is one thing to concoct explanations and plans on an *ad hoc* basis, in terms of a new situation or a new scientific finding, and another to see whether the ingredients of the human scene can be ordered under some integrating hypothesis of a profound and powerful nature. Horne wrote in 1904, "The artificial manufacture of educational systems is noisy in our day.... The educational truth is in the unification of those educational truths for which the separate factions are fighting." [3] The factions he referred to were those of the evolutionists, hereditarians, environmentalists, mechanists, volitionists, interest and effort theorists, and the like. It was obvious to a philosophical mind that the whole truth for education was being built by each faction on a fragment. There are many good books in Philosophy of Education available to show what can be done with integrating on less fragmentary, more philosophic principles. Some of the categories used are more fruitful than others. Some become tired out through usage, for a given generation. Robert Ulich shows in his *The Human Career* how the study of education can be freshened and illuminated when new-old categories like theonomous, logonomous, and autonomous are substituted for the names of the *isms*—realism, idealism, etc. Harry Broudy's *Building a Philosophy of Education* shows the creative, critical, integrating process at work. Any acquaintance, if it be at once serious and lighthearted, with the major gambits and ambits of the few inclusive, systematic philosophies of education can give a sense of how to play the game and will provide strong points of reference for judging doctrines and situations. Rupert Lodge notes in the introduction to his *Philosophy of Education* that there doubtless has never been an educational thinker who was completely the realist, idealist, or pragmatist of his

[3] H. H. Horne, *The Philosophy of Education* (New York: Macmillan, 1904), p. viii.

thorough-going, and sometimes purposely whimsical, description. But letting the mind play over the full possibilities of complete integration according to a great principle gives insight and release from pettiness,—and it suggests the wisdom of knowing Philosophia in all her *personae*, lest Procrustes take over.

A NOTE ON "PHILOSOPHY OF EDUCATION"

MAX BLACK

The label is misleading. It suggests that "philosophy of education" is related to education in the same way as "philosophy of science" to science. But science is not commensurable with education; and philosophy of education cannot resemble philosophy of science.

The chief purpose of the philosophy of science is to further the understanding of science, by means of the critical analysis of scientific concepts and methods. It is, in a sense, parasitic upon science—for without science there could be no "meta-science." The bewildering complexity of scientific methods, the luxuriant proliferation of scientific theories, invite the clarification that philosophical analysis can provide. So long as scientists continue to be so successful when about their proper business, and so inept when they philosophise about it, there will remain work for the philosophers of science to do.

Education is not technical in the way that science is. There are no distinctively educational concepts or well-defined procedures for educational investigation. There are no universal criteria of educational validity—there is no "educational method" analogous to "scientific method." If philosophy of education had to follow in the footsteps of philosophy of science it would have no subject matter, and no proper aims.

The reasons are not far to seek. "Education" is, and should be, a term as comprehensive as "life" or "experience." The great educational theorists have used it to refer to nothing less than teaching-and-learning in all its possible manifestations, exemplifications, and ramifications. Even when they discuss something as narrow as spelling or handwriting, the large conception dominates their thought. And any less ambitious approach to educational problems quickly degenerates into a fussy

FROM M. Black, "A Note on 'Philosophy of Education,'" *Harvard Educational Review*, 26, Spring, 1956, 154–155. Copyright © 1956 by President and Fellows of Harvard College. (Reprinted by permission.)

pre-occupation with trivia. But teaching-and-learning is an aspect of nearly all experience, not a "subject" separated from other "subjects" by well-marked boundaries.

Consider the different kinds of things that "teaching-and-learning" must cover: every concrete teaching episode involves transmission of information, of experience, of skill, and of attitudes. (And remember the corresponding ambiguities, notorious among philosophers, in the notion of "knowing"—as acquaintance, knowing *that*, knowing *about*, knowing *how to*, and their unlabelled variants.) It would be quixotic to expect a single theory to organize such a congeries of concepts: there is no such theory.

Had philosophers undertaken to establish, not a philosophy of science, but a philosophy of *investigation*, they would have faced similar embarrassments. For "investigation" shifts in meaning as "education" does—and for similar reasons. Philosophy of science is saved from the pursuit of the unattainable by the severe limitations that scientists have imposed upon the general task of investigation. But education has not accepted and should not accept similar limitations.

In practice, philosophy of education becomes nothing less than philosophy, without qualification or restriction. All serious discussion of educational problems, no matter how specific, soon leads to consideration of educational *aims*, and becomes a conversation about the good life, the nature of man, the varieties of experience. But these are the perennial themes of philosophical investigation. It might seem a hard thing to expect educators to be philosophers. But can they be anything else? If they don't try to think for themselves about philosophical questions, will they not run the risk of being directed by philosophical slogans they can scarcely be expected to understand?

EDUCATION AND
THE PHILOSOPHERS

RAPHAEL DEMOS

What contribution can philosophy make to education? Let me delay my answer by putting another question: what has philosophy to contribute to science, if anything? The answer to this one is: *nothing* (in a certain sense of "contributing"). Philosophy does not tell science how to conduct its experiments; it does not correct, far less provide, scientific theories. The philosopher knows nothing about

FROM R. Desmos, "Education and the Philosophers," *Harvard Educational Review*, 26, Spring, 1956, 156–157. Copyright © 1956 by President and Fellows of Harvard College. (Reprinted by permission.)

the laws of motion on his own account; about such matters he takes the word of the scientist. He only records scientific discoveries and theories on the tape of his mind. In the past, philosophy had been praised as the queen of the sciences; this statement is so absurd as to be really true, when one calls to mind the contemporary queens who reign without ruling.

But in another sense philosophy has a great deal to say about science, although the scientist may pay no attention. Here the relation of the art critic to the work of art provides a good parallel. The art critic says a great deal about the art work although very often the artist does not listen. Just as the art critic does not contribute to the creation of the worth of art so the philosopher does nothing to bring about scientific knowledge. But both are *judges* in their own respective spheres. (So we have an analogy of both art and philosophy to law: a judge does not commit crimes; he only pronounces verdicts on them.) However, there is a difference between the roles of art critic and philosopher. The former is allowed to take a painting apart, to go into details and criticize the arrangement of colors and shapes. The philosopher is not a critic of science in that sense at all. But he can take up— and it is his duty as a philosopher to take up—fundamental conceptions of science like those of cause, law, external object, probability, evidence and so on, and either criticize them, or at the least, analyze and clarify them.

Now, philosophy is to education as it is to science (roughly). Education is a going concern which the philosopher finds but did not create. I suppose that, as an enterprise, education is as ancient as man. Not of course that there always have been school buildings and professional teachers; but I should think that people have always had some notion of some fairly organized preparation for life, a schooling in the sense of an initiation into society. So, like science, education has a self-dependent continuing career. It is not then for the philosopher to legislate to the educator. But, also, as he does with science, the philosopher can analyze and reflect on principles in education. Education has its own fundamental conceptions (taken over without analysis) and its own basic premises (assumed without proof). The philosopher will be a Socrates, probing and questioning, pressing for clarification, asking for a reason why this or that premise is accepted. In this restricted field, the authority of the philosopher is unlimited. Education is replete with phrases which are practically clichés: life, adjustment, experience, education, culture, human nature, society, the individual, and so on. Everybody refers to "progressive schools" but has anybody using this phrase reflected on what progress means? Professor Broudy[1] refers most aptly to the need of a "semantic purgation"; I would go further than anything semantic and speak of a purgation, criticism, clarification of basic *conceptions* and *beliefs*. The job, then, of the philosopher is not to evolve educational systems by any a priori speculation; it is to take education as he finds it and do with it as Socrates did with the whole of life. Socrates was no metaphysician; he claimed he had no message of his own ("I know that I know nothing"); but he was a ruthless critic of the messages of others.

[1] Harry S. Broudy, "How Philosophical Can Philosophy of Education Be?" *The Journal of Philosophy* LII (October 27, 1955), 612–622.

As with all analogies, our comparison of education to science is imperfect. So let us compare education with politics. Certainly philosophy has much more to say about political than about natural science. This is because politics involves norms and values, as natural science does not. I would place education midway somewhere between politics and science, as a human discipline. Surely education has standards and presupposes norms (how the young *should* develop); it is concerned with the good life, a topic belonging to ethics, in turn belonging to philosophy. Unless prodded and badgered by philosophers, unless bitten by Socratic gadflies, educators might tend to assume that the existing accepted values of society are the right ones. In more than one sense, education is the most vital activity of society—so vital that it cannot be left to educators alone.

Having spoken of the duties of philosophers, let me now practice my preachment. My sermon will be very brief indeed. There is a danger today of what I may call educational imperialism—a danger coming more from social pressures than from teachers. By educational imperialism I mean the tendency to load *all* the ways of preparing the young for life upon the school. I don't see how the back of this camel can carry such a big load without breaking. In older days the job of preparation for living was shared also by the family, the church, and in small towns, by the way of life as practiced from day to day. The youngster learned good habits simply by doing the chores expected of him. Today, we ask the school to train not only the mind but also the emotions, to mold character and to provide ideals—also to teach jobs. Especially the family has been retreating in this country; the parents pass on their duties to the teachers. Democracy is opposed to monopoly and to centralization; it means distributing diverse functions among a diversity of organs. So we need other camels too—or work horses or oxen; let the family, the church, the farm and business share the burden of providing the *diverse* qualifications for life. Then, the school can concentrate on its own unique function, the one it can do best—which is to shape and sharpen the mind, or rather, to shape the whole man by developing his mind.

TOWARD A PHILOSOPHY
OF THE PHILOSOPHY OF
EDUCATION

WILLIAM K. FRANKENA

With many others I share a feeling of concern about what is offered to our future teachers in some quarters as the philosophy of education. The remedy for this situation is, of course, not to write papers like this on the aims and content of the philosophy of education, but to encourage people to teach the philosophy of education who are better trained in philosophy than teachers of this subject usually are. It may be, however, that by way of doing the former, one can accomplish something in the latter direction. This paper is written in that hope.[1]

Something must be said first about philosophy. Looking back over its history, it appears that philosophy has done three sorts of things. It has sought to work out a conception of the universe as a whole in all of its aspects, and of man's place in it. In this endeavor it has been synthetic, making use of the results of the various sciences of the day and adding to them the fruits of the aesthetic, moral, and religious experience of mankind, in order to see life steadily and see it whole. It has also been speculative, venturing more or less questionable hypotheses in order to fill out the picture or to find a meaning where none was obvious.

Besides seeking such "world-hypotheses," as S. C. Pepper has called them, philosophers have sought to afford some wisdom in the conduct of human affairs. That is, they have tried to provide, not only a picture of the world we live in, but a guide to action, whether individual or social, by discovering and formulating goals, norms, or standards to serve as pillars of cloud by day and pillars of fire by night.

In their twofold pursuit of the real and the ideal, philosophers have often been engaged in a less exciting but still essential kind of enquiry—analysis or criticism. This includes a critical evaluation of the assumptions and methods used by philosophers, as well as by scientists and common sense people, and a careful attempt to define such terms as "real," "true," "good," "right," "cause," "matter," "substance," and "time," which play so important a part in both ordinary and systematic thinking. Here, whatever his ultimate goal may be, the proximate goal of the philosopher is simply conceptual clarity and methodological understanding.

Let us call these three philosophical activities, respectively, speculative, normative, and analytical philosophy. Then it may be claimed that they constitute three branches or *parts* of any full-fledged philosophy—that any "compleat philosopher" must do all three of them, as Plato, Aristotle, and Spinoza did. On the other hand, they may be regarded as three distinct *kinds* of philosophizing, so that philosophers must choose between them. This view of them is often held today. Thus Dewey and his followers argue that philosophy should eschew speculation and become a normative enquiry—a "search for the ends and values that give direction to our collective human activities." Other philosophers, following Russell and Wittgenstein, contend that philosophy should be neither speculative nor normative, but

FROM W. K. Frankena, "Toward a Philosophy of the Philosophy of Education," *Harvard Educational Review*, 26, Spring, 1956, 94–98. Copyright © 1956 by President and Fellows of Harvard College. (Reprinted by permission.)

[1] In writing it I am partly indebted and partly reacting to (among others):
H. S. Broudy, "How Philosophical Can Philosophy of Education Be?," *Journal of Philosophy* LII (Oct. 27, 1955), 612–622.
K. Price, "Is a Philosophy of Education Necessary?," *Journal of Philosophy* LII (Oct. 27, 1955), 622–633.
C. L. Stevenson, "The Scientist's Role and the Aims of Education," *Harvard Educational Review* XXIV (Fall, 1954), 231–238.
H. D. Aiken, "Moral Philosophy and Education," *Harvard Educational Review* XXV (Winter, 1955), 39–59.

should devote itself entirely to logic and analysis. The most doctrinaire of them are the logical positivists, but other analytical philosophers take more generous points of view, and analytical philosophy should not be identified with positivism, as it frequently is by unsympathetic writers.

The point I wish to make here is that on the three-parts theory of the nature of philosophy as a whole, the philosophy of education will have three parts, one speculative, one normative, and one analytical; while on the three-kinds theory philosophers of education must choose between being speculative, being normative, and being analytical in their approach to their subject, as contemporary philosophers in general have been doing. My own disposition is to hold to the three-parts theory for both philosophy in general and philosophy of education in particular, but I cannot try to argue this now, and shall content myself with saying simply that I should like to see either of two states of affairs prevail, (a) one in which each philosopher of education is engaged in all three kinds of enquiry, or (b) one in which some philosophers of education are engaged in one kind of enquiry, some in another, and some in the third. In either case the three sorts of philosophizing would all be going on with respect to education, and this is the chief desideratum.[2]

We must now take a look at education, in order to see how philosophy may come to bear upon it. At once a distinction must be made between education as a process and education as an academic discipline. In the former sense, education is the process by which society makes of its members what it is desirable that they should become (not merely what it desires them to become), either in general or in so far as this may be carried on by what are called "schools." In the second sense, education is the discipline which studies this process in one way or another, its findings being reported and passed on in professional courses in schools of education.

By the philosophy of education one might, then, mean either the philosophy of the process of educating or the philosophy of the discipline of education. To help us to see how it should be conceived, let us examine the discipline more closely. It consists or might be thought to consist of three parts. First, there is the factual "science" of education. This is especially concerned to gather facts, particular and general, about the process of educating. It may be descriptive or experimental, describing or experimenting with methods of instruction, observing the consequences, etc. To this extent it will make its own contributions to scientific knowledge. But it will also collect from history, psychology, and other fields, any further facts which may be relevant to the business of educating human beings.

Next, there is the normative part of education. This makes recommendations, instructional or administrative, with respect to the process of educating. It proposes ends, goals, or norms for this process which teachers and administrators are to promote, and it advocates the means by which these ends are to be achieved. It also seeks to justify its recommendations about ends and means, so far as this is possible, by reference to such facts as may be discovered or collected by the science of

---

[2] They are, of course, going on after a fashion already; the desideratum, it seems to me, is that they should all be going on in *professional courses* on the philosophy of education.

education and to such moral principles as it may itself borrow from ethics in general.

Finally, the discipline of education has or might have an analytical part. This would be concerned partly with analyzing the concepts of the factual science of education, for example, "intelligence" or "growth," and with evaluating the assumptions and methods of this science. But it would also be interested in the normative part of education, analyzing its concepts, for example, "good," "justice," etc., and scrutinizing the methods by which it seeks to justify its recommendations.

The connection of philosophy with each of these parts of the discipline of education is now readily apparent. Consider the factual science of education. For the most part, this will be scientific, not philosophical in character, and will belong among the social sciences. But one of the fields from which it may borrow facts or hypotheses is speculative philosophy (including for the moment theology). For example, it may borrow from philosophy the naturalistic-humanistic view of life and the world, as so much of our recent educational philosophy does; or, like traditional theories of education, it may adopt the beliefs in a superior reality, a spectator theory of knowledge, and an immortal destiny, which Dewey has so long decried. To the extent to which it depends on or applies such doctrines, a "science" of education will not be really scientific, it will be philosophical; in fact, it will be an adjunct of speculative philosophy, whether it is aware of this or not (in saying this, I do not mean to bury such educational philosophy, nor even to dispraise it).

There is another possible connection between education and speculative philosophy. One might derive from a study of the process of education some hypothesis about the nature of the world, for example, the idealistic thesis that the history of the universe is the self-education of Mind. Here, however, the goal of enquiry is not insight into education but insight into the nature of the universe, and hence such thinking cannot properly be called philosophy of education, even though thinking of the reverse sort may be.

As for the normative part of education—this seems to me to contain the heart of the philosophy of education. All of it may with some propriety be called philosophy, since it consists of judgments about what should or should not be done in the process of education, together with the reasons for these judgments; indeed, it is really nothing but a branch of normative philosophy as a whole. However, some hesitate to include recommendations about the means to be used by the schools under philosophy, and would prefer to regard the science of education as consisting of two parts, as political science does, viz., a factual part and a part which makes recommendations about means. But, in any case, theories about the ends of the process of education are properly called normative philosophy.

It should be pointed out that the recommendations made by the philosopher of education, whether they concern means or ends, will normally be based partly on normative premises taken from ethics (and so from philosophy, though, of course a given philosopher of education may work out his own ethics in his capacity as a philosopher, and need not borrow from anyone *else*), and partly on factual premises derived from common sense, science, or philosophy. For example, any recommendation he may make about the treatment of religion in the schools will depend in part on his views about the aims of education, which will rest on his moral and social philosophy in general, and in part on his views about the validity of religious beliefs and the importance of religious literacy.

The analytical part of education as a discipline belongs entirely to philosophy—analytical philosophy. In so far as it is concerned to study the methods of educational science it is just a part of the philosophy of science in general, and there is no point in speaking of it as philosophy of education, unless the science of education has features which are peculiar to it. The analysis of the concepts and methods of the normative part of education, again, is to a considerable extent just a part of ethical theory; it is not as such philosophy of education, although philosophers of education should be at home in it. However, there is left as a proper part of the philosophy of education the analysis of concepts which are peculiarly central to either the scientific or the normative parts of education, for example, "growth," "learning," "independence," "intellectual freedom," etc.

I want particularly to stress the importance of doing such analytical work as a part of educational theory. Even if the object is the guidance of the educational process, and not just clear and distinct understanding, the analysis of crucial concepts is still essential—thought and action alike require us to be clear-headed in our use of crucial terms in the field of education as well as elsewhere. As H. D. Aiken has put it, ". . . the task of clarifying such golden words as 'liberty,' 'justice,' 'democracy,' 'person,' and 'love' is . . . essential to the well-being of any people whose way of life is expressed in terms of them. For if they are unclear or confused or inconsistent, then the way of life is so also."[3] If this is so, then it is imperative both that philosophers of education master the methods and results of contemporary analytical philosophy, and that analytically trained philosophers enter the field of educational theory.

This review of philosophy and education, first separately and then in relation to one another, has enabled us to distinguish at least the outlines of (1) a speculative philosophy of education which looks for hypotheses about man and the world which may be relevant to education as a process, (2) a normative philosophy of education which discerns the goals to be achieved and the principles to be followed in the education of human beings, and perhaps also makes recommendations about the means to be adopted, and (3) an analytical philosophy of education which seeks to clarify crucial concepts. Of these the first and second can now be seen to belong to the philosophy of the process of education and the third to the philosophy of the discipline of education.

On the three-parts theory of philosophy, each philosopher of education should engage in all three sorts of enquiry. On the three-kinds view, one philosopher of education will choose the first, another the second, and still another the third, or perhaps all of them will choose to do one of them and avoid the others. As I have

---

[3] *Op. cit.*, p. 57. Broudy and Price also emphasize the importance of analysis, *op. cit.*

indicated, I hope that all philosophers of education will take part in all three sorts of enquiry, or, if not, that some will choose one and some another.

In any event, it will be clear from what has been said that the educational philosopher need not and should not work in isolation. Just as the educational scientist borrows from and contributes to other sciences, so the educational philosopher borrows from and contributes to speculative, normative, and analytical philosophy in general, besides drawing upon the work of the educational scientist. Even if he limits himself to analysis, he will still make use of the findings of analytical thinkers in ethics and political theory, and may reward them with analyses of his own.

NOTE ON A PHILOSOPHY OF EDUCATION

JAMES GUTMANN

If one agrees with John Dewey that Philosophy is to be defined as "the generalized theory of education," many questions concerning the aims and content of "the philosophy of education" are seen in significant perspective. The very phrase, "philosophy of education," is almost redundant for the generalized theory of education constitutes education reflecting on itself. Or, more specifically, when teachers think about what they are doing, about the aims and content of their teaching, they are willy nilly practicing philosophy. That differences of philosophic adequacy, of grasp and depth, distinguish different levels of purpose and attainment, goes without saying. As in all philosophical endeavor, both analysis and synthesis, both discrimination of relevant data and construction of theory are essential to thorough reflection on problems of education.

That this is a job for all teachers worthy of the name, it seems to me, also go without saying. On the other hand, the label of "Philosophy of Education" is doubtless here to stay as applicable to a special department or set of courses at least as long as there are Teachers Colleges. Scholars will presumably think most effectively about educational problems in the light of their own experiences in their several disciplines and in transmitting what they have learned to their students. The assumption that these elements of all teaching are identical is as fantastic as is the belief that education can be isolated from scholarship.

To the extent that the scholar is "man thinking," the unscholarly educator is a contradiction in terms. From Socrates to Whitehead philosophers have never

FROM J. Gutmann, "Note on a Philosophy of Education," *Harvard Educational Review*, 26, Spring, 1956, 149. Copyright © 1956 by President and Fellows of Harvard College. (Reprinted by permission.)

separated their philosophies of education from their ethical and social theories nor, indeed, from their metaphysical speculations. Burnet did not discover an un-published work when he edited "Aristotle on Education" and Buchner found "The Educational Theory of Immanuel Kant" embedded in the matrix of the Kantian canon.

Just as the divorce of scholarship from teaching is untenable in any serious and complete conception of education, so the cleavage between professional and liberal education is impossible if the former makes any claim to philosophic dimensions. "Philosophy," wrote William James, "in one sense of the term is only a compendious name for the spirit in education which the word 'college' stands for in America." One can but hope that contemporary teachers have not lost this spirit and that they realize that if it disappears any "philosophy of education," however grandiose its claims, will be neither philosophy nor education.

"UNLESS EDUCATORS BE PHILOSOPHERS, AND PHILOSOPHERS BE EDUCATORS..."

PETER A. BERTOCCI

Philosophy is part of the human quest for the "things that matter most." I would define *philosophy*, briefly, as man's systematic search for the most dependable in the total situation. As long as philosophers keep alive a sense of responsibility for clarifying that total situation and the human being's place in it, they will never consider the philosophic task completed without a philosophy of education. Indeed, the philosophical enterprise withers in irrelevance unless its investigations are related, sooner or later, to the human task of knowing in what directions the examined life is worth living.

A *philosophy of education* is not a description of what is being done in the educa-tional process at any given time. It is an attempt to evaluate as systematically as possible, in the light of all human experience and knowledge available, what the aims and presuppositions of educated living are. A philosophy of education is not, first and foremost, a philosophy of schooling in a given society or state. Why?

FROM P. A. Bertocci, "'Unless Educators Be Philosophers, and Philosophers Be Educators . . .,'" *Harvard Educational Review*, 26, Spring, 1956, 158–161. Copyright © 1956 by President and Fellows of Harvard College. (Reprinted by permission.)

Because we cannot take for granted that any particular society or system of school-ing is motivated by aims consistent with the nature of the life good to live (to use Kilpatrick's phrase) in this kind of universe. Yet what differentiates philosophy of education from its close neighbors, ethics and social philosophy, is not its neglect of either but its more specific focus on the total educative process.

The aim of a philosophy of education is to help human beings become fully conscious of what is involved in evaluating the direction of their experience with a view to the life worth living. With this background, I say unblushingly that unless philosophers become educators and educators become philosophers both philoso-phizing and educating lose living contact with the underlying human need, to know what is dependable in persons and their universe, and to live in accordance with their findings.

In a word, the divorce between "philosophy" and "education," like many other divorces, created more problems than it solved. It left both partners with a threaten-ing, if not actual, irrelevance to the fundamental human question: "What life is worth living, what learning is worth undergoing, in this kind of universe?" Thus, the philosophers who left the "Cave" of education and forgot to return escaped the derision of the cave-dwellers only to be disregarded and to feel, at critical moments, like interesting parasites even on the back of the academic community. The educators who never made the ascent were always in danger of unshackling prisoners from their chains but still leaving them among the shadows of life, about which they, now unchained, could talk more glibly.

These remarks are made not so much to castigate "educator" or "philosopher" as to provide a background for an appeal that in any attempt to remarry philosophy and education in the persons of our undergraduate and graduate students we become fully aware that more than a new juxtaposition of courses is required, though we may have to begin with no more than that. Let us have a well-rooted, systematic re-integration and not merely a desegregation as we ask ourselves how nearly we can approach an adequate program in each particular situation. Plato's *Republic*, or ideal state, was conceived before he attempted to work out the *Laws*, in which he sought to realize the way in which the Athenian situation of his day could move closer to the ideal state. In what follows, I shall simply hint, without any originality, at what it seems to me our "laws" should constantly keep in mind.

1. If we are to educate persons, we cannot know what to teach, how to teach, and for what to teach, without understanding what persons have done (achieve-ments), what they can do (capacity), what they want or need (motivation), what their ideals or objectives are (what they approve and disapprove). A philosopher of education does not begin *de novo*, but *in mediis rebus*. His data are the experiences of men, both as organized in the existent sciences, and as expressed and interpreted in the social, political, aesthetic, moral, religious and logical activities of human beings. How shall he, as philosopher of education, evaluate these data, both from the point of view of truth and from the point of view of relative value? His first problem, logically, both during and after he makes himself as aware as possible of these data (that is experiences organized and interpreted from other more limited

perspectives), is to decide what his criterion of truth and of value shall be. Whatever tentative criterion of truth and value he has been using in the process of assembling his data, he needs to become fully conscious of the criterion by which he is to judge truth and value.

The philosopher of education is in a curious predicament here. He wants to know the nature of the persons to be educated, so that the educative process may be guided by the most reasonable beliefs about man. But he cannot know the nature of man without taking full account of, and interpreting, man's experiences and theories of value. This predicament is one to be appreciated rather than deprecated; it should keep him constantly aware of the need to keep his statements about "fact" in touch with his statements about "value," and vice-versa.

The historian of educational philosophy will know that fundamental in every philosophy of education is a criterion of truth, a criterion of value, a concept of man, and of the things which do or should matter most to him. In our own day, the plethora of data which comes to the philosopher of education from the biological and social sciences makes the task of "being informed" difficult indeed. Yet, no *philosopher* of education can stop with them. For he must see them with due respect to the presuppositions of the given sciences. He must distinguish implicit or explicit valuations from non-valued fact. Then, still intent on developing an adequate philosophy of man, he must turn to a similar analysis of the so-called value realm of experience. There simply are no short cuts to a philosophy of human nature. A philosophy of education may be judged by its sensitivity to the complexity of experience, knowledge, and valuation in the human situation.

2. The actual process of trying to understand the facts and values in human experience will already have taken the philosopher from man himself to a systematic appraisal of the world in which he lives. What men are and have been has depended to a large extent not only on what they have believed about their own nature and values, but also on what they have believed about the nature of the total world in which they found themselves. "Know thyself" inevitably involved them in "Know thy world"—and this was motivated not only by concern for sheer survival but for understanding, and for quality of survival. What kind of a universe are we dependent on? How does it nourish our different levels of need? What demands does it make upon us? If a man must "face reality," as the psychologist tells him, he had better know what it is, or at least better know what view of reality underlies his purposes. Part of the education of any man, if not the most important part from the point of view of quality, will involve a more than minimal half-conscious and uncritical realization of what main options for living are open to him.

3. I have been suggesting that nothing short of the fullest awareness possible of "man's place in the cosmos" is the constant problem of the philosopher of education. It is this constant background that makes him all the more sensitive to questions more immediately confronting him as he seeks to illuminate (not simply "apply") the meaning of his general conclusions to the actual social situation in which he finds himself. He does not simply *deduce* his more specific educational

aims from his general principles. But he turns to the problems actually confronting his neighbors, near and far, and, without pontificating, tries to work out the patterns of value by which the methods of educating should, at each level of the educative process, be infused and toward which they should aim. He dare not, if he would be wise, discuss such questions as church and state, the nature of adult education in a democracy, the relation of freedom to social order, the relative place of school, family, and other institutions in the development of personality, without the help of other investigators and administrators.

The philosopher of education is not an administrator, though particular ones might well be. Yet he knows that as a responsible citizen he is a philosopher-educator, and he knows that the students he teaches will be better educators, whatever their final vocation, if they understand what human education involves. The philosopher of education who knows and understands the basic issues which have divided men in their attempts to understand man and reality is all too aware of the hazards of his occupation, but he dare not remain either in the Cave, or in the Sun. He is always journeying back and forth. For, to adapt the Platonic image perhaps, the men in the shadows of the cave and their search for whatever sun there may be, must be as vital to him as his own search.

There is no more comprehensive task for philosophy, as here conceived, than the philosophy of education. Its very comprehensiveness is its value and its danger, for the philosopher of education knows both the dangers in philosophy and the risks in the educative process. As he goes about his work, can he possibly forget the words of Aristotle as he began the *Nicomachean Ethics* (I, ii, 7): "To secure the good of one person only is better than nothing; but to secure the good of a nation or state is a nobler and more divine achievement." But no sooner had Aristotle said this than he added, in the next section: "It is the mark of an educated mind to expect that amount of exactness in each kind which the nature of the particular subject admits."

SOMETIMES ONE WONDERS . . .

ROBERT ULICH

It may be a sign of humility, or a sign of vanity, or a sign of both (for the two often go together) that every reflective man asks himself from time to time whether his work really contributes something to the welfare and betterment of mankind. And there may be hours of doubt and despair. For example, "philosophy of

FROM R. Ulich, "Sometimes One Wonders . . . .," *Harvard Educational Review*, 26, Spring, 1956, 172–174. Copyright © 1956 by President and Fellows of Harvard College. (Reprinted by permission.)

education," what is it? A hybrid between theory and practice? Or a bridge crossed from and toward different banks of the stream of culture by philosophers ignorant of the complexity of education, and by educators unaware of the depth and greatness of the philosophical tradition?

Look at the present controversy about education. How often can one feel secure that either a critic or a defender of American schools has taken the time to really study the great philosophies of education? To select the most serious man of the first group: Robert M. Hutchins. Has he ever read Comenius, or Pestalozzi, or Herbart? Or even the medieval writers? If so how can he lay so much emphasis on the great cultural tradition and at the same time insist that the schools should be concerned with the "intellectual virtues" and nothing else? In his ardent opposition to the attempt of the modern public school to take the moral and vocational aspects of human culture into the area of its responsibilities, he even contradicts his admired Plato, for whom "musical education," i.e. the cultivation of the emotional basis of the personality, as well as early practical experience, or a sort of vocational schooling, are the fundamental requisites of human maturity. The same he does with his often quoted Aristotle, for whom "*oikeia hedone*," i.e. genuine, warm and personal interest in the performance of one's tasks is one of the important elements in education. This, after all, is not far away from John Dewey's theory of interest that Hutchins likes to blame for the defects of our schools which, alas, undoubtedly exist. Actually, Dewey is not at all original in his emphasis on the emotional involvement of the pupil. Every great educator, whether Christian or secular, whether ancient, medieval or modern, has done so. Dewey's originality has been grossly exaggerated by both his adversaries and his followers.

But have even those who consider Dewey the "father of modern education"— implying thereby hopefully that this is the same as good education—really read him? Many of them, it seems to me, know but parts of his *Democracy and Education* and some of his popular writings such as *School and Society*, but not his major philosophical opus. The quotations which one can so frequently read are often interpreted without due respect for their original context and, thus, have done more harm than good, even to Dewey himself. However, in this regard he is in noble company. Thinking of all the distorting references to the great religious documents, the classical authors in philosophy, politics, and poetry one cannot help being reminded of the famous saying: "God save me from my friends. Against my enemies I'll help myself."

Thus, the philosopher of education may derive some comfort from the fact that the influence of ideas on human reality has always gone over arduous and unsymmetric routes. All theoretical thought that reaches beyond the immediately useful and gives dialectical instead of simple and straightforward answers, has to be contented with a small niche in the multiverse of human interests. Up to the first decades of this century, when one suddenly discovered its utility, even theoretical physics was a sort of sanscrit within the sciences.

Under these circumstances, we might just as well leave education to the "practitioner," or to the clinic and the laboratory. Our psychological experiments are, in regard to education, just in the beginning; much has to be done in this field. So why not go there? The parents cry for better guidance for their children and the school principals for science teachers. Perhaps modern school architecture and a large playground may do more good to our youngsters than the centuries old, yet still undecided, battle between religion and secularism, supernaturalism and naturalism, freedom and authority.

But then I read the following sentence in the aphorisms of the Frenchman Gustave le Bon who, though already a scientist of renown, turned his productive mind toward the problems of human behavior and became one of the leading sociologists of our age. Philosophically, he was not far from Auguste Comte, though more critical about the effect of science on human behavior. He was one of the advocates of technical education and certainly not a friend of religion. Religion was to him more or less within the realm of "les illusions" with all the dangers of "crédulité."

"Passions and mystical influences are driving forces in the life of nations of such a power that in comparison to them all considerations of practical interests vanish."

"Material forces are formidable, psychological forces invincible." [1]

How did Le Bon arrive at these conclusions? Answer: By analyzing the growth and decay of societies, the nature and origin of wars, the contributions and defects of modern industry, and the merits and demerits of various forms of national education. I do not want to say that Le Bon, whom most of us know as the author of a famous work on mass psychology (*Psychology des Foules*) was always right in his diagnoses. In his search for the "mystique" in other nations he sometimes resorted to rather "mystical" explanations. However, when a man of his interest and knowledge sets the power of spiritual and mental influences above that of technical and material forces, he must have some reason for this conviction.

Here we are. Whatever the weakness of the individual philosophers—even of those who really deserve that great name which should be restricted only to the few really creative thinkers—in their totality they fulfill two important functions.

First: they analyze *"les passions et les influences mystiques"* of which Le Bon, though without sufficiently explaining what he really means, speaks in his aphorisms. Apparently, he considers them sometimes of negative, sometimes of positive quality, depending upon the direction in which they flow. Philosophers, especially those who talk about human goals, may even not merely explain and direct, but add to the passions and mystical tendencies in man; a Plato, a Spinoza, a Hegel, a Marx have certainly done so. However, the most powerful influences and the lasting affections of mankind in regard to its eternal problems come, not from abstract thought, but from religious prophecy, though, to a degree, its role is now taken over by statesmen or demagogues who appeal to the nationalist sentiment. But they build on shaking authority, and in order to be effective they have to mix

[1] Translated from *Hier et Demain*, pp. 219 and 7. The terms "mystical" and "psychological" have for Le Bon a wider connotation than for most of us. "Mystical" includes religious, spiritual and cognate experiences, and "psychological" could also be translated by "mental."

their pleas with pseudo-religious feelings and promises. Even the Russian atheists have done so.

Second, the philosopher evaluates. In spite of all possible relativism in his thought, he suggests to his listeners what he considers right thinking, right choosing, and right acting. And though his individual influence may be limited, in its totality philosophy helps to form that climate of opinion and, still more, that sense of direction and final purpose without which all human activity would end in cultural chaos.

Hence, the actual work of the school without continual philosophical self-evaluation would end in mediocrity, if not in self-destruction, for undirected and morally indifferent learning can be one of the most demonic forces. On the other hand, philosophy of education without continual regard for the work of the teacher and its relation to the life of the nation would end—and has often done so—in theoretical inbreeding and futility.

Only when practical interests respect the speculative, and the speculative serve the practical, can humanity and its cultural endeavors thrive. And it is exactly philosophy of education which should best be able to bind the thinker and the doer into a covenant of mutual responsibility.

PHILOSOPHY OF EDUCATION IN THE UNDERGRADUATE CURRICULUM

LASZLO J. HETENYI

In the various pre-service programs for teachers, the courses and course sequences commonly cluster around a small number of questions—each deceptively simple, each the center of heated argument.

The first great controversy springs from the question: "what do teachers teach?". Do they teach subject matter, or do they teach children? In any meaningful sense I feel this to be a false dilemma. Every teacher teaches something—be this something a skill, a constellation of concepts, a set of attitudes, a body of facts, or

FROM *Educational Theory*, 18 (Winter, 1968): 52–59. (Reprinted with the permission of the publisher and the author.) This article is an up-dated version of a paper presented to the Midwest Philosophy of Education Society, November, 1966.

what have you. Likewise, every teacher teaches somebody. One may lecture into a vacuum, one does not teach without somebody doing the learning. A teacher teaches *something* to *somebody* and to ignore either element makes the concept of teaching meaningless. If one accepts this contention, the "what?" question is appropriately answered by the identification of subject matter (conventional or otherwise) while the consideration of pupils and their concerns is included in the question "whom do we teach?" The answer to the first question is reflected in the curriculum by courses in a whole host of studies usually identified by state certification authorities as majors and minors; the answer to the second is seen in equally significant work in psychology, sociology, educational psychology, and so on.

If anything, arguments become even more heated when we ask "how do we teach?". In response to this question, teacher education programs offer methodology, field observation, supervised teaching, internship, and the like. This is not the place to argue with Mr. Conant, Mr. Koerner, nor yet with Mr. Bestor and his cohorts. Suffice it to say, that even critics of pedagogy agree that some means must be found to make the teacher skillful in specific behavior aimed at instruction. The combatants in this old war wage their battles about the best ways by which this phase of pre-service preparation should be brought about, but even the extremists agree that the outcome must yield instructional skills.

In this brief summary of the questions asked in a good pre-service program, I am struck not by the inclusions but by a curious omission. It is not often that students are invited to investigate systematically or extensively *why* one should teach. Why should there be schooling; why should we select those subjects we do select; why should we encourage school attendance and discourage dropping out, etc., etc.? When we do ask such questions we almost always provide simplistic or purely operational answers—such as, "by reducing dropouts we increase the percentage of those gainfully employable," or "only thus can we produce effective voters,"— and thereby reinforce the prevalent habit of answering fundamental questions with superficialities or clichés. As a result, when students become teachers they participate in staff meetings, make curricular decisions, instruct pupils, and formulate objectives for their schools without ever becoming aware of the presuppositions from which they operate, without perceiving alternatives, without subjecting to rational analysis the processes which led to their conclusions. Unless we assume that every teacher will engage in graduate work to remedy these shortcomings (a dangerous assumption indeed), we have left the most significant part of a teacher's education to chance, to the idols of the den and the theatre, to that dubious commodity we call common-sense. I suggest, therefore, that no teacher should be graduated until he has had to wrestle with some of the underlying human questions as these pertain to education. If this belief has warrant, then Philosophy of Education should be a necessary part of all undergraduate programs in teacher education.

I am well aware that the mere mention of "Philosophy of Education" places one in a thicket of controversy. Setting aside the feasibility of such study by purportedly immature undergraduates, there remains the fighting term "Philosophy of Education" itself. The literature is replete with disagreement concerning the nature of the discipline we call Philosophy of Education. Perhaps I will not be charged with over-simplification when I say that the essence of this division boils down to two contrasting views.

There are those who maintain that Philosophy of Education is an autonomous discipline, related to, but not part of, general philosophy and, likewise, related to, but not identical with, the practical analysis of educational problems. Foster McMurray[1] chose this stance. Albert J. Taylor[2] took a similarly dim view of what academic philosophy has to offer to education and, as far as education is concerned, banished epistemologists and metaphysicians from the State. William O. Stanley, one of the most respected voices in education, adds his considerable support to this position:

I am saying that Philosophy of Education is a distinct discipline . . . but I am saying more than that. I am asserting that most of the really pressing issues in educational theory and practice . . . may be adjudicated apart from a general agreement on ultimate metaphysical, epistemological and theological questions.[3]

C. D. Hardie,[4] and many others take similarly separatists approaches.

On the other hand, Charles F. S. Virtue, asserts "the inseparability of general philosophy and the Philosophy of Education"[5] and goes on to say that "General Philosophy is the matrix of educational philosophy, and that responsible evaluation of philosophies of education requires at least a modest exposure to metaphysics, epistemology and axiology."[6] Kingsley Price,[7] likewise stresses the necessity of relating the Philosophy of Education to metaphysics, ethics, and epistemology. Harry Broudy is not satisfied vaguely to relate Philosophy of Education to formal philosophy, he sees the connection as inexorable:

In this book the Philosophy of Education is regarded as the systematic discussion of educational problems on the philosophical level, i.e., the probing into an educational question until it is reduced to an issue in metaphysics, epistemology, ethics, logic, or esthetics, or to a combination of these.[8]

George Kneller agrees and offers the following definition of Philosophy of Education:

Philosophy of Education I consider to be the attempt to work out a systematic framework of concepts and values which will assist in the selection and judgment of educational goals and policies. But these goals can be considered realistically only to the extent that they are

[1] Foster McMurray, "Preface to an Autonomous Discipline of Education," *Educational Theory*, V, 3 (July, 1955), pp. 129–131.
[2] Albert J. Taylor, "What Is Philosophy of Education?," *Educational Theory*, VIII, 2 (April, 1963), pp. 95–109; 118.
[3] William O. Stanley, "Current Tasks in Educational Philosophy," *Phi Delta Kappan* (October, 1958), p. 12.
[4] C. D. Hardie, "The Philosophy of Education in a New Key," *Educational Theory*, X, 4 (October, 1960), pp. 255–261.
[5] Charles F. S. Virtue, "General Philosophy and Philosophy of Education: A Word from an Academic Philosopher," *Educational Theory*, VIII, 4 (October, 1958), p. 203.
[6] *Ibid.*
[7] Kingsley Price, "Is a Philosophy of Education Necessary," *Journal of Philosophy*, LII, 22, pp. 625–626.
[8] Harry S. Broudy, *Building a Philosophy of Education*, Second Edition (Englewood Cliffs, N. J.: Prentice-Hall, Inc., 1961), p. 14.

related to other more general questions, such as, the nature of the reality to which we belong, the meaning of life, of man himself, of the society he lives in, and of the political responsibilities he must assume. Since these are among the questions of philosophy itself, I maintain that the ultimate issues of education are expressed inevitably in philosophic terms.[9]

Faced with such sharp differences represented by such persuasive spokesmen, I am tempted to take no clear stand, to equivocate, and so to chart a safe course twixt Scylla and Charybdis. This, alas, is not a live option. If one would speak of Philosophy of Education as a necessary part of teacher preparation, one must be explicit about what one will do and what one hopes to accomplish. Once these points are spelled out, there is no safe middle ground in the controversy.

I have indicated earlier that the reason for including Philosophy of Education in undergraduate programs is to provide an occasion for students to grapple with the "why?" questions posed by education. But if the "why?" is to be discussed in anything approximating depth it must be discussed on a level that goes beyond education. If, for example, a particular method of instruction is championed on the basis of empirical findings, one should ask something about the grounds for accepting empirical evidence—or why one disagrees with those who do not accept such evidence. Or take the issue of religious instruction in the public schools. This is often discussed practically, or legally, but one would have to go beyond practicality, even beyond law, if one would come to grips with the "why?" questions on a fundamental level. Since this is the very kind of activity which I presume to advocate, I necessarily must cast my lot with George Kneller and Harry Broudy and be prepared to duck brick-bats from those who disagree. For that matter, there may be some ducking to do for having put these two distinguished gentlemen into the same camp!

Having opted for a view of educational philosophy which is essentially anti-separatist (certainly in an undergraduate course), I hasten to add that I do not advocate presenting a series of philosophic systems from which by simple deduction the rabbit of educational prescription is made to appear. Nothing could be less useful than to imbue the student with the comforting delusion that once you have settled on a few axiomatic beliefs you can, by a series of syllogisms, arrive at curriculum, methodology, school organization, and the like. Likewise, it is of no profit to select a number of classics in educational philosophy—contemporary or ancient—and have students catalogue the answers they propose to problems of education. If these are pointless undertakings, what are some of the alternatives?

One task of such a course is to make students aware of their own hidden assumptions, their emotionally held, well-nigh unconscious premises and to make them similarly aware of such premises in the thinking of others. It is an enlightening experience, for example, to raise questions about the doctrine of Transubstantiation (and find, by the way, that few Catholics in the class know what you are talking about), gradually have students who accept this doctrine discover that they are operating on different epistemological bases when they claim to know the nature

9 George F. Kneller, "Philosophy, Education, and Separatism," *Educational Theory*, XII, 1 (January, 1962), p. 35.

of the Host before and after the moment of transubstantiation—and then to demonstrate to the materialists in the crowd that they too employ unexamined premises when they accept the results of laboratory experiments as ultimates of reliable cognition. One also finds considerable consternation in the class when a discussion of social and political systems does not end by invoking the laudatory term "Democracy" or the epithet "Totalitarianism." Students are surprised to discover that in classing one system above the other they tacitly assume many logically antecedent propositions.

Through a series of exploratory sessions, designed primarily to bring to awareness that which hitherto has been unexamined and taken for granted, the instructor can establish a classroom climate in which a discussion of educational theory and practice leaves the realm of pooled prejudices and in which disagreements are turned into occasions for analysis. In relatively short order most students learn to spot and to articulate deliberately hidden premises or inadvertently suppressed assumptions by instructor and fellow students.

A second, related, objective of the course aims to sharpen the student's ability in the rational examination of arguments. It is here that the rigor and precision of linguistic analysis can come into play. The instructor must delicately balance pushing students to the limits of their capacity against the bewilderment and eventual boredom which would ensue were he to proceed too formalistically. It is not too much to ask of undergraduates that they define their terms and identify referents for them, that they recognize vagueness or ambiguity, and that they develop some sensitivity in spotting deliberate or accidental equivocation. Needless to say, the language of education should be the focus of such study.

Some specific attention to inferential processes is also of value. Once again the instructor would be grossly mistaken were he to immerse students in the works of Quine and Cooley or, for that matter, into the writings of more traditional logicians. The class would almost certainly respond with naked hostility or escape into peaceful slumber. Yet, it is possible for students to develop considerable skill in following the logical threads of an argument. What is more, the enterprise needs to be neither dull or repulsive to undergraduates. Many students thoroughly enjoy sharpening their own ability to argue logically and many more can become fiendishly clever in detecting logical flaws—especially in the instructor's presentation. When imaginatively led, classes become adept at, and inclined to, test the cogency of educational writers. At first, the group shows numerous and glaring, not to say ludicrous, shortcomings. On the inductive side, students frequently confuse inference with evidence and when pressed, become disturbed by their ensuing inability to evaluate the reliability of inferences. In the context of controversial educational issues, the identification and organization of evidence, convergence hypotheses, generalizations, and reliability statements become meaningful intellectual tools, instead of exercises in the esoteric. One can even try to include elementary statistical concepts and explore their use in the processes of induction. With due care and by curbing one's appetite for detail, statistics (at least on this level) can lose the power to frighten even the attractive future kindergarten teacher in the front row who "just can't cope with figures." Much the same can be said about the perennial problems of deductive analysis. A formalized treatment of syllogisms turns the class to stone, but developing such arguments in context of live issues, letting students discover their own fallacies, but stopping short of introducing a complicated technical vocabulary, yield rich rewards.

Alan Montefiore of Balliol College, Oxford, speaking at a recent meeting, described a somewhat similar approach and stressed its applicability to the education of teachers.[10] He identified nine topic areas and indicated how out of their discussion fledgling teachers gained insights into many central concerns of education. He proposed the issue of individual responsibility in a world of causality, the morals—politics—law complex in its relation to education, connections between factual and valuative statements as productive starting points for class discussion. Once students grapple not only with the concepts themselves, but with their use in social, political, and educational theories, a modicum of skill replaces the primitive attempts at rational argument which characterized the early sessions of the course.

The process primarily undertaken to increase analytical sophistication provides opportunities to introduce quite a few classical formulations of the problems under discussion. Montefiore cited one of his own more successful experiences to illustrate his point.[11] He started by raising some concrete problems in the schools and posed the apparent impossibility of reconciling individual responsibility with causality. Eventually he guided class discussion to Hume's demonstration that causality, far from contradicting, was a necessary condition of individual responsibility. Treating the instance paradigmatically, he made a telling point concerning the effective use of historical philosophic materials. No one would pretend that learning the name of Hume, or memorizing passages from his work has any significant value for prospective teachers! But familiarity with selected documents in proper context helps a teacher perceive that the questions which agitate him have exercised man throughout history and that answers provided by the great minds of the past do not close a subject for all eternity. As Montefiore used Hume's *Treatise*, so one can use Plato's *Republic*, the Dewey-Tufts' *Ethics*, or, for that matter, St. Augustine's *De Magistro*. Let me emphasize that I see no special virtue in introducing such works for their own sake, but let me also express my conviction that when a discussion of concrete educational problems leads students to a *meaningful* reading of a major piece of writing in philosophy or education, then the inclusion of a classic is certainly no pedagogical sin.

In some ways a climax in the course can be built by selecting a series of case studies or a particularly controversial work (such as, Goodman's *Growing Up Absurd*) and analyzing its central problem(s) with the techniques perfected throughout the course. Students usually find this not only an exciting undertaking, but also acquire a healthy respect for the difficulty of tracing an argument, especially a polemically presented argument, to its philosophic underpinnings. Once a class has

[10] Alan Montefiore, "The Place of Philosophy in the Education of Teachers," (Published in the *Proceedings* of the 31st Educational Conference of the Educational Records Bureau, 1966).
[11] *Ibid.*

been through this experience, there are not many among them willing to make sweeping pronunciamentos about education. The few who persist in the habit reap a harvest of jeers from their fellows.

Without prolonging the discussion unduly, let me now raise some questions about the success of such a course in an undergraduate program for teachers. It is, of course, hard to say what one means by success. I certainly have no conclusive evidence that those who have taken such a course are better teachers than those who have not. Reliable measurement of teacher effectiveness is, after all, hardly a readily available commodity! There are, however, a few straws in the wind and these point in a positive direction.

At Oakland University, we have tried to ascertain the graduates' perceptions of their education in light of their experiences in the first years of teaching. Results of a five-year follow-up study are as yet fragmentary, with returns from only the first three years analyzed. At the end of the first year of teaching each alumnus was sent a questionnaire asking him to evaluate his undergraduate preparation for teaching. Those of us in Philosophy of Education approached the returns with some trepidation, knowing full-well how Philosophy of Education usually fares in such studies. On a five-point scale, ranging from "no value" to "great value" (with the mid-point of three described as "some significant value" and four as "substantial value") I am happy to say that Philosophy of Education came out with an average score of 3.38. In other words, our initial respondents felt that their background in Philosophy of Education was somewhere half-way between having had "some significant value" and having had "substantial value" in their first year as professionals. The second and third classes of graduates responded in almost identical terms (3.49 and 3.39 respectively).

Even more interesting to us was an analysis of responses from graduates who completed questionnaires in two consecutive years. There were thirty-nine such instances in the Charter class and fifteen respondents increased their evaluation of the course while only eight decreased it in their second year of teaching. The second graduating group after two years showed increases in six instances, decreases in only four, with the bulk remaining constant. My statistician friends tell me not to become too sanguine when the "N" is relatively small. But they also tell me that, when the original scores cluster on the high side, to find that increases outnumber decreases in two consecutive groups is, to say the least, suggestive. It remains to be seen whether this happy state of affairs will continue as the study progresses through the remaining years. For the moment, our indicators tend to support the two hypotheses which prompted us to include Philosophy of Education in the undergraduate program:

a) that philosophic analysis of educational problems can be of value to beginning teachers and that they can and do become aware of this value in relation to their professional roles.

b) that, as the new teacher's insecurity and the accompanying preoccupation with limited practicalities decreases with experience, his concern for some of the basic issues in education (the ones I called the "why?" questions) assumes a more central position in his thinking. At this time he is likely to look back on his studies in Philosophy of Education with increased appreciation.

The results of our follow-up studies provide enough support for us to continue experimentation with a Philosophy of Education course in the pre-service professional sequence for teachers.

So far I have spoken only of professional growth, but Philosophy of Education, I feel, has much to contribute to the personal, human development of students. Once again, the evidence is less than conclusive (how could it be otherwise?) but suggestive. Here our information contains several strands from a variety of sources. The first piece of evidence comes from the follow-up study mentioned previously. In addition to questions about professional values, the graduates were asked to comment on personal values they felt their academic training contributed. Here they rated Philosophy of Education at 3.41, 3.33, 3.37 in successive years. These figures again are well in the positive range. What is more, respondents rated this area above several courses which the university prescribed in the fond hope of providing a good general education for all students. Nor can one attribute the differences to the customary preference for electives, since Philosophy of Education is strictly required of all prospective teachers.

A second indicator came from those few Liberal Arts students who freely elected this course. In the early years of the university, tight programming provided few electives and those that were chosen had to prove themselves in the student culture. It is especially interesting to note that Philosophy of Education held its small beachhead among electives in spite of the common complaint that it demanded hard work, included a substantial reading list, and built a reputation as a course in which high grades were not handed out with any liberality. Still, a small but continuous trickle of students who did not plan to teach chose the course as an elective.

A third hint comes from the faculty community. In reorganizing the undergraduate curriculum, the university's Committee on Academic Affairs unanimously recommended, and the Academic Senate with very little dissent voted, that the course in Philosophy of Education be one way by which students in any and all divisions of the university might fulfill the Western Civilization requirement in general education. This was the first, and thus far only, introductory course in a professional sequence so designated. Since the faculty acted neither out of caprice nor through lobbying by the School of Education and since both the Committee and Senate stated that they based their judgment on the six-year record of the course, the conclusion seems inescapable that in at least *one* institution, at least *one* approach to the Philosophy of Education is accepted as a significant contribution to general education. Should this happy state of affairs continue and should it develop that what one young, rather flexible institution can do is also viable elsewhere, then the bridge between general and professional education, perhaps the vital link between academician and educationist may yet turn out to be that much maligned, controversial discipline: Philosophy of Education.

SOME CONCLUDING
CONSIDERATIONS

F. F. CHAMBLISS
GENE D. PHILLIPS

A problem which ought to be of great concern to the educational philosopher, and one which seems especially pressing in these times of searching examination of the nation's schools, is that of reaching the minds of the populace with discussions of problems which concern it. There is a considerable gap between the kinds of problems which the great bulk of the populace think about and those of educational philosophers. And in one sense, this is as it should be: there are some kinds of questions (such as technical ones about metaphysics, epistemology, value theories) which belong in the realm of competence of the educational philosopher, and which farmers, businessmen, classroom teachers, laborers, and others would properly find outside their area of discourse. In a different sense, however, the mass of the populace deserves to know that there are attempts being made in the realm of theory to discuss problems of the educational process; and, further, that theory needs to be translated into terms of a kind which might enable the mass of the populace to gain some sense of the issues at hand.

There seems to be little doubt but that what C. Wright Mills has called "the mass media of distraction" have to a frightening extent tended to distract the public from the main issues, in the realm of education as elsewhere. It is known that in some instances certain journals have explicitly refused to publish alternative viewpoints in the present controversies about education, on the grounds that such discussion is not what their readers want. Refusals in that manner indicate that propaganda, in its worst sense, is being spread by certain strong interest groups. In addition to such conscious attempts at distraction, there are no doubt well-meaning attempts by various media which are also distracting, even if unintentionally so. But one can still believe that the having of good intentions alone does not constitute an intelligent study of anything.

However, in addition to the difficulties which educational philosophers actually face in contributing to the mass media, there is a further problem which needs to be confronted with respect to the enhancing of communication between the ivory

FROM *Journal of Education* (Boston University), 141 (October, 1958): 29–31. (Reprinted by permission.)

tower and more mundane affairs. How, in fact, can the educational philosopher translate his special concerns to the man in the street, so that they will be meaningful? If mass media are used by educational philosophers, will communication actually take place? Baldly stated, how can an educational philosopher make sense to a plumber, a farmer, a laborer, a housewife, or to any others who might ask, "What is your reason for existing? What good are you to us?" When one considers seriously how difficult it is for an educational philosopher to make meaningful, even to his own classes of prospective teachers, the problems in educational theory which he discusses, there is little wonder that he finds difficulty in talking sense to the less-formally educated populace. Yet the emotionally-toned appeals of the mass media represent a serious challenge to serious thinking about problems of the schools, which problems deserve the attention of the population. In what ways can the educational philosopher reach the minds of that population, while maintaining his professional competence and at the same time refusing to use the kinds of tactics and strategy which result in unintelligent emotionalism? Or may ways be found to use such tactics and strategy to produce something more desirable than unintelligent emotionalism?

The assumption which is made here obviously is that the educational philosopher ought to attempt to bridge the gap between his "purely philosophical" discussions and the realm of more widespread endeavors wherein those discussions must ultimately become effective. In his contacts with prospective teachers, he is engaged in a long-range plan to make theory become effective in practice: to the extent that teachers try out educational theories in their teaching, and insofar as such theories direct the minds of students for action in their everyday lives, discussions of educational philosophers may make a difference in things in the long run. But, in the meantime, what of the short run? The claim here is that there is a need for more immediate and more direct efforts at reaching the common man with serious discussion about the kinds of problems with which educational philosophers are concerned.

What is more, it seems worthwhile to suggest that the flow of influence might not all be in one direction. Educational philosophers might well consider the possibility of their learning something from the common man, as well as their "teaching" him about what it is that they are doing. It would seem that a lack of understanding of the various concerns of the common man on the part of educational philosophers is a serious obstacle to communication, as is the lack of understanding in the reverse direction. Educational philosophers communicate with each other (to a somewhat limited extent, at least). Conscious efforts are needed, not only to improve that communication, but also that more difficult kind, which calls for attempts to become involved in ways of thinking that are quite different from those which are far too often peculiar to the ivory tower of educational philosophers solely.

The difficulty in direct communication involving the gap between the realm of educational theory and the realm in which that theory may someday become effective is a species of a genus of problems in almost any realm of intellectual life;

for example, literature, law, theology, and the like. It is the hope of some that, in a democracy, all individuals can become intelligent about the forces among which their lives go on. And it is the further hope that the schools can become a significant institution for realizing that intelligence which perhaps has been more potential than actual up to now. There seems to be a crying need, in the pressure of today's events, to appeal to the intelligence even now realized in that potentiality, and to seek ways in which those individuals can make the best use of that intelligence in discussing problems which ought to be of concern to both the educational philosopher and the common man.

In brief, attempts are needed here and now, in the "short run," to make sense out of educational theory in the market place of ideas. Perhaps a more honest consideration of the ideas and sentiments of the relatively unlettered on the part of the "intellectuals" would help to make more meaningful those notions that have been put forth again and again about the potential worth of all sorts of endeavors of men: e.g., the claim that beauty is not a quality of certain so-called "works of art" alone, but is potentially a quality of all sorts of "ordinary" activities; the claim that the "good" and the "religious" are not peculiar to certain objects and writings alone, but are potentially qualities of a vast, largely untapped universe of a society's inheritance, the claim that the "intellectual" is not a modifier of specific subject matters alone, but is potentially a characteristic of those endeavors which have been called "practical" or "vocational" merely; and so on and on.

It seems that if such notions are ever to become anything other than theories merely, i.e., if ideas are turned into working-hypotheses to be tried out in the flow of experience—there ought to be attempts to make meaningful, in the thinking of a much wider population, the efforts of such manner of theorists as are educational philosophers. To do so would call for serious and honest attempts at sympathetic understanding, on the part of the populace for the kind of work which educational theorists do, and, in turn, on the part of educational theorists for the kinds of work and ways of thinking of the populace. The lack of such attempts at the present time might well become a concern for serious consideration by educational philosophers.

Ideas have been expressed in the preceding pages about the proper role of the educational philosopher in relation to himself and others. They have been stated in a variety of ways. The discussion has not been intended to conclude any such future activity, as it is known such a limited effort should and would not do. It is hoped, however, that more men can take more time from day-to-day exigencies to reflect publicly their beliefs, concerns, and dispositions about education—its new directions; thus, the role of the educational philosopher can know new dimensions of discipline and purpose.

SUGGESTIONS FOR
FURTHER READING

The following articles and portions of books deal, broadly speaking, with the metaphilosophical questions to which this work devotes itself. In particular, the issues of the nature and functions of philosophy of education are discussed. Although this list is by no means comprehensive, the student will find the widest possible variety of viewpoints brought under examination.

Austin, G. "The Philosophy in Philosophy of Education," *Educational Theory*, 3, #1 (January, 1953), 68–71.

Ayers, R. H. "Cryptotheologies and Educational Theories," *Educational Theory*, 15, #4 (October, 1965), 282–292.

Barnett, G. (ed.) *Philosophy and Educational Development*. New York: Random House, 1965, Chaps. I and II.

Barton, G. "De Principiis Non Disputandum Est," *School Review*, 72, #2 (Summer, 1964), 209–229.

Belth, M. "Prospects for a Discipline of Education," *Educational Theory*, 12, #4 (October, 1962), 193–204.

Benne, K. D. "Group Dynamics and the Conditions of Rationality," *Ed Forum*, 16, #1 (November, 1951), 43–55.

Best, E. "Common Confusions in Educational Theory," in R. D. Archambault (ed.), *Philosophical Analysis and Education*. New York: Humanities Press, 1965, pp. 39–56.

Bode, B. "Where Does One Go for Fundamental Assumptions in Education?" *Education Administration and Supervision*, 14 (September, 1928), 361–370.

Brameld, T. "Educational Philosophy and Teacher Training," Chap. 23 in *Ends and Means in Education: A Midcentury Appraisal*. New York: Harper, 1950, pp. 222–229.

Brameld, T. "Educational Philosophy: Its Needs and Function in the Training of Teachers," *Harvard Educational Review*, 17, #3 (Summer, 1947), 162–167.

Brameld, T. "The Study of Culture in Teacher Education," in *Cultural Foundations of Education: An Interdisciplinary Exploration*. New York: Harper, 1957, Chap. 13.

Brauner, C. J. *Education as a Subject of Study*. Dissertation, Stanford University, 1960.

Broudy, H. S. "The Role of Analysis in Educational Philosophy," *Educational Theory*, 14, #4 (October, 1964), 261–269.

Broudy, H. S. *Building a Philosophy of Education* (2nd ed.). Englewood Cliffs, N. J.: Prentice-Hall, 1961, pp. 11–19.

Broudy, H. S. "The Role of the Foundational Studies in the Preparation of Teachers," Chap. 1 in S. E. Elam (ed.), *Improving Teacher Education in the United States*. Phi Delta Kappa, 1967, pp. 1–22.

Brubacher, J. S. *A History of the Problems of Education*. New York: McGraw-Hill, 1947, Chap. V.

Brubacher, J. S. *Modern Philosophies of Education*. New York: McGraw-Hill, 1939, Chap. 1.

Burns, H. W. "The Logic of the Educational Implication," *Educational Theory*, 12, #1 (January, 1962), 53–63.

Burnett, J. R. "Observations on the Logical Implications of Philosophic Theory for Educational Theory and Practice," *Educational Theory*, 11 (April, 1961), 65–70.

Clayton, A. S. "The Relevance of Philosophy of Education to Questions of Educational and Social Policy," *Proceedings* of the P.E.S., 1960, pp. 78–90.

Clements, M. "Theory and Education," *Educational Theory*, 12 (April, 1960), 124–128.

Dettering, R. W. *The Contributions of Semantics to the Philosophy and Practice of Education*. Dissertation, Stanford University, 1956, 304 pp.

Eastwood, G. R. *Philosophical Analysis and Language in Education*, Dissertation, University of Minnesota, 1962, 441 pp.

Elvin, H. L. "Education and Our Social Thinking," *Educational Review*, 17, #1 (November, 1964), 2–17.

Ferree, G. W. *Selected Tools of Analytic Philosophy and Their Application in Education*. Dissertation, University of Florida, 1960, 192 pp.

Frankena, W. K. "Philosophical Inquiry," Chap. 10, in J. E. Goodlad (ed.), *The Changing American School*. 65th Yearbook of the N.S.S.E., Pt. 2., 1966, pp. 243–265.

Frankena, W. K. "The Philosophy of Education and Its Problems," Chap. 1 in *Three Historical Philosophies of Education*. Chicago: Scott, Foresman, 1965, pp. 1–14.

Gayer, Nancy. "How to Get the Fly Out of the Bottle," *Phi Delta Kappan*, 43, #7 (April, 1962), 276–283.

Greene, Maxine. "Philosophy of Education and the 'Pseudo-question.'" *Proceedings* of the P.E.S., 1960, pp. 56–61.

Greene, Maxine. "Philosophy of Education and the Liberal Arts: A Proposal," *Educational Theory*, 9, #1 (January, 1959), 50–54.

Greene, Maxine. "The Uses of Literature," *Educational Theory*, 7, #2 (April, 1957), 143–149.

Gruen, W. "Scientific Philosophy and Education," *Educational Theory*, 9, #4 (October, 1959), 227–234.

Hailparn, M. *Philosophy, Methodology, and Philosophy of Education:* a Study of Neutralism in Philosophy and Philosophy of Education. Dissertation, Columbia University, 1965, 202 pp.

Hardie, C. D. "The Basis of Any Educational Theory," Chap. 4 in *Truth and Fallacy in Educational Theory*. New York: Cambridge University, 1942, pp. 66–147.

Harrington, J. *A Critical Presentation of Four Philosophies of Education*. Dissertation, University of Houston, 1954, 319 pp.

Harvard Committee. *The Graduate Study of Education*. Cambridge, Mass.: Harvard University Press, 1966, 125 pp.

Jenilson, T. H. *The Concept of Theory in the Writings of Three Major Educational Theorists*. Dissertation, University of Maryland, 1960.

Jones, R. "Towards the Integration of the Foundations of Education," *Educational Theory*, 13, #2 (April, 1963), 74–83.

Kilpatrick, W. H. *Philosophy of Education*. New York: Macmillan, 1951, Chap. 1.

Levit, M. "The Field View, Color, and Educational Philosophy," *Educational Theory*, 10, #2 (April, 1960), 89–96.

Lodge, R. C. "The Essence of Philosophy of Education," *Educational Theory*, 3, #4 (October, 1953), 352–356.

Maccia, Elizabeth S. "The Separation of Philosophy from Theory of Education," *Studies in Philosophy and Education*, 2, #2 (Spring, 1962), 158–169.

Mason, R. E. "Grounds of Acceptable Theory in Education," *Studies in Philosophy and Education*, 1, #2 (January, 1961), 44–65.

Merritt, J. W. "The Province of Philosophy of Education," *Educational Theory*, 11, #1 (January, 1961), 45–51, 60.

McClellan, J. E. "Philosophy of Education in American Colleges and Universities," *La Educacion*, 5 (1960), 84–98.

McMurray, F. "Preface to an Autonomous Discipline of Education," *Educational Theory*, 5, #3 (July, 1955), 129–140.

McMurrin, S. M. "What about the Philosophy of Education?" *Journal of Philosophy*, 59, #11 (October, 1962), 629–637.

Morgenbesser, S. "Viewpoints from Related Disciplines: Contemporary Philosophy," *Teachers College Record*, 55, #5 (February, 1959), 255–260.

Morris, V. C. "Detente in Educational Philosophy," *Educational Theory*, 15, #4 (October, 1965), 265–272.

Neff, F. C. "Philosophy of Education: Its Nature and Scope," Ch. 1 in *Philosophy and American Education*. Center for Applied Research in Education, 1966, pp. 1–9.

Neff, F. C. "Education's Reflective Frontier," *Educational Forum*, 25, #1 (November, 1960), 97–103.

Newsome, G. "In What Sense Is Theory a Guide to Practice in Education?" *Educational Theory*, 14, #1 (January, 1964), 31–39, 64.

Newsome, G. L. "Ordinary Language Philosophy and Education," *Proceedings* of the P.E.S., 1958, pp. 90–99.

O'Connor, D. J., F. Brezinka, and K. Price. "Discussion: Philosophy of Education," *Harvard Educational Review*, 33, #2 (Spring, 1963), 219–236.

O'Connor, D. J. "What Is An Educational Theory?" Chap. 5 in *An Introduction to the Philosophy of Education*. New York: Philosophical Library, 1957, pp. 92–110.

Phenix, P. H. "Educational Theory and Inspiration," *Educational Theory*, 13, #2 (January, 1963), 1–5, 67.

Phenix, P. H. *Philosophy of Education*. New York: Henry Holt, 1958, pp. 14–19.

Phenix, P. H. "Teacher Education and the Unity of Culture," *Teachers College Record*, 60, #6 (March, 1959), 337–343.

Pilley, J. "Educational Theory and the Making of Teachers," *Educational Theory*, 3, #1 (January, 1953), 31–40.

Pinilla, A. "The Meaning of a Philosophy of Education," *Educational Theory*, 4, #3 (July, 1954), 200–205.

Powell, J. P. "Education and the Philosophers," *The Australian Journal of Education*, 9, #22 (June, 1965), 133–136.

Price, K. "What Is a Philosophy of Education?" *Educational Theory*, 6, #2 (April, 1956), 86–94.

Reid, L. A. "The Idea of 'Application' of Theory to Practice." Chap. 6 in *Philosophy and Education: an Introduction*. New York: Random House, 1962, pp. 86–96.

Reid, L. A. "Philosophy and the Theory and Practice of Education," in R. D. Archambault (ed.), *Philosophical Analysis and Education*. New York: Humanities Press, 1965, pp. 17–37.

Reisner, E. H. "Philosophy and Science in the Western World: An Historical Overview," in *Philosophies of Education*, 41st Yearbook of the N.S.S.E., Pt. 1. Chicago: University of Chicago Press, 1942, pp. 9–37.

Scheffler, I. "Toward an Analytic Philosophy of Education," *Harvard Educational Review*, 24, #4 (Fall, 1954), 223–230.

Scheffler, I. "Philosophical Analysis and Education. Introduction to I." *Philosophy and Education: Modern Readings*. Boston: Allyn & Bacon, 1958, pp. 1–10.

Schilpp, P. A. "The Distinctive Functions of 'Philosophy of Education' as a Discipline," *Educational Theory*, 3, #3 (July, 1953), 257–268.

Shermis, S. S. *Philosophic Foundations of Education*. New York: American Book, 1967, Chap. 2.

Smith, B. O. "Views on the Role of Philosophy in Teacher Education," *Journal of Philosophy*, 59, #22 (October, 1962), 638–647.

Soltis, I. "Philosophy of Education: Fourth Dimension," *Teachers College Record* (April, 1966), 524–531.

Squire, W., and S. Morris. "Philosophy of Education and the Training of Teachers," *Educational Review*, 17, #3 (June, 1965), 181–188.

Stanley, W. O. "Current Tasks of Educational Philosophy," *Phi Delta Kappan*, 40, #1 (October, 1958), 11–16.

Stanley, W. O. "The Social Foundations Subjects in the Professional Education of Teachers," *Educational Theory*, 18, #3 (Summer, 1968), 224–236.

Strain, J. P. "A Critique of Philosophical Analysis in Education," *Educational Theory*, 14, #3 (July, 1964), 186–193, 228.

Sun, Huai Chin. "Some Desirable Emphases in the Philosophy of Education," *Educational Theory*, 10, #3 (July, 1960), 217–223.

Swanson, R. S. *The Operational Definition and Measurement of Educational Philosophy*. Dissertation, University of Minnesota, 1955, 208 pp.

Tesconi, C. A. *A Comparison of the Philosophy of Education with the Philosophies of Art, History and Science*. Dissertation, University of Cincinnati, 1965, 462 pp.

Thompson, J. W. "Method-ideology and Educational Ideologies," *Educational Theory*, 12, #2 (April, 1962), 110–116, 123.

Ulich, R. *Professional Education as a Humane Study*. New York: Macmillan, 1956.

Walton, J., and J. L. Kuethe (eds.). *The Discipline of Education*. Madison, Wis.: University of Wisconsin Press, 1963.

Wilhoyte, R. L. "Is It Meaningful to Assert That Philosophy and Philosophy of Education Are Logically Related?" *Educational Theory*, 15, #1 (January, 1965), 13–18.

Zankov, L. "The Didactic Foundations of Teaching," *Soviet Education*, 5, #4 (February, 1963), 3–12.